BEAUTY IN THE MIRAH

"The Memoir"

SHAMIRAH SMITH

Beauty in the Mirah LLC.

BEAUTY IN THE MIRAH

I

I stepped into the therapist's office feeling overwhelmed, hopeless, defeated, and all together broken. I wasn't even sure if the therapist could help me. All I knew was that I needed help. I had prayed. I had cried. I was confused, and I didn't know what was wrong with me. "It's nice to meet you," my therapist said, as he shook my hand and tried to make me feel comfortable. She was a psychologist, so I'm sure she read my body language and saw that it was all over the place. "So, what brings you here? She said as she smiled, crossed her legs, and grabbed her notepad. I had paused for a second to think, and then I blurted out, "I'm depressed, I'm crazy, and I think I have Borderline Personality Disorder," I said all at once as I broke into tears. "Ok, calm down," she said, as she handed me a tissue. "Just take a deep breath, and tell me why you feel like you are crazy, depressed, and have BPD?" She asked, totally bombarded with my out pour of emotions. She reeled me back into reality and allowed me to get myself together. "I don't know. I just feel crazy," I said, still crying, and at that moment, I was feeling lost and worthless and slightly embarrassed. "Ok," she said, as she jotted in her notebook.

She asked me a series of ten questions, and my score had determined that I had a depressed mood. "Yes, according to the test I just gave you, you display symptoms of a depressed mood. I have Not diagnosed you with depression; let's be clear, there is a difference. There is something causing you to be depressed, and I am here to help you find what that is," she told me sincerely. "I am here to support you and be your guide and cheerleader along the way. Whatever we talk about here is confidential. This is your Safe Place," she said with a warm smile on her face. "Ok," I said, as I dried the tears from my face. "Let me tell you, first of all, you are not crazy, and we will get to the bottom of your depressed mood, but let me ask you," she said as she paused a moment. "What makes you think you have borderline personality disorder? She asked very curiously. "That is a huge statement to make about yourself. Have you ever been diagnosed?" She asked me. "No, I didn't even know what that was until my husband brought it to my attention," I told her, feeling confused. "What do you mean? Why would your husband say you have BPD? Is he a psychologist? She asked me. "No, he is not.

We were in the car the other day, and he played a from YouTube from a psychologist. It talked about people who have this disorder, and my husband said I act just like them," I told her, embarrassed. "Wow, ok, so what are the things you do to make him feel that way? She asked, very concerned. I act crazy; I throw things, I get mad to the point I begin having panic attacks and feel like I can't breathe. My husband feels like I am out of control. He told me I needed to go and see a psychologist asap to get on medication to control myself," I told her as I began to cry again.

"Ok, well, first let me say, I do not see you as Borderline personality at all," and she went on to break down the disorder and all the characteristics of it. "Secondly, let me ask you, why does your husband feel the need for you to be on medication? She asked, very empathetic. "I don't know, he says I have brain issues, and I need help. He told me, if I don't get the help that's he's going to leave me, so that's why I am here. Before I leave, are you going to write me a prescription for psych medication? I asked her. "No, I am not. One because I am a psychologist and not a psychiatrist, so I cannot write you a prescription. And secondly, I don't feel that you need to be on medication. I think you are a young woman who is sad, and displays some depressed mood, but not enough to where you need medication," she told me.

I felt relieved and sad at the same time. Relieved because a clinical psychologist confirmed that I wasn't crazy and I didn't have BPD, but sad because if I was fine, then why was I having all these unexplained emotions, and why did my husband feel that I was crazy. I was so confused and had so many unanswered questions. "So" she said, as she sat up in her chair and crossed her legs again. "You seem like a very bright young lady. You appear to be very intelligent and in tune. I also noticed that your husband's opinion really matters to you, and he has a lot of influence over you. Tell me about where you all are from, and how you both met," she said to me with her notebook in her lap.

We are from Atlantic City NJ, home of the Casino's, Trump Taj Mahal and Trump Plaza. The Miss America Pageants, The infamous "White House Subs" and the Epic "Marty Smalls Balls" held by Atlantic City Mayor Marty Smalls. Atlantic City has so much culture, history and memories. My mom would tell me stories about Atlantic City in the 80's, and I loved hearing them. They lived like they were in the "Paid in Full" movie, and their era was bomb. Though I loved my mother's stories, I had my own memories and experiences. Of course one of the memories was meeting my husband. "We've been together for seventeen years currently. When we first got together, I was eighteen, and he was nineteen just turning twenty" I said to her as I began going down memory lane.

"What's up, Tray?" I said, as I walked into my friend's house in Pleasantville, NJ, to chill with him. To my surprise, there was a short boy sitting in the corner with a huge afro. "What's up, Mirah" Tray said, as he greeted me back. "This is my cousin Damian," Tray said as he introduced me to his cousin. "HI, "I said, really paying him no mind. "How old are you?" I asked him, as he sat in the corner looking like an

11 yr old. "I'm 16," he said, with a shy smile on his face. "Oh, you look mad young. I thought you were like twelve," I said, being smart. I was about 14 at the time. Back then, I was so sweet but also a little sassy, and anything would just come out of my mouth. "Nah, I'm 16," he said, as he was still smiling. "You should give my cousin your number," Tray said to me, being way too overzealous. "I don't know, I don't just give my number out to people I don't know," I told him. Damian was sitting there, literally still smiling.

He looked so innocent and harmless, and I knew he wouldn't be bold enough to call me, so I just gave in and let him have my number. "Ok here," I said, as I wrote my number down on a piece of paper. I had left Tray's house and walked back home. When I got there, to my surprise the phone had rung, and it was Damian on the other end. "What's up?" he said, sounding a little shy. As soon as I was about to respond and engage in a conversation with him, Tray had called on the other line, and I had told Damian I would call him back, but I never did.

Fast forward about a year later, around February 2001. I had bumped into him at the bus station in Atlantic City, NJ. He had seen me before I saw him. "What's good," he said, smiling from ear to ear. "Hey, Damian!" I said in my young flirty voice as I was happy and surprised to see him. This time he didn't look like a young little boy. He looked his age. He was looking fly too. He had on an orange, white and blue jacket, a crispy white tee under it, and some jeans that fit him nicely. He had on a pair of orange and blue Bo Jackson sneakers, and this time his hair wasn't in an afro. He had it in cornrows braided towards the back with an orange, blue, and white fitted cap. He looked really cute and well put together. "You look cute," I told him. "Thank you," he said, smiling as always. "Give me your number again, I lost it," he said, as he pulled out his cellphone, and I gave him my number. "Make sure you call me," I told him. "I am, I'm about to catch the bus to Florida to my aunt's funeral," he told me. "I'm so sorry for your loss, be safe," I said to him, as I hugged him, and he walked out of the station to get on his bus.

Later that night, he called me, and this time we talked for a little while. We laughed together, and he told me when he got back from Florida that he wanted to take me out. I agreed and looked forward to seeing him, but yet again, time had slipped away, and we didn't link up or talk on the phone after that night. I'm sure he had girls he was dealing with, and I had guys I was dealing with, so we didn't make each other a priority. We were young and living our own lives.

In the meantime, I had a little heartache. Typical young love, nothing too serious. But serious enough that I was tired of dealing with different guys, and I wanted a steady boyfriend. So much so that I literally prayed to God that he sends me somebody. I wanted someone who was smart, funny, cute, dark-skinned, a low haircut with waves who was crazy about me, and he had to have money. I literally prayed for these things, and I trusted that God would answer my prayer. My best friend had a boyfriend who was like my brother. He always called me sis from the first day I ever met him.

"Yo sis, you cool as hell. You would be perfect for my brother," My bestie's boyfriend Tyriek told me, as myself, him and my bestie chilled together. That was like his fifth time telling me about his brother, so I finally asked him, "Bro, you always talking about your brother. Where is he?" I asked curiously, because he talked about him all the time, but I never saw him. "He's in Jail," he told me. "Oh my God, bro, you bugging. How am I supposed to meet your brother if he is locked up?" I asked him. "What is he locked up for anyway? I asked, "and he told me his charges," he said, as he was eating his chicken wings. "Bro, you are tripping. Your brother is never coming home," I said, totally ending that conversation. The whole time he mentioned his brother, he had never told me his name. It turns out the brother he was talking about happened to be Damian, and I had already known him. They were not blood brothers; they were best friends.

Damian had come home on bail. Him and Tyreik had moved in together along with one of Damian's cousins. My bestie would always tell me how she would be over there having so much fun, and that their house was lit. I had a boyfriend at the time, so I had never gone over there with her, but she would always tell me about Damian. Him and her were really close at one point and had a good relationship. Plus, she was his best friends' girlfriend, so it made sense that she was over his house a lot. I had known Damian, and I was surprised to learn that he was in jail for the type of charges he had. He was such a sweet person, and I could not see him doing that, so I was glad that he was home and doing well.

Fast forward to 2003. It was a Saturday, and I was hanging out with my bestie, and another one of my friends in Atlantic City. We were in Crown's Chicken on the avenue waiting for our food. "I want to see my boo, but I'm scared to call him," my bestie said in her young teenage voice. "Girl, why are you scared?" I asked her. "If you're scared, then let me call him for you," I said to her. I was about 17 at the time. I was intelligent, super sassy, and outgoing. I was the bold friend who was always down for anything. "Ok, call him for me," she said, as she dialed his number and gave me her cell phone. When I called, a guy's voice answered. "Hello?" he said. "Heyy, what you doin? I want to come see you," I said, pretending to be my bestie as I was trying not to laugh.

My bestie and my other friend were in the background, cracking up. "That's not Tyriek," my bestie said, letting me know that I was not talking to her boyfriend. "Who's this?" The guy asked, sounding like he was smiling from ear to ear. "It's Tia," I responded as I giggled, trying to sound like my bestie. "This is not Tia," he said to me, with a smile in his voice. "Yes, it is, and I'm about to come and see you," I said to him, flirting. "Well, Tyriek ain't here, but whoever this is, you can come through," he told me, with an upbeat voice. "Well, when is Tyriek going to be back? I'm going to be there in like 20 minutes, and I have 2 of my friends with me," I told him. I don't know. He should be back soon, and that's cool if you bring your friends with you," he told me, and we hung up.

"Girl, you are stupid! My bestie said as we all burst out laughing. "Girl, who was I talking to?!" I asked, still laughing. "Girl, that was Damian," she told me. "Damian? Oh, girl, you know Damian had a crush on me forever," I said to her. "No, he didn't," she said to me. "Girl, how are you going to tell me? I know when someone has a crush on me," I said to her as I was not laughing anymore. "I met him a long time ago through Tray. I talked to him on the phone a few times, he used to like me," I told her. "Well, you knew him back then, and I'm sure he wouldn't like you now. Me and him are cool, and he don't be giving no girls no play," she said to me. I had looked at her and burst out laughing. "Girl, please, I wasn't thinking about him. He used to like ME. And even though he don't be giving other girls no play, I bet you I could be his girlfriend by the end of today," I told her super confident. "Girl, bye. He is not going to make you his girlfriend today or any day," she said to me. "You want to make a bet?" I asked her, as I laughed at her lack of confidence in me. "Ok, let's bet. I bet you that Damian will not make you his girlfriend," she said. "I bet you that he will," I said as me, and she shook pinkies sealing the deal. We did not even make terms for if we won the bet. I low-key felt like she was trying to play me. At that point, I had just wanted to prove a point to her.

We had got our food. I got a four-piece wing and a beef patty, and we started walking to the westside, where he lived as we ate our food. We talked and laughed on the way there. My bestie knocked, and Damian opened the door standing there smiling from ear to ear. He had on a white wife-beater, a fitted cap to the back with his braids showing, some blue jeans, and a pair of red, white, and blue Bo-Jackson sneakers on. "What's up?" he said, still standing there. "You going to let us in or what?" I said, as I was joking and serious at the same time. "Shamirah, I knew that was you on the phone, I know your voice," he said to me, and I smiled. "Come in," he said, and we walked in and sat down. In my head, I was thinking of when the right time was to execute my plan. But as soon as I went to have a conversation with him, my bestie had called him to the kitchen because she so-called wanted advice about Tyriek.

At first, it was cool sitting there because that gave me time to figure out how I wanted to approach him, so that I could win this bet that me and my bestie had made. But after a while, it seemed like they were in there talking forever, so much so that I began to get sleepy and hungry. "Girl, I'm about to go," I said to my other friend who was with us, as she was sitting there waiting with me too. "I know, right." she agreed. I was talking to a couple of guys at the time, and one of them lived right around the corner. I wanted Red Lobster, and I knew he would have taken me there, no questions asked. He was crazy about me. He had a car and was really cool. He was so big on me. He bought me things and did anything I asked him to. I had lost my cellphone at the time, so I asked my friend to use her cell so I could call him, and right before I did, Tyriek came walking through the door. "To what do I owe this pleasure?" he said, smiling and excited with his over-the-top personality, and he gave my friend a hug and me. Once Tia realized that Tyriek was there, she and Damian had finally come out of the kitchen. "Oh, hey Tia" I wasn't expecting to see you," he said, giving my bestie a hug. She was head over heels over Tyriek, so at that point, she wasn't talking to Damian anymore, but they had taken up so much time that I was tired, hungry, and over it. I didn't even care about winning the bet anymore, I was just ready to go.

We all were sitting in the living room. My bestie and Tyriek were on one couch. Me, my friend and Damian were sitting on the same couch, and somehow, he was sitting right next to me. He sat there smiling, and to be honest, it was a little awkward at that moment. "What's good sis? How you been? Tyriek asked me. "I'm good. I'm just hungry," I said to him. "Oh word, you hungry? Damian was just about to go to the store and get some food," he said, as he was so excited that we both were in the same room, after years of suggesting that we needed to meet one another. "Yeah, I'm about to go to the store if you want to come," Damian said as he was smiling. "Ok," I told him because at that point, I was super hungry. The store was about two blocks away; it was not far at all.

On the way there, we made small talk. "So, it's been forever, how you been?" I asked him. "Coolin, Coolin" He said to me, as we walked. "What you been up to?" he asked me. "Nothing much, just going to school and can't wait to graduate in a few months," I told him, as I walked and enjoyed the beautiful weather. "That's what's up," he said. "How old are you now?" he asked me. "I'm 18," I said to him. "No, you not, you look super young, let me see your ID," he said to me. I pulled out my ID, and we both started laughing, which broke the ice a little bit. "So, do you have a girlfriend? I asked him, "Nah, I don't have no girl," he said, still smiling. "Why not?" I asked. "I just don't want one. I'm busy focusing on my money," he told me. "Ok, cool, I definitely understand that" I said to him, and in my head, I thought, "Well, maybe this will be a little harder than I thought after all."

When we got to the store, he opened the door for me. Inside was a small deli in the hood. I was walking around trying to see what I wanted. "You can get whatever you want. I got you," Damian said to me. "Ok," I said, as I smiled to myself. I would have paid for my own food, but I thought that it was super sweet of him to offer. I picked up a bag of Funyuns and a Mystic juice, and he ordered us a hot sausage. He liked his, the same way that I had liked mine; with cheese, ketchup, mustard, and onions on it. "Thank You," I said, as we got our food and left.

On the way back, I was eating my Funyuns, with the clear understanding that he did not want a girlfriend, so I was not going to bring it up again. We had small talk, and out of nowhere, he said to me, "You know what, I think I do want a girlfriend," as he was smiling. "Why did you change your mind?" I asked him, curious and shocked. "I don't know; I think maybe it would be cool to be with somebody," he said, and I could tell he was sincere. "Oh, Ok," I said to him, and in my head, I said, "Oh ok, I might win this little bet after all."

When we got back to the house, we all laughed and joked and had a good time. Soon it was nighttime, and Tyriek suggested that we go to the liquor store. He was the only one who was 21 at the time, so he was the only one who could buy liquor. We had walked there and laughed and bugged out the whole way. Damian and I walked next to each other, and he was a true gentleman. It had gotten cold, so he gave me his jacket, and I thought that was super nice of him. He was being very sweet, and I liked his energy. He was laid back and not too aggressive, and I liked that. He had a way about him that made me feel comfortable. When we got back to their house, they were drinking and having fun. I didn't drink because they had Bacardi O, and I didn't drink that. All I drank back then was Alize or Hypnotic and Hennesy, which was called the incredible hulk. They were all acting wild and being silly and having a good time.

I was enjoying myself. Damian and I had loosened up a little with one another. "Come here," he said to me as he guided me to the kitchen. "Sit here," he said, and he lifted me up and sat me on the counter. I was so small and petite back then. "I like your shoes" he said. I had on a pair of burgundy baby doll shoes with some black jeans and a tightly fitted burgundy sweater, and my hair was down with a China bang, and I had on a pair of big hoop earrings with my name in them. "Thank You," I said as my feet were dangling, and he kept looking at my feet, admiring how small they were.

He stood in front of me smiling, next thing you know, he put his body in between my legs, and he was standing there talking to me, and touching my legs at the same time. He had been drinking. I don't remember what he was saying, all I know is he was smiling the whole time. Before I knew it, he was right in my face, and out of nowhere, he tried to kiss me. I was thrown off, so I began to nervously laugh, and he wound up kissing my nose instead. We laughed for a minute, then I gave him a real kiss on the lips. From that moment right there, I felt a connection with him, and I think he felt it too. He smiled at me, and I innocently smiled back at him. He then took me down off the counter, and we continued to enjoy the night.

It had got late, so it was time to go. "I'm going to call you a cab, so you don't have to catch the bus home," he told me. "You going to pay for a cab from Atlantic City to Mays Landing? That's a lot of money," I said to him, and he laughed. "You good," he said as he handed me $50. "When you get home, make sure you call me," he said. "I lost my cell phone, and my house phone doesn't have long distance on it," I told him. "Oh word, I have an extra phone that you can have," he told me, and he pulled a phone out of his pocket, and to my surprise, he gave it to me. He had called the cab, and me and my friends all got in, and we talked about how much fun we had.

When I got home safe, I had called Damian as he asked me to. "Hello?" he said, sounding like he was asleep. "My bad for waking you up, I was just letting you know that I was home," I told him. "Ok, cool, that's what's up," he said, as I could tell he was smiling. There was a silence on the phone like he wanted to say something, but he didn't. "So, I guess you can call me tomorrow," he said to me hesitant. "Ok," I said to him with another pause. "So, what are we doing?" I asked him. "What do you want to do?" he asked me. "I would want to be boyfriend and girlfriend," I said to him very shyly and hesitantly. "Ok, that's what it is then," he said as I could tell he was smiling. "Really?" I asked, shocked. "Yeah, you my girl now," he told me. "Ok," I said as I was smiling too. "Ok, goodnight," he said to me, and we hung up. When I had got off of the phone, I felt like a giddy schoolgirl, and I had butterflies.

I was not expecting to have a boyfriend. I had always wanted one, but I had never found anyone that I had really liked, but Damian was different. His soul matched my soul, and he just felt right. I know I had made a bet with my bestie, and I still wanted my bragging rights. But I was also curious to see how it would be to be in a relationship. I was 18 and a senior in high school, so being in a relationship was not the main priority, but none the less I was excited. When I went to school the next day, I blasted it in my bestie's face that Damian was my boyfriend. "Girl, you lying," she said to me as we were at the lunch table. "No, I'm not. You can call him and ask him," I said as I pulled out the cellphone, he gave me. "Ok, you won, you got it," she said as she clapped me up. By the end of the day, I had told all my friends I had a boyfriend, and everyone knew. I was so happy. Having a boyfriend was exciting to me.

I was still a senior in high school, and I also went to Vocational school for fashion and design in the afternoons. The vocational school buses went to a lot of different cities. Even though I lived in Mays Landing. I would catch the Atlantic City school bus after school to see Damian. Sometimes my friends and I would even drive over to his house and hang out. His house was always fun and was always full of people, and we enjoyed going over there. Plus, the fact that I was in high school with a boyfriend who had an apartment was really cool to my friends and me. Me, Damian, and our friends hung out a lot doing regular things that teenagers do, like going bowling, movies, and just having fun. I really enjoyed being around him.

He was always happy and smiling. He knew a few guys that I talked to in the past, so when we went out, he made it known that I was HIS girl. He would always have his arm around me and show me a lot of affection. I had a little after-school job at Red Lobster, and he would pop up there sometimes with his cousins to get something to eat, and he would order the same thing every time. He always ordered the Cajun chicken pasta. I always got butterflies when I would see him coming through the door. I was a hostess, so I saw everyone, and I knew everybody's business because Red Lobster was the hot spot, and every guy who was trying to romance a girl took her there.

One day after vocational school, I got on the school bus to Atlantic City to Damian's house. He lived a few blocks from the bus stop. When I got off the bus, I had butterflies. It was not many times that I had come to his house without my friends. I was all alone, and I was a little nervous. When I got to the door, he opened it smiling from ear to ear, happy to see me, and I was happy to see him too. He gave me a hug and took my book bag from me and sat it down. Normally there were a lot of people there, but this day it was just him and me. Though I was nervous, he made me feel comfortable. He was always nice and always respectful, so I tried to ignore my nerves and just relax and spend time with him. "Let's watch 106 and Park," I said to him.

A few weeks before that day, I had gone to 106 and Park with my school. We had so much fun, and we were anticipating seeing ourselves on the show. I absolutely loved the host, Free, and I had finally got a chance to meet her, and I was super excited. She was so pretty and down-to-earth in person. "Oh yeah, that's right, the episode you are on is supposed to come on today, right?" he said to me as he was turning to BET. "Yup, you remembered," I said to him as I smiled and was flattered. "We had watched the show, and when it went off, we were sitting next to each other on the couch, and it was a little bit of awkward silence. BET was still on, and music videos were playing. "Can you dance?" he asked me, smiling. "What?" I said as I giggled. "Can you dance?" He asked again. "Yeah, I can dance, I guess," I said shyly. "Dance to this song," he said as one of 50 cent's songs was playing from his Album "Get rich or die Trying," which was both me and Damian's favorite album at the time. He had put me on the spot, and I was so shy and caught off guard. He had grabbed my hand to pull me up, and he started dancing. "C'mon" he said as he pulled me to him and motioned my body with his, and we were dancing together.

I was so embarrassed and uncomfortable, but it was fun, and we just laughed and laughed. When the song went off, we had sat down. "You know what we should do," he said to me. "What?" I asked him.

"We should take our clothes off and chill," he said to me. "Right here?" I asked as I looked around the living room. "Yeah," he said with a sneaky smile. "What if somebody comes?" I asked him. Nobody is going to come, my cousin left for the day, he's the only one with a key, everybody else has to knock," he reassured me, and he got up and put the bolt lock on and sat back down next to me. "Go ahead," he said to me. "Go ahead what? I'm scared," I said to him. "What you scared of?" he asked, and he got up and started taking his clothes off and kept his boxers and socks on. "Oh my God," I was thinking in my head. I was nervous, but I didn't want to look like a punk either. Nobody wants a boring girlfriend, so I just gave in and took off my clothes, leaving on my brown leopard bra and panties set, and I sat down next to him. He was looking at me, and I could tell that he was admiring my body. I was short and thick and had a really flat stomach and a cute butt, and my boobs were about a B cup. I had a cute figure, and I could tell that he liked it. "Let me look at you," he said as he stood me up and turned me around, and he was smiling.

The music was still playing, so we began to dance again, and this time he was feeling all over me, and I could see that he was starting to get erect. We were listening to Busta Rhymes and Mariah Carey's video, "Baby if you give it to me." It was getting a little intense. We were in our zone vibing and enjoying the music, when all of a sudden, we heard a bang and a kick on the door. "Oh my God!" I said as I jumped because it scared me. "Open the door, you bitch ass nigga" I heard his cousin yell through the door. He could not get in because the bolt lock was on. "Hold On!" Damian said, as he tried to hurry up and put his clothes back on. "Hurry up!" his cousin said, as he was trying to peek through the window.

Damian and I were cracking up. He threw me my clothes, but I didn't have enough time to put them on, and his cousin was beating on the door, yelling and cursing. "I'm going to unlock the door for him. Run upstairs when I count to three, ok," he said as his hand was on the lock. "Ok," I said with my clothes in my hand. When he counted to three, we both darted upstairs as his cousin burst through the door and tried to chase us. Damian hurried up and closed his room door, and locked it. We were laughing so hard that my stomach was hurting. "I thought you said nobody was coming," I said to him, still laughing. "My bad, Cuz popped up out of nowhere," he told me, and we laughed some more from the thrill. Damian popped in the R&B singer Genuine's CD and played "In those Jeans" on his stereo. "Are we going to put our clothes back on?" I asked him. "Nah, we good, we just going to chill like this," he said to me.

We sat on his bed talking and listening to music. Eventually, we ordered some food and just hung out and talked and enjoyed each other's company. As we were lying in the bed talking, and we started kissing, and he began rubbing my chest and caressing my body. Eventually he put his hands in my panties, and he could feel that I was wet, so he had climbed on top of me. I saw him reach for a condom and he put it on and we began kissing again. Next thing you know I felt him try to slide in his penis. "Wait," I said to him as I softly pushed him off of me. "What's wrong? He asked me compassionately. "I don't know if I'm ready to do this with you," I told him as he sat there with an erect penis. "Do what?" You, my girl. We been together for like a month now, you don't think it's time?" he asked me, this time he was not smiling at all. "I don't know. I was going to wait," I said shyly. "Wait for what?" this time his tone was firm, and I could tell he was aggravated. "Ok, you know what, you got it," he said as he got off of me and laid down next to me and he was silent.

After about five minutes went past, I asked him, "Are you going to say anything to me?" "Nope," he responded in an aggravated voice. "As a matter of fact, you can just leave," he said to me, as he turned his back to me. "What? Leave? It's like 1 o'clock in the morning, and you want me to leave? Are you going to walk me to the bus stop or call me a cab?" I asked. "I'll call you a cab, and you can go," he said with his back still turned to me. "What's wrong?" I asked him. "You coming over here and supposed to be my girl, and you fronting about some p*ssy," he said to me, aggravated. "I'm not fronting. I'm just saying that I wasn't ready for all of this with you. Before you I was with one other person, so I just wanted to take it slow," I told him as I was getting upset at the fact that he was getting upset with me about having sex. "I been with you, I been rocking with you. I haven't had sex with no other females. I'm loyal, and now you acting like I can't even have sex with my girl. You can leave and I will call somebody else over here," he said to me as he was getting up to get his phone to call me a cab. "If I leave, are we still together?" I asked him. "Nope," he said, and I sat there and thought about it for a minute.

I really liked him; I didn't want to lose him. I had never seen that side of him before. He was angry, and I did not want to make him mad. I wanted him to be the happy Damian that I was used to. "Ok," I said in a low voice, and I laid back down. "What you say," he asked me. I said, "Ok, we can do it." "You sure?" he asked me as he started to get back in the bed. "Yeah, I'm sure," I said in a monotone voice, and I laid there. He began kissing all over my neck, then he started sucking and licking all over my breast. I was getting wetter and wetter, then he went down and began kissing in between my thighs, and he went to lick my vagina, but at that point, it was so wet that he had come up and began kissing me, and I felt him began to slide his penis in and it hurt so bad. "I'm just going to do it slowly," he whispered in my ear," and I said "Ok," and I began sucking on his ear and his neck, and he finally got it in, it hurt, but it felt good. Damian had got into a grove, and he was being gentle, and I let him know when he was being too rough. We were having sex and making love. Damian was having sex with me like he loved me, and I could tell he was enjoying it, and I was too. I had sex before him, but with him, it was different. It was like our souls were intertwined, and with him, it was special.

After he nutted, he went and got us a towel. He laid next to me, hugging and kissing me, and then he wanted to do it again and again. My vagina was hurting so bad. Damian wanted to lay up with me and be lovey-dovey, but I needed to make sure my insides were ok. I had gone to the bathroom to make sure that I was not bleeding. There was a little bit of blood, but I was alright. After that, Damian was back to his happy self, and he continued being lovey-dovey and we continued to build our bond and chemistry.

The next day he was so sweet like his normal self. My bestie had come over to see Tyriek, and we ordered breakfast from Abes, and I told her all about my night. Damian was walking around smiling from ear to ear, and he even had a glow. Soon after breakfast, I caught a cab home to take a shower and change my clothes. I had caught a cab back over to his house. When I came through the door, there was a huge Valentine's Day type of basket. It had a huge teddy bear in it, balloons, candy, and all types of other cute stuff, and it had the plastic wrap over it.

Damian and I met on March 28, 2003. By this time, it was about the end of April, so I definitely was not expecting to see a Valentine's Basket. "You got this for Me!?" Thank you!" I said, as I admired it and gave him a hug. "What made you get this? It's not Valentine's Day," I said to him. "I thought of you, and I wanted you to have it" he said, smiling from ear to ear. "Well, thank you, I love it. It's so nice that I am not even taking it out of the plastic. I'm leaving it right here," I said, as I sat it on the table stand in front of the door. "I am putting it here so everybody can see what you got for me," I said to him as I was super appreciative and happy. "I got another surprise for you," he said to me. "What is it?" I asked. "I'm going to take you somewhere that's really special to me," he told me, and I was flattered.

It was a beautiful day out, and the weather was perfect. He had called a cab, and we rode through the city. There is something about being in Atlantic City in the evening when the sun is about to go down. The air is just beautiful, and the vibe and energy are wonderful.

You have to be there to understand what I mean. After riding around the city, we pulled up to Resorts Casino. I was only 18 so even though I grew up around the casinos, I had not been in many of them, so for me it was like a whole new world. When we walked in, it was gorgeous. There were chandeliers and glass everywhere. We got onto the elevator, and he took me to this nice restaurant. "Aww, this is really nice," I said to him as I looked around. "This is where my dad used to work," he told me as we ordered our food. I loved seafood, and it was a whole seafood buffet.

We sat there and ate and enjoyed each other then afterward, he took me on the Casino floor, and we walked around. We didn't gamble because he told me that since we were not 21 that if we hit the jackpot that we wouldn't be able to get it. We joked that with just our luck, we would hit it. We went outside and walked on the boardwalk. By this time, it was nighttime, and we enjoyed the breeze. We walked holding hands and went on the pier where he played a few games, and he won me a teddy bear. He even got me an airbrushed shirt that read Mirah and Damian. We went to a 99-cent store on the boardwalk and bought the wooden mats you sit on the beach. We sat by the water and listened to the waves and talked for what seemed like hours.

I loved being with him, and I felt safe with him. He had just turned 20 in April, which was a few weeks after we met. But for a young person, he was very wise and very intelligent. He was not like most of the guys I knew. He was just different.

"Let me tell you a funny story," I said to him as he made it easy for me to tell him anything. "What?" he said, smiling. "I think I prayed for you," I said as I started giggling bashfully. "I asked God to send me a boyfriend who was cute, who dressed nice, and was super sweet and into me like I was into him," I said as I laughed. "That's funny that you say that because I prayed to God that he would send me a girlfriend too," he said as he laughed. "Seriously," I asked him. "Seriously, Wilahi," he said to me. Wallahi means swearing by Allah (God) in Arabic. "Oh wow," I said, surprised and amazed at the same time.

"I think God sent you to me," he said sincerely, as he looked out into the ocean. "I think so too," I said as I laid my head on his shoulder. We didn't talk much after that. We just enjoyed each other's vibe, as we looked out into the ocean, processing the fact that we were God sent to one another. I could feel Damian's energy, and we both were filled with gratefulness. Afterward, we didn't get in a cab. We got ice cream and walked all the way from the boardwalk back to his house on the west side, which was kind of far, but we talked the whole time, and we were there in no time.

2

It was the end of my senior year, and I had a lot going on for regular high school as well as vocational school. In my Fashion design class at Vo-tech we had our fashion show. It was so much fun. Damian was there, and he met my teacher whose initials are P.W. I loved her. She was like a second mom to me, so I asked her if she liked him, and she said yes. Damian came to most of my school events, and afterwards my friends and his friends would party and have the best times. Though at my regular high school I was getting ready for graduation, I did attend my senior year prom. Damian really wanted to go, but I had already gone my junior year so I did not want to go again. On the day of my senior prom, I was in New York at a fashion show with my fashion design class.

I felt bad about not going to prom with him. "Damian, are you upset we didn't go to my prom?" I asked him as we laid on his bed. "Nah it's cool if you didn't want to go" he reassured me. "I'm sorry you didn't get to see me in a pretty dress" I told him as I rubbed his chest like I always did. "It's ok, if I want to see you in a pretty dress, I will wait for our wedding day," he said comforting me. "Aww, that was so sweet," I said to him as I gave him a kiss. My mom had told Damian about the big graduation party that she was throwing for me and he was so excited. I was too. All he kept talking about was how he couldn't wait to come to my graduation and see me walk, and I was excited to have him there.

When the day of graduation came all my friends and family were there. Me and all my friends that I grew up with were excited to walk. It was a bittersweet day because it was our last day of high school. Me and my bestie were excited because we knew our boyfriends Damian and Tyriek were in the bleachers cheering us on. We had the graduation speech, got our diplomas, and turned our tassels to the other side and threw our hats in the air. Afterwards everyone had found their loved ones to celebrate. I took pictures with my family, as they were giving me cards flowers and balloons. I was so happy, I kept looking for Damian, but I did not see him, and I was calling his phone. My bestie called Tyriek's phone and he didn't answer his either. We both just figured they were late, and that maybe they would just meet us at my house at my graduation party.

The party went on and it was a success. My whole family and all my friends were there. After hours passed it was over and still no Damian and Tyriek. At this point me and my bestie were getting worried. Neither one of their phones were ringing, they both were going straight to voicemail. After my party a friend of mine threw a hotel party. We all went there and were drinking and having a good time. Me and my bestie were trying to be present, but we kept wondering what happened to them, and why they didn't show up. I had an anxious feeling at the point, and I didn't want to party anymore so me and my bestie left.

The next day I had woken up early and tried to call Damian's phone. It was still going to voicemail; at that point I was extremely worried. At about noon I got a phone call from his cousin Lonnie letting me know that Damian was in jail, and that he had got locked up on the way to my graduation. They had got pulled over, and one of his friends had a gun in the car and didn't own up to it, so Damian and the two other people who were in the car went to jail as well. His cousin had let me know that Damian let him know that I knew where he kept his money stashed, and his cousin needed me to meet him so I could go and get it. I had caught the bus to A.C and met up with his cousin. I had known his cousin for years. I just had never known that they were related. He had pulled up on me in the ugliest car I have ever seen. When I saw him, he had got out and gave me a hug and we made small talk before getting in the ugly car. "Why the hell you driving this?" I asked him as I laughed. "Because I'm low, nobody would ever expect me to be in this" he said. "They definitely wouldn't, this is horrible" I said to him as I joked with him.

We had pulled up to where Damian lived, and of course nobody was home because everyone was in jail. "Damn, I forgot the door is locked," his cousin said as he tried to turn the doorknob. I had gone around the house checking to see if any windows were unlocked and they weren't. Me and his cousin were a little puzzled because if we couldn't get in, then that meant that we couldn't get the money to bail Damian out, so me getting into that house was crucial. We had walked to the backyard and saw that the upstairs window was cracked. "You think I can get up there?" I asked his cousin. "You trying to get way up there??" his cousin said as he laughed and pointed to the window in disbelief. "Yeah, if it's open. I'm going to try, give me a boost" I told him. "Damn you a rider," his cousin said to me, as he pushed me up so I could get into the window. It was on the second floor, so it took me a few tries, but eventually I was able to get in the house and I got the money out of Damian's stash, and I came out through the front door to meet Lonnie, and we sped off to meet the bails bondsman like we were in a movie.

A couple of hours later Damian was home, and he felt so bad about missing my graduation. He was pissed at his friend for not taking responsibility for the gun. That night we had chilled at his house, and we had had sex a few times. To my knowledge he was home, and it was not his gun so everything was good. I was not into the streets. I grew up in a middle-class lifestyle, so at that time I didn't really understand jail and how the system worked. He had told me that even though it was not his, that he still was charged. His friend didn't own up to it so everyone in the car was charged, and the charges wouldn't be dropped until his friend either took the charge or they went to trial. Either way I felt good, because I knew that it was not his, and I felt that everything would be ok, and that we would be able to continue on with our lives.

As I sat on the bed eating my hot wings and cheese fries Damian told me that he wanted to talk to me. "What's up?" I asked him, as I stopped eating and laid on his chest. He was so comfortable like a Teddy bear. He was not fat or anything. He had a nice build, and he was solid. Laying on him felt like heaven to me. There was literally no place I would rather have been, then lying there in his presence. As I laid there, I grabbed his hands like I always did. "I love your hands" I said as I was caressing his palms. To me he had the best hands ever. They weren't super big or super small. They were a perfect size, and they were firm and strong. Plus, he could fight so that meant he also hit hard and, that was so attractive to me.

He laid there and received all my love and affection, as we were so comfortable with one another. "What did you want to talk to me about?" I asked him, as I looked up at him. "I got a court date coming up soon for a real big case" he told me with much concern in his eyes. His demeanor had changed, and I could tell that it was serious. "What is the case about?" I asked him, scared to hear the answer. "It was something that happened a while ago, you remember I was locked up for the case, I told you about, right?" he asked me, and I nodded "yes". "I am still out on bail for that, and my trial is coming up soon" he said to me, and he began giving me the details.

I was shocked at the things that he told me. I could not even see a person like him being involved in anything like that. He was so sweet and kindhearted, so I could not even imagine him being caught up in certain situations. "Wow" I said as he finished telling me. "Well, I'm here for you and I got you. You are special and you are not that person. You are not the things that you have been charged with. I will say a prayer and ask God to see you through all of this, and everything is going to be ok" I told him as I hugged him reassuring him. "Ok" he said to me not seeming too convinced. "This is a big case and it's a real big deal, so I just want you to know in case anything happens, that I do love you. And I understand if you don't stick with me" he said sincerely. "What? Why would I not stick with you? I love you, and I got you" I reassured him. "I'm looking at a lot of time" he said, as he paused not knowing what my reaction was going to be. "How much time?" I asked him curious. "Like 60 years" he told me, as he seemed like he didn't even want to say it out of his mouth. "60 years??" I said as I was in disbelief. "Yup, so I got one of the best lawyers and God willing I beat the case. "Oh my God" I said as I felt sick to my stomach. "It's going to be ok though. The court date is not for a couple of months, so for now let's just not think about it, and just have fun" he said to me trying to cheer me up.

I felt so bad. I could not believe the information that I had just received. I was a little bummed out. He turned on some music and laid me back down on his chest, and he immediately changed the subject. "So, what's your favorite ice cream?" he asked me. "What? What kind of question is that?" I said as I laughed. "I just want to know" he said to me. "I don't know, I guess strawberry" I said to him.

We began having deep conversations about life, our pasts, religion, our likes, and dislikes, you name it, we talked about it. After talking for what seemed like hours, we laid there in silence and just enjoyed each other. "Where you see us in five years?" I asked him. "Five years is a long time" he said to me. "I know right, that would be crazy if we made it that long, right" I said to him. "Yeah, it would" I agreed. "Do you see us together? I asked him. "Yeah, I do" he said as he was rubbing my back. "Me too" I said to him as I smiled. "The only thing that would make me not be with you is, if you do something disloyal like cheat or something like that" he told me. "I feel the same way" I reassured him.

"What is one of the things that you like about me the most?" he asked, smiling. "I like that you are responsible, funny, loyal, giving and I love the way you love me" I said to him as I smiled. "Oh, and I like the fact that you don't have any kids. I would never date a guy with kids, because at this age it's too much responsibility. So, I like the fact that you made it this far with no baby mamas" I joked with him. "Word" he said smiling. "Hopefully one day we can have kids. It would be me and your first child, and we will have all of our kids together. That would be cool because a lot of people we know have more than one baby mother or baby father" I told him. "Word" I don't want kids anytime soon. I just want to enjoy life" he told me. "Me too" I said as I felt so secure. "Plus, you like my kid, I'll just spoil you" he said jokingly. "Whatever" I said as I nudged him a little bit.

He was joking but it was true. He really did spoil me. He bought me things, and he always made sure that I was good. He used to try to dress me. He used to tie my shoes for me and everything. He truly did treat me like his little princess. He waited on me hand and foot, he got my nails and hair done. He had certain people around and they would come and clean the house, so I never had to clean up or do anything. We had stopped catching cabs and started renting cars. He always took me to nice spots to eat. We never cooked, so we ate out all the time. We had a ball.

He had such a nurturing spirit, and I loved that about him because I always craved that love from a male. I didn't grow up with my father. He was in and out of my life, and we didn't have the best relationship at all. I had a stepdad who was no better. All I saw growing up was drama and neglect from drug addicted men, so being with Damian was like a breath of fresh air. He was my boyfriend, and even though he was young, he was very mature, and had a persona like a father. I think that is one of the things that drew me to him. I loved how he put me first. Actually, we both put each other first, and I loved the fact that we didn't have any kids, because we were able to give one another our undivided attention. My deal breaker was a man with kids and Damian completely agreed. We talked a little bit more then we began foreplay and had sex and went to sleep.

3

The next day I went home to my mom's house to spend time with my family. I hadn't seen my mom in a while, so I spent most of the day over there with her, my brother and my sisters. Later that night I went back over to Damian's house. I normally didn't call first, I just told him what time I was coming, and I would just pop up. As I was walking from the bus stop to his house to see him, I was super excited. When I got there, he and a few other people were in the living room and the house was ram sacked. Damian had a pissed look on his face. The first thing I noticed when I walked through the door was my huge basket with my Teddy bear in it was slit open. "What happened?" I said as I was confused. "Fucking police raided the crib" his cousin said. "They ain't find nothing, so they let us go" his cousin added. "What?" I asked confused. "They raided the house for what?" I asked. "It happened not too long ago. We were all just in here in handcuffs, I'm glad you weren't here" Damian told me as he had started cleaning up the house. "That's crazy" I said to him as I was so disappointed, and that they ruined my basket. "Why the hell did they tear my basket?" I asked. "I don't know babe; I will get you another one" Damian said to me, and I began helping him clean up.

Even though the house was turned upside down by the police, Damian was still in good spirits. We ended up having a fun night, even though it did make me a little paranoid wondering if the police were going to come back. I had never been in a raid before, and it seemed like a scary situation to be in. But me being young and naïve I didn't even care as long as I was spending time with Damian. He made me feel safe like everything was going to be ok. Him and the people there weren't tripping so I wasn't going to trip about it either. After everything was clean, we laid in his bed, and he wrapped me in his arms and we went to sleep.

A few days later it was the fourth of July and Atlantic City was lit and packed. There were locals and outer towners enjoying the city, the beach and the boardwalk. It was super-hot and humid that day. I had on a blue jean mini skirt and tight fitted sage colored top which was really cute and figure flattering. I had on a pair of sage colored sandals to match, and my hair was curly. I really looked cute that day and when Damian saw me, he was smiling from ear to ear. He had come and picked me up in a rental car, and we had gone on the boardwalk to see the fireworks and to enjoy the fourth. It was so packed on the boardwalk that you could barely walk. Damian didn't want me to get lost in the crowd, so he stood in back of me holding me tight by my waist. He was flirting and saying funny things in my ear. We were just having a great time. Even though we were surrounded by thousands of people it felt like we were the only ones there. The mood and the air were just right. It was nighttime so you could feel the breeze off of the water and the temperature of the weather was perfect. We had seen many people we knew while we were there. We stopped and spoke and talked and laughed with everyone as they were enjoying themselves too.

We had gone on the Pier and played games and Damian had won me several Teddy Bears and prizes. Afterwards we walked down the boardwalk holding hands as we looked up past the casino's buildings at the fireworks. They were beautiful and Magical. It was so nice being able to spend that moment with him, and looking at his face I could tell he was enjoying it too. It was getting late, so we were going to go back to his house and kick it. As we were walking off the boardwalk, we ran into a girl he used to talk to. I knew of her through a mutual friend Though me and her were never friends, we were on speaking terms. "Hey Damian" she said to him and "Hi Shamirah" she said to me, almost distant and cold. "Hi" I said to her as I didn't really even want to speak at all. I was wondering why she was even speaking to my boyfriend anyway. "I was up here with my boyfriend, but he ditched me, now I don't have a ride home, "she said to Damian as she was upset. Damian looked at me for reassurance to give her a ride, and I looked at him like "No" but being the good guy, he was, he said "Ok, I will take you home." It was her and another girl and they both lived like thirty minutes outside of the city and I did not want to ride all the way out to where they lived. "It's Ok, let's be a blessing and take them home," Damian said to me as he opened my door and the two girls got in the back seat.

As we were driving it was awkward tension, as I said she used to talk to him. They were never boyfriend and girlfriend, and me and her were not friends but you could tell she felt a way about me and him being together. Actually, a lot of girls were jealous of the fact that I was with him because of how good of a person he was and how he adored me and put me on a pedestal. A lot of girls that he used to talk to wondered why he didn't treat them like that. I guess it was just something about Me. There was something about me and his connection that made our relationship special. Damian saw that I was uncomfortable, so he grabbed my hand and put it on his, for assurance to let me know that I had nothing to worry about, and he gave me a reassuring look. Even though I was a little upset, once he gave me the look, I could not do anything but smile. He was so charming, and I could not stay mad at him.

Once he saw that my tension had eased he had put on our favorite R&B artist at the time "Genuine" I can't remember the title of the song but I know it was beautiful and some of the words were "It was better to loved and lost, then to have never lost at all" and me and him were grooving as we rode thru the night. As the music played. All I heard next, was the girl he used to talk to in the back sniffling and crying. "You Ok?" Damian asked her as he turned the music down. "I'm good," she said almost with an attitude. I was not sure why she was crying. Maybe she was upset seeing me and him together. Or she could have been upset that her boyfriend ditched her on the boardwalk. Either way, I was ready for them to get out the car and be dropped off so me and him could continue our night. Once we pulled up to their house they got out. The one girl said, "Thank you for the ride" and the girl he used to talk to just got out and closed the door without saying anything and she was still crying.

We had listened to music and held hands the whole way back and enjoyed being in each other's presents. When we got back to his house in the city, he parked the car and we got out. I thought we were going in the house but instead Damian had sat in a chair on the porch and pulled me onto his lap like I was a little girl. "You good?" he asked. "Yeah, I'm good. Why you ask me that?" I asked him. "I just want to make sure you good" he said with his usual bright smile. I sat there on his lap with him holding me, and it felt like the best feeling in the world. I felt so safe and protected and loved and cherished in that moment. I did not want it to end.

We had sat out there for a while just enjoying the summer night when a man walked up. "What's up man!" the man said lively to Damian. "What's good Pinky!" Damian said to the guy, and I burst out laughing. It was not funny, but it was. The man was a weird pinkish color almost the color of a hotdog. He was dressed clean, and he had a funny sense of humor. "Ain't nothing man. I see you sitting with your lady. I don't mean to disturb you, but I wanted to know if you wanted to buy some ice cream" he said as he was pulling a small cooler. "Aw man, pink man you disturbing me and my lady for some ice cream? Let me see what you got" Damian said as he joked with him, and Pinky opened up the cooler. At first, I didn't want any ice cream because his hands looked weird but then I saw strawberry shortcake ice cream which was my favorite, and Damian picked it up and gave it to me, and he gave the man the money. Him and Pinky joked a little longer then eventually he left. "Why did you call that man, Pinky? That was rude" I said to him, still sitting on his lap. "That's his name, he's a good dude. He was burned when he was younger, and his skin peeled. That's why he looks that color" Damian told me. "I been knowing him since I was a kid, he knows it's all love" Damian said to me as we ate our ice cream and continued to enjoy the night. We had come in the house and took a shower together, we got in the bed, and we had sex and went to sleep.

"Good morning" I said to him as we got up the next day as I came from the bathroom. "Good morning" he said as he got up in his boxers to use the bathroom and brush his teeth. When he came back in the room, he had got back in the bed he started feeling all over me, being flirtatious and kissing me. He then slid my panties down and we started to have sex, it felt so good. He loved morning sex, he loved night sex, he loved afternoon sex, he loved to have sex with me all the time every chance he could. Afterwards we got in the shower to get dressed for the day. Every day with him we did something fun, I never knew what we had planned. We mostly just went with the flow and always had a good time no matter what we were doing. "I want to take you somewhere that's special to me" he said as he was getting dressed. I had on a pair of white roc-a-wear sweatpants with red stripes going down the side. I had on a red tank top and a pair of all white air force ones. I had my hair down in a China band with my usual big hooped earrings ready for the summer day. "Where we going?" I asked him. "I'm taking you to meet my mom," he said to me. "What?!" I said excited and nervous at the same time. "I can't see her wearing this" I said as I wanted to change my outfit. "Nah, you good that's perfect" he said to me as he finished getting dressed and we left.

On the way we had stopped to get something to eat, and he got his mom something as well. I was so nervous to meet her. I just hoped that she liked me. At that point I had not met any of his family except for two of his older brothers. Meeting his mom was serious to me and I was not prepared. When we pulled up to the house, I had butterflies in my stomach. "Don't be nervous, " Damian said to me as he opened my car door to let me out. As we were walking up to the door, this brown skinned lady with short curly hair and a red and white dress came out the door with the biggest smile and her arms opened wide. She gave me a big hug and she kissed me on the cheek. I was taken back with happiness. I had looked to the side of me where Damian was standing, and I saw him smiling from ear to ear as he was pleased by his mother's reaction. She still had her hands on my shoulders, and she looked at him and said plainly, "Damian, this is your wife and you are going to marry her," and she kept looking at me and smiling. Before I knew it, I looked up and I saw three little boys run out the house from behind her and they were jumping and flipping and playing like boys do. They had to be about 11, 10 and 9 somewhere in that age range, "Who are they?" I asked Damian. "Those are my little brothers" he said to me as he smiled, and they all ran up to him.

I could tell that they loved and admired their big brother. He introduced me to all three of them and told me their names. They were so cute, and they all had their own personalities. I absolutely adored the youngest one. He was so cute. He looked just like Damian, and I loved his spirit. His mom asked if we could drop the kids off to his dad's house which was about an hour away from the city and he agreed. On the ride there, the kids talked and laughed and joked like boys do and Damian joked with them.

I enjoyed every minute of it. It was nice to see how he interacted with his family and how much they loved him. We had pulled up to his dad's house and I was nervous all over again. Though I wasn't as nervous meeting his dad as I was meeting his mom, it still was a little overwhelming to be meeting both parents on the same day. His dad was sitting in the yard in his chair and Damian introduced us and his dad shook my hand and smiled. His dad's wife was also there, and she introduced herself. They pulled chairs out in the yard and all four of us sat back there and talked and laughed. We talked about setting up a date to get on the ferry to the Baltimore Harbor to get some seafood and have some fun. Though Damian was allergic to seafood, he was down to go, and we all looked forward to it.

We were there for hours and soon it was time to go. We had come through the door to say bye to the boys and all three of them were sitting on the floor recording music on a recording machine that they had. They were so close, and you could tell they all loved each other. They were like little best friends. They were basically inseparable, and how in tune they were sitting on the floor together making that music was an image I would never forget. They looked so adorable, and that moment was so special. I wish I would have taken a picture. But the picture is captured in my mind and is a beautiful image that I will never forget.

On our way back to the city we had stopped pass a bar in Pleasant-ville NJ called Wash's to get some food. We had ordered some hot wings and fries to go, and planned on eating our food when we got back to his house. Pleasantville was literally only about eight minutes from Atlan-tic City, so we knew our food would still be hot when we got there. We were about three blocks from his house when in back of us we heard police sirens and I looked in the rear-view mirror and saw the blue lights. "What happened?" I asked Damian, confused because we had not done anything illegal, so I did not know why they were stopping us. "I don't know, I guess they on they bullshit again, " he said as he pulled out his license. One of the officers came to the car and immediately asked where we were going. "Damn man you not even going to tell me why you pulled over?" Damian said in a joking yet serious manner. The officer had called Damian by his last name, so I assumed that was not their first encounter with one another. Another officer had pulled up, this time he came to my window and asked ME where we were going as he shined his flashlight all through the car. "You know my house is a couple of blocks away," Damian said to the officer who was talking to me. "Don't be a smart ass" the officer said to him in a joking, yet serious manner and they all interacted as they had met before. "I'm just trying to get home and eat my food with my girl, you see the food in the back seat" Damian told them as he pointed to the hot food. "We can't let you go until we search the car," one of the officers told Damian.

We were young at the time. I was 18 and he was 20. Damian was smart and he knew his rights. I had not had too many encounters with the police so I didn't understand what was going on at that moment, but I knew that I was very uncomfortable. "Nah, y'all not just going to search my car for no reason. Y'all didn't even tell me why y'all stopped me, and y'all harassing my girl" he told them. They called him by his last name again and told him that he would be arrested if he didn't let them search the car. "Y'all ain't going to find nothing" Damian had told them. At that point there were about two other cop cars on the scene.

We got out and me and him were standing next to each other outside of the car. They had rambled through everything and didn't find anything. Lastly one of the cops grabbed the bag of food and said he had to search it. "What?" Damian said to the officer as he was crossing the line more than he already was. "That food is hot as hell, why would you search the food?" Damian asked, getting pissed. "Alright, I understand. I still have to check it" the officer said to him as he seemed like he wasn't even that comfortable doing it. "I'm not going to go through it, but just open the bag for me" the officer told him, and Damian opened the bag. "Ok, cool" the officer said as he flashed his flashlight in the bag and saw there was nothing suspicious in there. Damian closed the bag and they said we were good to go. I was pissed because it reminded me of the time when the police raided his house and didn't find anything and they ripped my basket that he had bought me, now this.

At the time we were so young we didn't understand that we were being racially profiled and harassed by the police. They were violating our rights in every way. Damian seemed like he was used to it, but that still did not make it ok. He had family members that had got in trouble with the law so just by his last name already having a reputation to it, he was an easy target as well. Damian had a few words with the officers. One of them had even apologized for putting us through that and it ended well. Us and the police were all about to leave and out of nowhere Damian's brother came running up yelling "Don't take him! Take Me!! With his hair looking wild. He had on a red baseball Jersey that was not buttoned up so his shirt was wide open showing his chest and stomach. He had on a pair of baggy jeans with no belt and a pair of Timbs that were not tied so they were flopping off of his feet. The sight was so hilarious that me, Damian and even the police burst out laughing. "What you doing bro? And where did you come from?" Damian asked, still cracking up. "I got a call that the police were taking you, " his brother said to him, as he was out of breath from running. "Everything is good bro, we on our way back to the crib" Damian told him. The police were still cracking up and they got in their cars and drove away, and me Damian and his brother went back to his house. That night was one to remember, I had not laughed like that in a long time. We had got back to the house and chilled. At that point the food was cold and we didn't even want it anymore. We had just chilled and had sex and went to sleep.

About a week later we had been out all-day having fun. It was about 8 o'clock at night when we came back to his house. His roommates and a few other people were there. We laughed and kicked it with them for a while and ordered some food and went up to Damian's room. Next thing you know all we heard was "Atlantic City Police, Come downstairs with your hands Up!" from a loud voice. "What the hell is going on?" I said as I looked at Damian. I was scared to death. "I don't know what the f*ck is going on" he said as he was confused too. "I know you all are up there, and the police began saying his roommates last names calling them down. Damian opened his room door and saw his roommates hiding in the back room. "Yo, I don't know what the f*ck is going on" he said with a concerned look on his face that I had never saw before, and I began to get even more scared. "I'm going to count to five if everyone who is upstairs doesn't come down, I am going to let the K-9 loose" he threatened. "Oh my God Damian, I am scared, let's just go down" I said to him as I began to cry. "You good, calm down" he reassured me as he opened up the room door and yelled "We coming down" and he held my hand and we walked downstairs.

When we got down there, his roommates were already on the floor faced down with their hands behind their backs. There were about five officers in the living room with helmets and body shields. They had huge rifle guns pointed at us, and one of the officers was holding the K-9 on the leash. It was such a scary sight, all I wanted to do was go home. "Get down" the officers said to me, and Damian and I was utterly disgusted. I did not want to lay on the dirty floor. Damian kept his room and his area very clean but the rest of the house where everyone else was not always the cleanest. There were a bunch of guys living there, and they did not always clean up, so to lay on the floor was a complete disgrace. As I laid there, dust was getting in my nose, and I wanted to cry. "Where's the bat?" One of the officers asked. "What bat?" his cousin asked. "We got a call that someone up the street was beaten with a bat, and they said the person with the bat ran into this house" the officer said. "We been here all night, nobody beat anybody with a bat," his cousin added.

The officers looked around. They didn't tear the house up like the time before, so I guess in their observation they did not see any evidence of a bat or anyone in the home who looked like they got into an altercation or anything. They let us up and made us sit on the couch with our hands behind our backs. "Alright, we are not going to arrest anyone, we got a phone call, so we had to come and investigate" one of the officers said. "We haven't done anything, so what is all this for?" one of the roommates said to the officer. "We were just checking, " the officer said as they did their report, and they all began to leave without apologizing for anything. I was glad when the dog left, it was scary and intense.

"That was some bullshit, you alright? Damian asked me when they left. "Yeah, I'm good" I told him as I was still shocked by what had just happened. At that point I felt dirty from being on the floor and I was ready to go home to my mom's house to take a shower. After what had just happened, I did not want to stay at his house. Damian understood and he took me home and I took a shower and we stayed at my mom's. My mom's house was nice, and it was big so we stayed in the den. "To-night, was crazy, " I said to him. "I know right, I'm sorry that happened" he said to me sincerely. "It seems like the cops are always harassing y'all" I told him. "Word" he said as he sat there like he was thinking about it. "I'm serious, it's always something, did you ever think about moving out of that house?" I asked him concerned. "Maybe we can get a place together somewhere else and move out of the city" I told him as I held his hand. "Word, you right. I do need to move, that crib is hot and it's always sh*t going on there" he said to me. "Yes, it is, we can get a place together. You don't have to be there and deal with all that " I reassured him. "I got you, I'm on it" he reassured me, and we got some blankets and watched movies for the rest of the night.

4

A few weeks later it was the end of summer, and it was time for me to go to college for the fall. Damian took me to buy a few things like my bookbag and my supplies and he got me a pair of black and red bugs bunny Jordans for my first day of school. I thought that was super sweet of him. He was just as excited about me starting school as I was. I went to Atlantic Cape Community College. I went to the Mays Landing campus as well as the Atlantic City Campus. I knew once school started, I was not going to be able to be with Damian 24/7 like I was the whole summer. We would have rentals or just catch cabs or busses wherever we needed to go. But once I started school my classes were mainly on the Mays Landing campus, which was about a five-minute drive from my mom's house in Oakcrest Estates. It was easier for me to get to school staying home at my mom's because I could either catch the bus right up the street or borrow her car to go to class.

School had started and I loved it. My major was Performing Arts, and my Minor was education. I took theater, dance, public speaking, and visual arts all in which I loved. I was in an advanced literature class and my teacher loved all my work. In college I was also a part of a small sorority called "The Pink Ladies" which was a group full of intelligent vibrant boss entrepreneurial women that I am still friends with until this day. One of the women in the Pink Ladies with me was my girl Mika English the owner of GREW by. M.E. Mika created her own hair care product and it took off. She has a store located in Pleasantville

NJ and sells her products on her website www.grewbyme.com. I loved college and I was so happy. I mainly stayed on campus all day since I did not have a car. On my breaks in between classes, I would call Damian on the phone and talk to him the whole time. On the days where I had classes in Atlantic City where he lived. He would come to the school and get me, and I would go to his house after I was done school. It was very fun, and Damian was very supportive of me going to school.

One day after I was done with class. I had called him and told him that I was catching the bus to see him and to meet me at the McDonald in the Renaissance Plaza in the city. He told me OK, but he had a little laugh in his voice. "Why are you laughing? " I asked him. "You going to be there, right?" I scolded him. "Yeah, I'm going to be there" he told me, and I told him I loved him. I went outside to catch the bus like I normally did. When I got to the city, I walked from the bus station to the McDonald in the Renaissance Plaza where we were supposed to meet. I called him and he did not answer. I sat in there for a few minutes and ordered fries so I wouldn't look like a weirdo just sitting in there for no reason.

About 20 minutes went passed, and he still had not shown up. That was not like him so I began getting worried. I didn't want to wait for him anymore, so I was about to just walk to his house to find out what was going on. I had walked out the McDonalds doors and as soon as I got outside; I had seen him pull up in a green Q45. He had one of his good friends in the front seat and Damian was in the driver's seat. He was smiling from ear to ear. "Whos' car is this?" I asked him, still a little annoyed that he was so late. "It's My car, get in" he said to me as he pulled up to me. "Is this your car? "I asked his friend, thinking Damian was playing a trick on me. "Nah sis this is really his car. He got it for you" his friend told me. "What?" I said in disbelief. "I'm serious" Damian said, as he pulled over in the parking lot to show me the car. He had got out and showed me everything. His friend had got out of the front seat and Damian showed me the Betty Boop seat cover and floor mat that he got for me because he knew that I loved Betty Boop at that time. "I know you in school now, and I don't want you to have to catch the bus so I grabbed this car so you can get back and forth" he said as he was really proud. "Awww " I said to him as I gave him a hug and a kiss, then I got in the front seat.

We dropped his friend off and we cruised all over in his new car. It was really nice, and I loved having our own car and it all felt really good. Damian kept his word and from that day on I never had to ride the bus to school or anywhere else ever again. He dropped me off and picked me up everywhere I needed to go. He was like my personal chauffeur, and he did not mind. I lived about five minutes from school, and he lived at least a half an hour away. Yet he still drove all the way from A.C to Mays Landing just to drop me off right up the street. Then he would drive back home to A.C and a few hours later when my classes were over, he would drive all the way back out there to pick me up and take me home. Then drive all the way back to his house unless it was a day where I came to his house with him. I asked him if that was too much for him to do, and he would always say no and that he didn't mind. Damian really did spoil me, and he was always there no matter what and I appreciated him for that.

It was a Thursday, and on Thursdays I had class in Mays Landing but my last class was on the A.C campus. Damian would always pick me up and take me to my A.C class and when I was done, I would stay at his house, because that was my last class for the week. I was waiting outside for him like I always did at the spot that I always had. I was so excited to see him pull up smiling like he always did, and I was ready to spend the weekend with him and have fun as usual. A few minutes had passed and instead of me seeing him pull up in his car, my mom had pulled up in her car to pick me up. "Mom, what you doing here, where's Damian?" I asked her, confused. I got in the car, and my mom looked at me like she had to tell me something, but she did not want to say it. "What's wrong?" I asked her, scared of what she was going to say.

"Damian called me and said he was stabbed," she said. "What? How did he call you then?" I asked confused. "He had called me on the phone and told me to tell you that he was stabbed. And that he was on his way to the hospital. And that he loved you" she told me, almost looking like she wanted to cry. "Oh my God" I said as I started to panic. "Calm down, I'm going to take you to the hospital" she told me, and she drove me to the Atlantic City Medical Center where he was. She dropped me off and she did not stay.

When I got to the waiting room, I saw that his brother and some other family members were already there. Everyone looked worried. I was scared to ask any questions because I could not bear it if I got the wrong answer. "He's ok" his big brother said, as he walked up to me and hugged me because he saw that I was a mess. "Thank you" I said to him, and it felt as if a million bricks had lifted off of me. Since he was stabbed and it was considered violence, we had to be registered to go upstairs to see him. Eventually they let us upstairs to the floor that he would be on.

The doctor came out and told us that Damian was in surgery and that his lungs had collapsed twice. While in the waiting room I was a nervous wreck again, praying that he was going to be ok. After what seemed like forever, they had wheeled him out of the back, and he seemed out of it. We were all happy to see him, and the doctor said to us "Is there a Shamirah here" and I told him that was me. The doctor said I just wanted to make sure because when he woke up from surgery, he was asking about Shamirah." They wheeled him past me. He looked at me and whispered "Sorry" I touched his hand and kissed it and told him that I loved him and that I was here and that I was not going anywhere.

Once he was settled in his room his family visited and left. I laid on the bed with him and I cried and told him how happy I was that he was ok. I asked him what happened, but he was still out of it, so I just sat there to give him comfort. Eventually visiting hours were over and I had to go. I was so sad, and I did not want to leave. I didn't know where his car was, so I just walked from the hospital across the street to the bus station. It was a cold night, and my walk was so lonely. I was so sad and worried about Damian. I had gone home, and I could barely sleep. I went to see him first thing in the morning as soon as visiting hours started.

When I came in the next day, he looked a little better. He had told me that over the night his lungs had collapsed again, and he had another emergency surgery, so he was being monitored the whole day. Damian was in the hospital for about a week, and he seemed to get better about the third day. He was finally able to talk and move and he was much more like himself. His Mom, dad and his dad's wife and brothers had come to visit him, and everyone was glad that he was ok.

Once they left, he finally told me what happened. "I was on the avenue getting some sneakers at the Hip Hip Shop when I bumped into so and so. We had words and he swung on me. I swung back and knocked him out. On his way down, I hit him again and I guess it woke him back up. As I was punching him, I felt something sharp on my side. He stabbed me and turned the knife and it hit me in my lungs, after that he ran. I didn't feel it at first, I guess because of my adrenaline. But then I looked down and my shirt was drenched with blood, so I just started walking to the hospital which is several blocks away. All I remember is people saying oh my God he's bleeding, and I just kept walking. Once I got to the hospital doors I just collapsed and next thing you know here I am" he told me. "Wow" I said as I felt bad, and I was mad at the dude who did it. "They had to cut my clothes off of me, they're in the closet" he said as he pointed to the closet for me to get them. His clothes were in a brown paper bag, and I was almost scared to open it. Damian took the bag from me, and he opened it. His clothes were covered in dry blood. Since it had sat for days, his blood was burgundy and smelled like old blood. "Why did they even give that to you?" I asked in disgust. "I don't know" he said as he put the clothes back in the bag, and I put the bag back in the closet.

He stayed in there for a few more days and then he was finally released home. His torso was wrapped in bandage really good, other than that everything else was back to normal. He had a lot of people come and visit him at his house, and it was just nice being back with him outside of the hospital. I helped him as much as he would let me, and he was in good spirits. I tried to tell him to take it easy, but he wanted to move around even though he was still healing. We had laid in his bed listening to Ochino Sparks "If I could do it all again, I promise to you I would do it different" we both were smiling and were so happy that things were almost like normal.

It was the afternoon. It was a beautiful day, and the sun was shining so bright. He had his windows open, and we were enjoying the city breeze. The vibe was perfect. "You know what I miss though?" he asked me, smiling. "What?" I asked him as I already knew the answer. "P*ssy" he said to me, and I laughed. "How are we going to do it and you're hurt? You can't even use your waist or mid-section" I told him. "Nah, I'm good" he said to me. "No, I don't want you to get hurt" I told him. I told him to just lay back and get comfortable and I gave him head instead. At that time, I was not a pro at giving head, so he always taught me what he wanted me to do. For him I don't think it was better than having sex with me. But he had to take what he could get at the time until he healed up some more.

Things were good after he got out of the hospital. Life was pretty much back to normal. I continued to go to school and spend time with him. We had fun like we always did. One day I went to the mall with my friends to shop and catch up and have some girl time. While I was there, I stopped past Victoria's Secret to get my Love Spell and Pure Seduction lotions and sprays like I always did. Damian loved how I smelled. While I was there, I came across "Vanilla Lace." It smelled so good, so I bought that too. I had also bought an all-white lace bra and panty set with thigh high stockings and the garter belt. It made my cute shape look super sexy. That night I had went to Damian's house with my spend the night bag. I had all my sexy goodies in it that I bought that day. I had taken a shower at his house, and I got out and put on my lingerie and sprayed myself with the Vanilla lace. He had room-mates so I came out of the bathroom with my bathrobe on and walked to his room. "Damn you smell so good" he said to me as he smelled my neck. "Thank You" I said as I took off my robe and he saw my sexy lace. "Damn babe" he said as he laid back on the bed and smiled at me looking surprised and turned on at the same time. "Let me see" he said as he spun me around to take a good look at me. "That's nice" he said as he looked like he wanted to tear it off.

Damian had turned off the lights and lit a candle and turned on some Jodeci. He had already taken a shower, so he was already in his boxers. "Dance for me" he said to me as he laid back to watch me. I was always shy when he asked me to dance because I was not the best dancer. But the mood was perfect, and I did feel sexy, so I just winded my body to "I want to Freak you" by Jodeci and I got into it. I could see him getting erect and I knew he was enjoying it. Eventually he pulled me on the bed and began kissing me. He started kissing my lips, then my neck, then my breast, then my stomach, then between my thighs, and then he began kissing my vagina and he told me to stand up in front of him and he knelt down a little and began eating my vagina while I was standing up. It felt so good, and I was enjoying every minute of it. He then stopped and turned me over and laid me on the bed and stuck his penis in me and we were having sex from the back. Soon he nutted and rested for a minute then we did it again.

We were in the room having a good time when outside the door in the hallway, we heard a lot of commotion. It was his two cousin's play fighting and having fun. "Let's stop" they might hear us" I said to him. "Don't worry about them" Damian said as he kept grinding. We kept going against my better judgement. Next thing you know "BOOM" the door came flying open and his cousins saw us having sex. I was so embarrassed, and Damian jumped up and closed the door and put his clothes on and came out of the room snapping on them. When he came back in, we laughed about it, and we laid in the bed and cuddled and talked. "I love you" he said as he kissed me on my neck. "I love you too" I said as I hugged him tight as I laid on his chest. "Look at me" he said, as he compassionately grabbed my face and made me look at him. "What?" I said to him softly. "I love you and I'm not going anywhere ok" he said to me sincerely. "Ok" I said innocently looking at him. "I'm serious" he said to me, and I could see in his eyes that he was sincere. I felt so secure in his arms, and I knew that he meant every word he said. I loved him because he was a man of his word and he never left me. He was always there. He kissed me on my forehead again and we fell asleep in each other's arms.

About four o'clock that morning we were awakened to a loud BOOM. It sounded like a boulder had come through the house. Before I could even react, the room door was kicked down by men with shields who were dressed like G.I Joe. They had flashlights and guns all in our faces. "Get up!" They were yelling, and one by one I saw everyone coming out of their rooms in plastic handcuffs. "Ma'am do you have clothes on?" one of the officers asked me as I was under the covers "No I don't" I answered as all I had on was my bra and panties. "Ok, we are going to let you get dressed, " he told me, and they provided me privacy to put my clothes on. As I was getting dressed, I was scared out of my mind at what was going on. When I opened the door, the officer was standing outside the door, and he put the plastic handcuffs on me and took me downstairs with everyone else.

There were about six of us down there. All the guys had boxers on because everyone was asleep in bed. There was one other female besides me. We all sat in the living room as they rummaged through the house flipping everything upside down. At that point, sadly I was used to it.

I was just waiting for them to get done so I could go back to sleep. By now the sun was coming up and the swat team was still there, actually more police and detectives had come. They all talked as we sat there. I had a bad feeling; this time was different from any other time. This time felt serious, and I didn't feel like it was going to end well.

They had come into the living room and told everyone they were under arrest, and my heart dropped. I looked at Damian's face and he looked so disappointed. I sat next to him the whole time on the couch, and he leaned over to me and said, "You good, I'm going to bail you out asap." I was thinking to myself how he was going to bail me out when he was going to be in jail too. They all were able to put their clothes on and one by one they got taken into the police cars and off to jail. One of the officers walked up to me and told me that I was not going to jail, and I was so relieved but still sad that everyone else was going, especially Damian. "You are not going to jail because we found your driver's license and since this is not your residence. We are going to let you go" he told me. I saw the girl going to jail and I asked her why they were taking her because she didn't live there either. They had found weed in her purse so that's why she was going. I knew Damian had bail money so I just wanted to wait until he was processed so I could find out his bail and get him out.

Soon everyone was gone except me and a few officers that were finishing up. I sat there empty and sad. The house that was once full of fun had no more life in it, it was somber. I was just waiting for all the officers to leave so I could gather all my stuff and go home to my mom's house and work on getting Damian out of jail. As the officers were leaving, one of them had the audacity to give me his card and tell me if I got any info to call him. When he left, I threw the card on the floor and began getting my things. Damian had left his cell phone with me, and his mom had called. "Hey mom mom" which was her nickname for me. "I heard what happened. I just wanted you to know that everything is going to be ok" she said to me and I broke down crying on the phone with her. She told me to be strong and be his backbone. The way she was talking to me was like she knew he was not coming home or something. I appreciated her encouraging words, but I knew I had to get dressed to begin working on getting him out of jail.

I went downtown to the courthouse in Atlantic City where he was seeing the judge. One by one everyone who got arrested was released on bail and the girl got a ROR. I was excited because I knew once Damian had seen the judge that he would be coming home. I waited and waited for hours, and I heard nothing. Eventually I left. I figured that he would just call me and let me know how much the bail was and when to pick him up. I had my mom's car, so I drove home and got in the shower and anxiously waited for his call.

Finally, at around 8pm, I got a call from the Mays Landing County Jail. "Hello!?" I said happy to hear from him. "What's up?" he said, sounding somber. "What's wrong? How much is your bail?" I asked him waiting for his response. He paused and sounded like he was super upset but was trying to hold back his emotions. "How much?" I asked him again. "I don't have a bail" he said to me disappointed. "What? What do you mean?" I asked him confused. "I was already out on bail from my other case, so the judge revoked my bail and said I was a flight risk, so he's not giving me a bail" he said, and I could not believe what I was hearing. "So, you're stuck?" I said as I began to cry. "Don't cry, it's going to be ok. I need you to call my lawyer tomorrow to get a bail hearing" he told me, and he gave me his lawyer's name and number to call in the morning. I was so sad that I could not stop crying. We were on a collect jail call so I knew that I could not stay on the phone with him forever. I did not want to hang up. If I could, I would have gone and stayed in the jail cell with him, that is how much I loved him.

The next day was Saturday so I could not reach the lawyer, so I left a message on his answering machine. The county jail had visits on the weekends, so I went to see Damian. It was surreal that 24 hours beforehand, I was with him, and we were making passionate love, and next thing you know I was visiting him in jail. I had been to the county before to visit people. Actually, me and Damian would go visit people who were locked up all the time. I just never imagined that I would be seeing him on the other side of the glass. When I walked in, the line was long as usual. It was dirty and I did not want to be there. I got anxious when I got up to the front, when it was my time to give all my information to the guard to go to the back and see him. Being back there made me feel like I was in jail too. When I went to the back to sit and wait for the inmates, of course there were people I knew. It was kind of embarrassing to be there seeing him. We were an admired couple, and I did not want people to see me at jail visits and to see him locked up.

I sat at the desk and finally he came down. The way the visit was set up was that you and the inmate were separated by glass, and you talked to them by phone. I did not want to touch the phone, it looked so dirty. Thank God I always kept tissues or wipes in my purse. I had wiped the phone down and picked it up to talk to him. "Hey, what's up?" I said as I could barely look at him without crying. "Nothing, did you get in touch with my lawyer?" he asked as he could barely look at me either. "No, I have to call him on Monday, but I did leave a message" I told him. Damian tried his hardest not to make eye contact with me. When he finally did, he looked sad. "Everything is going to be good; you hear me?" He said to me firmly in his protective dad voice that he always spoke to me when he wanted to reassure me that everything was Ok. "I hear you" I said to him like I was a little girl. "I need you to call the lawyer on Monday and I will call you later on at night so you can tell me what he said. And I need you to go to the city to get my car from my house and bring it out here to Mays Landing and park it at your moms house" He told me. "Ok, I got you, " I told him. The visit was soon over, and I left.

5

The jail was like five minutes from my house, so I drove home and laid down and cried. I was so lonely without Damian, and I didn't like being home at my mom's house. My mom was always nagging about cleaning, and I didn't get along with my step dad. It was miserable there to be honest. That's why I always stayed at Damian's house. His house was like a breath of fresh air. Being with him helped me escape my life at home and my childhood problems. Growing up my stepdad was on drugs, and there was a lot of arguing and drama in my house. The atmosphere was always hostile. The only time it was sort of peaceful was when my stepdad was in jail. The house was light, and my mom seemed happier, but every time he got out, things were back to being dysfunctional. They would fight all the time. My step dad would leave and go on drug binges which would stress my mom out. Since he was not a responsible parent, I was always the one who had to watch my little sisters who were his daughters. It made me resentful because a lot of my childhood I could not enjoy because I always had to babysit. I had my brother Waheed too. He was about two years younger than me; he pretty much played football and did his own things.

I was the oldest, so a lot of responsibility fell on me. My mom was diagnosed with OCD, so I always had to clean the house like Cinderella. It was a lot on me mentally growing up. I was never peaceful. I always felt like something bad was going to happen at any moment. Even on the days when my mom and stepdad were cool, I would still feel like at any moment the mood was going to switch and sure enough it did, a lot of times. By the end of the day, they were arguing and calling each other horrible names. I always felt like I had to protect my younger siblings. Even though they got on my nerves, I still loved them and wanted to make sure they were ok. I basically took the blunt of everything. When my mom was mad at my stepdad, she took it out on me. When my stepdad was cool with my mom, he always told on me to get me in trouble. The only time my mom really talked to me and dealt with me was when her and my stepdad were not speaking. When they were cool, it was like they were all one big family and I always felt like an outcast.

My mom had five children. Me and my brother had different dads. My stepdad was my three little sisters' dad. My brother and my stepdad had a good relationship, so a lot of times it would be all of them laughing and joking and I would be on the sidelines cleaning up or something like that. My stepdad was very immature, and he always kept drama going. Another reason why I hated being there was because he always stole from me. Every time he stole something my mom would apologize for him and replace it. She always said she was going to leave him, but she never did. I was resentful to her too because she knew all the mean stuff he would do, and she would always defend him. Every excuse was "I'm sorry, but he can't help it because he has a drug addiction." He played on her with his addiction and used it to manipulate all situations and she let him.

The worst time and when I could not take it anymore was one summer before going into the ninth grade. I had worked that whole summer, no friends, no fun just work, work, work. My mom had an at home daycare, and she let me watch some of her kids, so that I could make money to buy my school clothes. I was going to ninth grade, and I wanted to be fly for my freshman year. My mom would get me stuff every year, but she had five kids to buy clothes for so especially with me being the oldest, I could not get everything I wanted. She agreed to let me work so I could make my own money, and I was super excited. I had watched two different sets of kids. One girl and two boys in each set. The girls were ok, but the boys were BAD. Monday-Friday I would watch the first set and Sat-Sun I would watch the second set. Both of them I had to stay at their houses. Basically, I was never home all summer because I baby stated seven days a week. I was a social butterfly and for the whole summer I had no social life, but I did not care. All I kept thinking about was getting those checks, and what I was going to buy when I went shopping, and that was my motivation.

By the end of the summer I had saved a little over $800 and that was a lot for me just being 14 years old. I was hyped up. Me and my cousin, who was like my best friend, would talk on the phone about what we were going to buy. We were going to catch the bus to the mall and go school shopping together. There were about two weeks left before school started. I had finished my last day of watching the kids. I was excited to see my friends again and get back to my normal life. I did not have a bank account so I would hide my money in my sock in my drawer. My stepdad had stolen money from my drawer before, so I decided to move my money somewhere I thought he wouldn't find it. I had a teddy bear in my room, and I took some scissors and made a small slit in the neck part, then took some of the cotton out and stuffed the $800 in there and put the cotton back in and sat the teddy bear back on my bed.

I had gone out for a few days with my friends. I had not focused on my money. I figured it was safe. It was about three days before school started, me and my cousin got dressed to go shopping. I went to get my money out of the teddy bear and it was GONE. I flipped my room upside down looking for it and it was not there. I felt sick to my stomach like I was about to throw up. All I kept thinking in my head was "Nooooo, Not again!" I did not want to think that my stepdad stole from me again. My heart could not take any more betrayal, and that was the most money I had ever had in my life. Plus, it was for school. I had worked so hard for it dealing with those bad kids. I was panicking so I went to my mom's room and told her what was going on and she looked upset. She had a look on her face like she knew in her heart that he took it, but she did not want to believe it. "I'm so sorry that this keeps happening to you" she told me sincerely. "I get paid in a few days and I can give you something. I just went school shopping for the kids, and I have to pay the rent and bills, so I don't have much. I do feel bad for what he did. I know you wanted to get your school clothes with that money" she said as she felt bad for me.

The day before school came, my mom gave me $60. I had $60 to get a teenage wardrobe to go to my first day of high school in. I was beyond hurt, and at that point I began having hate in my heart towards my stepdad. I would imagine horrible things happening to him because I hated him that much. I went shopping with my cousin and she brought up damn near the whole mall she had bags galore. I was only able to get two pairs of jeans on sale from the gap and a shirt from rainbow. I did get my hair done. It was in a wrap with a China bang. On the 1st day of school, I wore my blue jeans from the gap and the red shirt I got from rainbow. I looked cute and all, but it was nothing compared to what I wanted to wear. After I started high school, I began to get after school jobs because I liked how it felt to get money. So, after that I worked at McDonalds. I worked at Wilson's Leather in the mall and numerous other places, and I kept money in my pocket. I always had my hair and my nails done and I always kept my money on me. I no longer left money at home for fear of it being stolen. I did not trust it at home, and I never felt safe there either. My stepdad stealing that much money was traumatic for me. I thought that my dislike for him could not get any worse, but a few years after that he betrayed me again in one of the worst ways.

Ever since I had become a teenager and my mom noticed that boys were into me, she would always tell me that whenever I was ready to lose my virginity, that I could always come and talk to her first.

Although I was like most teens, and did not want to talk to my mom about sex. I did appreciate the fact that she had left the door open for me to do so. I was seventeen years old, and I had a good friend that I would kick it with all the time, and we got so close that we became more than friends. We were never boyfriend and girlfriend, but we had a dope bond and a mutual understanding that we weren't together, but we messed with each other heavily. One night me and my cousin were at the bowling alley, and we bumped into him, and his friend and they invited us to their hotel. We were chilling at the hotel and having a good time. I was drinking my favorite drink back then "Alize" After years of having dope chemistry we were finally in a position where everything felt right, and I lost my virginity to him. I did not have any regrets. He was someone I cared about and had an awesome friendship with, so I could not see myself losing my virginity to anyone else.

The next day I was home in the tub, and I was on the phone with my best friend telling her about what happened like teenage best friends do. To my knowledge no one was home. I was on the phone telling all the details and having a good time talking to her. We had hung up and I had got out of the tub. As soon as I walked out of the bathroom, my stepdad was standing by the door listening to my whole conversation. I was so embarrassed, and I felt so violated. "I heard everything you said," he said with disappointment. "Ok," I said, not knowing how to respond as the whole situation was awkward. "I'm going to give you the chance to tell your mom. If you don't tell her, then I will," he scolded. My mom was not home. She was out at the time, and I was not sure when she was going to be back. "Ok, I will tell her," I told him, and he said Ok and went downstairs. I went into my room to get dressed, and I was nervous to my stomach the whole time. I was eventually going to tell my mom, but I did not plan on telling her this soon.

Finally, my mom was home, and she went into her room. I was giving her time to get situated as I was working up the nerve and trying to find ways to tell her. I had remembered what she always told me about talking to her if I ever had sex, and I was just going to come to her honest and sincere. I knew what I was going to say and how I was going to say it and I finally had enough nerve to go and knock on her room door. "Knock, Knock, Knock" as I stood there knocking on her door. "Come in" I heard her say and I took a deep breath. "Hey mom, I want to tell her something" I said as I came into her room. To my surprise my stepdad was already in there with her sitting next to her on the bed, and my mom's eyes looked like they had fire in them. "What?" she said to me very upset. I started to get it out, but before I could finish my mom had cut me off. "You sneaky little bitch," she said to me and I was shocked. "What did I do?" I asked her in shock and fear. "So, you want to be out here having sex, you little hussy" she said to me, and she got up and hit me. "I was trying to tell you" I said to her, as I was trying to hold my tears in.

I was so upset and angry, I looked at my stepdad's face as he sat there on the bed with a smirk on his face. He went into the room and told my mom as soon as she got home. He did not even give me time to tell her the way I wanted to like he said he would. He was such a liar and a snake. He took that moment from me. I was not sure what he told her or how he told her. All I knew was, that she was furious with me. "You are such a disappointment, get out of my room" she said to me, and I felt so low and ripped apart. Before that day my mom had never called me a bitch before, and she always told me I could come to her. I never thought that was how she would react. I think if I came to her on my own, her reaction would have been a lot different. I am sure my stepdad had added in lies and my mom did not even want to hear what I had to say. "You are on Punishment, the only place you can go is to school and back in this house, and you are not allowed to talk to that boy anymore" she yelled to me and closed her room door. I felt sick to my stomach. I could not believe what had just happened. That day made me hate my stepdad even more. I hated him with a passion. It was like he did everything in his power to constantly get me in trouble, and this time it was serious.

My mom did not speak to me for a while after that and the air in the house was so uncomfortable. I had gone to school but was not allowed to go anywhere else for a month. Of course, I still talked to the guy I lost my virginity to on the phone, and he would sneak past my house. I would go to the mailbox to check the mail just to see him. I was home one day cleaning up. I had my cell phone and a pair of bamboo hooped earrings sitting on the couch. My stepdad was in the living room, and I saw him next to my stuff. I saw him open the screen door and throw something, but I did not see what it was. When I was done cleaning up, I went to get my stuff off of the couch and I noticed my earring was missing. I had looked for it everywhere in the house and I could not find it. One day I was walking home from school and in the parking lot by the woods by my house I found my earring ran over and bent. It had instantly come to me that he threw it out the door that day and he watched me look for it. He was so mean spirited towards me. Being back home was miserable and since Damian was now in jail. I was stuck there back in the hell hole I tried to escape from.

While I was home, I fell into depression. I would not eat, and outside of calling Damian's lawyer, writing him and going to see him in jail, I would sleep all day. I had lost a lot of weight and I felt guilty every time I ate, because I knew he was in jail and could not eat what he wanted. Plus, food reminded me of him because when he was free, we would go out to eat all the time. I would write him every single day and tell him how much I missed him. I kept calling his lawyer, and he would request bail hearings that dragged on for months. At first Damian had no bail because he was a flight risk. At another bail hearing the judge gave him a bail but it was $100,000.00 cash. It was all becoming so overwhelming. It had felt like he was never coming home. Though things were rough on me, Damian stayed upbeat in his spirits. At that time, all of his friends and cousins were in jail with him, so he would call me and tell me all these jail stories about all the fun they were having. Even though

I was sad that he was in there, I was happy that he was around people he knew, and he was doing ok.

One night he had called me and sounded excited. "What's up? Why you sound so happy?" I asked him. "Guess who in here?" he asked me. "Who?" I asked curious. "Your dad" he said to me. "Wow" I responded. I was not close with my dad at all, and we barely spoke. Him and Damian had basically met in jail, and they developed a close bond to the point that my dad called him his son. Damian would call me and tell me about my dad all the time. He would tell me how intelligent he was. Even though I was not close with my father, I appreciated their bond, and I was glad that they got along. My dad gave Damian a stamp of approval as my boyfriend and their bond grew from there. Damian was in jail for a few months. I had taken a semester off from college then eventually went back. I was so stressed dealing with his legal cases and going to his court dates and jail visits, that I began to fail school. I did not want to totally flunk out, so I withdrew the rest of my classes until I was mentally ready to attend school again.

My brain was so clouded with the criminal justice system that I had written a paper for my advanced English class titled "Guilty Until Proven Innocent" which was a paper that depicted what I was going through in my personal life as far as seeing the inmate's side of fighting a case, and dealing with the judicial system which was not in favor of young black men. The more I talked to his lawyer and went to the court cases and saw how the prosecutors operated, it was clear to me that no matter how innocent a person was, they were "guilty until proven innocent" instead of "innocent until proven guilty". My professor loved it so much that he asked if he could keep it for future classes and I told him yes. My English class was the only class that I was not failing because it gave me a chance to do what I loved to do, which was write. But I did eventually withdraw the class as well to not receive an F.

Once I was no longer in college, I knew I could not just stay home and do nothing with my life, so I decided to get a job at the Walmart up the street in Mays Landing. I had worked in the jewelry dept. It was not my ideal job, but it gave me something to do. I had a lot of fun at work and almost everyone I knew worked there and we had the best times. Working at Walmart was lit, and it kept my mind off of missing Damian so much. Life for me seemed like it was getting a little better. I wasn't as depressed. I was making money and I was back to being some-what of a social butterfly. I had missed Damian, but I had begun to get used to the fact that he was in jail, and I began living my own life. I still called his lawyer like crazy to set up court dates and wrote him and went to see him every weekend. I was optimistic that he would be able to post bail soon, so I was in good spirits and knew that everything would be ok.

6

One day I went to the County Jail to see him, and he didn't look happy to see me like he usually did. "What's the matter?" I asked him concerned. "You dyed your hair red," he said to me as he noticed the auburn rinse I put in my hair. That's one of the things I loved about him, he always noticed everything about me. He always paid attention to detail. "Yeah, I did. Do you like it?" I asked as I smiled. "Yeah," he said giving a small smile, but I could still see that something was bothering him. "What's the matter?" I asked again. "I have something to tell you" he told me, barely even able to look at me. "Me? What?" I asked as I became anxious. "Once I tell you, promise you not going to just get up and leave," he said to me, and I began to get worried. "What? Just tell me" I told him.

"Right before you came, I had just canceled a visit," he told me. "A visit from who?" I asked confused. "This girl came up here with a baby, and she said that he was mine," he told me, and I thought what I was hearing was a joke. "What? A baby? You told me that you didn't have any kids" I said to him. "I don't!" he blurted out upset. "She tripping, and that's why I told her that she had to leave the visit. Before she left, she told me that DFCS would be sending a paternity test to the jail" he told me. He said that the guy that she thought was her son's father was tested, and it came out not to be his, so she wanted Damian to be tested too, so she could find her child's father.

I was so confused and hurt at the same time. The thought of him having a baby made me sick to my stomach. I felt nauseous at that moment. We always talked about past relationships, and he never mentioned her ever. I was confused as to where she even came from. He told me that they were never in a relationship. He said that she was just someone he had sex with, and he forgot all about her. She lived at his grandmother's house because she was friends with his cousin. I had actually seen her before when she was pregnant, but I had no idea that she was potentially pregnant with my boyfriend's baby. At that point, I was disgusted with him, but I told him since he did not believe it was his, then we should just wait and see what the test says and just go from there. Damian did not seem convinced that it was his son, and due to the circumstances surrounding the girl, I believed him. And I put it out of my mind until they got the paternity test.

A few weeks later he had a bail hearing, and the judge lowered his bail. At this point, he had been in jail for about six months. The judge lowered his bail from $100,000 cash to $60,000 with a 10% bond. The bails bondsman had called me while I was at work, and they were ready to get him out and I was super excited. I had given the money to his brother to go and get him and I was just waiting for the phone call from him telling me that he was home! While I was at work, it was around 10 pm. I was closing up the jewelry center; when his brother and his cousin came to the jewelry stand where I was. "What's up, bro?" I said to him smiling as I wanted to hear the good news. His brother was not smiling, and my smile quickly faded as well. "He's not getting out tonight," his brother said to me looking pissed. "Why what happened?" I asked, concerned. "We went to give the bail bondsman the $6,000, they took it and come to find out the judge hit my brother with a $10,000.00 cash bond," he told me. "What!?" I said I was pissed.

They would not take 10% so I had to call the lawyer the next day to see if he could get the judge to lower the bail. The judge did not agree, and we had to come up with the $10,000. We had got money from his dad and his wife and a few people who owed Damian money from the streets. His brother and a few other people had put up money as well. We were exactly $2000 short on the nose. I did not know where I was going to get the money from. I was wrecking my brain because I had already tapped into all of our resources. I was so stressed out, but I had prayed about it and given it to God. Literally, a few days later, my mom had given me my mail and it was a refund check from school and the amount was $2001.01 on the nose. I had forgotten all about my financial aid check beings though I had withdrawn from school. There is so much I wanted to do with that money. My main goal was to buy myself a car. But I knew that I wanted Damian home and now with the $2000 check, we had the total of $10,000 and was able to bail him out.

The next day I called his brother and let him know that I had the rest of the money. He came and got it and the whole balance was paid. Damian called me later that day sounding excited. "I'm coming home!" he said to me over the phone as I could tell he was smiling from ear to ear. "I know!" I said with a smile on my face. "Where you get the bread from?" he asked. "I used the money from my refund check, now out of my check I have $1.01," I told him as I laughed. "Aw man, I definitely appreciate it. You know I got you when I come home," he told me. I told him that I loved him, and we both hung up.

When Damian got out of jail, it was the middle of the night, so I didn't see him until the next day. His brother had brought him to my house to pick up his car and we drove back to the city together. I was smiling from ear to ear being back in his presence. It all felt surreal. I had gone to hug him, and he had felt hard. I could tell he had been working out. On the inside, I was beyond excited, and I was trying to contain myself. Damian didn't have his place anymore, so we went to his brother's house to chill. While we were there a lot of his friends and cousins came by to welcome him home. Everybody was happy to see him and were having a good time.

I was chilling in the living room while all the guys did their thing on the porch and outside. I understood that everyone had wanted his time. I was just happy that I was in the same place as him, and he was not behind glass. "What's up?" he said as he came into the living room and sat next to me. "Nothing," I said as I smiled at him, and he put his hand on my leg and began kissing me flirtatiously. "You good?" he asked me. "Yeah, I'm good, "I told him as he looked at me happily. "We about to leave soon alright," he said, reassuring me since he was spending so much time with everyone else. "Ok, I'm good, enjoy yourself and your company," I told him, and he went back onto the porch to finish kicking it with his friends and enjoying himself.

I was in the living room watching a movie when his brother's wife at the time came in. "Hey sis," she said to me. "Hey," I said as I was happy to see her. "Girl, you lost mad weight," she said to me noticing how small I had got. While Damian was in jail, I had lost close to 20lbs. I was already only about 125 when he was home so losing 20lbs made me about 105lbs. He didn't mind it, but I don't think people were used to seeing me that small. Damian was not surprised that I had lost weight because I saw him the whole time he was in jail. He liked me the way I was, and he didn't trip about my weight loss. "I know girl" I was stressing I said to her as I laughed, and she sat down next to me on the couch.

"You still look good though, plus now that your man is home, he going to have you thick all over again," she said motioning her body in a sexual way, referencing me and Damian having sex, and me and her burst out laughing. "But girl! Guess where I was at today?" she said to me ready to give me all the tea. "Girl where?" I asked her curious. "I had gone to their grand mom's house today, and I saw the girl there. AND I finally saw the baby today," she told me. "Oh wow, did the baby look like Damian?" I asked her a little scared to get her response. "No, not really, I don't think that's his baby," she said to me. I had instantly felt relieved.

The whole time Damian was in jail, we never talked about the possibility of it being his child outside of the time when he first told me about it. Other than that, it was never a conversation piece. Up until that point, I had honestly put it out of my mind. But now that he was home, it was time to face reality and get it all figured out so we could go on with our lives. Her bringing up the fact that he might have a child made me feel sad on the inside. I did not know for sure, so I did not want it to ruin the night. I put it out of my head and told myself that we would cross that bridge when we get there. He had just come home, and he had not taken the test yet. While he was in jail, they were supposed to test him, but they never did. In the middle of our convo, Damian had come in and told me that he wanted to take a ride, so we got in the car and left.

We had driven to the west side of Atlantic City where the bay was. When we drove back there, we drove through a few bushes. Once we entered, there was a small open space where the water was and it looked out into the city and it was so peaceful and serene. "Where are we? I asked him, as he opened the passenger side door for me to get out. "This is the Bay my dad used to take me to when I was little," he said as he put a blanket on the hood of the car, and we sat up there and looked at the water. "Wow, this is really peaceful," I said as I enjoyed the atmosphere.

Atlantic City could be a dangerous place, there are drugs, violence, and murders as well as all of the commotion from the casinos and night-life. But being back there felt like we were miles and miles from the woes of city life. It was an amazing vibe, and I would not have wanted to spend that moment with anyone but him. "You said your dad used to bring you here when you was little, so this place must be special to you," I said to him as I sat next to him on the hood of the car with my head on his shoulder. "Yeah, it was. My dad would take me fishing back here, and we would talk and spend time together. It is just as peaceful now as it was back then" he told me as he smoked his black and mild. "I thought you would have got them things out of your system by now," I said to him as I pointed to the mild. "I did, but I'm chilling so I'll just take a few puffs," he said to me as he smoked it. Damian was not a weed or a cigarette smoker, but he would smoke black and milds from time to time. "You want to hit it?" he asked me. "No, I'm good. You know I don't smoke," I said to him as I looked out at the water. "What's on your mind?" he asked.

I knew what was on my mind and my heart, but I was not sure if I should express it to him, because I was not sure how his reaction would be. "Nothing," I said to him. "I know you Shamirah, something is on your mind, what's up?" he asked. "Well, sis said she went to your grandmom's house today and saw the baby," I said to him as I looked back out into the water. "Oh yeah, what did she say?" he asked me still smoking his black and mild. "She said the baby don't look like you and she don't think it's yours," I told him. "I don't think so either, especially due to the circumstances. I don't even remember even being with that girl, at all," he told me. "Well evidently, she thinks it's your baby, so you had to have sex with her at some point," I said to him.

He went into detail about how he met her, and the circumstanced surrounding how they hooked up. I was shocked at what he told me because I looked at him so highly. I never thought he would be with a certain type of woman. He was so picky and particular about the women he liked, and nothing about her seemed like anything he would have been with. "I love you. I never loved her, nor had any type of relationship with her. I want you to know that even if it comes out that her son is mine, that does not change anything between us. I still love you. I still want to be with you, but if he's my son then I do have to take care of my responsibility. She is not somebody I want in my life. So, if you wanted, we could raise the baby together" he told me sincerely. "I don't know Damian; a baby is a big responsibility and I don't have kids so I don't think I want to raise somebody else's. I'm in college and I want to do films and be famous. I have dreams and goals and I am not ready to be a mom right now, I told him. "I definitely understand how you feel, and I would not want to have to put all of that on you at all. But if he is mine, I do at least want you to be a part of his life. You are a very smart and special person and I would want him to be around a woman like you in his life" he told me. "I appreciate that," I said to him as I was still a little uneasy. "But let's not think about that for now and just enjoy the night," he said to me as he wrapped his arm around me.

"Well Shamirah, wow, that was a lot," my therapist said to me as she sat there finishing up her notes as I told her my story. "You and your Husband have been through a lot in such a short amount of time. After all the police raids and him going to jail and him possibly having a child, with all due respect I would like to ask you; what made you stay with him?" she asked me as she looked at me with her glasses slouched on her face and her pin in her hand ready to take more notes. "And before you answer, just take a minute to truly think about it," she said as he paused and put her paper down and gave me her undivided attention. "Think about it. What made a smart, vibrant young woman straight out of high school with a world full of opportunities and dreams of being a writer and a movie producer and a head full of so many awesome ideas and endless possibilities. What made a young woman like that put her life on hold?" she said to me as she looked me in my eyes.

I took a few minutes to truly ponder on it. The therapy room was silent and I twiddled my fingers as my therapist gave me time to think about it. "I loved him," I said to her after giving myself about two minutes to think about it, and she picked up her pen again. "Ok, you loved him," she said to me as if she wanted me to say more. "Yes, I loved him and I felt like he needed me and I did not want to leave him to fight his cases and to deal with everything he had going on alone," I told her. "Ok," she said to me as she sat back in her chair and crossed her legs. "I felt like I could save him and show him a better life," I added. "Ok, why did you, an 18-year girl straight out of high school, with not much life experience think that you could save someone else?" she asked me in a very stern but compassionate way, and I sat and thought for a minute. "I don't know, all I knew was I loved him and I didn't want to leave him because he needed me," I told her. "Ok, while you were going through him being in jail and finding out that he may have a child, how did it make YOU feel?" she asked me sincerely.

"This is your safe zone, so you can be honest," she said to me. "It made me feel sad and hurt " I told her. "Ok, it made you sad and hurt, " she repeated. "At that time did you express to your then boyfriend, now husband or anyone else that those things made you sad and hurt?" she asked me. "No," I said to her. "So, you held it all in, and even though you were sad and hurt you put your feelings to the side and hid them because what?" she asked me. "I wasn't worried about my feelings; I was just worried about being there for him," I said to her. "And Shamirah I do understand that, I truly do," she said to me. "But you cannot try to fill other people's cups when yours is empty. It seems like you gave a lot emotionally and even though it was a lot on you, you just kept taking on loads" she said to me.

"I never really looked at it that way, " I said to her. "Yes, even though we love people it is still ok to have boundaries. It seems like you and your husband adored each other and he really loved you. I am sure he was unaware of what you were feeling internally especially since you didn't tell him at that time" she said to me. "Outside of everything you told me, it seemed like you all had a great relationship and had a lot of fun, and were crazy about each other. So, what happened along the way that brought you in here today? She asked me as she picked up her pin and sat back to listen. "Well when Damian got out of jail everything was great," I said to her as I began to tell her the rest of the story.

After the night talking by the Bay we had gone on with our normal lives. He was so sweet to me, and I was so glad that he was home. "What you doing? He said to me as he had called me on my phone while I was at my mom's house. "Nothing, getting dressed and waiting for you to come and get me," I told him as I was putting my clothes on. I had on a pair of red pants, a red shirt with hearts on it, and a black blazer with some black shoes, and my hair was in jet black Farrah Faucet feathers. I was so small back then and my shape was so cute. I had talked to Damian on the phone the whole time that he was on his way to get me. When we were not together, we talked on the phone all the time for hours. Sometimes we were not even saying anything and we would even fall asleep on the phone. He had pulled up and told me to come outside. When I got to the door, I saw a silver Lexus outside but I did not see him. "Where you at?" I asked him confused. 'I'm outside, " he said to me as he rolled down the window smiling from ear to ear. "Whose car is this?" I said as I walked outside surprised. "It's my car," he said as he got out and hugged me and showed me the car. It was very nice.

It was silver and it had nice chrome rims on it. The inside was cherry wood grain and it was very fancy. The seats were leather and I remember him warming the seat up for me and taking me to the passenger side so I could sit down. When I had opened the door, he had a nice seat cover for me, and he had the Betty Boop mats that had in his other car. He always customized my seat to make me feel comfortable. "Aww thank you," I said to him and I sat down to feel how warm the seat was. "I love it, " I said to him as we both sat in the car in front of my mom's house. He played music on his stereo to show me how the system sounded and we just vibed out. My mom and stepdad had come out to see his car and they all talked for a while and a couple of guys from the neighborhood came and talked to him as everybody was enjoying themselves. I was cool with all my neighbors; we all were like family so they knew Damian and they would always show love. Everyone liked him and thought he was perfect for me. He was a likable guy. My brother and my little sisters like him too.

Damian had come to my sister's fourth Dora the explorer Birthday party and celebrated with us and bought her gifts. He also was there for my other little sister's birthday who was crazy about Bratz and Polly Pockets at the time. All the Bratz were sold out at "Toy's R US" so we drove around all day going from store to store to try to find them. He was determined to get her what she wanted to make her happy. He was just a good guy with a good heart and he was the perfect boyfriend. So kind, caring, and attentive. He did anything and everything for me. He literally treated me like gold and made me feel like I was the most special person in his life. It almost was like an obsession. He always wanted me with him. I never drove myself anywhere because he always said that he would take me, and if he took me somewhere, he would be with me. When I wasn't with him, he wanted to know who I was with and what I was doing.

When we weren't together, he always made sure we were on the phone. We never really spent time apart. Our lives were so intertwined with one another. At that time all my friends had gone away to college or was doing their own thing. So, I really didn't have many friends around. Damian was my friend and he is who I hung out with. I was around him and his family and that was enough for me, and I was happy. I guess you could say I was obsessed with him too. I didn't care that I didn't have any friends. I liked that he drove me everywhere and was always with me. I didn't want to leave his side. We were both obsessed with one another and we didn't care.

Later that night we were in the parking lot listening to Usher "Lovers and Friends" just talking and enjoying the night sky through the sunroof. "Come here," he said as he grabbed my hand and rubbed it on his penis through his jeans and I could feel that he was hard. Damian was always very sexual with me. He always wanted to have sex, all the time, anywhere. "Stop doing that right here, we're right in front of my mom's house," I said, as I giggled and hurried up and moved my hand so that no one would see me. It was about 11 o'clock at night and anybody could be walking by at any time. My neighborhood was lit so I was not about to take any chances. "Let's drive to the Clubhouse where the pool is. It's closed now, so I'm sure nobody is over there" I said referring to the Clubhouse in my neighborhood which was in the next court from where I lived.

The Clubhouse was where the office, the gym, and the pool were. It was late at night so no one was over there so we parked there and chilled. "Ok here," Damian said as he pulled his penis out and motioned me to perform fellatio. "Ok," I said as I took a deep breath and I put my mouth on his penis and began stroking it. "You have to close your mouth tighter," he said as he was trying to explain to me how to do it the way he liked it. At that time, I still was not good at giving fellatio. I had the technique all wrong so when he asked me to do it, I would feel bad because I didn't think he liked it but Damian worked with me until I got it right. While I was doing it, he had told me to stop and he pulled out some Vaseline. "Where did you get Vaseline from?" I asked as I wiped my mouth and laughed. "Here just jerk it with this'" he said as he handed me the Vaseline and I scooped it in my hand and began jerking him off and he was enjoying it.

Next thing you know, we saw blue lights in the back of us and he immediately zipped up his pants and sat up in his seat. I had a handful of Vaseline with nowhere to wipe it. "Is everything ok?" The cop said as he flashed his flashlight on the driver's side where Damian was sitting. "Yeah, we good officer," Damian said to him. "Do you guys know that this is private property and you can't be here after hours?" The officer asked as another officer pulled up. "Oh, I didn't know that. I live right here at 5114 Radnor Court " I said to the offer and he asked for my ID and I showed him. "What y'all doing out here anyway?" He asked me. "We are just chilling, listening to music," I said to him and he looked around the car with his flashlight again like something was suspicious. "Could you both step out of the car?" he asked, and we got out. I still had a handful of Vaseline and I kept trying to rub my hands together to get rid of it but it was way too greasy.

The one officer questioned Damian and the other officer questioned me and we told them both the same thing, that we were listening to music and finally they let us go and just told us to leave because it was private property. The police were not rude or anything. I think they knew we were doing freaky stuff and they were trying to get to the bottom of it. When I and Damian got back in the car, we burst out laughing even though I was so mad at him. I still had a handful of Vaseline, so we drove to my mom's house and I cleaned off my hands. Damian did not have his apartment anymore and he was only home for a couple of weeks at that point so he was staying at his brother's house. I had grabbed some clothes from my mom's house to spend the night with him. We drove to the city and chilled at his brother's, and finished what we started in the car and had a great night.

7

The next day we got up and got dressed and we went to see his mom who lived around the corner in Atlantic City. We sat there and talked with her and laughed for a while, then we had left to go on the avenue to the Hip Hop shop to get some sneakers. As we were walking Damian looked at me like he had something on his mind. "What's up?" I asked him concerned. "You know how I told you about the possibility of me having a baby right?" he said to me, and immediately my stomach went into knots. "Yes," I said, wishing this conversation would just go away. "Well, I think I'm going to go to the courthouse and get the test today," he told me. "Today?" I asked him as I was thrown off. "Yeah, today. I have been home a couple of weeks now, and I don't want to put it off any longer. I'm going up there and I'll pay for it myself" he told me. I felt sick to my stomach. Even though I did not know if the baby was his, I didn't know for sure that it was not his, and that was scary for me. "I already told you how I feel. I love you and I got you, but I have to know" he told me. I didn't respond, there was not much for me to say. He had already had his mind made up, and nothing I said was going to change it. Plus, I wanted him to get the test so we can know the results and move forward with life. This topic was always the elephant in the room, and it was time to address it.

I did not want to be there when he took the test, so I had told him to take me home while he went. I was nervous and felt nauseous all day. I didn't want to talk to anyone, not even to Damian. I just felt sad. I chilled in the den for most of the day watching tv and trying not to think too hard. While I was home, my mom and stepdad were arguing per usual, and it had gotten really violent. I was downstairs and I heard thumping and clashing upstairs. It was so loud that I went up there to make sure my mom was not hurt. When I opened the door, they were fighting and there was debris everywhere. I saw my stepdad hit my mom. As they were fighting, she scratched him on his back, and it left a welt and he went berserk. "You hit me you bitch, you going to jail tonight" he kept yelling. "You stupid bitch" he was saying as he was trying to find the cordless phone. My sisters were young, and they were crying and looking scared. I put them back in their room and consoled them the best I could. He had finally found the phone and he called 911 and told them that my mom attacked him. The whole time before the police came, he was taunting my mom calling her all types of bitches and telling her that she would see how it feels to go to jail. He was laughing at her all the while my sisters were crying "No daddy, please don't send my mom to jail." It was so sad to see them like that. I lived with this dysfunction, and I hated that they were going through it now too.

My mom wasn't saying anything to him, she had tears in her eyes and she had got dressed and put her hat on and a jacket and waited for the police to come. When they pulled up, he laughed hysterically like he was possessed by the devil and told her "Bye Bitch." When the police came in, they asked what happened and my mom told her side, and he told his side. Just moments before they came in, he was laughing like a mad man, but all of a sudden, he was hurt and in so much pain. He put on an act for the cops like he was a victim and he showed them the scratch. The police deemed my mom the aggressor and they put her in handcuffs. They put her in the police car and took her to jail. My mom was silent the whole time they were locking her up. She didn't say a word. She just looked numb. The police car had driven away, and my sisters were still crying. Instead of consoling his children, my stepdad was talking so much trash and boasting about sending my mom to jail.

At that point, all the neighbors were outside being nosey. My step-dad was yelling, "I bet that bitch won't put her hands on me anymore," he said laughing like the immature mad man that he was. Everyone was just looking at him in disgust. Everyone knew he was a drug addict. They knew my mom held the house and the kids down. They knew he was a deadbeat. That was my mom's house, she paid the bills. He contributed nothing at all. Yet when she was locked up, he was walking around the house as he owned it. It was disgusting to watch and every-thing in my being wanted to do something to him. I hated him with a burning passion. He was the scum of the earth in my eyes. At the time my mom had two cars, a white Kia car, and a white truck. He was not allowed to drive either of them because he did not have a license and he was irresponsible. My mom told him that she didn't want him smoking cigarettes in her car. Well once they took my mom to jail in no time, he hopped his non-licensed having ass in her Jeep and lit up a cigarette and drove somewhere and didn't come back. I didn't even care. I was glad that he was gone. I had made sure that my siblings were ok, and I had called Damian and told him what had happened, and he was at my house ASAP. He got the kids some McDonalds and then we left my sisters there with my brother who was old enough to watch them. We left so that he could bail my mom out of jail.

She had got out a few hours later and had caught a cab home. When she got back, she was pissed. She packed up all of my stepdad's clothes and said that she was done with him. He was gone for a few days, and I had stayed at my mom's house to make sure that she was Ok. Damian had stayed there too to make sure everything was good. A few days had passed, and my stepdad came home. Instead of my mom giving him his clothes to get out. They had wound up making up and I was in pure disbelief. "You are not mad at him for what he did?" I asked her. "Yeah, but I was wrong too. I should not have put my hands on him" she said to me, and I was in disbelief. My stepdad was dysfunctional, and so was my mother for taking him back. After all of that, and from that point on I decided to wash my hands of both of them and move on with my life. I had spent all my time with Damian wherever he was, I was at too, to avoid being at my mom's house at all cost.

I had still been working at Walmart in the jewelry department. Since Damian was home, I wanted him to get a job to stay out of trouble, so I told him to fill out an application and he did. I had got hired there while he was locked up and though I missed him, the job was fun and kept my mind occupied. I had met a lot of cool people working there, and me and my friends had the jewelry department jumping. All the workers were always in jewelry talking and playing around with us. Working at Walmart was one of the most fun jobs that I ever had. While I was working there, there was the manager of one of the departments named Kurtis. He was a cute young white guy. He never really said anything to me, but every time I saw him at work, he would give me "The Eye" and I could tell that he liked me. I always would look at him and smile and say hi and keep it moving.

One day while I was at work, Damian had called me and told me that he had had an interview at my job around 3 pm. I was excited because I would have a chance to see him, and I was excited for him to get the job. I was in the jewelry dept when I saw Damian and Kurtis walk past the counter. Kurtis was giving me the eye as usual without saying anything and Damian was looking at me smiling from ear to ear. I was cheesing, smiling at him too but we didn't talk because I knew he was on his way to his interview. Since Kurtis was the manager, clearly Damien was getting interviewed by him for his department, so I just smiled and waved at them both and that was it. It was about an hour later. I was in my department kicking it with my friend laughing like we always did. Next thing you know I see Damian and Kurtis walking back past the jewelry dept. They seemed really cool like they hit it off really well. They both were talking and laughing and again I didn't say much. I just looked at them both and smiled. As they walked past, Kurtis had stopped, and he was red as a cherry. "Hey, I been noticing you for a while and," he said as he paused and looked at Damian who was standing next to him and he continued. "And I was just wondering if I could take you out some time," he said as he seemed to be relieved to get it out. I stood there stuck and embarrassed. Me, Damian, and my friend looked at each other and we all started laughing. "Kurtis, I can't go out on a date with you, this is my boyfriend," I said as I pointed to Damian and Damian was standing there as the situation was so awkward. "Ohh my bad!" Kurtis said to Damian very apologetically. He seemed embarrassed and he was super red. "You are good bro," Damian said to him smiling. The way Damian was, I was surprised at how calm he was about Kurtis asking me on a date. They had walked away in awkwardness and me and my friend burst out laughing. "Girl, what the hell was that about?" My friend said cracking up. "Girl, I don't know, " I said as I was laughing too.

Damian had got hired on. I worked 3p-11p and he worked the over-night shift 11p-7a so when he was coming to work, I was getting off of work. I would stay and kick it with him until the store closed at 11:30. Every night Damian would come to work with a cappuccino from Dunkin Donuts. Some nights on his breaks we would go to Dunkin donuts and make a little date out of getting his cappuccino. The over-night crew was lit, and they all would go on break at about 3 am. Every night I would be out there waiting for Damian and all the guys would make jokes about us because we were so inseparable. On his breaks a lot of times we would be in the car just kicking it, and he would eat something lite. It was the middle of the night, so he wasn't all that hungry. We would drive from the Walmart parking lot to another parking lot where it was no cars, and we would have sex in the back seat of his car. We always had fun times and did spontaneous things. Afterwards, I would go home up the street to my house and call him on the job phone. Everyone knew it was me calling. He was like my drug. I could not get enough of him.

"What you doing?" He said as he called me one night on his break around 3 am. "Nothing," I said as I was lying in bed listening to music.

"Turn on 99.3 the BUZZ," he said to me, and I turned on the radio station. I listened to the song and when it went off, I heard Damian on the radio giving me a shot out and it was so sweet. "Aww thank you, that was nice," I said to him as I had butterflies. He was always doing sweet things for me, and I appreciated and loved his heart. He had a big heart, and he was very thoughtful. He was the type of guy who everyone loved. When we came to the hood, he was the guy who gave all the kids $1 or bought them ice cream from the ice cream truck. He was the one who everyone in his family looked up to. I looked up to him too. He was my boyfriend and young like me, but he was wise like a father figure, and I listened and did everything he told me, and I always took his advice. It got to a point where I didn't think with my own brain anymore. I just relied on him to think and make decisions for me. Damian spoiled me mentally and physically and I became codependent on him and at that time I had not realized it. I was just in the glory and blindness of being in love.

Since Damian didn't have his apartment anymore, sometimes we didn't want to chill at his brother's house, so we started getting hotel rooms to spend time at. We would get paid from Walmart and get our room. We would go and get some Chinese food or whatever and come back to the room and chill. We would get rooms with Jacuzzi's and it would be so romantic. We were in our glory, and we did whatever we wanted. We laid there and watched movies. We took showers together and we would have sex and enjoy each other's company. I would get creative and get lingerie and special things to take with us to the room to have fun. One time I bought a bunch of bags of gummy bears, and I poured honey on my breast and my vagina and made a gummy bear bikini for Damian to eat off of me. We would do fun sexy stuff like that and have a good time.

One night we were in a room, as we were in the bed there were police outside on the loudspeaker saying someone's name that sounded like his, and we were trying to figure out what was going on. The room next to us had been raided and it was a huge scene. The rooms we were staying at, at the time were low budget so ever since then we had started staying and better and fancier rooms with more privacy. I would drive my mom's white Kia all the time back then. One night we had a room at Resorts Casino, and we drove the car to the liquor store to get something to drink. The parking lot was narrow, so I had a hard time getting in. Damian kept asking me if I wanted him to park and I told him No. I pulled in and sat in the car while he went in. When he came out, he asked me again if I wanted him to pull out of the parking lot and I told him "No I got it." I had hit the gas with the car in reverse and the next thing I knew, I heard something that sounded like a crushing sound. "Oh sh*t," I said as I knew I hit something, and I was scared to find out what it was. Damian had got out and walked to the back of the car and I could see his face through the rear-view mirror, and I knew that I had messed up. "Come here," he said as I got out of the car and walked to the back. I had hit a fire hydrant and it put a huge dent in my mom's back bumper and there was yellow paint all over the dent and her car was white. I was so nervous to have to tell her what happened, she was going to kill me and never let me drive her car again. The whole night in the room I really couldn't even enjoy myself because I kept thinking about the car.

The next day we checked out and I had no choice but to take her car back to her. Me and Damian were both silent on the way. I knew once I got home, I was in deep sh*t and I had a sick feeling in my stomach. "I don't know what to do, " I said to him, as I wanted to cry. "We will figure something out. I'll try to find a shop real quick" he said as he was looking up shops on his phone. As we were in traffic on the black horse Pike literally out of nowhere right next to us was a little beetle car that read "Mobile Car Repair "on the side and it was like it was heaven-sent. "Beep the horn!" Damian yelled to me as I began beeping the horn to get the guy's attention. He saw me and Damian coax him to pull over and we pulled into the MGM car wash parking lot. Damian showed him what happened, and the guy popped the dent out and painted over the yellow paint from the fire hydrant. It was not perfect, but it was better than it was, and I was hoping that my mom would not notice that anything had ever happened.

When I got home, I hurried up and gave her, her keys and me and Damian caught a cab back to the city where his car was. I was so scared all day thinking she was going to call my cell phone, but thank God she didn't, and everything was ok. A few weeks later she had gone to Walmart and when she came home, she said "the back of my car looked different. I think somebody in the Walmart parking lot bumped into my car because I see some yellow paint on my car" she said to me and all I could do was chuckle to myself and say, "People always hitting people cars at Walmart" and I shook my head and from that day on my mom never said anything else about it thank God.

8

In the meantime, life was great. Damian was really into music so he had artists that he would take to the studio to do records. Outside of being at work and chilling together. I spent a lot of time with him in the studio and it was so much fun. We would be in there for hours while the artist wrote and recorded their songs. It was always good vibes and fun times. I used to have a rap book in high school so everyone would joke with me to get in the booth. But I was way too shy to do it, so I would just kick it with everybody and watch them be creative. They made good music and I felt that Damian had stars on his hands. Where we were from there were a lot of distractions. Outside of the booth people were dealing with real-life so the music did not take off how it could have. But it was fun watching and being a part of them creating great songs.

Damian had taken me on a date to a bar in Pleasantville, NJ and he had decided to order raw oysters on the half shell and they looked so disgusting. But he dared me to try it, and I did. I put cocktail and tobasco sauce on it and swallowed it without chewing it and it was actually pretty good. Ever since that day I and he always ordered raw oysters on the half shell every time we went out to dinner. We would go and shoot pool with his manager Kurtis. He and Damian became really close and we would hang out with him and his girlfriend's outside of work. We always had a good time. Damian's brother had got married. Me, him, his dad, and his two older brothers went to a bar to celebrate and play pool. We had fun and laughed the whole time. I was the only girl hanging out with the guys, so of course I was really chill and laid back and I let them do their thing. I was about 19 at the time so his dad was making jokes about me being in the bar and asked me if I was old enough to be there. I joked back with him and told him, yeah and I continued to watch them enjoy themselves.

I had sat at the bar trying to look grown. Damian sat next to me and asked me what I wanted. He was 21 at the time so he was able to buy drinks. "I don't know," I said in a naïvely, smiling. "I guess I will get an apple martini," I said to him trying to sound mature, but I didn't really know what to order. I had never sat at a bar and ordered a drink before, so I was feeling real grown and sexy as I sat there with my man ordering a drink. "What can I get you all?" the bartender had asked us, and Damian ordered me a drink that was in a martini glass and it was purple. To this day I don't know what the drink was called, but it was delicious. I had drunk about 3 glasses of it that night and I was lit and feeling nice and tipsy.

We had stayed at the bar for a while and had a good time, so the drinks wore off a little bit. Me, Damian, and his brother left to go back to his brother's house and his dad and his older brother had stayed. When we got to his brother's house his new wife who was also like my sis was there and she had cooked, so we had hung out and laughed at ate. "We about to play a game," she said as she pulled out a checkers-like shot game. "How you play?" I asked her. "Whoever loses has to take a shot," she told me as me, her, Damian, and his brother sat around the table excited, and his brother pulled out a bottle of Tanqueray. "What is that?" I said as I saw the bottle. At that time, I did not drink white liquor and that bottle just looked like trouble. "It's Gin," his brother said to me, and he let me try a little bit. It was disgusting. I was so nervous to lose, because I did not want to drink a shot of it. We had begun playing the game and of course, I was losing so I was taking shot after shot. The Gin was so nasty, but I had so many shots that I did not taste it anymore. Next thing you know everyone was tipsy or drunk. We were laughing and had a ball.

I remember the room started to spin and I did not feel good. "You ok?" Damian asked me as he was trying to hold me up. I was so drunk at that point that I could not even stand. "I'm ok," I said as the room spun around me. "Do you feel like you need to throw up?" Damian asked me. "I don't know," I said to him as at that point I could not even feel anything. My whole body was numb. "Come on, let's go outside," he said to me as we walked out the back door to the backyard. It was nighttime and the cool air felt good. I could remember was Damian holding me up, and I was looking straight up at the sky looking at the moon. It was so bright, and it looked so big like it was coming towards me and I thought the moon was going to fall on me so I tried to duck for cover. "What's wrong with you?" Damian asked, still holding on to me. "Nothing I told him as I held onto him, and we stood there and laughed. The air was cool and all I remember feeling was my legs getting warm and I felt wet. "Yo, you just pissed on yourself," he said to me as he looked down. I had peed on myself and on his sneakers. We were standing in a puddle of pee. I was so drunk I could not believe what I did. All I could do was laugh.

Damian had picked me up and took me to the back room in his brother's house, there was a bed back there. I remember him taking off my pants and underwear and he left out the room to wash them in the sink and he sat them on the heater in the room to dry. I remember him wiping me with a soapy rag and drying me with a towel and wrapping the towel around my waist and giving me a cover to stay warm. He had laid in the bed with me in pitch black until my clothes finished drying. I had appreciated him taking care of me, that was how he was. He was such a caretaker especially when it came to me. Even though I was drunk out of my mind, I knew I was safe with him. We laid there in the bed and he was rubbing all over me. Even as pissy as I was, he still had sex with me.

In the morning we woke up and my clothes were dry, so I got dressed and we went into the living room. Me Damian, his brother, and his brother's wife had laughed about the night and how drunk I was. His brother and his then-wife were like my brother and sister, so I was not embarrassed at all. I was happy that we got to spend their wedding night with them and create memories. Damian had driven me home and we laughed and held hands the whole ride, enjoying each other's company. We had made plans to get on the Ferry to Maryland with his dad and his wife a few days later so I was looking forward to it. I was so in love with Damian, and he was in love with me and we were so happy and on cloud nine. I was on a natural high from him and life in my eyes was perfect. He had dropped me off at home in the afternoon. I was going to take a shower and get dressed so we could go to dinner that night. While I was home, I was talking to my mom and telling her what had happened the night before. My stepdad was not home so there were good vibes and happy energy in the house, so it was a great day so far.

Later that day, I had gone into the bathroom to take a shower and I had sat on the toilet when my phone rang, and I saw it was Damian. I had not heard from him all day, so I got butterflies and was excited to talk to him. "Hello?" I said as I picked up the phone bubbly and happy. "What's up? What you doing?" he said, but I could tell something was wrong. "What's the matter?" I asked because he did not sound like his usual self. He sat on the phone in silence for a minute and he began to scare me. "What's up?" I asked him curiously and he was hesitant to talk. "I got the DNA test back today," he said to me with no life in his voice. I sat there in silence. Scared to ask what the results were. "What it say?" I asked hesitantly. Damian did not answer me and immediately my stomach dropped and I knew. "It said he's mine," he said with no emotion in his voice. I paused for a second to process it; then I just burst out hysterically crying on the phone to the point where I felt like I was having a panic attack. "No, No No!!" I kept saying.

I was surprised at my reaction. I did not know I would be that hurt and feel that much pain. I had never dealt with the emotion of the baby possibly being his. I had just kept it out of my head and hoped the results would come back negative. Damian was silent the whole time, he did not know what to say. I think he was in shock as well because he kept saying that he didn't think it was his. "I understand how you feel. I'm fucked up about it too" he finally said as I was still crying. "I'm going to give you some time," he said to me very compassionately. "No! I don't need time" I said to him trying to talk in the midst of being hysterical. "What you mean?" he asked me. "I don't need time; I can't do this," I told him. "What you mean? You want to break up?" he asked me. "Yes," I told him as I was angry and hurt. He had never hurt me before, but the pain I was feeling was unbearable. Even though he didn't cheat on me I still felt betrayed. If I would have known he had a girl pregnant, I would not have been with him at all.

Even though he did not know about the baby either, I still felt like I was in a situation where I was not given an option to choose what I wanted. I wanted a man with no kids, and he was no longer that man. He was the love of my life who adored me, he gave me all his time and all his attention, and I was not ready to share him with anyone. "I told you that nothing between us was going to change," he said to me as he sounded hurt that I was hurt. "It don't matter Damian, you have a baby and I don't want to be with you," I told him, still crying. "Ok, that's not what I want, but I do understand how you feel, " he said to me sincerely. I could tell that he was disappointed, and that he did not want to tell me. It took a lot for him to do so, but at that moment, I was disgusted by him and I felt betrayed. "I don't want to talk anymore," I said, still crying. "Ok, I understand. Just know I do love you, and this is not what I wanted and this is not how I want it to be" he said to me and I hung up on him. When I got off the phone, I felt like my whole world had shattered and fell apart. Just earlier I was on cloud nine and just like that my world was turned upside down.

"Ok let's pause right there," my therapist said as she sat her note-pad on her desk and leaned forward to look at me. "I am so sorry that you went through all of that, that sounds like it was emotionally hard for you," she said to me sincerely. "Outside of obviously being hurt by finding out that your partner had a child that you knew nothing about, what was the feeling that triggered anxiety and caused you to feel like you were having a panic attack?" she asked me curiously. I was silent for a moment, and I thought about my life growing up. I thought about how I didn't have my father or a positive father figure in my life. I didn't know it at the time, but I was yearning for love from a male. I had my grandfather Charles Smith who was awesome, but he passed away right before I turned 13, so he was not there for those pivotal teenage years when I needed advice and love from a male. I also had my God dad who was an awesome father figure and loved me like his own. But he had his own lifestyle as well and I did not see him as much.

Even though Damian was young, in a lot of ways he was like a dad to me. He was loving, caring, and nurturing. He gave me whatever I asked for and he always made sure that I was safe. He was warm and comforting and gave good advice as a father would. I never had my dad. I never really felt like I belonged anywhere. Even though I lived at home with my mom, my stepdad, my brother, and my sisters I still did not feel like a family with them. I always felt alone. I never had a place of feeling like I had someone, so when I got with Damian it felt like he was all mine. All his love was for me. His whole world revolved around me, and I loved it, and vice versa. I was all about him and he was my world. We both were intertwined with each other's lives and whatever he lacked he found it in me and what I lacked I found in him.

We loved each other dearly but we had also developed a trauma bond. My brokenness and need for love were attracted to his need to give it. So, when it came out that he had a child, I knew that he was no longer all mine and I had to share him like I had to share everything else in life. I no longer felt like his number one, because he had a whole child to take care of and it broke me. In that moment of finding out, it felt like I was a lonely little girl all over again with no one to save me. I think I started to have a panic attack because I remember being a little girl about five or six and my mom was being mean one day. I think she put me on punishment, because I remember being in my room. I was sitting in the doorway, and I was so sad. I remember starting to cry and I said to myself "I want my dad" then I immediately remembered that I didn't even see my dad at all; and that my dad was not worried about me, and that he was never coming to get me. I remember at that moment feeling helpless and I had a feeling of anxiety as well. I just could not describe what I was feeling as a child. I felt so alone all the time and it was really a sad feeling like I had a hole in me, and something was missing.

My mom had me young and she did the best that she could, but she had a lot of emotional scars herself, so she was not always able to be her best emotionally as a mom, so I was left to fend for myself emotionally and I had to figure it out. I remember one day; I was about seven or eight and I was walking home from school. I was excited because my little sister was having a birthday party and the whole family was coming over to celebrate. As I got closer to my building, a car was parked on the street and when I got closer to it a guy had called my name. When I looked in the car it was my dad. He was sitting in the driver's seat smiling and told me to get in. I got in and he made small talk. I told him it was my sister's birthday, and that we were having a party at my house and I asked him to come. He told me that he would come, and he asked me what she wanted for her birthday. I told him to get her a doll and he told me that he was leaving to go and get it, and that he would be right back. I got out of the car and ran upstairs and told my mom that my dad was coming to the party, and she said "Ok" as she was putting up the decorations. She didn't really say much about it afterward.

When all my family started coming, I was telling all of them that my dad was coming. When my grand pop came to the party, I told him that my dad was on the way, and he saw how excited I was, and he smiled and looked at me but he did not say anything. The party had lasted a few hours and nighttime had come. We played and sang happy birthday and opened gifts and soon people started leaving and my mom and my aunts started cleaning up. I kept looking out the window waiting for my dad, but there was no sign of him. I was sad but I still had hope that he was coming. My grand pop was one of the last people to leave and I sat with him. He didn't say much but he knew I was sad.

All my family knew that my dad wasn't coming. I was the only one who had high hopes. When my grand pop was leaving, he gave me a hug and told me that I was coming to his house over the weekend, and that we were going to have fun. I spent a lot of time at my grandpops house when I was young. That was like my second home. 809 Cedar Lane, Pleasantville NJ, and 609-641-80#@ was the first address and phone number that I was taught, and I didn't even live there. I have a lot of special memories of being there with my aunt and my cousins. It was a nice house with a big backyard and a pool and there were always cookouts and parties going on. My grand pops house was the hot spot and because of him, I had an awesome childhood. That very day at a young age I learned not to trust my dad and that he was a liar. So even though I was young, I had put him out of my head, and I focused on not worrying about him. I knew that I would never believe anything he ever said again.

At a young age, I always liked to write. I remember writing poems and short stories starting at the age of six. So, writing has always been an outlet for me. It always made me happy. I would be in my room watching Sesame Street and I remember making up stories and writing them down. I was in the 1st grade, so I am sure that I spelled a lot of things wrong, but I enjoyed doing it anyway. From early on I knew that I had a vivid imagination, and I had a passion to write and draw. When my dad did not show up, I found out that shortly after that, he had gone to jail, and he stayed there for a long time. While he was in jail, he would always write me and call me. He paid more attention to me in jail than he did on the streets. I enjoyed talking to him, but I still never fully trusted him. I would go and see him with my aunt and my nana and cousins. Sometimes at the visits, he would talk to me and sometimes he would be focused on everyone else. To me a lot of times the visits were uncomfortable. I didn't really like having to go and see him, but my mom would encourage me to so I did.

The next time I remembered my dad being home from jail, I was seventeen years old. I was still skeptical about him, but I thought that a lot of years had passed so I would give our relationship a try. My dad had called me one day and asked if I wanted to go and see a movie and I agreed. He had picked me up in a navy-blue Nissan Maxima. He pulled up smoking a black and mild and I got in the car and told him how much I liked it. "I got this car for you," he said to me, still smoking his mild. "Really?" I said excitedly. "As soon as you pass your driver's test, I'm going to give it to you," he said to me as we drove off. "I'm taking my driver's test next week," I told him. At that point, I had already passed my written test and I was scheduled to take the driving portion, and if I passed, I would have my driver's license. I was super excited that my dad had a car for me when I got my license. "Maybe he has changed," I thought to myself, and I felt good on the inside. We saw the movie "The Ring" which was terrifying to me. I hated scary movies and the ring had me super scared. Even though I was sitting next to my dad, we did not have the type of relationship where I could grab him for comfort on the scary parts and he didn't try to comfort me either. So, we sat there, and it was kind of awkward. I had gotten through the movie, and he had dropped me off home.

He reassured me about giving me the car. He told me that he would drive it until I got my license and after that, it was mine. I went into the house and told my mom what he told me, and she was excited for me. All that next week she and my godfather had shown me how to drive. Although I was nervous, I had passed my driver's test on the first try. A good friend of mine took his driver's test on the same day and he passed too. My mom took both of us to the DMV and we got our license and we were both so excited. I told him that my dad got me a car and that we were going to go riding, and we both joked and laughed on the way home.

As soon as I got in the house, I had called my dad to tell him the good news, but he did not answer. I had called him all day and no answer. I had called him the next few days and still no answer. Finally, about a week later I got in contact with him. "Hello, I been trying to call you," I said to him in a cautious voice. "What's up?" he said, sounding aggravated. "Nothing, I just wanted to tell you I got my license," I told him as I had proudness in my voice. "Ok," he said, sounding short-tempered. "Are you still going to give me the car as you said?" I asked him nervously. "What?" he said rudely. "Are you going to still give me the car?" I asked again, taken back by his mean response. "No, that's my car," he said to me. I was shocked. I did not know how to respond to him, because I had never had that type of interaction with him before.

I did not know if he was playing or serious. "Do you want to talk to my mom?" I asked him. "No, I'm talking to you, and I'm telling you that you are not getting the car," he said to me. "Then why did you say you were giving it to me when I got my license?" I asked him. "I didn't tell you that," he said as he blatantly lied. "You did tell me that," I said. At that point I wanted to cry. I was holding my tears back, but you could still hear the cry in my voice. "I didn't tell you nothing and I'm tired of you," he said out of nowhere. "Tired of me?" I asked, shocked. "How could you be tired of me when I have never really been around you?" I blurted out to my surprise because I was not a smart-mouth child. "I wasn't there because of you," he said, and he blurted out more things that I can't remember because once he said he was not there because of "Me", my mind had gone on stuck. I could not believe that he said that.

At seventeen years old, all the abandonment he caused me. I still tried to open my heart to him, and he had the nerve to push his actions back on me. He took no responsibility but blamed me. I felt sick to my stomach. I do not remember the rest of the conversation. All that I knew was once I got off the phone with him, I never wanted to talk to him ever again. When I hung up, I was crying in pain. I had felt so hurt and belittled. I told my mom what had happened, and she gave me a hug and told me to be done with him. A week later she bought me a lemon from my aunt that needed to be fixed. The car did not work, but my mom promised to get it fixed and running so that I could have a car. It was not the car I wanted but I appreciated her for it. The car had never got fixed and it sat in the parking lot until it had got towed away. A few weeks later my dad went back to jail. Come to find out the people he bought it from had never given him the title and they reported the car stolen and he was locked up. I never got the full story or the full truth. After that, my dad was in jail for several years. I had felt broken and hurt by his words, so I did not really speak with him the years he was in jail.

While he was there, he had written a letter to me and was letting me know that he had written a book about his life's story. My dad grew up in the 80's. His book talked about Atlantic City life in the '80's and everything that was going on in that Era. My dad had reached out to me to ask me if I could write the intro and explain how his actions and absence affected me and my life. He asked me several times, but I did not get around to doing it. I had so much anger and rage towards him, that I was scared that I would say things in the book that would hurt his feelings. I never explained that to my dad, but he must have picked up on my energy, because he had called me on the phone from jail and told me that it was ok to say whatever I wanted to say in the intro, and that he was prepared to hear the truth. He told me that he won't be hurt and that he just wanted me to express myself.

"Ok, stop right there," my therapist said as she took off her glasses giving me her full attention. "Did you ever write the intro? And if so, what did you say?" She asked me. "No, I never wrote it. I was too angry to begin to get the words out" I told her. "Ok, I do understand, I want you to hear me out," she said to me sincerely. "I understand that you have a lot of issues surrounding your father and I heard you say that he has done hurtful things to you," she said to me. "But I want you to just step back for a second and take out the fact that he is your father and the expectations you have of him and just see him as a person. A person who was a person before becoming a father. A person who may have had their own issues and struggles in life. I know a lot of times we have expectations of our parents. But sometimes if you just see them as human, it will help you better understand them when they make mistakes. No human is perfect, and I am not making excuses for your dad. But I do want you to let go of those expectations so you can free yourself, and you can begin to heal from your past. Once you let go it will be easier to forgive and make peace. Does that make sense?" She asked me. "Yes, that makes a lot of sense," I told her as I sat there and thought about what she said.

"I want to give you an assignment. I don't want you to do it today, because I want you to take your time and get out all that you want to say" she told me. "I want you to write a letter to your dad and give it to him when you feel like you are ready. I want you to get your thoughts out of your mind and heart and onto paper. You have to release the pain you are carrying" she told me sincerely. "Ok," I said to her in agreement. "Ok, now let's get back to the original question that I asked you in regard to you finding out that your then-boyfriend at the time had a child. What I heard you say is; it caused you anxiety and hurt because the lack of relationship with your father, and your boyfriend played a major role in your life, almost like a father to you and you felt like you would lose him and his attention because now he had a child to take care of. Did I hear that correct?" she asked me. "Yes, that is correct " I said as I had to acknowledge my feelings even though it was hard. 'Ok, so after you told your boyfriend that you could no longer handle being in a relationship with him, what happened next?" she asked me as she put her glasses back on and picked her notebook back up.

"After I hung up on him, I had a panic attack once I processed everything. I had stayed in the bathroom for a while because I did not want anyone to see me like that. I was so embarrassed about the situation that I did not tell anyone about it. I just kept it to myself. I would not eat or anything. I felt anxious all the time. I was angry at Damian. I felt like he had stabbed me in my chest on one hand. On the other hand, I had to keep reminding myself that he did not know either, and that he did not hurt me on purpose. My mind was having a back-and-forth battle between love and hate, and hate was winning.

I had not talked to Damian for about over a week, and one day he called me to check on me. "Hello" I answered in an uninterested voice. "What's up?" he said, unsure of how I was going to respond. "Nothing," I said being very one-worded with him. "I was just checking on you and seeing if you were good, " he said. Normally you could always tell that he was smiling. But this time there was no smile in his voice. There was sadness. We were silent on the phone as I really did not have much to say to him. "Have you seen your son yet?" I asked him. "No not yet, " he said to me. "It's been a week since you found out, why haven't you seen him?" I asked. "I wanted you to be with me when I see him, " he said to me. "What?!" I asked confused. "Why? We are not even together" I said to him. "I know, but you are a part of my life and I want you a part of this too. The first time I see him, I want you to be there to share it together," he said. "You have to be joking right?" I said to him as I could not believe what he was saying.

On the other hand, I thought that was considerate of him to include me, but it was pissing me off at the same time. I had so many emotions at the time. "I can set up to go and see him, are you going to come?" he asked me, and I paused. "I don't think so," I told him, and he got silent. "Listen Shamirah, I did not know I had a son either. This is messed up for me too. This is not what I want, but it is what it is. I want you to be a part of my life with my son. I understand how you feel right now, but I don't want you not to be a part of the equation" he said to me. "I'm not dealing with no baby or no baby mama drama," I told him. "Man, his mom is irrelevant. If you were on board, I would get my son and me and you would raise him. She's not even a factor at all," he told me as he was agitated by having a baby with her. "It all sounds good, but I'm just not beat right now," I told him. "So, you really want to stay broken up?" he asked me sincerely and I paused.

I really wanted to be mad and curse him out and be mean, but deep down inside I still did love him, and I did not want to be broken up. I had missed him and all the fun we had. "I don't want to, but I have to," I said to him as I began to cry. "You don't have to at all. I still want you, and I'm sorry all this happened, but I told you I still got you, and that nothing was going to change between us" he reassured me. "I don't know. I will think about it. I will talk to you another time" I told him. I never brushed him off the phone or was ever that short with him before, but this time I was. "Well, put it like this, I'm not going to sweat you forever," he said, and he hung up the phone.

I knew how Damian was. I remembered the time he got mad when I would not have sex with him. I remembered how mean he could be, and I did not want to have him start being mad at me. I also thought of how good of a guy he was, and how much love he showed me, and how special he made me feel. I loved and cared for him. He was special in my life and I did not want to lose him. Damian had called the next day and I agreed to go and see his son with him. He had picked me up in his Lexus and he still had my Betty boop seat cover and floor mat on my passenger side, and his car was so clean and smelled so good. He looked cute too. He had on a button-up Polo shirt, some jeans and some Timbs, and a fitted hat with his braided hanging from the back. He was smiling from ear to ear, and I knew he was happy to finally see me.

He had gone in his backseat and pulled out some roses and handed them to me and I thought that was sweet of him. He opened the car door for me, and we sat there for a minute as he was still smiling. I guess he was taking it all in, because it was a good possibility that he would never see me again. "Thank you for coming, " he said as he held my hand then tried to kiss me on my lip, but I pushed him away. I was not ready for all of that. I was still feeling some type of way. "I know this is hard for you, but I got you. You are number one in my life, and I love you" he told me as he kissed my hand and I did not respond or say anything back.

We had driven away to see his son, but before we went to his house, we had stopped to go shopping for him. We went to the Shore Mall to pick him up some clothes. We were in the baby department, and it was so weird to me. I had never had a reason to go in the baby dept before and it was definitely different being in there with my so-called boy-friend, who was shopping for his son who we just found out about. All of it was uncomfortable but I tried to go with the flow anyway. We had picked out some cute outfits to bring to him and we went to the register to pay for everything. We got our bags and went to see him. When we got there the mother had brought the baby downstairs to us. We did not go into the house. We took him to the car, and he cried at first but then eventually he was ok. Damian had told him he was his dad. He was a little over one year old so of course, he did not understand.

After a while, he began to play a little bit, but we were in the car and Damian wanted everyone to be more comfortable. We put some of the new clothes on him and got his car seat and took the baby to Damian's mom's house where we could spend quality time. Once at his mom's house, she got to see the baby and she was so excited. Me and Damian spent time with him too. We ate and tried to get him familiar with everyone. Damian's younger brother Drew had lived there with his mom. When Drew met the baby they instantly clicked and he loved him right away. Later on, that night we took the baby back home to his mom and gave her the new clothes and Damian let her know that he would be back to get him.

After that day Damian had got his son a lot and began to grow a bond with him. Though I was always uncomfortable with the situation, I tried to get used to having his son around. His second birthday came, and me and Damian went shopping and got him his first toddler 4-wheeler and we spent his birthday with him. I tried my best to be supportive and present even with all the pain of the situation. I was happy that Damian wanted to be a part of his son's life because every child deserves to have their father in their life.

9

It was now December in New Jersey, and the days were filled with cold temperatures. I loved winter and being with Damian made it even better. The winter before then I did not get to spend it with him because he was in jail. Since he was home this time, we made sure that we enjoyed every moment. On cold nights we would be cozied up in his mom's house enjoying his family. His mom cooked every night. She always made fried chicken, macaroni and cheese, and string beans and she always had cornbread too. It was Christmas time so the city and everywhere else we went was lit up so pretty and the air felt magical. Back then we celebrated Christmas, so we were excited to go shopping for everybody and get them gifts. Me and Damian both worked at Bally's Casino at the time. I worked in the Promotions dept, and he was a Sous chef at the Restaurant upstairs. We would see each other at work in passing. Most of the time we would run into each other downstairs at the laundry area where all the Casino workers picked up their uniforms. When we were off, we cruised the city on Snowy days listening to good music and enjoying each other's company.

Damian was really close to his cousin who was in jail at the time, and we had made plans to go and see him. Me and him had been out all day and that night he wanted to be romantic, so he parked the car at Park Avenue Park in Pleasantville and we sat out there and listened to music and laughed and talked. We had to leave to go and see his cousin at about 4 am in morning and at that time it was about 1 am. We must have been really tired because instead of driving home we had fallen asleep at the park. It was freezing cold that night and Damian had the heat on in the car. He gave me his coat and we were knocked out. The park was not the safest and thank God no one had robbed us or shot us through the night. When we got up it was about 4 am and we began to drive where his cousin was to see him at the jail. We had stopped at Wawa to use the bathroom other than that we still had our clothes on from the night before. I remember waking up from laying on one side of my hair and it was flat. My curls had fallen and the other side was perfect. "We are dirty," I said to Damian as we both laughed on the way to his cousin. We chewed gum and thought nothing of it. The only ones who knew we slept in the car and didn't wash, or anything were me and him. I loved him because no matter what, we were always down with each other and always had the best of times. I would never have done anything like that with anyone but him.

We went to the jail visit and enjoyed his cousin. Afterwards we left and he dropped me off at my mom's house and I took a shower and got some sleep, and he went home to do the same. Later that night he came to my house to pick me up and he spent time with my mom and my brother, and we laughed and enjoyed each other. In the winter my mom always baked cookies with the kids and played her Christmas music which was a mixture of the Kelly Price Christmas album, Cece Winans, Mariah Carey, and other artists. My mom's house was always decorated for all the Holidays, especially for Christmas. She went all out, and it was nice. Everyone was in the holiday spirit. My mom asked if we wanted to put up the tree so we did. It was me, my mom, my brother, my three little sisters, and Damian. Of course, as he was helping, he was smiling from ear to ear. He was always so happy, and his spirit was so warm and my whole family loved him. After we were done my mom put on the grinch and we watched movies the rest of the time and Damian had left later that night.

The next day I went to Damian's mom's house, and she was preparing for Christmas as well. Me and him had helped her put up the tree and decorate her windows. Afterward, we did a poinsettia to pick names out of a hat to see who we would buy gifts for. I had his sister and his mom. His mom got me and no one else revealed who they had. We all laughed that night and his mom and brothers played spades and everyone was having a great time. We had looked out the window and it had begun to snow. The night was perfect, and I was enjoying every minute of it. I loved family and I loved his family and I appreciate how they opened their arms and hearts to me and always made me feel welcome. It was a blessing for me to be experiencing all those memories and being truly happy, because the year before Damian was in jail with no bond and I had no idea if and when he was coming home. I was so sad and miserable. Fast forward a year later, he was home and we were having the time of our lives. I was so grateful for every moment. Me and him would go out to the malls and shop for Xmas gifts for our family and he was so excited. Damian was a giver and so it was fun to watch him be so happy to make others happy. We had a big family, so we tried to split our time with everyone.

On Christmas Eve we spent time at my mom's house and left their gifts there with them to open on Christmas morning. We stayed the night at Damian's mom's house and woke up with her on Christmas morning to open gifts. His mom bought me a gold xoxo bracelet and a gold ring with a Garnet birthstone representing my birthday month. Damian had got me a heart xoxo Necklace and bracelet set with "I love you" plated on them written in cursive. It was so pretty, and I loved it. A few weeks before then, we were in the jewelry store and I was looking at it because I liked it, and the fact that he remembered and went back and bought it meant a lot to me. We had all opened our gifts and enjoyed the morning. Me and Damian got dressed to go to his dad's house to spend time with his father, his stepmom, and his little brothers. When we got there his brothers were playing with their gifts and his stepmom and his sister were in the kitchen finishing up Christmas dinner and Damian spent time with his dad. I helped his sister and stepmom in the kitchen and to my surprise, his stepmom handed me a square Macy's box. I opened it and there was a long sage-colored silk bathrobe in it. It was so pretty. "Thank you!" I said to her as I gave her a hug. We had all sat down and ate Christmas dinner. We talked and laughed and enjoyed the holiday spirit. Spending time with his family was beautiful and it was so nice watching his brothers play together. They all had a tight bond, and it was so cute to see.

After we finished, it was time to go. We hugged everyone and told them goodbye and got in the car to go back to the city which was about an hour away. "I had fun," I said to Damian as I got in the car and put my seatbelt on. "Me too," he said as he turned on some R&B music and we enjoyed each other's company. As we were driving it began to snow. "Aww look," I said as I pointed to the snowflakes. "Mmm Hmm," he said as he smiled and turned up the music and we enjoyed the winter vibes. He had the heat blasting in his car and it was so warm and toasty. He had stopped at Wawa and we got Chai Tea and enjoyed the rest of the ride home watching the snowflakes falling.

A few weeks passed and it was New Year's Eve and Damian went all out and bought Moet and Moet Rose. We spent New Year's Eve with our friends drinking and playing games. We had so much fun. We had the streamers and noisemakers as we watched MTV's Ball drop-in Times Square. "5, 4, 3, 2,1!!" We all yelled as Midnight came and it was now 2005! I kissed Damian and hugged him, and he popped the bottles and we toasted. "Happy New Year!" I said to him as I was so happy to be spending New Year with him. The year before then he was in jail, and I was sad and alone. Ever since he had come home everything had been so special and perfect. He was everything I wanted and more. What also made me happy in our relationship was the fact that he felt the same way about me that I felt about him. I loved the fact that even though he made me happy. I made him happy too. I loved that I was a comfort and a safe haven for him. When he looked at me, I saw love and proudness in his eyes. He adored me. To him, I was an angel and he made that known to everyone. He protected me when I was not around and always had my back. He would tell me about hating females that would try to talk about me to him when I wasn't around, and he wasn't having it. He would put them right in their place and dismiss everything that they would say. To Damian, it did not matter how the world saw me. It only mattered how he saw me, and he knew me better than anyone. He didn't believe lies and rumors about me which meant a lot to me. We were each other's protectors and I never had to question his loyalty and he never had to question mine. We were like Mickey and Minnie mouse. We were made for each other.

January 5th had come which was my birthday. I had to work that day in the Casino. I loved all my co-workers, they made going to work fun. When I got there My friend who I had previously worked with at Walmart had got me a cake with my name on it and Balloons. My whole department had shown me birthday love. Just so happened that day I was working upstairs in a different area, and they happened to be having a party up there, so I got to join in for my birthday. I had a ball at work that day. When I got off at 4 pm, I went home to get dressed. Damian pulled up at my house with a bouquet of balloons and I spent my birthday with him.

The next day we went to breakfast. "Remember when you spent your school check on me and bailed me out of jail when you wanted to get you a car with the money?" He asked me out of nowhere. "Yeah," I answered wondering where that came from. "Remember I always told you I got you," he said to me smiling. "I know, " I said to him trying to figure out where the conversation was going. At that time, I was back enrolled in college at A.C.C in Mays Landing. Damian would still drop me off and pick me up, and on the days, he was busy I would have my mom's car. I drove her car most of the time, so he didn't have to come all the way from the city just to take me up the street. I appreciated her letting me use her car but sometimes she would be petty about it, or my stepdad would have it. When that happened and Damian was busy,

I would have to get on the bus to school. There were many days that I stood at the bus stop freezing and Damian really did not like that, but I had to do what I had to do to make sure I got to school. "I don't like when you at the bus stop. I know sometimes I'm ripping and running and can't come to get you" he told me apologetically. "I know. It's ok, I'm grown so sometimes I have to figure it out, I'm good." I told him as I smiled. I knew when he could, that Damian always made sure I had a ride, so I knew his intentions were good. "I got a surprise for you," he told me with his sneaky smile. "What?!" I asked curiously because my birthday was yesterday, so I had no clue of what he wanted to give me that he didn't give me for me already. "I'll show you when we leave," he said. I was ready to go to see what he was talking about.

We had breakfast in Pleasantville, and we left and drove to the city in a parking lot where we met up with two Italian guys. When we pulled up, they were smiling. "Who is that?" I was thinking to myself, and my face was probably scrunched up too. "Wait here," Damian said as he got out of the car and clapped the guy up, and the other guy walked away and then pulled up with a small red car. It was a 90 something Hyundai. It was so small and cute. I was wondering what was going on. The guy handed Damian the key and Damian walked up to the passenger side of his car where I was sitting. He was smiling from ear to ear. "Here, this is your car," he said to me as he handed me the key. "What!" I said shocked and I got out of the car to look at it closer. It was an old car, but it was in perfect condition.

It was so Tiny, and it fit me perfectly. I got in and tried it out and I felt comfortable. "You like it?" Damian asked me. "Yeah, I like it," I said as I was looking around. The guy had handed Damian the title and they shook hands and got in their car and drove away. "Thank you!" I said to him as I was shocked, he got me a car. "Now my babe don't have to be at the bus stop or driving your mom's car. You got your own whip," he told me proudly. "Thank you!" I said to him. "Ok get in," he said to me, and I got in and he told me to drive it to my house and he would follow me. "You know, I'm not good at driving," I said to him as I was nervous. "You good," he said to me reassuring me that I was going to be ok. "Ok," I said as I took a deep breath and I followed him out of the parking lot.

We had taken the expressway from Atlantic City to Mays Landing. I felt like I was driving like a turtle because all the cars were passing me. When I finally got home, Damian pulled up behind me and told me that I did good, but I needed to drive faster, and I started to laugh. He stayed and talked to me for a minute then he drove off and left. I was excited to go into the house to show my mom my new car, but when I told her about it, she seemed uninterested. She had an attitude, and her vibe was cold. I was not sure what was wrong with her, but I was used to her being wishy-washy, so I just blew her off and went about my business.

My mom must have realized she was being rude to me because the next day she came to me and asked me if I needed her to put the car under her insurance. Then she took me to best buy to get a BOSS stereo system to put in my car, and we went to Walmart to pick out some seat covers. I had got red ladybug theme seat covers and steering wheel cover with the floor mats, mirror ornament, and some cherry scented air freshener. I chose Ladybug because they did not have Betty Boop and that was the next best thing. I had the inside of my car looking really cute and the outside was clean. From that point on I was all over the place in my little car. All my friends called it "The Red tomato" I had some good, good times in that car and I was grateful to have it and grateful to Damian for getting it for me.

10

A few weeks had passed, and he came to pick me up to take me to Red Lobster because he said we needed to talk. When we got there, I was a little nervous because I could not imagine what we needed to talk about. "What's up?" I said as I sat there eating my biscuit while we waited for our food to come. I always ordered the same thing, the Ultimate feast and raw oysters on the half shell for my appetizer. "I just needed to talk to you face to face," he said as I could tell by his energy that something was bothering him. The last time we had this type of energy in a conversation was when he was telling me that he possibly had a son. I was just praying that he was not about to say that he had another child that I did not know about. "What's wrong? You seem sad" I said to him concerned.

"Remember I always told you about the case I had when we first got together?" he asked me. "Yeah" I responded. "And remember I told you it kept getting postponed?" he asked. "Yeah" I responded curiously. "Well, my court date is coming up now and I may have to take it to trial. If I lose, I'm going away for a long time, no less than 10 years" he told me. I sat there for a minute and did not respond because I did not know what to say. I began to feel sick and really did not even want to eat anymore. "Ok, so what if you don't take it to trial then what?" I asked when I finally spoke. "If I take a plea instead, I'm still looking at some time. I am going to get my lawyer to get me as little time as possible. But the thing is: I think I can beat the case so I want to take it to trial and get acquitted" he told me. "If you go to trial you have to depend on a Jury to find you not guilty to be acquitted. A young black man from Atlantic City with the charges you have in the Atlantic County judicial system, and you think that a jury will find you not guilty?" I said to him, making him understand the odds that were stacked against him. "I know all of that, but my lawyer is a monster and I feel like the case can be beat. There is no evidence and no witnesses" he said to me. "I don't know Damian; I just don't think that's a good idea," I told him. I knew that he valued my option, but I also knew that at the end of the day, he was going to do whatever he wanted to do and that scared me. When is the court date?" I asked him. "Feb 17" he replied. "Wow, that is a couple of days after Valentine's Day," I said to him. "Yup," he said as he still looked concerned. I can tell by him telling me that it took a load off of him because his energy was lighter.

Our food came but I did not have an appetite. "Don't stress yourself about it, " he said to me as he ate his food. "Everything will be good, " he told me. When Damien dropped me off at home, I went to my secret place to pray. I prayed and asked God to have Favor and Mercy on him and to please not allow him to do a lot of time. My biggest prayer was for him to do no time at all. One thing about me in my life is that when I prayed, God answered. There was not one thing in life that I had asked God for that he did not give me. I knew that God showed me favor in my life. I also knew that God had favored Damian as well. He was a very blessed person. He had the heart of a Martyr and a giver. After I prayed, I had peace and I knew that somehow, someway everything would work out and I closed my prayer and went to sleep.

11

A few weeks had passed, and it was now February. I was talking to my co-workers about what we wanted to do for Valentine's Day the next week. I was scheduled to work, so I went to my supervisor to request time off, and I was approved. I was so excited to spend my first Valentine's Day with Damian. I went shopping at the Hamilton Mall to buy an outfit. I bought a pair of black and pink patent leather pumps with little silver chains on them and a pink top with a heart on it, and a black blazer to go with it. I got my hair done in long Farrah Faucet feathers, and I also bought a sexy Teddy for that night. I did not know what Damian had planned for us, but whatever it was, I knew it was going to be nice. I had boyfriends in the past for Valentine's Day, but with Damian, it was different and special, and I was looking forward to it. Valentine's Day had come, and for some reason, it felt like Christmas. Damian was just as excited as I was. I had talked to him earlier that day, and he told me to come to his mom's house around 5 pm. I had bought his mom some candy, and I got him a heartfelt card.

When I came into the house, he had greeted me with a bunch of Valentine's day balloons, two teddy bears, one was red and one hot pink that read "I love you" and they both had 2005 written on the teddy bears feet. He also handed me a heartfelt card and a heart-shaped box of chocolate. At that time, I did not eat chocolate, but his gesture was nice. We had taken a bunch of pictures and laughed with his mom before we left to go on our date. "You all have fun, " his mom said as she gave us a hug. I had sat my teddy bears and balloons on the table.

I went to put the box of chocolates down too, and Damian told me to bring them with us. "Ok," I said to him, as I thought to myself, why did he want me to bring the chocolate. But I grabbed it anyway, and we left. He had opened the car door for me, and we drove to the end of the Dove, but all the suites were booked up. We drove to about five different restaurants that night, and they all were all booked. After driving around for about an hour with no luck, we sat in the car and thought about spending our Valentine's Day back at his mom's house. "I thought you made reservations somewhere," I asked him as I sat in the car, a little worried that we were not going to be able to enjoy our night. "I did," he told me. "Then why are we driving all around?" I asked him, confused. "Because the place I made the reservations I wasn't sure if you wanted to go there. "Why wouldn't I?" I asked him. He let me know that he made the reservations at a low-key spot, and I had no problem with it. "They having a Valentine's Day Dinner there. We were supposed to meet my mans and his girl, but they couldn't make it," he told me. "Ok," I said as I laughed. "Just because they couldn't make it doesn't mean that I would not want to go," I told him.

This particular bar was our spot back then. We went there to Party every weekend. His friends and my friends used to be there, and we would have a ball. Me and Damian would dance the whole night. Around that time Young Jeezy's album "Snowman" was poppin and they would play his album heavy along with Rick Ross and T.I. We were up north but those three down south artists had the city jumping. "Ok cool," he said to me, and we drove there. When we got there, there were not many cars outside, so I could tell it was not packed like the rest of the restaurants we had gone to. Damian had opened the door for me, and I was getting out, and he reminded me again to bring the chocolate. I was thinking in my head why he would want me to bring chocolate to a restaurant. But again, I just did what he asked me to and bought the box of chocolates with me.

When we walked in, we were escorted upstairs where we normally party. It was normally a room with a DJ, a few chairs and tables, and a dance floor. That night they had it set up so pretty and romantic. There were tables with tablecloths and table settings with wine glasses and plates and napkins and roses. The lights were dim and romantic, and they were playing soft music. It was too cute. There were about fifteen tables set up, but the only people there were us and another couple across from us. We figured it was a little early, so maybe more people would come. The waiter came to our table and lit the candles for us and handed me a pink rose. "Can I take you all's order?" they asked" They had a set Valentine's Day menu. I ordered steak and potatoes, and Damian ordered the same.

While we waited for our food, they had brought out some hot rolls with strawberry butter. That was the best butter I ever had in my life. When our food came everything was delicious. Me and him sat and talked the whole time. We stared into each other's eyes like in the movies. No extra people had come. It was just us and the other couple, and I would not have had it any other way. To me that made it more special; it was just us in our own little world. The service was great. The food was great. The atmosphere was great. I had an all-around good time. Once it was time to leave, Damian paid for the check and tip, and we left. I was about to forget the box of chocolate, and he reminded me to grab it. "Why did you even want me to bring this?" I asked him, and he did not answer me; he just smiled.

We had driven to a hotel right next door. "Stay right here for a minute," Damian said to me as he got out of the car and went into the room. I sat there in the car feeling on cloud nine. I was having a great night, and I couldn't pick a better person to be with than him.

Being with Damian was like a fairy tale for me. He made me feel so special, and he did any and everything in his power to make me happy. He was truly an awesome boyfriend and friend." Ok come on," he said as he opened the car door for me to get out, and he grabbed the box of chocolate, and we went to the room. When he opened the door. I could not believe my eyes. The room was dimly lit by a fireplace and a few candles. There were fake rose petals all over the room, and he had filled the Jacuzzi with bubbles. "Oh my God," I said as I felt like I was in a dream. "You did all this for me?" I said as I wanted to cry, and I instantly became shy and taken back. I had boyfriends in the past, and I had family that loved me. But Damian made me feel a different type of love. One that I never felt before, ever. The love he gave me was overwhelming, and it almost made me feel like it was too good to be true. Every day with him was like a good dream that I did not want to wake up from. "C'mon, let's get in," he said as he began taking his clothes off. I took off mine, and we were both naked and got in.

He had opened champagne and poured us some. While we were in there, he just kept looking at me, smiling. I was used to him smiling, but this smile was different. He had a nervous happiness to him. "Do you love me?" he asked. "Yeah," I answered. "Would you be with me forever?" I asked him. "Yeah, I want to," I answered him. "Ok," he said as he sat back and drank his champagne. He sat the box of chocolate by the Jacuzzi, and as I was drinking my champagne, he asked me if I wanted some chocolate. "No, thank you, I'm not hungry. I just ate all that food," I said to him. "Please, just try one, and I'll try one too," he said to me, and he handed me the box. "Ok" I said as I opened the box. In the middle of the candy was an opened box with a ring. "Oh my God!" I said as I was in shock. "Damian, what is this?" I asked, happy and confused. "Will you marry me?" he asked me as he looked into my eyes, and I could tell he was sincere. "Yes!" I said as I hugged him and kept looking at the ring. He put the ring on my finger, and we began kissing. I felt like I was having an outer body experience. I could not believe that he had just proposed to me. I was twenty years old, and I was engaged to be married. I was in my glory.

We had got out the Jacuzzi and dried off, and Damian laid me on the bed, and we had passionate sex the whole night. There was so much love, and affection behind it, and I enjoyed every moment of it. The next day we got dressed and went to Kmart to print out all of our Valentine's Day pictures to have as memories of that day. We both were still on cloud nine. I called everyone to tell them I was engaged, and he called everyone to tell them I said yes! It was beautiful, and everyone was happy for us, especially his mom, dad, and his stepmom. They knew about it the whole time. That day was so special to me, and it definitely was a night that I would never forget. The next few days were amazing, and we were like two love birds. I was looking at pictures of wedding dresses and decor in magazines. I went back to work showing all my friends my ring. Everyone was so happy for us, and we received so much love.

12

Our excitement was short-lived as his day of court had come, and we both were nervous. I had knots in my stomach and had felt like I had to throw up that whole morning. We got dressed for court and drove to the Mays Landing Courthouse. On the ride, Me and Damian were both silent. There was a sad aura in the air. When we got there, his older brother and a few other people he was close to, were there. They all clapped each other up but no one was smiling, and you could feel the nervous tension. Damian had gone into the courtroom to talk to his lawyer, and they were in there for a while, while we waited in the lobby.

When he came out, he told us that since he had already put in a plea of not guilty that his lawyer told him that he could take a plea that day or take it to trial. Since he had already told his lawyer previously that he wanted to take it to trial, they already had a jury picked that was already in the courtroom. "What you going to do bro?" his brother asked him with the sincerest look on his face. "I don't know bro. I think if I take it to trial, I can beat it," Damian replied, looking unsure. "Bro, I don't think you should take it to trial," one of his brother's good friends told him. "What is the plea they gave you?" I asked him. "A three flat with almost a year already served. Plus, I'm a first-time felon so my lawyer said he is going to get me as little time as possible" Damian responded. "What Nigga, you better take that" his brothers friends said. "I don't want to take it," Damian told him. "Nigga if you lose trial, you looking at ten years or better, and you know if you lose, they are going to smoke your ass" the guy added. Then a couple of the other guys chimed in.

The whole time me and Damian's brother stood there looking at Damian. I nor his brother had to say a word. Both of our faces said, "take the plea." Everyone else could give their opinion, but we were close to him. We would be the ones hurting, not them, so their opinions were irrelevant at that point. "I know you want to go to trial and everything, but I have a bad feeling if you do," I told him as I pulled him to the side. "They have no witnesses and no evidence, so they have no case," he told me. "But they must have something if they are willing to go to trial, and the prosecutor already don't like you. She is ready to smoke you.

All she has to do is convince the jury that you are guilty and it's a wrap. You're going away for no less than ten years," I stressed to him as I was about to cry. Damian didn't say much, he just stood against the wall thinking. As we were standing there, his lawyer came out. "Time is ticking, and the judge wants to know your decision," his lawyer said to him. "I just don't know what I should do, because I feel like we can beat it," he told his lawyer. "Yeah, I will fight my hardest for you, but I can't guarantee anything. If you want to go to trial, I'm ready, and we can bring the jury in," his lawyer told him. "I just need a few more minutes," Damian said to him. "Ok man, I got you" his lawyer said to him and went back into the courtroom.

Damian looked stressed like I have never seen before. He normally had all the answers, and he normally was so confident which made me confident. But this time he looked scared which made me even more scared. "I'll be right back" I said to him as I went into the bathroom. My stomach was hurting so bad that I had to throw up. My body felt so anxious and overwhelmed. I stood there in the stall and cried for a minute and prayed. "God, please help us and give us guidance, we don't know what to do" I said crying and pleading to God. I had heard someone come into the bathroom, so I wiped my tears and flushed the toilet then came out to wash my hands.

At the sink next to me was the prosecutor. She had on a black skirt suit set and a pair of black heels, and she did not crack a smile. She always looked mean. I felt like she wanted to see Damian go away for a long time due to his charges. I felt like even though the witness was not in court that it was her mission to prove him guilty to the jury, and I felt in my heart right then and there that he should take the plea and not risk going to trial. "Did you see the prosecutor?" He asked me as soon as I came out of the bathroom. "Yeah, I saw her in there and she was cold. " I told him. "Word, she walked past me and gave me the grimiest look," he said to me. "Damian, I think you should take the plea. A three flat with damn near a year time served is not bad compared to ten years is a no brainer. She is out to smoke you, and me feeling her energy in the bathroom after I prayed, gave me all the confirmation I needed. I will be heartbroken if you get ten years. You are a good person, and I don't want to see you in jail at all, especially not that long," I said as I was about to cry again. "Nobody else's opinions matter. It is me, and you that are together, and I think you should take the plea," I said as I looked him sincerely in his face.

He stood there for a while, thinking and knowing that time was ticking. "Alright, I think I know what I am going to do," he said to me, and his brother walked over. "What's good bro. What you going to do?" his brother asked him. "I think I'm going to take the plea bro," he said to him, and his brother looked relieved and clapped him up. I gave Damian a hug and let him know that everything was going to be ok, and we walked towards the courtroom to let his lawyer know his decision.

His lawyer let the judge know that he was taking the plea, and the judge dropped all the other charges and sentenced him to three years flat with twelve months' time served. Damian was to report to the court in 30 days to begin his sentence. For the thirty days that he was out, we spent every hour and every second together. If I was not at work or at school, I was with him. Every day got closer and closer to him leaving, and it was sad. It was weird having an actual date when you knew the love of your life was going to leave you. The only thing that gave me comfort was the fact that this all would be behind us, and once he came home, we could start our lives together without this case hanging over his head. Damian had done all his errands and handled all his business before going in.

We went on dates, and he was still as romantic as ever. I think he tried not to think much about it and just tried to enjoy every day as best as he could. The night before sentencing, we had got a room to spend time, but there was so much emotion that we didn't say much. We just held each other and read each other's thoughts. We comforted one another in a way only we understood. "I love you," I said to him. "I love you too," he said to me as he looked into my eyes. "I know you do. " I said to him genuinely. "No, for real, I really love you, and I got you when I come home. We going to have a good life and move to Atlanta and have babies," he said to me smiling. "Shut up, you talking jail talk already," I said to him as we both laughed. Me and him had talked about moving to Atlanta for a while. I wanted to go to school there for film and media. I always wanted to write movies and become a movie producer.

Me and him stayed up and talked for most of the night and we did not want it to end. It felt like time was flying and morning was coming way too fast. His sentencing was at 9am. So, we got up really early so he could get a good breakfast. We sat down to eat but neither of us had an appetite. We drove to the courthouse together in his Lexus and we held hands the whole time. I tried my hardest to hold my tears back, but I was just so sad. I was trying to be strong for him because he was the one having to go to jail, and I know that was a lot on him. When we pulled up to the courthouse, it felt like doomsday. We walked in the courtroom, and I gave him a kiss and a hug. His lawyer and the judge and the other court people were in there as the judge was reading everything. Damian stood there with a humble spirit. I still remember what he had on. He had on a burgundy red sox jacket with a yellow Polo shirt under it, dark blue jeans, some tan construction timberland boots, and a burgundy hat with his braids hanging from the back. Even though he was not smiling at the time, I still saw the happiness in his face. Even though he was going to jail we both were happy that the worst was over.

I sat there listening to the judge and he asked Damian something, and Damian said, "Yes." The judge looked at him and paused for a minute. "Young man, I can tell you are a good kid. Make sure you come home and do the right thing. I know you can, and I don't want to see you in here anymore," the judge said to Damian humbly. "Ok Judge," Damian said humbly, and next thing I know, the guards came behind him and put the handcuffs on him and I began to cry. "Don't cry, everything is going to be good," he said to me as I watched them take him to the back, and I could no longer see him. I sat there crying so hard. I could not hold it in. I felt so sad and empty without him. "It's going to be ok. He will be home before you know it," his lawyer said to me as he helped me up and we walked out the courtroom. "He's a good kid, when he comes home, make sure he stays out of trouble. Even the judge likes him, the judge does not normally give that lenient of a sentence with those charges," his lawyer said to me as I walked down the hallway with him, still crying.

We had left the courthouse to go to our cars and the lawyer told me to take care and I got in the car to leave. I sat in Damian's car in disbelief that about an hour ago we were just in the car together and now I was driving his car alone. I never used to drive Damian's car. I was always in the passenger seat while we were having a ball. I felt so empty, but I knew that I had to be strong for the both of us. I had driven home to my mom's house and cried for most of the day. I was so used to Damian pulling up to get me and him calling me or popping up with that big smile on his face. I missed him so much and it had only been a day since he was gone. I did not know how I was going to make it with him being in jail.

I had laid down that night to try and get some sleep and he had called me from the county jail. "What's up?" he said and to my surprise he was in good spirits. "Why you sound so happy?" I asked him as I was still sad. "I don't know man; I just got a good feeling" he told me. "That's good, a good feeling about what?" I asked him. "I just feel like all of this is behind me and I can finally get my life back. I don't feel like I'm going to be in here long" he said to me confidently. "Oh ok, I'm glad you are positive about it. I have been sad all day because I miss you" I told him. "I know. I miss you too, but everything is going to be good Insha Allah" he said. Insha Allah means "God willing in Islam.

Damian was Muslim ever since I knew him, and he was strong in his faith at that time. His love of God kept him humble and honorable, and I loved that about him. Whenever he had any issues, he knew how to pray and leave it in God's hands. Though we were together, and I was not Muslim we both had strong faith and knew that God had our backs no matter what. "Ok" I said to him as his confidence made me confident. "The quicker I get out the county and go to prison, the quicker I can see parole and come home" he told me. "You have to go in front of parole?" I asked him not knowing that was what he had to do, and it made me nervous. "Yeah, but Insha Allah everything will go good" he told me. "Ok" I said to him. "I love you, just stay strong, all of this will be over soon. Just go to school and go to work and I will be home before you know it" he said to me. "Ok" I said to him as I wanted to believe him. "Love you, Goodnight" he said to me. "Love you too" I told him, and we hung up.

I went to work and school that week. Though things were different without him I kept my head in the game and did what I needed to do. I had not really talked to him much throughout the week. I knew that I would see him on Saturday in the county so we could catch up. Saturday had come and I went up to the jail. When it was my turn in line, I went up to the guard to give them his name so they could call him down for his visit. The guard had looked through the books for a minute and looked confused. He had got on the phone and asked for Damian. As he was talking to the person on the other end. I felt like something was wrong. I had felt it in the pit of my stomach. The guard had hung up and he said what I feared. "He is not here ma'am, he was moved" the guard told me. "Do you know where he was moved to?" I asked him concerned. "No ma'am, you will have to wait until he calls you or writes you to let you know where he is," the guard told me. "Ok, thank you," I said to him, and I left. When I got in the car, I felt frustrated, then an overwhelming sense of peace came over me as I remembered that Damian told me the sooner, he leaves the county, the sooner he will be home.

I had not heard from him for about four days after that and I was getting worried. I could not write him or put money on his books or anything because I did not know where he was. Finally, after about the 5th day, he finally called, and I was so happy. "Are you Ok?" was the first thing I asked him when I finally talked to him. "I'm good" he said as I could tell he was smiling. He told me about two days after we talked that he was moved from the county jail to Mountain View Correctional Facility in Annandale NJ. It took a while for me to be able to visit him because first he had to put me on the visiting list, and I had to be approved. After a few weeks he finally called me and told me that I was approved to come and see him. I had no clue where the jail was, and I found out it was like a little over two hours away. I had my car but I was not the best driver and back then we didn't really have GPS so I was nervous because I did not want to get lost, but I definitely wanted to see him. Me being me I did my research and found out that there was a jail shuttle that went from Jersey City to Annandale, and I could take it there to see him.

Damian was there for about a month before I was able to visit him. He had visits every other weekend, and I had switched shifts with another coworker so I could make it up there. I lived in Mays Landing so I had to get up at 2am to get dressed and leave my house by 3 am and then I drove my car to the Atlantic City Bus Station to park it there. It was still the middle of the night and the bus station was filled with bums and homeless people, but I sat there and waited for the NJ transit to come at 4am to go to Newark. It got to Newark at about 6 am. Then I had to sit there and wait until 7:30 for the bus from Newark to Jersey City. The bus arrived in Jersey City at about nine-ish and from there I had to wait for the Jail shuttle that was coming at 10am. It was a long and tiring trip. There were a lot of other girls who were going to see their boyfriends too. Eventually, I got cool with a few people, so I didn't always have to wait by myself. I would go to the McDonalds that was in the Newark bus station and get my usual breakfast "A number #1 egg McMuffin meal with no meat, because I do not eat Pork." Eventually the shuttle would come, and we all would get on and do pickups in Jersey City along the way.

On our way to the jail seemed like a long road in the middle of no-where. When we drove closer, you could see that you were driving up the mountains. The jail was secluded and had an eerie vibe driving to it. Once I got there though, all those feelings went away. I was excited to be able to see Damian. The visiting hours was three hours long so we got to talk and catch up, but we couldn't kiss or hold hands or anything.

One time I had went to visit him and we were about a half an hour into the three hours visit and he asked me to get him a Mountain Dew out of the vending machine, so I did. He had drunk it and about five minutes later, he had to use the bathroom. The guard told him if he went to the bathroom then he would not be able to finish his visit. Damian tried his best to hold it, but he couldn't so eventually he did go to the bathroom and afterwards he was escorted back to his bunk, leaving me sitting there with over 2 hours left to wait to leave with the jail bus. I was not upset with him. He was human and needed to pee like humans do. I had felt like it was petty that he had to lose his visit over it, and I had come all that way to see him for such a short time. In that moment it made me feel like I could not wait until he came home because jail was in the way.

Once the visit was over, I took the buses back to get back to Atlantic City, then drove my car home. Damian had called me. "Sorry," he said to me on the phone. "It's ok, that was crazy," he said as we both started laughing. "Well, I can't come see you this weekend coming up. I have to wait all the way until next the week when you can have visits again," I told him and, we talked on the phone for a little bit, then hung up.

I was living my life and going to college. When I wasn't in school, I was going to Damian's dad's house where everybody was. I would spend time with them and check on his little brothers. Also, Damian's Lexus was parked at his dad's house, and I had bought a cover to put over it. Damian asked for no one to drive it, so I checked to make sure the car was ok. I wanted it to be in perfect condition when he came home. I was also spending time with one of my close friends who was more like a sister at the time. We would go to the mall and shop and drive around in my car laughing and blasting Destiny's child album "Destiny Fulfilled." We would go to each other's house and have girl talk and just have a good time. She knew as soon as me and Damian started dating. She was in my drama class in high school, and I would tell her everything. Her boyfriend at the time was in Annadale too so she was supposed to come up there with me the next weekend that I went to see Damian. Her boyfriend had written her and told her that her name was approved on the visiting list, so we had made plans to go together.

Damian would write me letters and tell me how much he loved me. He told me that when he came home that he really did want to move to Atlanta with me. My mom was making plans to move down there to get away from my stepdad and to be closer to my grandmother. Although I was not completely ready to leave Jersey, I was considering it. I wanted Damian to come with me. His letters were sweet, and I was looking forward to him coming home. About a week before the visit, he had called me and told me that he was going up for parole a few days later, and I was happy but nervous at the same time. "How do you feel about going before the parole board?" I asked him. "I feel good about it" he said somewhat confidently. "Ok well we have to say a prayer" I told him as I began praying over the phone. "We had small talk then we hung up. It was Friday, the day before I was coming for the visit, and he called me and I knew at that point he had seen parole.

He did not call me on the day he went before the board, so I did not know what to expect him to say on the other end of the phone. "Hello?" I said as I picked up. "Yo, what's up?" he said with really no emotion in his voice. "How did everything go?" I asked afraid of the answer based on his tone. "Man, you don't even have to come up here" he said to me nonchalantly. "What you mean? I asked as my heart dropped and I was expecting the worst. "You don't have to come all the way up here because I'm coming home!" he said with excitement in his voice. "What? You scared me" I said, relieved. "I went before the board and they approved my parole, so I'm coming home in like two weeks" he told me excitedly.

Damian was in there for about 4 months and as promised the judge gave him time served and he went before parole fast and thank God he was approved thanks to prayer and the Favor of God. I was happy knowing he was about to come home, and I began counting down the days. After we spoke that day Damian did not call me much and I figured it was because his time was so short, and he was trying to stay focused on coming home. When other inmates in jail know your time is short sometimes, they try to sabotage it, so I figured he was trying to say less.

"Ok, let me stop you there," my therapist interrupted. So, it seems as if you all had a great relationship. You all were happy together and individually. You supported him through court and his jail time, and you all made plans for the future together, correct?" she asked me. "Yes" I answered her. "First, let me say the engagement was beautiful, and y'all was so romantic at a young age," she said as she complimented us. "So, according to what you are describing, it seemed like a very healthy and loving relationship. I am just trying to understand where the tears came from that you came in here with today, because your now hus-band seems like a great man from what you have told me so far. Is there something that I am missing?" she asked.

I had chuckled a little bit before I answered her. "That day I was with him in the courtroom when he got sentenced seems like the last day, I ever saw him. The real him that I knew and loved" I told her as I began to get a little sad. "What do you mean? She asked me curiously. "That day in the courtroom, I remember it so vividly, what he had on, his hair, his hat, his boots, his cologne, and even though he was being detained, I still remember his smile and the light in his face and spirit," I told her. "Ok, but he went to jail, and he came home, was he not that same person?" she asked me, confused. Before I answered her, I sat back and crossed my legs, and began telling her the rest of my story.

13

The night before Damian came home, I was anxious and had butter-flies. I was ready to finish where we left off. I was excited to have fun and go on dates, be romantic, travel and start our lives together. The day of him coming home, I got up early and my God sister drove me up to Annandale to pick him up. The whole ride I was excited. We got to the front of the jail and sat there for a while before he came out the doors. Finally! I saw him, and I ran out the truck to hug him. He was smiling. He had on a white shirt and a pair of blue jeans and a pair of black shoes, all clothes that the jail gave him. "Oh my God I cannot believe I can touch you!" I said as I hugged him, and we got in the truck and drove away from the jail. I never wanted to see that place ever again.

On the ride home he was kind of quiet. I figured he was taking in all his newfound freedom. He had a smile on his face the whole time. But it was not his usual happy spirited smile. It was like a forced smile, and he had an energy that I had never felt from him before. I did not think much of it at all. It was a long day and a long ride, so I just figured that he was exhausted.

When we got to the city, my God sister dropped us off and we went to get Damian some white air force ones and he had clothes and sneak-ers waiting for him at the house. He took a shower and got dressed and looked like his normal self. "How you feel?" I asked him. "I'm good, " he said with a forced smile. He had just come home so he was paroled to his mom's house. Since he was on parole, he had an 8 pm curfew. We could not get a hotel room or chill like we wanted to because he had to be home when his parole officer called. Since he had just got out, we did not want to take the chance of them popping up and he wasn't home, because that would have been a violation. Also, since Damian was at his mom's house, she was in church heavily and she did not play about fornication so I could not spend the night with him. We were grid locked and totally out of our element. Normally we would have a hotel room set up. We would have got drinks and had a few people come chill with us to celebrate him being home. We definitely would have been having sex and doing all types of nasty things to one another. Instead, we were in by 8pm watching Madea with his mom at her house.

I had left that night and came back early the next day so we could have the whole day together. When I got there, Damian didn't really seem like he was in the best mood. He was a little distant, so I tried to give him his space. "Well, I know you haven't seen your car in forever, so let's go to your dad's house to get it" I said to him hoping that would make him happy. "Ok, let's go. I want to see my pops and my little brothers" he said to me as he started to put his shoes on to leave. We got to his dad's house, and he was happy to see everyone.

We ate with them, and he spent time, and we all went outside so he could look at his car. He had got in and sat down and looked around. "How does it feel being back in your car? I know you love your car," I said to him smiling. "Word, it feels good" he said to me, and he sat there for a minute. He got out, and him and his dad talked on the porch. His dad lived right up the street from the boardwalk, so we all took a walk up there to see the ocean and enjoy the breeze. "This is like old times being up here, right?" I said as I walked beside him holding onto his arm like I normally did. But this time, he did not put his arm around me like he normally did, so it became awkward. I figured he just wanted his personal space to himself. We had left the boardwalk because it was almost time for him to come in and report to parole, so we drove back to his mom's house. He drove his Lexus to his moms and parked it in the parking lot. I stayed for a little bit until it was time for him to go in, and I left.

The next day I had to work, so I had not talked to nor seen Damian the whole day. When I got off, I drove over to his mom's to see him. When I pulled up, he was sitting on the stoop talking to some guys and he was smoking a black and mild. When I walked up to him, he was smiling, but he was not like his normal self. Normally Damian would be happy to see me and breaking his neck to greet me and show me love. "What's up?" I said to him. "Nothing, coolin" he said to me still smoking his mild. I saw he was with a group of guys, so I went upstairs into his mom's apartment.

Eventually, he came in and kicked it with me and then we took a walk outside. As we were walking, I noticed his car was not in the parking lot. "Where is your car?" I asked him. "I sold it," he said nonchalantly. "What?! You sold it?" I asked shocked. "Yeah, I sold it. I just came home. I have to get on my feet, so I sold my car for the money," he told me. "Wow, I am surprised. You loved that car" I said to him. "Yeah, but I will get another one" he said to me. "Well, how are you going to get around now?" I asked him. "I am good. I can't go anywhere like that anyway. I can look for a job right here in the city and catch a cab to work," he said to me. "Ok, I just do not want you to get sidetracked. I want you to stay focused," I said to him. Damian's mom's house was in the projects, and he was surrounded by temptation. I did not want him to get caught up, especially since he was on parole. "I'm good, I got this," he said to me.

Damian was visited by his parole officer one day when I was not there. His parole officer had met his mom and checked out the apartment and deemed everything good. His officer would call from time to time, and eventually he was off of parole. I believe in total he was on parole for about 3 months, and he was released from his curfew. Just like his jail sentencing, his parole process was so smooth and easy for him as well, and it was nothing but the grace of God.

Once he was off, he was able to move around more. He had been close with a guy in his building who also happened to talk to a good friend of mine, and we all would hang out. The first night Damian was off parole, we had got a room at Caesars casino and had drinks and us four played the slots and casino floor games. We were having a ball. Damian was a little bit like his old self since he was free. After we finished playing, we all went back to the room to drink and eventually my friend and his friend had left, and it was just us two. We were finally able to get some alone time. We had quickies since he was home, but being alone in the hotel room, we were finally able to have sex the way we wanted to, and we both enjoyed every minute of it.

I was grateful that he was finally free from jail and parole, I was happy he had finally had his freedom back. We were still close. We were still boyfriend and girlfriend. We still did things together but things were not exactly like they were before he went in. Before Daman went to jail, we were together every second and every minute of the day. Now that he was home, we were more independent of each other. I was still working at Bally's and had developed relationships with a lot of friends. I would go out to night clubs and events, and I was truly enjoying my life.

While I was out, I would bump into Damian and he would be with his friends. We would dance with each other and show love, but we were not all up each other's butts how we used to be. I was glad we were having fun individually, but he was going out way more than he used to before he went to jail, and I always worried about him when he was not in my site. Atlantic City was a dangerous place to grow up. In the summer is when people were getting killed left and right, and it was people that we knew, so death was hitting very close to home. I would call him on his cell phone all the time to check on him. He would tell me he was good, and I would feel better. Then I would begin to feel anxious about an hour later and I would call him again. I was very over protective of him. We had been through a lot, and I always wanted to make sure he was safe.

One night I was home in Mays Landing. I was calling his phone, and he was not answering. I began calling around 12 am up until about 2 am. It was not like him to not answer his phone, so I was super worried. I got in my car and drove to the city to see where he was. I had pulled up to his mom's house around 2:30 am and I was still calling his phone and still no answer. Even though it was late, and I knew his mom was asleep and that she would be mad at me, I knocked on the door anyway. To my surprise Damian opened it. "What's up?" he said, looking confused. "I was calling your phone all night, and you didn't answer" I said to him, as I was relieved that he was ok. "I'm good. I was asleep" he said, and I almost felt embarrassed.

"Let me put my shoes on to come outside so I don't wake my mom up" he said to me as we walked down the breezeway steps and sat in my car. "You are shot out. You really popped up at my crib damn near three o'clock in the morning," he said as he started laughing. "Damian, it's not funny. I was worried about you" I said to him as I wanted to cry because I was really worried about him. "I'm good, I was in the crib, asleep, it's the middle of the night. What did you think I was with a broad or something?" he asked me. "No, I didn't think that. I didn't know where you were, and I didn't know if you were ok. There's a lot of stuff going on in the city right now and I was making sure you were good" I explained to him. "If I wasn't OK, what was you going to do?" he asked, making fun of me. "Damian, shut up" I said as I briefly laughed, and I hit him. We talked for a little bit in the car, and I left.

As I was driving home, I was overwhelmed with emotion. I was listening to music and crying just thinking about everything on the ride. I had drove home and when I got to Mays landing it was about

4am. I was driving past the mall riding past the Woodlands when I heard a siren behind me and I saw blue lights. To my surprise I was being pulled over. The cop took a while to get out the car. I was already crying so I was still crying when he walked up to the window. "Is everything ok ma'am?" the white cop asked me, and I shook my head yes. "Are you crying because I pulled you over?" he asked me. "No" I said to him as I was crying. "Ok ma'am, well I pulled you over because you have a headlight that's out, ok" he said to me. "Ok thank you, I will get it fixed in the morning, " I said to him. "Ok ma'am you be safe" he said to me. "Thank you" I said, as I rolled my window up and drove away. That whole night was emotionally draining, so when I got home, I went straight to sleep.

14

My mom had talked about moving to Atlanta for a long time. Finally, she had made up her mind and found a place in Lawrenceville Ga, not too far from my grand mom. I was sad that my mom was leaving. Although I was an adult 21 years old, I still lived home, and with her moving I really didn't have a place to go. I did not have time to prepare myself and get an apartment because my mom told me she was leaving so abruptly. My mom had packed up the house in a U-Haul and her and my sisters drove away in her car and just like that my family was gone. My brother and I stayed in NJ. My brother stayed with his best friend's family. I went to live with my aunt in Atlantic City.

My aunt was my dad's sister. I had grown up knowing my dad's family all of my life, but I had not lived with any of them before. Staying at my aunt was ok. Her house was always super clean. We both worked at Bally's Casino, but we worked opposite shifts so we barely saw each other. Damian's mom had moved into a house, and he stayed with her. My mom had left, and even though I had a lot of relatives in the area, I still considered Damian's mom and his family my family, so I was at their house all the time, and it made me feel happy. I would go over there and spend time with them even when Damian was not there. Being with them gave me a sense of belonging.

Me and Damian were getting along well, but we still were very much doing our own thing. When I was not at his mom's house, he

would always call me and ask where I was, and he would pop up out
of nowhere. I had begun to notice that Damian was very controlling. I
noticed it in the past, but it did not bother me because we were always
together. But since we were a little older and I became a little more
independent, I noticed his controlling ways even more. If I had plans
to go out with my friends, he would tell me not to go or suggested that
I chill with him instead, and that is exactly what I would do. Damian
had mind control over me. I don't know why, but I did let him control
me in a lot of ways. I wanted my own life, but I could not shake myself
from being under his control.

One night we were taking a ride in the city and he told me that his
good friend had just came home and that we were going to meet him.
When we pulled up by the store it was a light skinned guy standing outside. Damian and him were outside the car talking and the guy looked
into the car and said "what's up, you know you are my sister, right?"
I knew who he was, and I looked up at him and smiled. Ever since
that night Damian and him were thick as thieves and were together all
the time. When Damian started hanging around him, he had started
changing and acting funny towards me. On top of it there started being
girls around that I had never seen before. Damian had a music company
and next thing I knew he was handing out business cards in the city
with the same business name for his music company, yet the cards were
advertising an escort service. I had asked him what that was about, and
he said that he had the girls around because they were escorts, and that
was his new business venture.

Damian was beginning to change even more. He started being so
distant. One of me and his rules with each other ever since we first
started dating was that we never ate without one another. That was one
of the reasons why when he went to jail the first time, I had lost so
much weight. It was because I felt so guilty about eating without him.
One day Damian's mom had cooked chicken, macaroni, string beans
and cornbread, and she left my plate in the kitchen for me like she

always did. This particular day, I had come to Damian's house and him and his friend were in the living room eating. I said hey to them and began talking to his mom for a minute and didn't think anything of it.

I had gone into the kitchen to get my food and my plate was not there. "Ms. Rose. where did you put my food?" I asked his mom as I yelled to her from the kitchen. "It's on the stove" she said to me, and I looked for it one more time. I still did not see it. Damian and his friend were sitting there looking dumb. "Damian, where is my plate? I asked him, and he had a sneaky smile. "My bad yo, I gave it to him " he said pointing to his friends plate. "Word!" I said to him super disappointed. "My bad sis, I did not know this was your food" his friend said as he was eating. "Damian, that's messed up. Why would you give him my food?" I said to him as I felt so disrespected. "My bad, he said he was hungry" Damian said laughing as if it were a joke. "It's not funny, that was messed up" I said to him as I walked away and sat downstairs with his mom. I was so annoyed, and he did not even care that it bothered me. Damian was wrapped up in his own world, and he didn't cater to my feelings like he used to.

15

At the time, Keisha Cole was really hot, and her single "Love" was playing all over the city, so Damian's people had booked her at Lucy's Blues, a nightclub that was in the Tropicana casino in Atlantic City. Damian had invited me to go with him and a few of our other friends. I loved Keisha Cole, and by all of us going, I thought it was going to be romantic. I had met up with a few of my close friends there too, and we were having a ball. I had on a burgundy tank top with a waist-length burgundy sweater jacket over it, some tight jeans with burgundy and clear rhinestones on them, and a pair of burgundy cowgirl boots. My hair was in a hump with a long ponytail, and I had on big hoop earrings.

I looked really cute, and all the guys were checking me out. I wanted to dance with Damian and enjoy the night with him, but he was with his friends and was barely paying me any mind which was not like him, so I just ignored him and had fun with my friends. Afterwards, he whispered in my ear that he was going to meet me at my aunt's house, and I told him ok, and he made sure I made it to my car safe, and he left with his friends.

When I got back to my aunt's house, it was about 3 o'clock in the morning. I waited for him, but I fell asleep. The next thing I knew, he was chirping my phone; saying, "where you at?" he never used to call first he would always just burst through the chirp. Back then we had sprint Nextel chirps and everybody was walking around like we were on walkie talkies. "I'm asleep" I said to him. At that time, it was about 6am in the morning. "Come outside" he said to me as I was comfortable in bed, and it was freezing outside. "I'm not coming outside" I told him as I chirped him back. "Word? then let me in then" he said to me. "I can't because my aunt is home" I told him, and I put the phone on vibrate because the chirp sound was too loud.

Next thing I knew I heard my ringtone which was Ciara's song that sung "and I, know that you won't break my heart" I loved that song and that was my ringtone for Damian. "What?" I said as I picked up the phone annoyed that he was calling me so early when he was supposed to come hours ago. "I just want to see you" he tried to say in a sweet voice to win me over. "Alright, I'm about to come and open the door" I said to him, and I went downstairs and snuck him in and we went upstairs to my room.

He was freezing cold from being outside and I had on short pajamas and all he wanted to do was play and touch me with his cold hands. He was so annoying, but I loved him and I was glad he was there. We got under the covers, and he laid with me and he must have been so tired because we did not even have sex, he just held me the whole time and fell asleep.

In the morning he left, and I shortly saw him again when I got dressed and came over to his mom's house to see everybody. Damian's son Branden was living there at that point. His son's mom had left out of the picture for a while, and nobody knew where she was, then she eventually popped back up. Before Damian's mom moved to her new house his son's mom had started coming back around to see his Branden and eventually the son's mom had him back in her custody. While having him she would come past Damian's moms house a lot.

When she was out of the picture no one had heard from her or knew if she was ever coming back to get her son, because she had just up and left him. Damian's family was upset with her. But that being his son's mom no one stopped her from seeing him, and she was able to take Branden to live with her. She would come over almost every day. Damian's brother's wife at the time was living there. Me and her both being females we both picked up on the fact that things did not feel right, and we questioned her intentions for coming around.

Me and his brother's ex-wife were close as well as me and his mom. I would be there a lot and every time I came over, his son's mom was there being way too comfortable, as if she was trying to work her way in, and I peeped it all. His mom was not very fond of her, but on the strength that that was her grandson's mom, she was not going to turn her away.

When I would be there it would be super uncomfortable. I would never speak to her nor did she speak to me. His son could have visited his family without her being there, so it was never really clear to me why she made it a point to sit up under Damian's mom in the first place. Damian really didn't care for the situation either. He always told me not to worry about her and he paid her no mind. Her presence was questionable, and he was barely there when she was there anyway. He was always somewhere in the streets.

One day it was me and his mom there at his mom's house and the baby mom popped up. Me and his mom were having a very good conversation like we always had. When his son's mom came over you could feel the uncomfortableness in the air. I could even tell Damian's mom was uncomfortable too, but she was cordial and not rude even though the look on her face was saying "what is she doing here." I had walked off to the kitchen to get a water bottle because I was about to leave at that point.

His mom had said something to his son's mom, I don't remember what it was and to me and Damians mother's surprise, his son's mom responded "Ok, Mom" I wish I could have taken a picture of his mom's face and mine too. We both looked at each other like "What???" his mom was not rude, but she was taken back and did not know how to respond by her calling her mom. That moment was sooo awkward. The girl barely even knew his mother and yet she was calling her "mom", now at that point I knew she had an ulterior motive. I already did not care for her just because she always seemed like a sneaky snake of a person to me. I always got bad vibes from her, and I didn't deal with her at all.

I had left because I could not take any more of the fakeness. I had told his brother's wife and she did not like that at all. I had told Damian, and he was confused too and again told me not to pay her any mind and that she was doing the most. At that point, I just ignored her whenever I saw her because there was something off about her. I knew in my heart that even though she was never Damian's girlfriend that she was jealous of me, and she wanted my spot. She saw the way Damian and his family treated me and I knew she secretly wanted it to be her instead, especially since she had his son.

Damian's mom had moved to her new house and the first few days I stayed there, as well as his sister and his brother's wife, who was there while his brother was in the army. We helped unpack and set the house up. We were having so much fun and enjoying each other. We would be chilling, talking and laughing like family did. I didn't see his baby mom the first few days and I thought to myself "Good, thank God, she finally got the hint that no one wanted her there." She was not an ex of his, they had no relationship outside of having their son. She didn't know his mom. None of the family welcomed her except his sister. Her presence was just pointless and made her look like she was up to something. I figured she got the point and went about her life.

I came over there a few days after the house was settled and low and behold, who do I see "his son's mom" there with their son. This time her energy was different. She seemed sassier and way more comfortable. I had stayed most of the day and that night when I was about to leave, I had seen Damian's mom giving her a blanket to sleep, and she was complaining that it was cold, and she didn't want to sleep on the floor. "She lives here?" I asked his brother's wife, confused. "Yeah, I guess" she said to me, just as confused as I was. I was shocked and hurt. I had spent the whole day over there and nobody told me that his mom let her move in.

Word was, when no one was around she gave his mom a sob story about her having nowhere to go with her grandson, so she asked if she could stay, and his mom said yes. I understood that his mom did not want to see her in the street, but it didn't change the fact that me and his mom were close, and I thought out of love that she would have told me. Not that she had to because it was her house. But I wish she would have told me to mentally prepare me that my boyfriend was now going to be living with his baby's mother.

I felt so betrayed. It was also very embarrassing to me. As close as I was with my friends, I had never shared that with them because they would have thought I was crazy for staying with him and crazy for still going over there. I loved Damian and I knew it was not his fault. He didn't want her there either, but it wasn't his house, so he had to deal with it too. He didn't mind his son being there, but her being there made him uncomfortable as well.

When I was there, he never really talked to her, and you could feel the awkwardness. I didn't know anything about her outside of when he told me who she was as far as him having a baby with her. She didn't know me, but she gave off an attitude as if she didn't like me, and that I did something to her, or I was stepping on her toes. She gave off the vibe like she belonged there, and I didn't because she had his son. She was sadly mistaken because even with her there, he was always lovey-dovey with me as well as his mom and family showed me so much love and I could just see the jealousy on her face.

To me it always felt like she wanted to be me, and she wanted the relationship I had with his family. I also think she wanted Damian too. I think that she thought that she would move there, and they would favor her because she was the mother of his son and that eventually Damian would try to mess with her and that she would be with her baby's dad. That's the vibe I got, and my vibes never steered me wrong. Normally I am spot on and the only reason why it didn't play out how she wanted it to, was because Damian did not pay her no mind at all The reason why I kept coming around was because Damian would always tell me "she look stupid not you. You belong here, she don't" and he always made me feel secure. He would always apologize for his mom letting her stay there, because I would express to him how I felt about it and he understood. After about a month of living under the same roof Damian felt enough was enough and he didn't want to have to see her every day.

16

His dad had moved into a duplex, and Damian had moved in with him, his wife and his brothers, and finally, it was so much better! The energy there was so different, and I could visit my boyfriend without having to see his BM doing little sneaky things and being annoying. His dad didn't play that, so I did not have to worry about him letting her move there. At his dad's new house, it was so much fun. His little brothers were older at that point, and they would be in and out of the house with their friends. They loved me, and I loved them. They would call me "big sis," and I called them my "little brothers." I would watch them interact and just laugh and enjoy all of them.

Once Damian moved to the new house, he was still hanging out with his light-skinned friend and whoever else. He had more clientele with his escort business. He had girls here and there, and some would even pop up at his dad's house while I was there. No one ever came in or disrespected me at all. Damian would always say that they knew he had a girlfriend, and he only talked to them because of business. I didn't know if I believed him or not because he was moving funny. His light-skinned friend was always up to no good with women, so I didn't know what Damian was doing when I wasn't around.

He was doing his thing, so I began doing my own thing. I would be out meeting people and enjoying my life. I was in Club Deja Vu one night having a ball, and I bumped into him. He was with the light-skinned boy and his other friends. I was looking super cute. I had on a lace black peplum top with the back and arms out and a pair of tight capris with some open-toe black heels, and my hair was long with brown highlights. I was dancing and drinking with my friends, and he saw me and walked to me and whispered in my ear, "Don't get one of these niggaz fucked up," he said, and he touched my boobs and walked off. I laughed and didn't pay him no mind, and I continued to have fun. That was how Damian was; he wanted his cake and to eat it too. He would be wishy-washy with me but always wanted me to be available to him. But I was meeting more people and was out, and about all the time around the city.

I was doing my own thing. I had always felt like a star. I had aspirations of being on tv and in the industry since I was about 12 or 13. I always saw myself as a writer and movie producer. Another passion of mine was being on a reality tv show. Ever since the first season of the Real World with Tammy and the rest of the cast, I was hooked. I used to always say when I turn 18, I'm going on the Real World. But by the time I got of age, the show was no longer being shot. By that time, we had had other shows like Flavor of Love and Making the Band which I loved too. I was already with Damian, so I didn't want to go on a dating show. I was in college taking theater classes, and I loved to talk, so I wanted to get an internship at 99.3 the Buzz. It was our area's local radio station, but radio was not my major, so I did not pursue the internship.

I always wished that I did, because I always felt that I would have gotten the internship and that the outcome could have been awesome. Growing up, I had always wished I had been raised in New York. I loved the bright lights and fast-paced city life. I loved the music, and the whole vibe of NY. I always felt like that was where I belonged because it was full of opportunities that I did not have in South Jersey. I remember the whole Atlantic City and surrounding areas were super excited because Jay-Z was opening the 40/40 Club on Atlantic Avenue in Atlantic City. Everyone was talking about it. I really wanted to go until I found out it was by invite only. I watched them build it as I would ride down Atlantic Ave, and I always envisioned myself there.

Finally, on the day the Club was opening, the city had the whole area blocked off because only certain personnel could get through. I remember the whole day I was so excited to see what celebrities were going to be there. Even though I could not get in the building that night, I had driven my car up there and walked and stood by the ropes. There were police there and everything, but they let me, and a few other people stand there and watch who was coming in.

The event was star-studded. There was car after car pulling up with celebrities and important people, and they stopped at the red carpet with the 40/40 backdrop to take pictures. I was by no means a groupie, but I was happy to be there and felt like their world was where I belonged, and for once in my life, I was amongst the stars. We did not have Snapchat and social media back then, so I was not busy taking pictures or recording. I was very present and in the moment. Finally, Jay-z and Beyoncé pulled up, and the crowd outside went crazy. It was amazing, and even though I was on the outside looking in; I was still glad to be there and witness the opening of the 40/40 club in Atlantic City. Finally, everyone was in the club, and there was nothing left to see, so I got in my car and left. While driving home, I was just praying to God to make me a star.

After the 40/40 opened, it was always jumping and packed, and a lot of people would hold events there. My cousin "E" and I were super tight at the time. She was always super thick and had a big butt, and men loved her. I was short and thick, and men loved me too. A female celebrity who had produced a show on MTV was holding an audition at the 40/40 looking for video girls, so my cousin and I went. It was popping that night; the bartenders had drinks flowing everywhere. People were dancing, the music was jumping. It was just all-around good vibes.

Myself and E had auditioned. We had made it through a couple of cuts and made it to the end to be picked for the show. We had a ball. We danced and had a good time. We had gone to the bar, and the bartender had asked me what I wanted. "Just give me something sweet, " I said to him, trying to sound confident. I had watched him make my drink, and it was so pretty. "What is this?" I asked him. "It's a sex on the beach," he told me as he smiled, realizing I was a rookie. "Thank you," I said to him as I giggled and I tasted it, and it was delicious. Myself and E were sitting down talking and drinking when the video producer came up to us and started a convo telling us how excited she was for us to be on the show, and she gave us her email address to send pictures to. We kicked it with her for a little bit, but myself and E were both laid back, and we didn't want to overdo it.

We were excited to be going on an MTV reality show. The next day, we emailed the girl the pictures, but we never heard anything back, which was odd. To this day, I cannot remember the girl's name, the website, or the show we were supposed to be on. I am guessing that the pilot never made the cut, so the show never got off the ground. Either way, me and E had a great night full of awesome memories with some awesome people.

E and I had hung out a lot. That was my girl. One night I had met her at her house, and we got dressed. I had on a black top with some tight pants and black patent leather pumps, and I had on a long dark brown and blonde wig. I had looked cute, and I was feeling super grown and sexy. "Where you want to go, E?" I asked her as we were in my car riding. "Let's go to the strip club," she said. "Ok, cool," I said as we drove there. Although I grew up around strip clubs, that was my first time actually in one. E was used to going, that was her thing. I was 21, and they carded us and let us in. E was super comfortable, so I just followed her lead. E had a statue-esque presence about her. When she walked, she glided. Her whole demeanor was so confident, on top of her being sexy so naturally that had drawn people to us.

We had sat at the bar and watched the girls dance, and the bartender had come over to ask us what we wanted to drink. I had remembered getting a sex on the beach at the 40/40 club, so I ordered one. "Let me get a shot of whiskey," E told her, and she went to get our drinks. "You drink Whiskey?" I asked E as I laughed. "Girl, hell yeah," she said as we both chuckled. E was so goofy, and we were so goofy together. We always had a good time. Our drinks came, and we went to sit by the stage to watch the girls. It was not packed at all, and we were trying to figure out why. There were guys next to us, and they told us it was amateur night. We wanted to see real dancing, so we were ready to go. We drank our drinks and left. "Girl, we have to come back when the real dancers are there," I told her, and we drove to the city to another hot spot we liked to hang out at, and when we got there, it was jumping.

When you came into the club, you walked up some steps, and then there were tables. The pool table area, the bar, and the dance floor. Me and E had sat at the table right by the steps, so whoever walked in, we were the first people that they saw. I had my back towards the steps, so I could not see who was coming up, but E could. Me and her sat there talking while we waited for our drinks, and she sparked up a cigarette and started smoking. "Let me hit it," I said to her, and she handed it to me. I went to puff it, and before I could get it to my mouth, I heard a voice so "Oh, word, so you smoking now?" and when I turned around it was Damian standing right behind me with a huge sneaky smile on his face. "Put the cigarette down," he said to me like he was my dad. "No," I said to him, and he took it from me and put it out in the ash tray. "Why are you letting her smoke?" he asked my cousin. "Let her? She is grown," she said to Damian, laughing. "She not allowed to smoke," he told her, playing but serious at the same time. "I can't believe I came walking up the steps, and I see your ass smoking," he said to me, joking but serious.

"Whatever, Damian," I said to him, and I pushed him away to go with his friends.

He went to the bar and got us drinks, then he chilled with his friends, and everyone was having a good time. Me and him took pictures together and had fun. He had ridden with me to take E home because I had been drinking, so he drove my car. After we dropped her off, I went home with him, and we had sex. I was so drunk, and I was on top of Damian riding him. He said he was about to nut, and he tried to push me off, so he didn't nut in me because I was not on birth control at the time. I was so drunk I did not remember him trying to push me off, and I kept riding him. He did end up nutting in me, and he was upset. "Why didn't you get off?" he said to me, mad. "I didn't know," I said to him, still out of it. Most of the time, I was on birth control. But that particular time I was not, and since we didn't use condoms, he would always pull out, and he was upset that I didn't get off of him, and he nutted in me.

The next day he was really upset and was being mean to me, saying things like I "raped him," and that was pissing me off, so I left, and I did not speak to him for a few days. In the meantime, I was no longer working at Bally's. I had signed up for bartending school because I wanted to bartend at the 40\40 or one of the strip clubs. I went through the process, which took about a month, and I was finally in. I loved my teacher and my whole class. Everyone was so fun, and we were learning so much about mixology, and that was just a great time in my life. While I was at school one day, I wasn't feeling too good, and the girls joked with me that I was pregnant. "I am not pregnant y'all," I said to them as I joked back with them. We had taken a little break, and one of the girls from class went to Wawa right across the street from my school and bought a first response pregnancy test and gave it to me. "Here," she said as she handed it to me. "What is this?" I asked her. "It's a pregnancy test, go to the bathroom and take it," she said to me, and all the girls encouraged me to go.

I went to the bathroom and waited three minutes as the test said. I could not look at it, so I gave it to one of the other girls to look at it for me. "Well, you're pregnant!" She said excitedly, and everyone started hugging me and congratulating me. "What?" I said as I was in shock, and I had to let it sink in. For the rest of the class, I could not focus because I was in such shock. I had never thought much about it, but I was excited now that I knew I was pregnant. The next day I went to the Atlantic City Medical center to get blood work to confirm I was pregnant, and sure enough, I was. Damian and I were not on the best of terms, so I didn't tell him right away because I did not know what his response was going to be.

17

Later on that night, my bestie and a few of our other friends decided to go partying in Philly, and they asked me to go. It was a car full of us girls, and her brothers were in a car behind us. I will never forget driving there; going over the Walt Whitman Bridge into Philly and my friend putting her foot on the gas out of nowhere and flushing it. "Slow down! We all screamed as we were holding on for our lives. All I could think of was us on this bridge over the water, and if we crashed, we would fall over. Driving over the bridge was scary enough, and my friend didn't make it any better driving crazy. Finally, we were across the bridge and we all "Thanked God!" "Girl, what is wrong with you?!" My friend snapped at her. "I was scared, so I was trying to hurry up," she said as we all were still in shock.

We had pulled up to the club, parked and met up with my best friends' brothers. "Yo, y'all was driving fast as hell," one of her brothers said to us. "I know right, I'm pregnant, and she was trying to kill us" I said to them. "You pregnant?" her brother asked me, surprised. "Yeah," I told him. Once we got in the club, it was packed and had an upstairs and downstairs. I was dressed really cute and had on heels. I had on a small metallic silver purse that I had put too much stuff in, and it wouldn't close so I was paying attention to my purse the whole night, making sure that nothing fell out. We all danced and had a good time. They all were drinking. I had a sprite in my cup because I was pregnant and was not going to consume alcohol. As I was dancing with my bestie, a guy came up to me. I really did not even get to get a good look at his face. All I could remember was his silhouette, and that he was dark skinned.

He started to try to dance with me, and I wasn't interested so I turned my back. When I turned around, he was trying to grind on my butt, and I moved away. I could tell he had an attitude, and he said something slick. The music was loud, so I could not hear exactly what he said, then he walked away aggressively. I didn't care. I was just glad he got away from me because it was something about his energy that was dark. A few minutes after he walked off, I looked down at my purse and noticed my phone was missing. "Oh, my God," I said as I panicked and I searched my purse, and the floor around me and my phone was nowhere to be found. I went to the DJ booth and asked him to ask the crowd if they had seen a Nextel phone with a rhinestone case on it and he did. He asked them if they found it, bring it up to the DJ booth.

We were in the club for a while after that, and I was hoping that someone would turn my phone in. I could not even enjoy myself for the rest of the time, because I wanted my phone. I also felt violated that someone would just steal from me like that. As the night ended, we all had linked back up to leave, and we waited for all the crowd to clear to look for the phone. My besties brothers, security and everyone was looking for it. I even went back to the DJ booth as he was packing up to ask him if anyone turned it in, and he told me no. "Ma, I'm sorry about your phone, but I don't think you're going to get it back," he told me in a humble way. I had walked back to everyone and told them that we should just leave, and we all got back in the cars and left.

As we were driving back to Jersey, my bestie had got a call on her phone from my number. "Girl, whoever got your phone is calling me," she said, and she hurried up and answered it. "Hello, whoever this is, you need to give my friend her phone back" she said, pissed off. At first, the person wasn't saying anything. They were just breathing and they hung up. They called back about 5 minutes later. "If y'all want the phone back, meet me at the airport," the man's voice said, and he described what he had on and to meet him. Against our better judgment, we had made a detour and headed to the airport. When we went there, we didn't see anyone with that description, and we called my phone and there was no answer. "Man, f*ck this, let's go," I said as we drove off.

A few minutes later, the voice called back and gave us another location to meet him. My friends were willing to drive there, but I wasn't. He was sending us on a goose chase in Philly in the middle of the night. I did not know him nor his intentions, and he gave me an eerie feeling. I think he was trying to line us up. "No, y'all we not meeting him nowhere. We going back home, and tomorrow I will just have to get a new phone. He got that, fuck him" I told them, and we headed towards Jersey. He had called back again, and I got on the phone. "Yo, stop calling this phone you broke ass bum. You in the club stealing females phones you a clown ass nigga, you can have the phone and go suck a d*ck" I said to him as I was livid with him.

I hung up and blocked my number from her phone so he would stop calling us. When we got back to Jersey, they had dropped me off home. At that point, I did not stay in the city with my aunt anymore. I had moved with my grand mom in Absecon. It was about 4 am when I got home and to my surprise, she was up when I came through the door. "Are you ok?" she asked me. "Yeah, grand mom, I'm fine," I told her, confused as to why she asked me that. I had got a call from your number, but it was a guy on the phone, and he said you were dead. "What?" I said to her, shocked. "Grand mom, my phone was stolen, and I told her the story.

"Wow. Well, I am glad you are ok; you need to call your mom because we were all worried. He just said you were dead, and that was it. He hung up and didn't pick back up. I had called my mom and let her know I was Ok. Everyone was so frantic. I was pissed that he would go through my phone and tell my family I was dead. That was so evil of him. I knew at that point it was the guy in the club that I didn't want to dance with. He had an evil spirit and was in the club like an evil demon with evil intentions, and I was furious.

I got up the next day and went to Sprint to get a new phone early that morning, and I got my number changed. I called everyone to let them know I was ok. Almost everyone in my contacts had told me that a guy had called them saying different things. I was convinced that the guy was crazy and had issues. I told everyone to block my old number and gave them my new one, and that was that. Throughout the whole ordeal, I had not talked to Damian. I had not gotten a chance to tell him I was pregnant. Nor tell him what happened in Philly and about the guy stealing my phone.

When I got the phone, I had called him. "Hello, he answered as he did not recognize the number. "It's Shamirah, this is my new number. My phone was stolen last night, I explained to him. "Hmm," he said very nonchalantly, and I could tell something was wrong. "What's the matter with you?" I asked him. "I'm about to drive to the city. Do you want me to come over? I asked him. "Nah, I'm good. I had called you last night, and a nigga picked up and said he just finished f*cking you, and that you couldn't talk because you were in the bathroom crying," Damian said to me, and I could tell he was pissed. "Damian, that is a lie. A guy stole my phone, and he is crazy. He told my whole family that I was dead, and then he tells you some bullshit like that," I said to him as I was so mad and felt violated all over again.

"Well, the nigga sounded believable to me. I know you were up in Philly last night, and I don't know what the hell you was doing," he said, upset. "Damian, I swear to God, I did not do anything. I was with Tia and them, and my phone was stolen," I pleaded to him. "Yeah, whatever. I don't know what you were doing, but I'll holla at you," he said to me, and he hung up. "Wow," I said to myself as I was pissed. I wanted to tell Damian about me being pregnant, but after that conversation, I was super scared to.

I had left the mall and went to the hospital to get another confirmation test. When it was done, I had asked the nurse to call Damian to tell him. She had called him and put him on speaker. "Hello, Mr. Damian, this is the nurse from the Atlantic City Medical Center," she said to him as we sat in her office at the desk. "Hello, may I ask what this is about? 'He asked, confused. "I have a Ms. Shamirah Smith here, and she came in today to confirm a pregnancy, and I wanted to let you know that the results are positive and she is, in fact, pregnant," she said to him as we both looked at each other not knowing what his response would be.

He paused on the phone for a minute before answering. "Shamirah," he called my name to see if I was there. "Yes?" I said to him like I was a kid in trouble. "You play a lot of games yo," he said, and then he hung up on us. The nurse looked at me, and I looked back at her as I was looking stupid. We basically had a conversation without words. Both of our eyes and body language said it all. I was embarrassed, and she knew it. "Ok, Ms. Smith, here is your paperwork. You can take it to get Medicaid and whatever else you need. This is your proof of pregnancy. Good luck with everything," she told me as she handed me the paperwork. "Thank you," I told her as I took the papers and left.

On the drive home, I was so upset that Damian acted that way, so I popped up at his house to talk to him face to face. When I pulled up, he was on the porch smoking a black and Mild. "Why did you hang up on the nurse?" I asked him as I got out of the car. "Man, get the f*ck out of here with that BS," he said as he kept smoking. "What BS? I'm pregnant," I told him as I showed him the paperwork, and he would not even look at it. "I cannot believe you are acting like this," I said to him, disappointed. "You got me messed up," he said as he finished smoking his mild and went back in the house, and I followed behind him. "How I have you messed up because I'm pregnant?" I asked him, still showing him the paper.

He sat down on the chair and ignored me for a while, hoping that I would leave. But I didn't. "That's messed up that you would treat ME like this of all people," I said to him. "What?" he said as he turned and looked at me with the meanest face. "I haven't really talked to you. I don't know what the f*ck you been doing. Then a nigga answers your phone in the middle of the night and says he rocked you, and that you was in the bathroom crying. Then you pop up saying you pregnant. Get the f*ck out of here," he said to me rudely. Damian could be hard sometimes, but before that point, he had never talked to me like that. Nor ever made me feel that way. He made me feel low and dirty. I told him that my phone was stolen and what the guy said wasn't even true, and yet he still believed it. He would rather believe a stranger over me, and it hurt that I was pregnant by him, and he was being so cold about it.

We talked about having kids all the time in the past and how excited he would be, so his mean reaction had definitely thrown me off. "Well, as I told you, that guy was lying. I don't have sex with nobody, but you," I told him as I was sad and exhausted. "I'm leaving," I said to him, and I began walking to the door. Normally he would always walk me to the car and open the door for me and see me off. This time he just sat there and didn't walk me nor say anything.

When I got in the car, I began to cry profusely. My feelings were so hurt, and I felt so alone. My mom was in GA, so I had no close family around me for support. I couldn't go to his mom because I didn't feel safe with her anymore after she let his baby mom move in. I was sad and alone. I went back to my grand mom's house and went to sleep. Damian had called me later that night, and we talked. He didn't say the words "I'm sorry," but he apologized in his own way, and I accepted it, and we were on ok terms.

Over the next few days, we were cool. We hung out and spent time like normal, and it seemed like he was coming around to the idea of me being pregnant. He even told his mom and the people that were close to him. That made me happy, and I was in such a positive place in life at that point. I knew that I wanted to eventually move to Ga where my mom was. I was just staying in Jersey to finish Bartending school so that when I moved, I could Bartend in Atlanta.

About a week later, I had become really crampy. I googled it, and it said cramping during early pregnancy is fine, so I did not think anything of it. I had gone to bartending class like normal, and we were behind the bar making drinks. We were all laughing and joking like we normally did when suddenly my stomach began to hurt. I went to the bathroom, and I saw blood. I had called the girls in the bathroom to tell them what was happening. One of the girls called her mom, who was a nurse, and told her what I was experiencing. Her mom had said that spotting was normal, but I was not spotting. I was literally bleeding bright red blood, and it was a lot of it. Other than the bleeding, I felt ok, so my teacher gave me a pad, and I continued on through class and didn't think much of it.

The next day I woke up, and I was super crampy, and I was still bleeding. I tried to get through my day, but the pain got worse and worse to the point where it was unbearable. I had called my mom and told her what was going on, and she told me to go to the hospital. Despite her telling me to go, I was in so much pain that I could not even drive, so I laid in bed for another few hours. The blood flow was still heavy. I was getting worried, and I began to panic.

I had mustered up enough energy to drive from Absecon to Mainland Hospital in Galloway, NJ. Which was about a 20-25-minute ride. When I got there, I was in excruciating pain. I told them what I was experiencing, and I still had to wait in the waiting room which felt like forever. At that point, they were taking so long to call me to the back that I left Mainland and drove to Damian's house. I had not told him that I was bleeding for a few days and that I had gone to the hospital, so he did not know what was going on. When I got there, him his dad, and his uncle were there, and we were all in his dad's room. I had walked out to go to Damian's room, and I laid across the floor.

"What's wrong with you?" he asked me concerned. "I don't feel good" I just came from Mainland," I told him. "I'm in so much pain I feel like I'm going to die," I told him. At that point I was so weak because I had been in excruciating pain all day. "Well, get up and we're going to the hospital," he said, and he grabbed my keys. His dad and his uncle were clowning me and saying that I was faking and making jokes because they had been drinking. I was in so much pain, and they were making it worse, so I went and sat on the porch to get some air. All I remember was lying on the steps and looking up at the sky feeling like I was going to die. I had never been pregnant before, so I didn't know if what I was feeling was normal or not.

At that moment, I wished his dad's wife who had recently passed away was there to help me, because being surrounded by all those men who had no compassion was hard. Me, Damian, his dad, and his dad's wife had never made it on the Ferry ride to the Baltimore Harbor because she had sadly passed away due to cancer. As I was sitting there, my phone rang and it was my friend "D." She was calling to check on me and I told her what was happening, and she told me to go to the hospital immediately.

Damian had finally come out of the house and got in the driver's seat and drove me to the A.C medical center. We waited in the waiting room, and the pain got worse and worse, and I began to cry. The only thing that gave me a little comfort; was the fact that he was there with me. I laid on him, and he consoled me the best he could. His presence made it a little bit better. He had got a phone call on his cell, so he stepped outside to answer it. While he was out there, I had to pee, so I went to the bathroom. While I was in there, I felt something wet and slimy come out of my vagina. When I looked in the toilet, it was a big dark almost black looking blood clot. I wanted to see what it was, but before I could examine it, I heard the triage lady call my name, and not even thinking, I hurried up and flushed the toilet.

When I went to the back to see the doctor, I had told them what happened, and they confirmed that I had a miscarriage. Everything had happened so fast so when I went to the back, Damian was still outside. I didn't have time to get him, so the nurse had gone to the waiting room to bring him to the back. When he got back there, the doctor told him the news. He sat there, and he looked sad for me. The doctor had taken some bloodwork, and me and Damian sat in the room by ourselves until it came back.

"You Ok?" he asked me concerned. "No," I said as I felt heartbroken. I could not stop thinking about what I saw in the toilet. I wished I had got a chance to look at it to at least see my baby. I was not pregnant anymore, and I felt empty. Damian had stood up and walked over to me. "Everything is going to be good. Everything happens for a reason. We will have a baby again when the time's right," he said to me with compassion. "Ok," I said to him, appreciating his kind words. The doctor had eventually come back in and told me my test results and confirmed the miscarriage. The doctor told me that I was RH negative, something I had no clue about. "What is that? I asked him. "It is when your blood lacks a certain protein. Your immune system fights off foreign things in your body. So, your body basically rejected your fetus, causing you to have a miscarriage," he explained to me. "Oh wow," I said to myself as I felt even worse. "But do not worry, there is a shot we give to RH negative women called the Rhogam shot, and this will prevent you from having miscarriages in the future" he told me.

The nurse had gone to get the shot and it was huge. "Oh my God!" I said when I saw it, and everybody started laughing. "I hate needles, so I do not want that shot," I told them. "You have to, it's for your protection especially since you just had a miscarriage. Before and after any birth, you have to get the Rhogam shot," he explained to me, and me knowing that not taking it could prevent me from having kids, I had to suck it up and do what I had to do. The shot was so thick and long, so they recommended I get it in my buttocks, because that was where I had the most cushion. I got it. It hurt and I was glad it was over. He wrote me a script for pain, and I left the hospital and went back to Damian's house. Sitting there with him the reality that I wasn't pregnant anymore hit me and sadness came over me. He would constantly encourage me, which helped for a little while, then I would get sad all over again.

Finally, I had gone to sleep in his arms, and we were woken up to noise and a little person came running into the room. It was his son. I had not seen him in a while because I had not been to Damian's mom's house where he lived. He came in the room happy, and Damian played with him. Though I was happy to see him. It made me even more sad, and I really wanted my baby at that point. I began to feel depressed, so I left and went home to my grandma's house, and I cried for most of the day alone in my room.

After I had the miscarriage, Damian barely ever wanted to have sex with me. He was scared I was going to get pregnant again. I had gone to the OB-GYN and got on the Ortho Evra birth control patch, and I told him that everything would be fine. Once he knew I was on birth control, he would come around more and eventually, we started having sex again. Damian had become so up down. One day he loved me the next day he didn't. One day he wanted to be with me the next day he didn't, and it was sending me on an emotional roller coaster. At that point my head was all over the place, and I was losing control of myself. I would get so angry when he would act funny and I always asked myself what could I do better, so that he wouldn't treat me that way.

So, I would do my best to not piss him off. But it seemed like no matter what I did, he always still had an issue.

One day he had popped up at my grandmom's house and we kicked it and had a good time. I will never forget that day. He had on a black skelly hat, a white thermal long sleeved shirt, some jeans and a pair of tan Timberland boots. I remember us having sex and he didn't even take his pants or boots off. Which I did understand due to the fact that we had to hurry so we did not get caught. But what I remember the most was; after we were done, he had zipped up his pants and put his skelly and his coat on and he said, "you going to be pregnant now,". "What does that mean?" I asked him and he didn't answer me as he was putting on his things to leave. You are leaving? I thought we was chilling" I asked him confused. "We did chill," he said, smiling with that sneaky smirk. "Ok, whatever Damian, go ahead" I told him, and his friend had come and picked him up, and he left like I was a jump off. I sat there at home feeling a way. I was like damn, he had become so wishy washy, and I could no longer read him. He acted like he didn't want me, but at the same time he would not let me go. He always made his way back in my heart, and as soon as I opened it back up, he would snatch his love away again, and that made me emotionally unstable.

Even though he left, he had called me in the middle of the night and was being sweet, so the next day I decided to pop up on him at his dad's house. Again, all of a sudden, he was being so nonchalant and stand offish. "Are you not happy that I am here? Because you acting real funny right now," I said to him as he was smoking his black and Mild. "I'm good," he said being smart. That whole day Damian was in and out the house on the phone and doing his own thing. I was there talking to his brothers and chilling which was not out of the norm because I got along with his whole family and when I was over there. Nighttime had come, and me and Damian were in the room chilling. Normally when I am around him especially at night, he is all over me trying to have sex, but this time he wasn't. He actually seemed like my presence annoyed him. "What is wrong with you today? I asked him. "I'm good, you chilled here all day, I didn't tell you to leave, did I?" He asked me. "No, what do that have to do with anything?" I asked him. "It means I'm good, what else do you want from me?" he asked. "You are so rude," I said to him as I got an attitude. "How am I rude? I let you chill here and everything," he said as he was champing a black and mild. "Um, well whatever, you acting like I did something to you, that's the vibe you are giving off," I said to him. "Listen, it's been a lot lately. A nigga picked up your phone and said he rocked you. Then you pop up pregnant when I was barely even seeing you like that" he blurted out. "What Damian! You are STILL on that?!" I blurted out. "Yeah, I haven't forgotten," he said, smoking his mild. "That is so messed up. I told you my phone was stolen, and after all I went through with losing the baby, and you still going to bring this up?" I asked him. "Yup, I don't trust you" he said, and my mind was blown. I could not believe he said he could not trust ME of all people. The person who was the most loyal to him and held him down in every situation. My heart was shattered. "Oh my God," I said to him as I wanted to cry. "I don't," he said, still smoking. I didn't even respond. I had sat there in silence and was in deep thought. "He really don't love me anymore," I thought to myself, and I felt myself panic on the inside, and I went into fighter flight mode and thinking of ways to not make him not mad at me anymore.

About an hour had passed, and he laid down, and I laid on his chest like I normally did, and he didn't push me off so I felt like things were better. He seemed ok and calm. I knew his demeanor, and I knew how to work him. Even though he could be wishy-washy, he still had a soft spot for me and vice versa. We were like each other's drug. We were toxic for each other, but could not get enough of each other. It was scary and dysfunctional. I began rubbing his chest, and eventually he moved my hand. "What are you doing?" I asked him. "We not about to do this," he said as he sat up. "Do what?" I asked defensively. "I'm not about to have sex with you," he said, and it stung to my ears. In all my years of knowing him, I have never heard him utter those words nor ever turn down sex with me. "What? Why?" I asked him offended. "Because I'm not," he said, getting annoyed. "Last time, you got on top and didn't get off and then you popped up pregnant. You not tricking me again," he said. "Tricking you? Why do I need to trick you?" I asked him, offended. "First you say you don't trust me because the guy answered my phone, now you say I tricked you" which one is it, because you are all over the place" I said to him getting upset. "Both," he said to me in a cocky way. "You are full of sh*t," I said to him as my feelings were so hurt. He sat there, and he smoked his black and mild. He was quiet like he was thinking.

I was still in my feelings, and I should have left, but I didn't. I stayed. I stayed and thought of ways to make him love me and want me again. Eventually, he didn't pay me any mind anymore, and he turned off the light to go to sleep. I laid down next to him, and he turned his back to me. I laid in the dark and for some reason, I remembered I had a $100 bill in my purse, and out of nowhere I asked him, "If I give you $100, will you have sex with me?" He had turned around, thought about it and to my surprise, he replied "Show me the money first," and I got up and got it out of my purse. He had turned the light on to look at it and then turned the light back off. "Ok, Yeah, will have sex with you for the $100," he said, and I gave it to him. We had sex and it was the saddest prostitute-ish feeling ever. While having sex with him I had wanted to cry. After we were done, I was so pissed that I got up to leave. I kept thinking in my head that he was going to give the $100's back and that it was all a joke, but he never gave the money back, and I left feeling broken and empty. I had felt like I had hit the lowest of low and mentally. I could not do it anymore, and I had made the choice to not talk to him anymore.

Eventually, I got myself together, and I got back into the swing of life and was having fun again. I had linked up with my friend who did hair and fashion shows, and I started modeling. I would go to practice and had met a whole new group of girls, and I was having so much fun with them. I had my first hair show with them in Philly and we had a ball. We stayed at a hotel, and I got my hair and makeup done and got to wear things I normally wouldn't wear. It was just an all-around fun experience. It kept me busy, not focused on Damian and losing the baby. I had graduated bartending school, and I was ready to work at one of the strip clubs.

Where I really wanted to work was the 40/40 but they told me that I did not have enough experience yet. So, I would bar and club hop to get into the Bartending loop and I was having a blast while doing it. My life was full and fun, and I had no complaints. Every time I was not worried about him, Damian would pop back up acting all lovey dovey, and I would fall for his trap. After the miscarriage, things were a little different, but we were ok. He was doing his thing and I was doing mine. Sometimes he would be sweet; sometimes he would be mean. You just never knew with him.

One night he had called me over to kick it with him at his house. While I was there his vibe was off. "Why you ask me to come over here if you just going to act funny? I asked him. "You can leave," he said, being smart, which came out of nowhere. While I was not talking to Damian a friend of mine had introduced me to a guy who was cool with her boyfriend, and they were from out of state. The dude had seen me and was feeling me, so without my knowledge she had given him my number. He had called me one day out of the blue. I didn't recognize his number so when I picked up, and he told me who he was and where he got my number from. He was cool so we would kick it from time to time, and he would always say, "Just say the word, and I'll be in Jersey to see you asap." I never took him up on his offer because where we lived was small, and I didn't want people in my business and going back to tell Damian, so I just kept him at bay. Plus, I still loved Damian and I was not ready to fully move on yet.

While I was at Damian's house and he told me, I could leave; my phone happened to ring. I didn't answer it because I knew who it was. "Answer your phone," he said to me, being nosey. "No," I said to him. "What you got a nigga?" he asked me being jealous. "Don't worry about it. You just told me to leave right?" I said to him being smart. "That nigga don't really like you, he just want to f*ck," Damian said to me and it infuriated me how disrespectful he was with his mouth. "He treats me better than you do," I blurted out. "Oh, so you are talking to somebody" he said like he caught me in a lie. "I don't have to sit here with you, and take your sh*t. He is all the way in NY and if I call him right now to come, he's coming" I told Damian cockily because he was pissing me off.

My phone rang again and this time I picked it up. "What's up babe?" The man's voice said on the other end. "Nothing boo, when you coming?" I asked him. "Shit I would have been there, when you want me to come, I'm on it asap" he told me. "Ok, let me hit you right back" I told him, and I hung up. "Damian don't play with me" I said to him. Him being the petty person he was he decided to pick up the phone and call a girl as well. It was a few days after Valentine's Day, so he was referencing teddy bears and things that made me believe he was at her house

"Ok, let's stop there" my therapist said as she sat up and uncrossed her legs. "That was a lot, and I am so sorry for your miscarriage. I know that was hard for you. It seems like that was a very emotionally over-whelming time for you. How were you feeling at the time? What was your thought process?" she had asked me. "At that point I had enough, and Damian was making me feel crazy with anger. I could not figure out how I was so good to him, always there for him, and yet he could treat me so cold as if I did something to him. Both times he was in jail I supported him and stayed with him, even though I was super stressed out and I could have left at any time, but I didn't.

I was loyal. It seemed like once he came home from prison and he wasn't cased up anymore, he made me feel like he didn't need me anymore, and I felt used. "Wow, I understand, " my therapist said to me as she was taking notes. "It seems like your boyfriend at the time, now husband had provided a need for you at one point, and that need was no longer being met," she said to me. "Yes, he provided happiness, stability and love. But when he came home, he was a whole different person" I said to her. "I understand, and what do you think you could have differently back then?" she sincerely asked me, and I sat there and thought about it for a moment. "I guess I could have not been so needy and looking for him to provide all those emotional things for me.

I wish I could have learned to give those things to myself. I didn't know how to love me, and I never had emotional stability, so being with him when he was nice made me feel whole. But when he was mean it made me feel useless," I told her. "I understand. Do you think you gave him too much power over your emotions? She asked me, and I sat and thought for a moment again. "I had never thought about it that way before, but Yes," I answered her. "What you have to understand is; no matter how he moves or what he says, or how he feels, it should dictate how you feel about yourself. He is entitled to behave however he wants; that's HIS STUFF, that is not YOUR STUFF. You cannot allow people to project THEMSELVES onto you" she sincerely said to me. "When he was acting those ways, you could have set boundaries.

We teach people how to treat us. When we allow certain behaviors, it makes the other person feel like it's ok, and they will constantly push those boundaries if allowed to. So, he knew no matter what I say or do Shamirah will be there. That's what you taught him that you are Ok with even though sometimes you are not. You allowed it because a need was being met so you overlooked everything else," she said to me as she looked straight at me. "Yes, that is true," I told her. "I really did not know any better back then," I explained to her. "Yes, I do understand that. But you have to understand in life it is OK to have boundaries" she reassured me. "So, what happened next," she asked me as she sat back with her pen and pad. "I had ended up leaving his house and going home," I told her. "After that whole ordeal I had made it up in my mind that I wasn't dealing with Damian anymore, and I had made plans to move to GA with my mom

18

At that time, I was in church, and I was focused on the word and being in the Drama Ministry. I had grown up in church since I was about
13. I would go with my grandmom when I was younger, but at about
12/13 is when my mom got into church and had us going consistently.
I actually loved going to church and learning about the word of God.
At a young age I was in bible study, paying tithes, praying and obeying
God. So now that I was an adult, I had made the choice to go back. I
was very happy at the church I was in. I was not focused on Damian. I
was focused on doing activities with my church family. I was in an awesome and prosperous state mentally, physically, and emotionally and I
was focused more and more on leaving NJ and moving to GA.

Every time I wasn't worried about Damian, he would pop back up
asking me on dates and to hang out with him. Most of the time I took
him up on his offer, and then he would be nice for a while and then
resort back to his wishy-washy ways. He had come to see me one day at
my grandmother's house. We were watching soldier boys' video on BET
and then College Hill had come on. We were lying in bed spending
time, and it was cool. "You know I am leaving right?" I said to him as
I sat up on the bed. "Word? Where you going?" he asked. "I'm going to
Atlanta with my mom" I don't want to be up here anymore" I told him.
"Oh word, damn," he said as he seemed like he didn't know what to say.
"Yeah, I think that's best for me. Plus, I'm done bartending school, so I
can go down there and work and get into school for film" I told him.

"Word, that sounds good" he said taken back at the unexpected news. "I think that will be good for you" he said to me. "My stepdad is going down there this weekend to see my mom and I'm going to go with him," I told Damian. "Oh wow, I didn't know you was leaving so soon. How long are you going to be gone?" he asked me. "For a few days. My mom is going to show me around to give me a feel, and I will see if I like it" I told him. Oh Ok, cool" he said still a little thrown off.

I had ended the conversation at that point and began watching tv again, and he began to rub on me. "What are you doing?" I asked him. "You know what I'm doing" he said as he began flirtatiously playing with me and caressing me. He then got on top of me and began lifting up my pajama shirt. "Damian, I literally just off my period" I told him, just in case he saw any blood or anything that there would be no surprises. Plus being pregnant had made me read up a lot on pregnancy and the body. I had read certain days before and after your period you can ovulate. I didn't understand ovulation completely because I didn't look much into it at that time. But I wanted to let him know there was a chance that I could get pregnant, so I asked him please do not nut in me. He said Ok, and we had sex.

While we were having sex, I felt all this warm wetness in my vagina, and I know what it felt like when he nutted in me. "Why did you do that when I told you not to?" I asked him as I pushed him off. "Do what?" he said playing dumb. "You nutted in me!" I said to him, annoyed. "No, I didn't," he lied. "Yes, you did," I said to him as I got up, and the nut was running down my legs. I went to the bathroom to wipe myself and sure enough there was nut on the rag. Damian didn't address it, and we eventually left, and I dropped him off home in the city.

A few days later, I drove with my stepdad to see my mom and sisters in GA. It normally takes about 12/13 hours to get from Jersey to GA, but my stepdad was speeding the whole way non-stop, and we got there in about 9 hours. I did not enjoy being around him. He annoyed

me, but I had to suck it up. I had no choice but to be in the car with
him, and that was the sacrifice I made to see my family. When I saw my
mom and sisters, I was so happy. I had not realized how much I missed
them, and my mom's house felt like home. She had a cute apartment in
Lawrenceville in Alexander Mills. The neighborhood was nice and had
a pool and everything. The apartments in GA looked way better than
the apartments in Jersey. I liked the area and the vibe, and I was looking
forward to moving down there. I enjoyed my visit. We were there for a
few days, then we went back to Jersey.

When I got back, I felt so empty. I felt like Jersey was not my home
anymore because my close family was not there. About a week later,
to my surprise, my aunt and cousins were driving down to Ga because
two of my other aunts had moved there. My aunt had let me ride with
her, her husband and my two cousins. I was so excited to go and see
my mom again. To my surprise my stepdad found out they were going,
and he asked to ride with them too and they said yes. I did not want
to be around him, but I was stuck in the van with him for another long
period of time. When we got to GA, they dropped us off, and I spent
time with my mom and sisters for a while and went to sleep. We were
only staying for the weekend.

The next day I had went to the mall with all my aunts which was on
a Saturday, and unbeknownst to me they were going to be there all day.
I wanted to go back to my mom's house because I was there to spend
time with HER, but I spent the majority of the time at the mall. When
I got back to her house it was late, and the day was gone. The next day
was Sunday, and it was time to pack up and leave. I was so sad. I did
not want to go. I had not brought all my things so I had no choice but
to go back. To all of our shock, my stepdad did not ride back with us.
My mom had let him stay.

She moved all the way from Jersey to get away from him and his
toxic-ness and in just a couple of months he managed to swindle his

way back into her life. Even though I was upset that my mom got back with him, I was happy that he didn't have to ride back with us. I didn't feel like being around his energy. His energy was playful and aggravating. He was a play fiend and didn't know when to stop. He would play with me all the time and do this thing where he put his fingers into my knees and it used to hurt so bad, but it would make me laugh and when he was done, I would be so mad at him. When I got back to Jersey for the second time, I knew for sure that I was ready to go. I had started to get all my ducks in order to move.

19

About a week later, I had got my hair done. I loved it. My hairdresser did a long jet black sew in, so I had set up for me to take pictures at Walmart back when they still had their portrait studio. The pictures had gone great but the whole time I was having hot flashes and wasn't feeling like myself. When I was walking out of the portrait studio, I had run into one of the girls from bartending school and I was telling her I wasn't feeling that good, and that I would catch up with her later. She said to me "girl you better get a pregnancy test." Me being pregnant did not even dawn on me.

A few days before me taking the pictures I had been really crampy, but I just figured I was about to get my period. Once she said it a light bulb had went off and since I was already in Walmart, I went to the pharmacy isle and got me a first response pregnancy test. I had stood in line to pay for it and a wave of heat just came over me and I felt like the whole room was spinning. I felt faint and it felt like the line was moving in slow motion because they were taking so long. I didn't have any energy at that point, so I grabbed a bottled water out of the refrigerator by the register and drank it. Finally, I was up to the clerk and she rang my stuff up, and I darted out the door because I didn't not want to faint in Walmart.

When I got outside, I felt a little better since I had some fresh air. When I drank the water, I felt a slight bit better because I think I was dehydrated. Finally, after all of that I was over I sat on the bench at Walmart and focused on the pregnancy test. I was so nervous to take it, because after the miscarriage, I was not focused on getting pregnant again. I was ready to start a whole new life in Atlanta, and a baby was not a part of the plan.

I had called my cousin who lived across the street from Walmart in the Woodlands, so that I could go to her house and take the test. "Omg girl, I am so scared" I said to her as I came in the door. "B*tch, you pregnant" she said laughing and joking like we always did. "No, I'm serious, I'm really scared. Look I'm shaking" I told her as we both looked down at my hands. "Alright go in the bathroom and take the test" she said to me, and I opened it and read the directions. "Ok, I'm going to pee on it and leave it in the bathroom and You go and look at it" I told her. I had peed and I felt so nervous and anxious. I went into the living room and sat next to her and hugged her. "I'm so scared!" I yelled to her, and she was laughing. "Don't be scared. You and Damian been together forever. You will be fine," she told me. The three minutes was up, and it was time to look at the test.

My cousin hopped up, and I saw the nervousness in her face too. "Ok, here goes nothing" she said walking to the bathroom. She went in there and picked it up and looked at it and walked out the bathroom with the biggest smiler ever. "What it says" I asked nervously. "You are the MOTHER!" she said smiling. "Girl stop playing" I said to her hoping she was joking. "Look," she said as she handed me the test. I looked at it and surely there were two lines, and they were dark. "Oh my God" I said not knowing how to feel. I stayed there with her for most of the day for comfort. I didn't know what to do or if I should even tell anyone, since I told everybody the 1st time and I had a miscarriage.

Once I left her house, I drove to the city to tell Damian because I didn't want to wait like I did the first time. I came to his house, and I showed him the pregnancy test and anticipating his reaction. "Ok" he said nonchalantly. "That's all you're going to say?" I asked him. "I knew you was going to be pregnant" he told me. "What you mean?" I asked him curious. "The day I nutted in you; I knew you was going to be pregnant" he said. "What?" I asked him. "So, you did it on purpose?" I asked. "Not on purpose, but I didn't prevent it either" he told me. "Hmmm" I said to him as I sat next to him. "Well, I'm keeping it and I'm making a doctor's appointment soon" I told him. "Ok" he said and that was that. Over the next few weeks, I became extremely sick and nauseous. It was the beginning of June, so it was hot and humid, and the weather made me even sicker. Also, the fact that I could smell the pollan and the trees and everything was intensified. Every smell made me gag. It didn't help that I was living with my grand mom and she did not turn on her air conditioner, so I was in the house burning up and miserable.

One day I could not take it anymore and I had called my mom and asked her when she came up for my brother's graduation could I ride back with her. She told me yeah and to have all my stuff packed. I was so happy to be leaving. In those pregnancy moments I just wanted to be with my mom and my family. I was so sick that I had lost a lot of weight and I was really skinny. I would see Damian and it seemed like every time I saw him, I would start to throw up, so I tried to stay away from him. When my mom came to Jersey for my brother Waheed's graduation, she had pulled up to my grandma's house where I stayed and I happened to be walking up the street. "Oh my God, look at you" she said to me in disbelief. "You are so skinny" she said feeling bad for me. "I know mom" I haven't been eating" I said to her, and I got in the car and we drove to the graduation at Oakcrest High School Mays Landing.

At the graduation I saw everybody I grew up with. It was popping. People saw me and did not even believe that it was me. Everybody said "Wow, you are skinny" and they were not saying it in a good way. I had on a black one-piece romper and a pair of sandals so you could see my arms, legs, and feet and everything was so slim and frail. I had never been that skinny in my life. I was a little uncomfortable, but I didn't care because I was enjoying seeing my brother graduate, and that was all that was important to me. After graduation we celebrated. Later that night I had went to see Damian to say goodbye. I was so sad to leave him. I was going to miss him, but I knew if I wanted to have a healthy pregnancy that I needed to leave. Before I left, I told my grand mom that I was pregnant because she didn't know. She told me that it was good that my mom had come to get me because I would not have been able to raise a baby in her house, which I already knew. Leaving was sad but it was necessary.

The next day we got on the road to go to Georgia. On the ride my mom had packed sandwiches and chips and had a bucket of chicken. "Please eat" she said to me as we drove, and I had eaten on the ride more than I had eaten in months. It felt good to be back with my mom, where I was safe and knew I would be cared for. Being pregnant was new to me and I was clueless about it, and needed my mom's guidance. For most of the ride I talked to Damian on the phone, and I talked to him a lot when I got there. I had been in GA for about two weeks, and I really missed him and all my friends. I would talk to his mom on the phone every day and she kept me encouraged.

It seemed like when I got to GA, I had gotten even sicker. The air was different and had a lot of trees and I could smell every leaf, every bark, every pollen and particle and it was debilitating. If I was sitting in the living room and someone came into the kitchen and turned on the water in the sink, I could smell it and I would instantly have to throw up. Not to mention it was HOT. Georgia hot is different from Jersey hot. In Jersey it would be hot during the day but in the evening, it would cool down and there would be a breeze. Although it was humid, you could still get relief. In GA it was just dry hot and being pregnant it felt like the temperature was 1000 degrees, so I stayed in the house as much as I could.

After about two weeks of being there my mom had told me she was driving to Jersey to visit and asked if I wanted to ride and of course I did. Once I got there it felt so good to be back, and I called all my friends to see them. Damian knew I was coming, and I had popped up at his house. "What's up" he said smiling from ear to ear as he greeted me as I walked up on the porch. "Nothing" I said as I smiled as I was happy to see him too. His dad had lived in a duplex and him and his brother had moved into the apartment upstairs. He had moved before I left. I did not want to stay with him, because at the time he was working a lot at Harrah's casino and was never home.

I was pregnant and would have needed a lot of his assistance and I don't think he was capable of giving me what I needed. So, although I would have been my child's dad during my pregnancy. I felt like it was best to just go and be with my mom. We had gone upstairs to his apartment and talked, and he had let me know that him, his dad and his brothers were moving to Greensboro, NC. "Oh, wow when y'all leaving?" I had asked him as I was little excited that he would be closer to me. "We leaving next week" he had told me. "I know, your dad is leaving, but what made you go? Why didn't you just stay here?" I asked him. "I think I just want a change" he told me. "That's cool" I said to him as I was happy, he wanted something different especially since we had a baby on the way.

Damian had taken me downstairs to see his dad. "Hey Mr. B" I said as I walked through the door, and he smiled when he saw me. He gave me a hug and finished spraying the carpet with resolve, cleaning the house to move. "So, your leaving to NC?" I asked him as I smiled. "Yeah, yeah" he said in his laid-back demeanor. His dad was really cool and laid back. I know he liked me because I could always tell by his face. He was old school and didn't really mess with everyone, but when he loved you, you knew it. Damian had walked away to the back, and I was still there with Mr. B. I really wanted to cry because sadness came over me.

Even though Damian was moving closer, I still felt like he was far away. Even though we had our ups and downs I still wanted a chance to be with my child's dad, and with us being in different states I was not sure if that was going to happen. "Well, I guess this is it. I don't know if I will be seeing your son anymore now that y'all will be in NC" I said as I joked, but he could read through my emotions and knew that I was genuinely concerned. As he was still spraying, he looked up at me and said "He'll find you" he said as looked me in my eyes and smiled. And at that moment I felt peace and that meant a lot to me that he said that, especially coming from him. His dad could be a jokester and sarcastic so him saying those short words to me spoke volumes to my heart.

Damian had come back to the front room, and it was almost time for my mom to pick me up to go back to GA. He had my car parked in front of his house. I had given it to him when I left and told him to get it in his name. I took out everything I wanted and gave him the title. My mom had pulled up not too long after that and I gave Damian a long hug and told him I loved him. He told me he loved me too and that he would call me, and I got in the car with my mom and left.

When I got back to GA, I was getting bigger and farther along in my pregnancy. I was not working and the unemployment I was getting from Jersey had run out. I was beginning to get a little stressed. To make matters worse, I had got a call from the EHT police department telling me that they had found my car abandoned and they ran the tags and Vin number and found that it belonged to me. I had told them to just junk it. But by that happening I had gotten fines that I didn't know about so my Jersey license had got suspended which prevented me from getting my GA license, so I could not drive myself around and I had to wait to get rides which was super frustrating. I was used to moving around and doing what I wanted to do. GA was not like Jersey where you could walk or get on the bus or jitney or catch a cab wherever you needed to go. In GA you literally needed a car to go everywhere. I had Medicaid so I would get picked up for my doctor's appointments when my mom could not take me.

It was overwhelming. I became mean and angry while I was pregnant, and everyone got on my nerves. The house was already crowded with me, my mom, my stepdad, and three sisters and then my mom had gone to Jersey to pick up my brother and his girlfriend and they moved in too. The house was packed and noisy. My sisters would blast music all day since they were out of school for the summer. My brother and his girlfriend would argue all the time. My stepdad was in and out of the house opening and closing the door letting the stank outside air in, and my mom was barely home because she worked all day, so I basically was the one in charge having to deal with everybody. I would try to stop my brother and his girlfriend from their chaos, and somehow me and my brother would get into it. That house was out of control to the point that the neighbors started complaining and reporting us.

My mom knew we needed a bigger house, so she found a big, beautiful house in the Georgian Hills Subdivision in Gwinnett. The house was huge, and we were all excited to move into it. My mom was approved, and the agreement between her and the owner was that they went by her income and my stepdad's SSI income, and my stepdad and my mom agreed to pay the deposit and split everything moving forward and he agreed. We had gone a few days before the move in day to paint and get the house move-in ready. Every time we went to that house people would just start arguing and getting angry, mainly my brother and his girlfriend. My mom had let them get the bigger bedroom, which was the master and every time we went in there, there was a dark presence. We didn't really pay it any mind. We just wanted to finish painting to begin moving in the furniture. My room was so cute. I had painted it Sage, which was so calming. I was excited to finally have my own space and I was ready to get the room ready for the baby, not to mention the neighborhood was beautiful. It was like somewhere rich people lived.

The houses were huge and there were pools in the neighborhood and tennis courts, and I was excited to live and raise my baby there.

On moving day my mom had got a truck and my brother and sisters had moved that whole house. The furniture was heavy, and my mom lived on the second floor and it was summer. It was a hot and exhausting day. Tensions were already high because everyone was tired from moving. Of course, I did not have to move anything because I was pregnant, so everyone took their anger out on me because they felt like I was not doing anything. Once we all got to the new house and unpacked the truck. We took the furniture in the rooms they belonged in as the landlord came to get the money. My mom had her portion and right on moving day in front of the landlord my stepdad said that he didn't have his money. "What?" we all said. "What do you mean, you don't have your money?" My mom asked him as she was getting pissed off. "I don't have it, Stephanie, damn" he said, getting an attitude as if he wasn't the one in the wrong.

He knew the moving date. He watched her get the truck and him and all my siblings moved all that stuff in the house, and he did all of it knowing he was not going to pay for it. The landlord was so upset and thought they were trying to run a scam on him. My mom had to tell him that she didn't know that he didn't have his half. The Landlord had told us that we had to go unless he got the deposit. Everyone was upset and disappointed and begged him to give the Landlord the money, but my stepdad did not care. He was being very selfish and nonchalant and expected my mom to figure it out. He kept laughing and was a whole clown that day. He looked so stupid and pitiful, and I could not believe that he pulled a stunt like that. He was low for doing that.

My mom had left to go to our apartments at Alexander Mills to try and get our apartment back so we would have somewhere to live, since we could not live in the house. Thankfully they had not rented the apartment and they said we could move back in. While she was gone, there was chaos at the house. Everyone was pissed at my stepdad and him and my brother started arguing. He threatened to beat up my brother which was out of character even for him. Him and my brother were always close, so to see him being aggressive with my brother made me pissed. "You are not going to do nothing to my brother, we will f*ck you up in here" I said to him which was even out of character for me. It was like everyone was possessed. "Shut up!" he yelled to me, and when he said that my brother jumped in his face "Yo, don't be talking to my sister like that," my brother said to him as he got in his face and my brother's girlfriend tried to hold my brother back. He pushed her out the way and she went and sat down. I saw the look on her face, she was genuinely scared.

The tension in the air was so thick, you could cut it with a knife. You could just feel that something was about to happen. My stepdad had pushed my brother out his face and I immediately jumped up and pushed him. He had picked up a lamp and threw it. After that, all I saw was blood, and I did not know where it was coming from, and I went bonkers because I thought my brother was hit. I began tussling with my stepdad, and my brother picked up a chair to hit him with it, but he moved, and the chair hit me instead. "Yo, my bad," my brother said as he was even more pissed because I was hit by the chair, and they began to fight. I was in such a panic I did not know what to do. I was about six months pregnant and should not have been in that situation.

My mom's car was still parked outside because she left in the u haul. The keys were in my stepdad's pocket, so I grabbed them and ran. He saw me and began to chase me. We were outside, and he tried to get the keys back as my brother was blocking him from me. It had begun to rain. Now, we were outside getting soaking wet, but all I could think of was to get the keys in the ignition to go and find my mom. Finally, I was able to get in the car and when I did, my stepdad ran to the passenger side and opened the door before I could lock it and he grabbed the keys out of the ignition. At that point I knew we were screwed and stuck there.

It felt like torture being there with all this drama and no help. I jumped out the driver's side to grab the keys from him. Me and my brother both tussled with him and as I tried to grab the keys, I slipped in the wet grass and fell. After that, my stepdad ran in the house and closed the garage and my brother helped me up. I stood there and cried, my first thought was, was my baby ok, and my second thought was I felt defeated. My brother's girlfriend had opened the front door for us so we could come in out of the rain. My stepdad had ran and hid somewhere in the house because he knew he was wrong. We were not even focused on him anymore. All we wanted to do was leave.

When my mom finally came back, we had told her all about it and she was livid. She could not believe he acted like that to us, especially me since I was pregnant. She told him he had to go, and I don't know where he went. We were just happy he was gone. The landlord let us stay the night, and the next day we got up and my brother and siblings had to move the house all over again. It was disappointing to watch. Before we knew it, we were all back cramped up in that little apartment. My stepdad was not there because my mom had put him out. But of course, she let him come back eventually, and when he came back, he was even worse. He was super disrespectful to everyone. He came and went as he pleased. He was a bad vibe in the house, and there was so much tension.

One night I am not sure what he got into, but the police were chasing him not too far from our house, and he had jumped a fence to get away from them. Instead of hiding out, he came back to the house with his clothes all ripped. The police eventually found him, and he went to jail We were so happy he was gone. But he must have not done anything major because they let him back out and he was back at the house terrorizing us again.

We had taken pictures at the new house that we had to move from, and my mom got them developed. When we looked through the pictures, there were dark orbs everywhere and black cloud-like streaks in the pictures as well. "Oh my God, this house was haunted," my mom said as we all looked at the pictures in amazement, and could not believe that we were about to live in a house with dark entities in it. That explained a lot and gave me an uneasy feeling. "God knows what we don't know, and everything happens for a reason," I told them, my mom ripped up the pictures and threw them in the trash, and we moved forward and never thought about that house again.

20

There was so much going on and I would always tell Damian about it. I used to talk to him all day every day. He was settled in NC and seemed to like it. He had started going to school to sell life insurance, and he was in a good place in his life. Things were not the way I wanted them. My home was dysfunctional and overwhelming. I was pregnant without my child's dad. I didn't have any money or a driver's license, and I was becoming depressed. I would sit on the balcony at night and look up at the sky, and pray to God to change my situation. I told him I wanted my own place, a car, and that I wanted to be with Damian, and I wanted him in our daughter's life. I had found out what I was having, and it was a girl.

At first, I was disappointed because I wanted a boy, but after being consoled by my mom as well as Damian's mom. I had become ok with it. I was scared to tell Damian at first that it was a girl, because I did not know how he would react. "Mom Mom, do not be scared to tell him. He will be happy and love her, and I am happy to have my grand baby" his mom told me as I could hear her smile through the phone. She was so excited when I told her we were having a girl. His mom had called me mom mom all the time. That was her name for me. "And you know another thing mom mom" she said to me. "What?" I had asked her as I sat in the car in the parking lot of my doctor's office. "He will be happy, because he is having his first girl with YOU " she said to me, and that meant a lot.

After talking with her I felt confident enough to call Damian and let him know. "Hello," he said with curiosity in his voice because he knew I was going to the doctors that day to see what we were having. "So, I got the ultrasound today." I told him getting nervous all over again. "What is it?" he asked. "It's a girl" I said with no enthusiasm in my voice. "Oh Ok, that's what's up" he said as I could tell he was smiling, and it almost sounded like he was relieved. "Are you mad?" I asked him. "No, why would I be mad?" he asked me. "I don't know. I just thought you would have wanted a boy" I said to him. "Nah, I'm good, I don't want a boy. I already got a boy," he said. "I'm happy it's a girl," he said to me, and that made me feel better.

We had talked about names weeks before the Ultrasound and decided if it was a girl, we would name her Najah and I was so excited about our little family. Some days that I talked to him on the phone, he was super loving and made it seem like we were going to come together and raise her; and other days he would be wishy washy. At the time I moved to GA, I was under the impression that we were together. He would still act like my boyfriend, and we would talk 24/7. We just happened to be in different states.

I was in the kitchen one day late at night sitting on the floor talking to him. "So, when the baby come, are you going to move down here?" I asked him. "No" he responded. "Why not, I want my daughter to have a family. I did not grow up with my dad and I don't want that for our daughter" I told him. "I am not moving down there. You have to show me that you are mature and until then, I'm not coming" he scolded me. "I don't know what you mean. I am mature" I pleaded to him. "No, you're not" he said, beginning to badger me and put me down, like he normally did. Damian had played a lot of mind games, and I had always fallen into them.

He knew how to manipulate me and control me like a robot. "Well,

I will try to do better, just tell me what I need to do" I said to him as I sat on the floor with my ears wide open, ready to take mental notes. "I don't know. I will figure it out and let you know," he told me. "Ok, well we are still together, right? I asked him. "No" he said as he chuckled. "What you mean? I thought we were together" I said to him as I was thrown off. "I'm not with YOU" he said checking me. "Well, I thought we were, so when do you think we will ever get back together?" I asked him desperately. "I don't know, you have to get your mind right," he said to me so nonchalantly.

He could be so heartless towards me sometimes, and this was one of those times. "Well, I want to be with you, and I want my daughter to have a family," I said to him with a crying voice. "I don't want to be with you, and I'm not moving down there," he said firmly. "Oh my God" I said as I burst out crying with him on the phone. He knew my cries. He knew that it was a *my feelings are deeply hurt* kind of cry. I cried like a baby, and my heart was hurting, and he knew it. "Stop crying," he said to me, and I continued to sniffle and eventually got myself together. "Don't cry, everything will work out," he told me, trying to console me. He always would be the one to work me up, and then put the fire out like he was the good guy. But I fell for it, and he made me feel better. "Goodnight, get some sleep" he said to me as it was about 3 o'clock in the morning. "Ok, goodnight," I said to him, and I went to bed.

A few weeks later, I flew to Jersey to have my baby shower at Damian's mom's house. I had got picked up at the airport and on the way driving to his mom's house I saw someone walking down the street with a huge bouquet of pink and white balloons, and they walked just like Damian. When we pulled up closer it was his brother Drew. "Hey, Drew! You want a ride?" I yelled out the window. "Nah, I'm good" he said as he smiled, happy to see me showing his dimples. Me and Drew were very close, and he would always joke and be playful. We loved each other like brother and sister. "Awww, the balloons are so nice" I said to myself, and I was excited to get to the house to see what everything looked like. When I got there, it was decorated pretty, and Drew had come in with the balloons and everything was perfect. "Hey Santia!" I said as I saw Drew's baby mother at my shower. She lived there at his mom's house at the time. Santia was pregnant at the time as well. We were 2 months apart. They were having a daughter as well, and they had named her similar to my daughter's name. So, we both had daughters on the way.

We had talked for a little bit, and then my guests began coming. I was so excited. All my friends and family were there and I was so happy to see everyone. It was filled with so much love and laughter. Damian's mom was the host and she enjoyed everyone, and it was an all-around good time. Damian had called to talk to me because he could not make it. I was sad, but it was Ok. I had his mom and Drew there, as well as everyone I loved, so I was happy. I got a lot of gifts and baby tubs and clothes and all types of things. I had flown up and forgot that I would have to get all that stuff home to GA, which I was not going to be able to get it all on the plane. One of my aunts had paid to ship my gifts to my house in Georgia, and I was so grateful.

I stayed a few more days and spent time with everyone. My baby shower was at the beginning of December. I spent my last day at Damian's mom's house, and I was there with Drew the whole time. He was making fun of my stomach and showing me how to upload pictures on Myspace. Damian had called and was asking him what I looked like pregnant. "She cute, she still looks the same. Her stomach just got bigger" I heard him tell him trying to be discreet. I had not seen Damian for most of my pregnancy. I was going on nine months, and I had not seen him since I was about 3 months. I basically went through my whole pregnancy alone. Thankfully I talked to him every day, but it was not the same. I was lonely without him. Not to mention that pregnancy makes you super horny, and I could not have sex with him when I wanted to. When it was time for me to go, I hugged everybody and told them I loved them. "Drew you up next. We are both about to have little daughters soon!" I told him. "I know right, I can't wait," he said. Drew was a good spirited person and he loved kids and animals. "I love you; I will see you soon. " I told him. "I love you too sis" he said as he walked me to the car, and I left to go to the airport.

Once I got back to Georgia, my gifts from the baby shower were already there and to my surprise my mom had fixed up the room while I was gone. While I was gone my brother and his girlfriend had moved back to Jersey, and my sisters were back in school during the day, so the house didn't feel crowded anymore. It was so nice and comfortable. I unpacked all the baby's stuff and put her clothes in the drawer. Najah was so blessed. She literally had everything from clothes to toys, to sleepers, to diapers and wipes She had a swing, baby chair, blankets, body wash, literally everything. I felt so thankful because my pregnancy was rough financially.

I got a job when I was about 5 months pregnant at a Sports Bar in Lawrenceville called "Tailgaters". When I had first went to get the job, I had on a black lace shirt, and I was pregnant so my boobs looked nice and full. My shirt was peplum, so it covered my stomach and I had on some tight pants and some open toes shoes. It was during the day and luckily, the owner was there. He was a very handsome guy. He kind of looked like Idris Alba a little bit. He had come out to talk to me and did an on-the-spot interview. I told him about my bartending skills and showed him my mixology certificate. He kept staring at me and I was not sure what he was looking at. He was checking me out. I could tell he thought I was cute, and he liked my personality, but I could not put my finger on why he was staring so hard.

At the end of the interview, he took my application and said, "I can't let you work as a bartender, but you can work here as a waitress" he told me. "Why not a bartender? That's the position I applied for" I told him. "I can't let you work behind the bar because it gets really busy and you are pregnant," he said to me and all I could do was laugh. "How did you know?" I asked him. "I could just tell. You have that pregnant look, plus I could see your stomach," he said pointing down. "Oh wow, I thought I had covered it up," I said to him surprise that he peeped it. I was super tiny when I was pregnant, my stomach didn't even begin to show until I was about 7 or 8 months. He had hired me, and I worked at Tailgators as a waitress from about 5 months to 8 months.

It was cool and fun. I met a lot of people but it was not an environment for pregnant women. It was like a club so there was dancing and loud music, people smoking and drinking, plus it was very strenuous on my feet from walking orders all day. But I didn't mind it. It gave me exercise and something to do. I liked working there. Some people could tell I was pregnant, and some couldn't. Most of the regulars there knew I was pregnant and to my shock a lot of the guys still tried to talk to me and get with me. I never knew that guys hit on pregnant women so much, it was crazy. At first, I thought it was a Georgia thing, but even when I went back home up north for my baby shower I was in Philly and Jersey and they tried to talk to me too. I don't know what it was about me being pregnant, but guys were attracted to me like a magnet.

I worked at Tailgators and got my tips, but I had never got to keep them to myself because I always had to help my mom. So, while I was pregnant, even though I was getting money, I was not able to shop for my baby like I wanted to and that would make me so sad and stressed. My mom would always say, "I promise it won't always be like this. I promise before the baby come, you will have everything you need" and I believed her. So even though I didn't want to; I gave her my tips and helped her with the bills. So, seeing all that my baby had made me feel overwhelmed with joy, and I was happy that everything worked out. I was at the end of my pregnancy, so I did not work at the bar anymore. I was home relaxing, waiting for Najah to be born.

2 1

One day I was sitting in my room on the floor doing my hair. My room closet doors were mirrored. I sat there with my blue pajama two-piece pants set on. At this point, my stomach was huge. I had woken up that morning with a happy feeling in my spirit, and I did not know why. I had finished my hair and was fixing it in the mirror when I heard a knock at that door. I did not think anything of it because I didn't know anyone in GA, and I knew it was not for me. "Shamirah, go answer the door," my mom had yelled to me, and I wondered why she didn't just get it herself because her room was right next to the door.

When I opened it, my jaw dropped. It was Damian and his dad standing there. Damian had the biggest smile ever, and I was so happy to see him that I almost jumped in his arms. "What y'all doing here?" I said as I wanted to cry. "I came to see you," Damian said, still smiling. I let them in, and they sat down at the kitchen table. "He would tell me every day that he wanted to see you and that he missed you, so I said let me get on this road and take him to see his women," his dad said as he smiled at me and looked at Damian. When I looked at Damian, he was still smiling from ear to ear. "I look different, huh," I said to him as I touched my stomach, and he nodded his head yes. "Ok, well, I'm going to let y'all spend some time," his dad said as he left the house.

Damian and I sat there, and my mom came out of the room to say hi to him, and they talked for a little bit, and then he and I went to my

179

room. While we were in there, I let him see my stomach. He touched it and seemed like he was in disbelief. We talked and laughed, and I showed him the baby's stuff and the ultrasound pictures. He was sitting there and taking it all in. All of it seemed new to him. I guess him seeing everything in person made it all real. At that time, we didn't have FB or social media like that, where I was posting pictures or iPhone with facetime, so he didn't know what I looked like.

He tried to touch me, but I think my big stomach was a lot for him. He was used to my stomach being flat and me really not having any boobs. Now everything was accentuated. I know you want to have sex; we can do it; you don't have to be nervous. I told him. "I just don't want to hurt you," he said to me. "You're not going to hurt me," I told him, and I took my pants off. "Ok, just turn around; I don't want to be on your stomach," he said to me, and I turned around and bent over doggy style, and he did it from the back. It had felt so good to be finally having sex, and I could tell he was enjoying it too.

I was super wet, so wet that he could not contain himself, and before I knew it, he had nutted and it was over. I got us a rag, and we cleaned off and chilled for a little bit because we were going to do it again, but his dad called his phone, and it was time for him to go. I did not want him to leave. "You could just stay here for a few days," I told him. "Nah, I have to go back with my dad, he's my ride," he told me. "Ok, I understand, " I told him as I hugged him tight and kissed him. I could tell he was sad to go too. It was so unfortunate. I was glad that he came but him leaving me there pregnant made me miss him even more. He had called me on their ride back home to NC, and we talked the whole time. "Everything is going to be good with us," he reassured me. "I love you," he said to me. "I love you too," I told him, and we finally got off the phone.

It was now Christmas Day. I woke up in a good mood. Damian had called me, and we talked for a while. I had called his mom to wish her a Merry Christmas, and Drew answered the phone. "Ewww," he said to me. We always would joke with each other and say Ewww. "Ewww, Merry Christmas, big head," I said to him, and he gave his mom the phone. She was so happy and in a good mood. We talked for a while, then eventually hung up to enjoy our families.

Later that night, I got a phone call that I never imagined that I would get. "Drew was shot," Damian said on the other end of the phone. "What?" I said as I jumped up out of my sleep. "Drew was shot, and we all getting in the car on our way to Jersey," Damian told me. He, his dad, and all his siblings had raced up there 8 hours away to be by Drew's side. I could not go back to sleep. I was up praying and waiting for an update. Halfway through the trip, Damian called me. "Drew died," he said, and he just hung up. "What?!" I said, and I broke down and cried.

The next morning, I had got on the computer to book a flight, but they all cost too much, and I didn't have the money, nor could I borrow it from anyone. I wanted to be up there by their side, and it killed me that I couldn't. Damian had not called back, and I was still in disbelief. I had not talked to his mom yet, and I would not believe it until I heard it from her. I had called her phone, and she picked up balling crying. "He's gone mom mom. He's gone" is all I heard her crying, and I heard the heartache in her voice, and I could not even talk at that point. I just burst into tears. Normally his mom was strong and encouraging. I had never heard her cry before, and it broke my heart. "I love you," I said to her, and I hung up.

I could not bear it. I cried for days. Initially, I did not know what happened. But once Damian had time, he called me and told me that Drew had been shot in the house. He had a girl over, and she somehow accidentally shot him. He tried to get help, but when he got to the steps, he fell and the bullets ricocheted, causing him to have internal bleeding. It was so sad. His mom found him and couldn't save him, and that broke her heart. At the hospital, they tried to give him a blood transfusion, but it didn't work, and he passed. To this day, I miss him. I miss his laugh, his smile with his dimples. He was a young fly dude, so I always wondered how he would have been as an adult. Most of all I miss him for his daughter, who I know he would have loved to death.

The family was heartbroken. They had his funeral and came back to NC. Damian's spirit was so different, and I felt so sad. He had taken the test for his life insurance class and had failed by one point. "I just couldn't sit in that class anymore after what happened to Drew. They talked about death, and it was just a lot for me. My head wasn't in it anymore, and that is why I failed," Damian expressed to me. "I know, you still did a good job. You were one point off," I told him, trying to encourage him. "Yeah, I don't think that it's for me right now. I will find something else to do like construction, he told me. "Ok, everything will be ok," I said, trying my best to console him even though I was hurting myself. Drew's death came as a shock to all of us, and everyone took it hard. The girl who shot him said it was an accident, and the family believed her. It was just so unfortunate that she was even over there and that, that even had to happen.

A few weeks had passed, and it was closer to my due date. "Are you going to be here for the baby's birth?" I had asked Damian on my birth-day, which was January 5th, and my due date to have Najah was January 10th. Which was a few days away. "I will try," he said to me. "I hope you can be here; I really want you to see her being born," I expressed to him. "Ok, we will see," he said to me, and I had asked him the same question over the next few days. Finally, about two days before my due date, he had called me and told me he was on his way. He had taken forever to get to me. From Greensboro to where I was, it was about 4 ½ hours, but Damian had taken way longer than that. I was calling his phone, and it was going straight to voicemail. I was so worried about him, and I had not talked to him that whole day. Finally, late that night, the house phone had rung, and it was him calling from a gas station. He was close but did not have enough gas to get to the house, so my mom had met him and gave him the gas money, and he followed her to the house.

He had come through the door, and he had looked exhausted. "Where you been all day?" I asked him as he laid across my bed with his face in his hands. "Yo, you have no idea what I went through to get here," he said to me, not even lifting his face up. "What happened," I asked him, concerned. "First of all, I drove all the way here with no License. The truck is not even registered or insured, and I didn't even know if it was going to break down or not. I didn't have no bread for gas, so I was just winging it. On top of that, my phone had lost service, and I didn't even know where I was going. I just remembered that my dad said it was a straight run and told me the exit. Once I got off at the exit is when I called your mom to meet me at the Quick Trip, and at that point, I was on E," he told me long-winded. "Wow, I didn't know you went through all of that to get here" I told him. "Yes, I went through all of that to be here for my daughter being born," he said to me. "Ok well, thank you for being here. Take your shoes and stuff off so you can get comfortable," I told him, and he did. "Are you hungry?" I asked him, and I went to the kitchen to make him a plate. He ate and relaxed, and we went to sleep.

The next day was Jan 10, which was my due date. There were no signs of the baby coming. I had no contractions or anything. I had a doctor's appointment, and after the appointment, we planned on getting the baby a few things and going to take pictures. When I got to the appointment, the midwife checked my cervix, and sure enough, there was no sign of the baby coming. They ran the tests and listened to the baby's heartbeat, and everything was good. "Ok, so I can go now?" I asked her. "No, sweetie, you are going to have a baby today," she said to me, and I was confused. My doctor had come in and explained to me that they didn't want me to go over my due date and since my water had not broken on its own, they would have to break my water for me. "What?!"

I said I was scared. Damian sat right next to me the whole time, and I was so glad he was there. The look on his face when they said they were going to break my water was priceless. He looked scared for me, and we both did not know what to expect as this was our first delivery. My doctors were awesome though. They kept me informed every step of the way, and the midwife was so compassionate. "This is going to hurt a little," she said as I laid back on the OBGYN table, and she stuck her hand in me and twisted it to break my water" and said, "Ok, now go to the hospital, which happened to be right across the street."

From that point on, everything was moving fast. I got to the hospital, and they began strapping all this equipment on me and began giving me IVs. I was getting really nervous and anxious, and by looking at Damian's face, he was too. Eventually, they took me to the room where I would be giving birth. Everyone had come. Damian was there, my mom, my grandpop. My grandmom worked at the hospital at the time, so when she got off, she came into the room too. It was a full house. At first everything was happiness and laughter until my contractions started kicking in, and things began to get real. I remember constantly feeling like I had to poop, but nothing would come out.

My mom and grandmom walked me back and forth to the bathroom, because my stomach was in excruciating pain. I began to get scared, and I was so glad my mom and grandmom were there to keep me calm. The contractions were getting worse to the point it was unbearable. Finally, a doctor came in to give me my epidural. Everyone stood outside except my mom. She was able to stay in the room and coach me through it. I had to sit completely still as they inserted the long needle in my spine. Once it was done, I didn't feel anything at all. Everyone had come back into the room, and the nurse had turned the room light off and turned on this bright labor-light that was pointed directed at my vagina. She checked my cervix and told me it was time to push. The epidural worked so well that I could not even feel my contractions to push the baby out, so they lowered something in my IV, and I began to feel them, and they hurt.

Damian was there the whole time, holding my hand and holding my legs up to push. Finally, after hours of labor, Najah was born, and Damian cut the umbilical cord and was the first one to hold her. When I finally got to see her, she was so cute. She looked just like her dad. I was taken from the labor room to the hospital room that I would be staying in until I got out of the hospital. I had her at Gwinnett Medical Center, and my room was so nice and spacious. It was like staying in a hotel room, and I was very comfortable. Damian spent time with me in the room and bonded with the baby, and it was nice. I had finally had my own little family. Eventually, all my family began to come, and the room was filled with visitors. My stepdad had come up there to see the baby as well. At first, I did not want him to hold her, but I didn't want to be petty, so I let him have her, and I took a picture of them together. Overall, it was nice having everyone there for support. Eventually, they left, and it was just me Damian and the baby.

The next day Damian had got up early, and I saw him getting dressed. "Where are you going?" I asked him. "I am leaving," he said putting on his hat. "Why are you leaving, and I am not even out of the hospital yet?" I asked him confused. "I have to go, I have to get the on the road and get the car back," he said to me as he seemed eager to go. "Please don't leave; I don't want to stay in the hospital by myself," I begged him. "You have your mom and your whole family here with you" he said to me trying to comfort me. "It's not the same as having you here. You are her dad," I pleaded to him. "I know, and I would stay if I could, but I have to go back," he told me, and he kissed the baby and left.

Minutes after he was gone, the picture people came to take Najah's baby's pictures, and then the lady came with the birth certificate to sign. I filled out the paperwork as her mother, and I was so sad that

Damian was not there to sign her birth certificate. I had grown up all my life looking at my birth certificate, and even though I knew who my father was, my birth certificate said father's name "Unknown" and that hurt, and I didn't want my daughter growing up seeing her birth certificate and feeling the same way. Her father was there when she was born as well as she looked just like him. We were once sweethearts. My baby didn't come from a one-night stand so in my eyes, there was no reason that her dad's name was not on her birth certificate.

He had got home later that day and called me at the hospital, and I told him how I felt about the situation, and how it wasn't right that he left before signing her birth certificate. "My bad, I am sorry. I just had to go," he said to me. I promise I'm going to come back down there real soon, and I promise I will put my name on her birth certificate," he told me sincerely. "When are you coming?" I asked him. "I don't know yet," he told me. "Why did you leave abruptly like that anyway?" I asked him, concerned. "It was just too much," he said, taking a deep breath. "That was the first time being away from my family since Drew died and seeing you in labor, and all that blood was just a lot. I kept thinking about Drew, and I just needed to be around my family," he told me. "Oh, I understand," I said as I felt bad and understood where he was coming from but still hated the fact that he left. It was hard not having him there with the new baby and me, but there was not anything I could do about it.

I got out of the hospital and came home with Najah. She was so quiet that you would not even have known that there was a baby in the house. She was so cute and so sweet. I would hold her and take pictures of her all day. I would get the film developed and send them to Damian so he could see her. Everything was still pretty old school at the time. He would call every day so she could hear his voice, and when she heard it, she would smile and get so excited. My mom had helped me out a lot since this was my 1st baby. My sisters would always come into the room and play with her, and everything was peaceful. I had gone to sleep one night with Najah next to me in the bed, and I had a dream that felt so real. I was sitting up on the bed holding her in the dream, and Drew had walked through my room door. He was wearing a white t-shirt, some blue jeans and some white sneakers. He had looked exactly how I remembered him. "Ewww," he said, walking through the door smiling. "Ewww, what you doing here?" I said to him as I smiled back. "I didn't come to see you; I came to see my niece," he said as he sat down next to me and was looking at her.

At that point it was March, and his daughter had been born. "You just had a baby too" I told him in the dream. "I know," he said cockily. "I was in the hospital when she was born," he told me as he was smiling and looking at Najah. The house phone rang, and I woke up from the dream. When I opened my eyes, I had chills and goosebumps that stood up on both of my arms. I was asleep when he came but it felt so real. I believe when your loved ones pass away, they do visit you in your dreams. So, when he came, I knew it was really him and I was so grateful that he had paid the baby and me a visit, and I was so happy to know that he was actually there when his daughter was born. It gave me a lot of peace. Of course, I had told Damian and his mom my dream, and they both concurred that, that was him and he came to visit me, and when I told them what happened, it made them smile.

22

Living in peace at my mom's house was short lived when my step dad started up his drama per usual. At that point, he had some girl in the neighborhood pregnant. My mom had put him out, but when she went to work, he would come to our house to take toilet paper and food to take across the street to the girl's house. My mom would be at work, and my sisters were at school, so I would be the only one there. I did not want to confront him at first, because I had my baby there, and I didn't want that drama around her. I had told my mom what he was doing, and she confronted him. "I can do what the f*ck I want to do!" he yelled at my mom and disrespected her, calling her out and her name. The girl looked a mess, yet he was walking around the neighborhood with her. My mom had to see it constantly, not to mention she lived right across from us, so if we looked out the window or sat outside on the balcony, we could see her house, and a lot of times we saw her and my step dad sitting outside. It was disgusting to watch and embarrassing.

My mom was so hurt and ashamed, then he had the nerve to take things out of our house to take it over there. He and the girl were so trifling. He could not even provide anything for her, so he took from us. She was scandalous well because she knew he had a wife and a family right across the street yet, she still messed with him and flaunted him and her belly around the neighborhood. They both were hurtful and selfish and they belonged together. My mom wanted no parts of my stepdad at that point, yet he would not stop coming to our house. Finally, one day I could not take it anymore and I confronted him, and we got into a huge argument, and I told him how I felt and how much I hated him. "I hate you too," he had told me.

He was not even the same person I knew growing up. He was always a piece of work but at least he used to be humble. Now, he was just pure evil. He fought me. He fought my brother. He was disrespectful to my mom. He was a cheater. He had a baby on the way. He was just doing way too much at that point and I was mentally tired of him. He didn't live there so he didn't need to be there, and I expressed that to him. After we got into it, I went into my room and cried. "I hate it here," I said to myself as I held Najah in my arms. I had cried even more because I had felt like I failed her as a mom. I did not want her growing up in the same toxic household that I did. I wanted better for my baby.

I had gone to sleep, and eventually, my mom had come home, and she came into my room. "Shamirah, get up," she told me. "What happened?" she asked me, and I told her all the things he said to me, and how he was taking things from our house while we were struggling and giving it to his pregnant girlfriend. I just knew for sure that my mom would back me up and agree with me that it wasn't right. "Ok," she said, taking a deep breath, and I waited for what she had to say next. I thought my mom was going to say something like she was going to change the locks or get a restraining order or something along those lines, but to my surprise, she did not. "Ok, so you are going to have to leave," she told me. "Me?" I said as I pointed to myself, surprised. "What did I do?" I asked in shock. "Despite whatever is going on, that is still my husband, and you cannot talk to him like that. You being here is causing way too much drama in my house," she told me, looking right in my face. "I am causing the drama?" I asked her, still shocked. "Yes, you are, you and him don't get along, and I am in the middle of it and it is too much," she told me. "But mom, I was taking up for YOU. He got a girl pregnant and was taking things from here and disrespecting you, so I was standing up for you," I told her. "I am a grown woman. I don't need you to fight my battles," she told me in a bold manner.

I was so shocked and confused at that moment. My stepdad was the one doing wrong, yet I got blamed, and I had to leave with my 4-month-old baby at the time. "Mom, so where are I and my baby supposed to go?" I asked her. "I already called your grandmom, and she said you can come there, so you can pack your stuff, and I will drop y'all off today," she told me. My feelings were so hurt; she had already made preparations for me to leave. She always let him get away with everything, and she always took his side. She did it my whole life, so I didn't know why I thought this time would be any different. She had left the room, and I packed up all my and Najah's stuff. I had called Damian crying and told him what had happened. "Wow, that is messed up," he said to me. "Y'all can come and move here," he told me, and I seriously considered it. "Ok, I will see, but for right now, I will go to my grandmom's house to get away from here," I told him, and we hung up. I saw my stepdad outside on the way to the car, and he looked at me with a smile "ha ha bitch" was the expression he had on his face towards me. It was all good though. On the inside, I was happy to get away from that miserable toxic house. On the ride there, I did not talk to my mom; she was so pitiful in my eyes. She was so hurtful, and she never had my back when it came to him.

We had pulled up to my grandmom's house, and she was waiting on the porch with her hands on her hip. She had come to the car and carried the baby in the house while I got my bags. I had grabbed the car seat and bought it in the house, and my mom pulled off. The whole situation was awkward. "Mirah, you ok" my grandmom had asked me, as I sat down on the couch trying to gather my thoughts. My grandmom was my peace. She had such a sweet and caring spirit, so when she asked me, I just started crying. "Aww, its ok," she said to me as she hugged me. "Your mom don't make no sense. She is crazy over him, and she won't come to her senses," my grandmom said, consoling me. "You are here now, and I want you here. I would never see you and my great grand baby on the street. Go ahead to your room and unpack your bags and come and eat," my grandmom told me and that is what I did. It was so peaceful at my grandmom's house, there was no arguing, no fighting, no drama, or stress. My grandmom, my grandpop, my uncle, myself, and Najah lived there. I had my own room and my own space. No one bothered me, and I loved being able to spend time with my grandmom every day. She also loved having Najah there, they all did.

Najah learned to crawl and do so many things while living there. My grandmom would come home from work in the afternoon, and Najah would hear her voice and crawl to her room and my grandmom would have her for hours, which gave me a lot of free time. I would be on the phone with Damian or making my Myspace page or whatever else I wanted to do. Living with my grandmom was great. My grandparents were great people, and I was thankful that they took us in with open arms. Everything was good but I wanted to work towards getting my own place and I needed a job. I had gone back to my old job at Tailgators. I was not pregnant anymore. After I had Najah, I had a cute shape and weight. Before I had her, I was 120lbs. and after I had her, I was 130 lb., and I loved how I looked. The bar was already full of bartenders, so I went back as a waitress, and it was fun. I was not pregnant anymore, so all of the club elements did not bother me. A lot of my regular customers were still there, and everyone showed love. While working there I had lot of guys who approached me and who wanted to take me out. I turned a lot of them down because I still had hopes of getting back with Damian and that we would be a family.

One night I was in the kitchen at my grandmom's house. It was dark the only thing that was on was the light over the stove. I was talking to Damian on the phone. I was having a serious conversation with him about our relationship status. I had talked to him on the phone every single day since Najah was born and even before that. He flirted with me. He gave me hope. He talked about our baby and our future to-gether, so I felt confident enough to have a conversation with him. "So, when are we going to be back together?" I asked him boldly. "Probably never" he said to me. "What you mean?" I asked him. "I'm not trying to get back with you" he said to me which was contradictory to what he had just said a few days before then. I was tired of his games, and I was tired of him taking me up and down emotionally. "Ok, so you are saying that we are never going to be together?" I asked him for confirmation. "Yes,that is what I am saying" he said boldly. The whole time we are having this conversation I am thinking in my head of all the guys I've been turning down for no reason. "Ok well if that is your final answer then that is what it is going to be " I said to him sternly. "Ok" he said cockily. "Ok" I said as well, and I hung up on him.

The next day I went to work at the bar with a whole new attitude. I was single and could do whatever I wanted. So, when guys would ask me for my number, I would give it to them. I was living with my grand-mom, and I didn't have much at all. At the bar I talked to men, and I was given a cell phone and money. I got taken shopping for me and my baby. I went on dates. I was having fun. There was this one particular guy who came in the bar all the time who really liked me. I wasn't really interested in him, but he had money. He tried to talk to me one day and I was not interested. One of my other waitress friends had saw me and whispered to me "girl you better talk to him, he just paid my rent."

At the time my grandpop was picking me up and dropping me off at work. Sometimes I would get off at 4 and 5 o'clock in the morning and I didn't like him to have to come out that late, so I really wanted my own car, so I gave the guy my number and we began to talk. I needed to go to Jersey to go to court and to get my driver's license reinstated so one of my customers paid for my flight and paid my fine. I had come back to GA and went and got my GA license and I was ready to start driving. When I got my License back some of my customers would let me drive their cars, I was a free spirit working at the bar and I had so much fun. Since Damian told me he didn't want to be with me, I had nothing holding me back anymore.

Me and the guy talked for a few weeks and one day we were at the mall shopping, and he had asked me what I wanted. "What do you mean?" I asked him as we ate in the food court. "Whatever you want" he said to me in his accent. He did not know how to speak English well. For my baby, I need a car" I told him. "Car?" he said as he did a driving motion. "Si, a Car" I said to him doing a driving motion as well. "Ok, Ok, I take you this weekend to look at cars" he said to me, and I smiled and held his hand. I had felt really bad for leading him on but at that point that was the only way I was going to get my car. I wanted a new car to get a better job to eventually move out of my grandmom's house. That weekend had come, and we searched so many different lots and I didn't find anything so I was over it. That Sunday he had pulled up to my grandmom's house with a silver car. It was so cute. I had run outside to greet him. "You like?" he asked me smiling. "Yes, I like! You got this for me?" I asked him happily. "Si" he said to me smiling and he gave me the keys and I looked around in the car. "Thank you!" I said to him, and I hugged him.

Since he had drove the car to me, I had to drive him home to his house. I had drove the car for the first time and it rode really well. On the way to his house, he had given me the title and when we pulled up, he had checked under the hood and told me that everything was good. He had invited me into his house and handed me a beer. I did not drink it because I don't drink beer. "Today was good day right" he said to me in his accent smiling. "Si, Si, it was, thank you so much" I said to him as he sat right next to me, and put his arm around me. I had never kissed him or anything. I would just always hold his hand. I was not into him at all. When he had sat next to me, he was really close and wanted to be touchy-feely. I knew since he had bought me the car that he thought I was going to have sex with him.

He was drinking and I stayed for a while, so it didn't seem like I just got the car and dipped. But in my head that was really how it was. I had got what I needed, and I was ready to go. He played good music and was dancing, and we had fun but it was time for me to roll. "I have to go and get my baby" I told him as I stood up with my keys in my hand. "No, no baby stay" he said as he grabbed me by my waist and I was so turned off, nothing inside of me would bring me to want to have sex with him and him being persistent was making me angry. "No, I have to go, I will come back another time" I lied to him.

He saw that we were not going to be affectionate nor have sex or anything so eventually he got the picture and walked me to the car. "Ok, my love, drive safe" he said in his accent as I was sitting down in the driver's seat. "Ok, I will" I said as I smiled. He leaned in the car driving to kiss me and I turned my face, and he kissed my cheek. I had drove off and was relieved to be out of there. He was such sweet guy with a good heart, but he was not for me. He deserved a sweet loving woman who wanted to be with him in a relationship and who could love him. I was not on that type of time, and I was not the woman for him.

I finally had my car, and I was hype. I had taken it to the car wash and went to the Auto store to get seat covers and mats and air fresheners to make the car smell good. It was a nice, and it was clean and it was all mine! I would look out the window and admire my car and I would get in it and drive me and my baby wherever I wanted to go. I had signed the title and got the car in my name, and it was a wrap from there. When I had first got my car, I did not tell Damian for a while.

One day I had talked to him on the phone, and he said he wanted to see the baby. "I can bring her to see you" I said to him not thinking. "How you going to do that? Your grandmom going to let you take her truck? He asked me. "I just got my own car" I said to him. "What? When?" he asked. "I just got it" I said to him even though I had, had my car for about a month. "How did you get a car Shamirah?" he asked me.

"I worked and saved up my tips" I told him. "Hmm, that don't sound right" he scolded me. "Well, it's right. I saved my tips and I got a car" I said trying to get off of the topic. Damian was not stupid, and he was a snooper. He was the type of person that when you told him something, he will investigate it until he gets to the bottom of it. He would ask me about the car, and I would stick to the script that I bought it with my tips. He's the one who said he didn't want to be with me, and I was doing my own thing, so it was none of his business.

I had driven the baby to see him in NC. That was my first time driving out of state by myself and my first time putting that car on the road. I had got my oil changed and I was ready to go on the 4 ½ hour drive. I had my cell phone but I did not have a GPS so I just remembered my grandpop told me it was a straight shot from GA to NC and Damian had told me what exit to get off and to call him when I got to the gas station, and he would come and get me. The only problem was metro didn't have many towers back then so when I came out of GA my phone no longer had reception and I began to panic. I had got lost and it had turned to nighttime. I could not use my phone so when I got to a gas station, I had called him, but no one was answering. I was lost in a whole another state and I was scared. I had got more change and called again from the pay phone and thank God finally someone picked up.

Damian came with his brother and got me and the baby and he drove my car to his house as we saw how shaken up I was. When we got there his dad and brothers were there and everybody got to see the baby for the first time. "What's up sis, can you do my hair for me?" his little brother Khris asked me. "Yeah, I will do it" I said to him as he wanted it cornrowed. At the time, I could not cornrow to save my life. "Khris I will just grease your scalp for you ok" I said to him as he sat there, and I had the grease in my hands. It was too funny, and everyone laughed. I enjoyed being around his family. Me, Damian the baby and his brother Rich had went out to eat at a Chinese buffet. It was so nice to be out with Damian as a family. Najah was normally so good and well behaved. She was about 8 months old at the time. We sat her in the highchair and gave her, her food and she began making a mess and flipping over her plate. It was so embarrassing but comical at the same time. "Stop it" Damian kept saying to her and she would just laugh and keep doing it. When we had left our area looked like a disaster.

I had stayed there a few days and Damian was really cool. He acted like we were a family, and it was nice. I remember us going to the mall in Greensboro and me and him were both so broke. We went to get out the house. We had the baby in her stroller as we walked around window shopping. I remember walking pass all the stores seeing stuff that I wanted but couldn't get. "Don't worry about it, one day I will be able to buy you whatever you want, just like I used to" Damian said to me genuinely. I knew that he meant what he said, and I knew that one day it would happen. He used to spoil me, and at that point life had changed so much but I always knew in my heart that things would get better.

We sat at the food court and shared a slice of pizza between the three of us and I enjoyed every minute of it. I always appreciated the little things in life and always knew that everything would be ok. Of course, we had sex the whole time I was up there. I had enjoyed our visit, but it was soon time to get back to GA. I had gone to see Damian in NC on several different occasions. He saw Najah a lot when she was a baby and had a bond with her and even though we were not in the same state nor were we together, it felt good that he loved our daughter and made sure she knew who he was.

23

I had not seen Damian in about a month or so and there was a huge event in Atlantic City at the Harrah's casino the Pool After Dark, so I had flown back home to NJ for the party. I had stayed at my aunt's house, and I had bought the baby with me. The party was off the hook. The whole city was there and I got a chance to see all my friends and party with them. Everyone was telling me how good I looked and said "I looked ATL thick" Fun and good vibes that night is an understatement. The night was truly epic.

While I was in there having fun and drinking my drink, someone came from behind me and kissed me on my neck. "What the hell" I said as I turned around and to my surprise it was Damian standing there with the biggest Kool aid smile. "What's good?" he said to me as he hugged me. "What are you doing here?" I asked him shocked to see him. "Same thing you are doing here" he said still smiling. "And what you drinking?" he asked as he grabbed my cup and drank some of my henny & coke. "Give me my stuff back" I said as I grabbed it from him smiling. "You look good, don't get none of these niggaz in here f*cked up" he whispered to me in my ear. "Boy please" I said to him as I mushed him. "You heard what I said. I'm watching you" he said to me as he took my drink and walked away with his friends. I stood there and laughed and got another drink and finished partying with my friends.

We all went on the roof top and enjoyed the night sky looking over

the city. I was in my glory. I was back home with all my friends having
a great time and knowing that Damian was there too had made it even
better. I was truly enjoying myself that night and was on cloud 9. After
it was over everyone was leaving and Damian had found me. "Where
you about to go?" I asked him. "Back to my aunt's house to get the baby"
I told him as I was a little tipsy. "Oh, my baby is up here too? I want to
see her" he said to me. "It's like 5o clock in the morning. I'm sure she's
asleep" I told him. "You right, I got a room at Caesars you might as well
slide with me" he said to me. "Ok" I told him, and I let my friends know
that I was leaving with him and we went to Caesars and it was beautiful.
The way it looks inside the lobby is so Cathedral and pretty. We were
drinking on the way there and I was so drunk, we got to the room and
I don't remember much. I know we had sex and had so much fun.

Damian had the room for the weekend and the next day he took
me to my aunt's house and got a chance to spend time with Najah. He
had taken her with him to his friend's house and had her for most of
the day. That night he had come and got me, and we went back to his
room at Caesars. All I remember is walking through the casino floor
with him carrying her in her car seat. It was too funny, and a baby did
not belong in the Casino. We had wanted to go on the floor and have
fun so we took Najah to his mom's house so she could watch her. Since
his brother was shot in her old house. She moved to a new house, and
we took the baby there. "Aww bring me my baby" his mom said as she
smiled from ear to ear when she saw her. She picked her up and held
her and kissed her. "Y'all go ahead and have fun. I got granama baby"
she said making a baby voice. She was so happy to be watching her and
Najah had laid on his mom's arms and went to sleep and we left. We
had played on the Casino floor and enjoyed our night and came back
the next day to get the baby. "Mom, how was she?" Damian asked his
mom. "Oh, she was perfect. She laid on ganamas big arms and slept all
night" she said as she smiled.

We had taken the baby and went back to my aunt's house. I was getting my stuff together because I was catching a flight home the next day. I was walking in the city and the way that I went I had to walk past his mom's old house. When I was walking up, I saw a group of guys. The same group of guys that Damian used to be around. When they saw me walking up of course they all wanted to be nosey. I had Najah in her stroller with a blanket over it to protect her from the wind and air particles. "Oh, what's up" everyone was saying when they saw it was me. "What's up Sis" one of the guys said. "Let me see the baby" he said to me, and I pulled the blanket from off of her stroller uncovering her and they all almost simultaneously said "Damn, she looked just like Damian". "She got his whole face" One of them said. "Yup she looks just like him" I said sassy and then I put the blanket back over here and walked away. My brother Waheed had come to visit me and my aunt's house in the city and he got to see Najah and I enjoyed seeing him and it was time for us to get back on the flight to GA.

When I went to get my suitcase, it was opened and looked like it was rummaged through. I had opened it all the way and noticed my shoes were gone and I had gone into the compartment where I had my jewelry that I had bought with me to take to the jeweler to get fixed. Everything was gone. The bracelets that Damian and his mom had got me, my rings that my mom and his mom had bought me. My earrings everything. The only piece of jewelry that I had left was my xoxo necklace that Damian had got me, and the only reason why I had that was because it was around my neck. All my belongings were stolen, and I was pissed. To this day I don't know who took my stuff, but God knows and I am sure he dealt with the thief accordingly. So that put a damper to an end of an awesome trip. While I was in Jersey Damian was so lovey dovey. He talked about how he changed his mind, and that he did actually want to be a family, and that he wanted to move to GA. While I was there and spending time with him and the baby it made me want to be a family as well.

When I got back to GA, since I had my car, I had wanted to work on getting a place so Damian could move down. Plus, as much as I loved my grandparents, I was ready for a place of my own. Even though me and Damian had got on good terms and were trying to make plans to become a family. I still had a life of my own in GA. I was still working at the bar waitressing.

It was a slow Monday night and there was this guy sitting at one of the tables by the door. He was sitting there drinking a bottle of Remi Martin by himself. I had looked at him and saw him drinking liquor that he didn't buy at the bar, but I didn't say anything to him about it, plus he was not in my section. I had continued to wait my tables minding my business when I turned around and the guy was standing right behind me. "What's up cutie" he said to me smiling confidently and I immediately picked up on his up-North accent. "Nothing, excuse me" I said, brushing him off and trying to get past him because he was in my way. "Ok, but can I get your number before I go" he asked me confidently. I had looked at him up and down and out of nowhere I said "Maybe on Thursday" I said trying to be smart. "Ok cool" he said, still smiling, and he grabbed his coat and his Remy bottle, and he left. When he left, I did not think anything of it. Guys had tried to talk to me all the time and most of the time, I had blown them off.

I was at work a few days later on a Thursday night and it was a little busy. To my surprise I saw the guy walk through the door and he had come in and sat in my section this time. I walked over and gave him a menu "Let me know when you are ready to order" I said to him. "Today is Thursday, right?" he asked me, smiling. "Yeah" I said, looking at him crazy. "I asked you for your number, and you told me maybe on Thursday. Today is Thursday so I'm here to get that number" he said smiling. He had caught me totally off guard and all I could do was laugh. "Omg you remembered that? " I said to him as I smiled.

"Yeah, I remembered. I will always remember when it is something that means something to me" he said to me. "Sit down" he said as he pulled out a chair, coaxing me to sit. "I am working, I can't sit with you long" I told him as I sat down. "How much do you think you would make tonight?" he asked me. "I don't know, it's not that busy so maybe about $200" I said to him, and we went in his pocket and handed me two $100 bills and put it in my apron. "Ok, now you good" he said to me, smiling. "Thank you, you didn't have to do that" I told him. "I know, I wanted to. You good. I like you." he told me boldly. "Oh Ok" I said to him, a little intrigued by persistency. "I know you have to get back to work so I am not going to hold you, can I get your number now?" he asked as he was about to leave. I gave it to him, and he had put it in his phone and gave me a hug and left.

When he left, I was thrown off in a good way. His presence and demeanor were bomb. I was also low key flattered that he had remembered that I had said Thursday. I had no intentions on giving him my number, but it was really nice that he actually came back. His approach was super sweet. He had a crush on me and that was cute.

I had finished working the rest of the night and when I got off to my surprise, he had called me to check on me, and we had talked for hours. We had so much in common. We had laughed so much throughout the conversation. He had told me where he was from and a little about his life and why he came to GA. I had dug him and the more I talked to him, the closer we got. After that we had talked every day and we hung out a lot. He was so sweet and caring and always trying to help me. We had become really close friends. He had really liked me and wanted to be with me, but I was not ready to be in a relationship with a new person.

He had come to pick me up one day and took me to a car lot to get this infinity he wanted me to have. "I already have a car, " I told him as we walked around the lot. "Nah, you need something better" he said, trying to persuade me. "But my car I don't have payments" I told him. "Don't worry about the payments, I got you" he told me. As much as I liked the car, I did not want to have a car note, and I appreciated him for offering to finance and pay for it. But we had only known each other for a short while and that was too big of a gift for me to take from him, so I declined.

He also knew I wanted a better job than the one I had waitressing. I wanted something stable so that I could get an apartment for me and my daughter. He had offered to pay for me to take CNA classes so I could get a job at a hospital or nursing home until I found something better. At the time I did not want to do CNA work, so I didn't take the classes even though he always tried to talk me into it. I did eventually find a job in the Mental Health field working for the state. He was very happy for me and proud of me. He had asked me did I want to go on a cruise to the Bahamas and I said yes, and I was super excited, and we had made plans on going, but something came up, and we never made the cruise. The more I was around him, the more I liked him. He was someone I saw myself falling in love with, but of course Damian was still in the picture calling, and making his presence known.

It was November when I started my new job and the holidays were approaching. I was still living at my grandmom's house, and they didn't celebrate Christmas or anything due to their religion. So even though I had a baby I was not able to do all the fun holiday stuff with her at home which made me a little sad. I would always talk My friend about it and he said he would help me get a place. I was upfront with my friend and told him about Damian and how we may get back together, and it was a possibility that he was going to move to GA and we would be a family with our daughter. He would listen, but he wasn't feeling the idea, and he wanted Us to be together.

Our relationship had grown a lot, and we spent a lot of time together. Although I did like him a lot and had the biggest crush on him. I was not ready to abandon the idea of not being a family with Damian and Najah. My friend was around her and he really liked her, and she took to him well. He always showed love and he accepted being in her life with open arms. But at the end of the day, he was not her dad. Plus, the fact that he didn't have kids of his own, and I was not going to put that responsibility on him. Even though he didn't mind at all.

At that point I was torn between the two. I think I had loved two people. I loved how my friend made me feel and the type of person he was. I loved his energy and his spirit. I loved Damian because we had history and now that we had a daughter. I fell in love with the idea of having a family. I did not know what to do. I had talked to my friend about it and was upfront about everything. The advice he gave me was to do whatever was in my heart but either way, he would always be there. That had meant a lot, but I knew in reality if I chose Damian, that he could not be there because Damian was not having that. He was super territorial and possessive and that was not even an option to keep open communication with my friend if I was with Damian.

I had begun working and saved up my checks. By now it was January. Najah turned one on January 11th, 2008, and I had a small Happy Birthday for her at my grandmom's house. It was so cute, and she looked so adorable. Shortly before her birthday she had walked, and it was so exciting. I worked Monday-Thursday 10-hour shifts and was off Friday, Saturday and Sunday at my job, so that Saturday I had a birthday party for her at Chuck E Cheese with all my family and cousins. It was so much fun. My baby was growing, and we were building memories. The only sad part was that Damian was not there for any of it. Him being in another state was hard. We had talked all the time over the phone, but it was not the same as him being there in person.

The next month which was February. I had gone to apply for an apartment, and I was approved. I was so happy to finally be getting my own place. The blessings were pouring in at that point. The apartment was prorated, and I got my first two months free. My friend had paid to get the electric and cable turned on and it was time to move in. I was so excited. I had bought furniture off of my aunt and people at my job had blessed me with so many housewarming gifts, so I was at a great start going into my new place.

I had talked to Damian and told him I had the place. He was in Jersey visiting at the time and he said he would be down in GA to live in a few days. At that time, I was still in contact with my friend. He had given me money and told me to get whatever I needed. Also, as I was moving out of my grandmom's house as I was packing up my shoes, I had totally forgotten that I had a stash of tips in one of my shoes and I counted it and it was $800 even. God was just sending me blessings upon blessings. I was in a good place and space in life. I had a good job. I had a car. I had my apartment, me and my baby were healthy and thriving. Life was great.

My friend had known that Damian knew about the apartment and that he had made plans to move down. "I got you forever, you definitely a real one" my friend had told me. "Ok, that's cool, I'm just trying to figure everything out with my baby dad right now" I had told him. "I can def dig it. I would prefer you move on with me, but it's all good" he told me in his cocky and confident voice. I knew Damian was coming so I had never invited my friend to see the apartment. I was in my place by myself with Najah for about four days and my friend had called me and told me he had to go out of town and that he would hit me when he got back. I told him ok and to have a safe trip. I was a little relieved that he was gone because even though he was respectful. I just didn't want to take the chance of him calling me or popping up in my neighborhood. Once he left, I totally focused on Damian coming.

One night I was in my apartment, and I was trying to put the glass on the wall unit in the Livingroom by myself. It was so heavy that I winded up dropping it and it shattered all over the rug. There was glass everywhere. Me being in the house by myself I didn't know what to do. I didn't have a vacuum yet so I went to ask my neighbors if I could borrow theirs and of course they said no. I was so frustrated that I had called Damian crying. "What is the matter with you?" he asked me concerned. "I dropped the glass and it shattered everywhere and I have no way to clean it up and I don't want Najah to get cut by glass because it's all over the place" I cried to him. "Everything will be ok, just get a broom and sweep it up. When I come, I will get a vacuum cleaner, and keep Najah in the room to be safe" he told me and we hung up. My common sense should have told me to sweep up the glass, as well as I had more than enough money to get a vacuum. I was just alone, and I wanted support. Damian nor my friend was there. I was no longer at my grandmom's house. I was on my own and had to figure it out and I was not use to that. I was just ready for Damian to come to be there with me and Najah.

My apartment was set up cute and my house was clean, and it smelled so good. Najah had her own room that was decorated with Dora the Explorer. I would cook for me and her and we would spend time but being in the apartment by ourselves was lonely. Finally, after about a week later, Damian had moved down to GA. He had caught the bus from NC to Atlanta, and me and a girl friend of mine had gone to pick him up from the bus station. When we had pulled up the bus had not come yet, and we sat there and waited. I had butterflies in my stomach. Before that point I had not seen him in months. When the bus came, I saw him get off with his big duffle bag wrapped around him and I got out the car and ran to him and hugged him. He had hugged me back and he was smiling from ear to ear. "You are finally here!" I said to him as we got in the car. I had introduced him to my girlfriend. "I finally get to see who she been talking about all this time, " she said to him as she greeted him. "Word, word" Damian responded as he smiled.

We had drove off and he was sitting in the backseat. I saw him take off his hat and durag in the rear-view mirror and I had looked away for a split second. "Look" he said to me smiling and when I turned around, he had had his hair cut. For as long as I was with Damian, he had cornrows. I always told him he would look cute with a low haircut with waves, and he always told me that one day he would do it. "Oh my God, you cut your hair!" I said to him shocked because I had never seen him with a low cut before. "Yeah, I did it for you, I wanted a new look for my new start in life" he told me as he smiled. He looked really handsome. His hair was jet black and his waves were spinning. It looked just like I imagined it would. I turned around to touch his hair as I rubbed his head. "Very nice, you look really cute. I like it, " I told him.

We had pulled up to our apartment. "Home sweet Home" I said to him as he grabbed his bag, and we thanked my friend for the ride, and we got out. We lived on the second floor, so we walked upstairs and I opened the door with the key and showed him around. "I like it" he said, smiling as he looked around. I had taken his bag and sat in the closet, and we sat down on the couch to catch up. "So, you are finally here, how do you feel?" I asked him. "I'm good, I'm good" he said as he was trying to take it all in. Najah had been with my grandmom for the day so she had dropped her off to me. Damian had gone downstairs to the car to get her and said hi to my grandparents and they welcomed him with open arms. I was on the balcony watching them and Najah was so happy to see her dad.

She was one but she knew who her dad was. They came back into the house and Damian played with her. "Dada is here now" he told her as he hugged her, and she hugged him back. "I'm glad you are here" I told him. "Me too" he said. "So, as you know, I work Mon-Thursday 6am-9pm and then from 1pm-7pm. I know my shift is long but at least I have Friday, Saturday and Sunday off" I told him. "Word" he said to me. "So, since you are not working yet, Najah will stay here with you while I go to work" I told him. Before he came, we talked about him watching her. Najah was in daycare but I preferred her to be around family so we talked about him keeping her and that would also illuminate the daycare bill which was expensive. "Ok cool" he had said to me, and he finished spending time with her.

Damian had moved in on my days off so over the next few days life was great. Me and him talked about our plans and we vibed. It was our first place together, so I cooked and made breakfast and dinner every night. At the time I was not the best cook, but I did my best and we ate dinner as a family, and it was nice. It had been a while since we had been together, so we would put Najah to bed in her room and I would put on my sexy pajamas every night and we would watch movies and have the nastiest sex. We had sex everywhere in the house. We just could not get enough. We did so many different positions and when we were done, we would do it again. It was nice and we both were on cloud nine. Monday had come and it was time for me to go back to work. I had to be there at 6am so I normally left the house at about 5:20-5:30 am and most mornings it was cold and dark.

My alarm had gone off and I got up and left Najah with Damian and went to work. Something was wrong with Damian's phone, so I was not able to call him to check on them throughout the day. When I got home from work the house was a mess with toys everywhere. Najah's high chair had oodles and noodles all over it and everything was just out of order. "Here take her" Damian said as soon as I came through the door. "I just walked in. I didn't even get to sit down yet from being at work all day, and why does the house look like this?" I asked him, annoyed. "I had a long day watching her. I can't use my phone and she cried every time I tried to step on the porch to smoke a mild" I need a break too" he said as he clamped his mild to go and smoke. "Well Damian, you can't just let her trash the house" I told him as I started cleaning up.

He had gone on the porch to smoke, and I noticed Najah's diaper was wet. "Did you change her? I asked him as I opened the sliding door to talk to him. "Yeah, I've been changing her all day" he told me as he pushed the sliding door closed to not get smoke in the house. After he closed the door, I went to change her and clean up and I was so annoyed while doing it. "Damian, if you are going to watch her, I can't come home to this every time. I am gone from the house from 5am and don't get home until close to 8pm. My days are long and if you are going to help, then help " I said to him as I went to run Najah's bath water to get her ready for bed. "This is a lot, and I'm not used to this," he told me. "I understand, but being a parent is a lot, you are just going to have to adjust. You didn't have to deal with none of this for a whole year, but you are here now" I told him frustrated. "Ok, tomorrow is another day. We will see what happens' ' he reassured me.

I gave Najah a bath and got her ready for bed and I took a shower and got my clothes out to get ready for bed. Damian wanted to stay up and chill and have sex, but I had to explain to him that I was on a routine on my work days. I had to be up early so I could not just sit up all night and have sex. He was still thinking of us as the Old Us. The old Us could party all the time and stay up late and do whatever we wanted. We had no real responsibility. We were just living life. We now had a baby. I had a year to adjust to being a mom while he was in NC and Jersey doing whatever he wanted to do. I had a child a job and a routine so my life was structured and he needed to fall in line and understand everything was not all about fun all the time. We had a child and real bills and needed to deal with real life.

The next day I had went to work and since he could not use his phone the day before. I had decided to leave my cell phone because I knew I could call them from my work phone. While I was at work, I got a call from Damian, and he was angry. "What's wrong" I asked him. "I just answered your phone, and it was some nigga on the line" he said to me and told me the number and I knew exactly who it was. It was my friend. I was angry because I had already told my friend the situation and I had already told him not to call me and that I would call him, and it was for that very reason. I knew if he called and Damian found out, he would be furious. Damian was not the type of guy who let things slide. He was the type to investigate until he got to the bottom of it, and he wasn't going to let up until he did.

Even though we were not in a relationship when I was dating my friend, I still did not want Damian to know about it. He was super possessive, and I did not want the drama. Nor did I want Damian to know about him because I did not want to mess up our chances of getting back together. "I don't know who it was, maybe it was the wrong number" I told him. "That wasn't no f*ckin wrong number" he scolded me. "I know you was down here talking to niggas, and you got niggas calling your phone. I'm here now all of that shit is a wrap" he scolded me again. I was on the other end of the phone not knowing what to say. As Damian was talking, I was getting heated on the inside, because my friend defied me and called me when I specifically asked him not too. I felt like a little kid, and he got me in trouble.

When I got off the phone with Damian, I had immediately called my friend. "Hello" he answered. "Yo why the hell would you do that?" I yelled at him. "Do what?" he asked me. "Why would you call my phone when I told you my baby dad was here and not to call me because it would start drama" I scolded him. "Ayo my bad, I had forgot" he said. "Well, you can't be forgetting stuff like that, now I'm in some sh*t" I told him. "Damn he got you scared like that?" he asked me. "It's not about me being scared. This is somebody I have been with for a long time, and we don't rock like that. It's no way, he would be cool with me talking to you. Now that you called, he got his radars up, so at this point we can't even kick it anymore" I told him. "Word, it's like that? He said to me shocked. "You made it like that. I told you don't call me, and I was going to handle it, now you messed it all up" I told him. "My bad, I won't call anymore" he said, "It's too late, it's a wrap. We can't even kick it no more" I had told him, and I hung up. It hurt my heart to have to talk to him like that. He had never seen that side of me, and he didn't deserve to be treated like that, but he didn't have to deal with the consequences I did, and I knew him calling was not going to blow over easily.

"Ok let's stop there" the therapist said to me as she uncrossed her legs and sat up in the chair. "It seems like you were a little conflicted and didn't know who you particularly wanted to be in a relationship with, is that correct?" she asked me. "Well, I knew I wanted to be with Damian so my daughter would have her mom and dad together. But also had feelings for my friend and as well. I felt myself loving him more and more. I knew as time went on, we would get closer and closer, and I did not know what the future held for us and that was a little scary for me. I did love Damian. If we did not try, I would have always wondered what the future would have been like" I told her.

"Yes, I do understand that, but also it seems like you wanted to continue a relationship with the other guy but you had to cut it off so Damian would not find out, so it just seems like you were forced to let that relationship go and it is not something that you wanted to do, but you had to do. Is that correct? She asked me. "Yes and no, I did not want to sneak around Damian's back and be deceitful so I knew I would have to make a choice and I chose him because he was my daughter's dad. If we did not have a daughter together. I may have chosen the other guy because he seemed better for me personally. But I wanted my daughter to have a family so I put all of that aside so she can have the best upbringing as possible with her mother and father" I told her. "Ok, so how did it make you feel to make that decision?" she asked me.

"It made me feel bad because my friend was a good person. I wish we had met at a different time in life and maybe things would have turned out differently. But no matter how much I tried I was not over Damian. When it came to anyone no matter how good they were to me, I would choose him every time" I told her. "Ok, I understand. Please proceed with the story" she said, sitting back in her chair and crossing her legs.

Damian watched Najah for a couple more days and at the end of my work week he decided that having her all day was too much. "I thought you came down here to help me with her and now you are telling me you don't want to watch her" I said very upset with him. Having her all day I cannot move around. I need to get my bread up and I can't do that sitting in the house all day" he told me, upset. "I don't know how you expect me to go to work then" I said to him. "You have your mom and all your family here; you are going to have to figure it out" he said to me cold heartedly. I was not expecting him to act that way.

Damian could be rude, but this was our first time interacting as parents. I did not think he would give me a hard time about watching his own daughter while I worked. I had asked my mom to watch her, and she agreed. Thankfully my mom lived close to my job, and it was super convenient. The only thing was that I had to get her up with me super early in the morning and we would get home late. I would have to get her ready for bed to do it all over again. I had felt like she should have been home with her dad and on a routine. Instead, she was at my mom's house all day from 6am -7pm every day. Thankfully my mom and sisters were a big help, so I knew she was safe all day and she ate and was taken care of, so that gave me a piece of mind while I was working.

Although everything had worked out, it had still made me angry and resentful towards Damian, because he would be home all day doing whatever he wanted and I felt like he should have been helping out more with our daughter. We had begun getting into a lot of arguments and they would get worse and worse. He would always bring up me talking to guys when we were apart and accuse me of things that I was not doing. He would control what I wore and where I went. He clearly didn't trust me, and it was causing so much strife between us. Also, on my end I was annoyed because I felt like my life was peaceful before he came and I could do what I wanted to do, and since he was there now, he was smothering me. When Damian first moved down, I had missed my friend a lot and wondered if I had made a mistake. Damian would always ask me questions to try and trip me up into telling him things. He was very manipulative and was always fishing for information and once he got it, he would get upset and want to argue about it.

One day I was on the computer in the nook area we had in the apartment. I was minding my own business. Damian came in with bad energy and I knew it was about to be something. Out of nowhere he began asking me about my car and where I got it, when I already told him that I saved up my tips and bought it. He was not trying to hear it and he kept antagonizing me about it. "I know a nigga bought you that car, just admit it" he kept taunting me. I was on the computer trying to not feed into him, but he began pissing me off. I got up from the computer and began to walk to my room to get away from him. When I got up, he was standing in my face saying "Just say it, I won't be mad, just keep it real" he kept repeating. "Ok, ok a guy bought it" I blurted out so he could shut up, and before I could blink, I saw his hand coming at my face and he had punched me so hard in the mouth that I had spun around and fell to the ground. He did not use all this strength because all my teeth would have been knocked out, but it was still very painful. "I was in shock but most of all I was making sure that he didn't knock any of my teeth out.

I sat there crying asking him why he did that and he stood over me with anger all over his face. "I knew it, " he said to me proud that he finally got it out of me. "You a fuckin whore" he said to me still standing over me. My face had hurt so bad that I did not want to talk, but I kept saying "I am not a whore. I did not have sex with him" and I was telling the truth because I didn't. Damian was furious and he did not help me up. He just paraded the apartment ranting and raving about how much of a liar I was. My feelings were hurt. On top of that was the first time he had ever hit me in life. When we were in Jersey, we had our ups and downs, but we did not call each other names nor disrespect each other. Once he came to GA and we lived together we had started crossing boundaries and once those boundaries get crossed it is hard to recover from them, and the dynamic of the relationship changed in a horrible way. We were going through a lot, and it seems like the arguments never ended. Thankfully his mom would call us and talk to us individually and she would talk to him privately. It seems like when she talked to him, he would listen, and things would be ok for a while and then the drama would start again.

One-night Damian was about to go out to the club and a good friend of his came over to pick him up and he came in and they had a few drinks. Me and Damian had a disagreement and it got heated. We were all in the living room as me and him were arguing. "Chill yo" Damian kept yelling at me and I kept talking so he grabbed me by the shirt and pulled me in the room dragging me. I was screaming and punching him and when we got in the room, and he let me go. I had thrown something at him, and it missed hitting the wall. There was a lot of loud thumping and commotion going and Damian's friend was calling his name for him to come out of the room.

He was trying to get out, but I was grabbing him by the shirt, hitting him and screaming. "C'mon bro, let's get out of here before she calls the cops," his friend was yelling. His friend grabbed all of Damian's belonging and was helping him get out of the door. "Hurry up bro, let's go" his friend said as they hurried up and left. I was pissed off that Damian had embarrassed me like that. I had called his phone, but he did not answer so I began to text him. I had texted him mean things for hours and my texts were paragraphs long. Finally, I went to bed. He came home about 4am and he was drunk and he got in the bed and laid next to me and cuddled me. "You know I love you right?" he whispered in my ear. I was half asleep, so I did not answer him and next thing you know he was pulling my panties down and we were having sex.

We did this cycle over and over again. Argue have sex. Argue have sex. He would be mean, then come back to me with a whole speech about how much he loved me and just wanted us to get right. I would listen to him, and things would be ok for a while and then it would go back to being toxic. It was a vicious cycle. With all that was going on, I wanted to get closer to God, so I began going to church again. I would get up on Sundays and get dressed and me and Najah would go.

24

One Sunday I had come into church during praise and worship. When I went into the doors, I saw a man standing in the front singing and waving his hands and I could only see the back of him. Me and Najah had sat down, and the guy looked familiar to me. He looked like my step dad, but I wasn't sure because I had not seen him in church before that day. The church I was attending was the one my mom and him went to in the past. I started trying to get a good look at him and when he turned his face, I saw him from the side, and I knew for sure that it was him. Once it was confirmed that it was him, immediately my spirit said "Go up there." I was so nervous and I did not want to, but my spirit kept pushing me and I knew I had to go.

I left Najah in the chair and I walked up to the front of the church to the altar, and I touched him on his back. He turned around and saw that it was me and he immediately began to cry and hug me. "I'm sorry" he said as he was crying, and I knew he was genuine. "I'm sorry too" I said as I was crying as well. The spirit was flowing, and you could feel the peace and forgiveness flowing through our bodies. The Pastor and his wife and the rest of the church noticed as well, and the Pastor and his wife came and prayed over us and the whole church lifted their hands towards us in prayer. It was beautiful and it was a moment of much needed forgiveness and healing. After church he asked me for a ride to where he was staying because he no longer had lived with my mom. I had pulled up to where he lived and gave him a hug and we said bye and I pulled off and went home.

A couple of days later my mom had called me and told me that he had been locked up for robbing a gas station with a fake gun. He had gone to jail and fought the case for over a year, and he finally was found guilty and was sentenced to fifteen years for armed robbery. The courts didn't care that the gun was fake, they still threw the book at him. He was in jail for a total of three years and one day my mom had called me about 5am in the morning crying. "He died" she said as she said his name and I will never forget the feeling that went through my body. I was so sad, and I could not believe it. I did not know the words of comfort to say to my mom. I had gone over to her house in the morning to stay with her as some of the family came down to be with her.

It was a very sad time. He had a small funeral and burial, but I did not go. I do not take death well and I wanted to remember him how I last saw him. Happy, Peaceful worshipping and serving the Lord. Neither one of us knew that would be our last time ever seeing each other. But God knew, and I am grateful that he gave us the opportunity to say we were sorry and to forgive each other. That was a blessing from God.

Of all of the bad things that my stepdad did in life, what I knew for sure was despite everything, that he loved God. He struggled with addiction from whatever pain he had endured in life. None of us are perfect and we all face trials and tribulations. DMX was his favorite rapper because he could relate in so many ways. What I chose to remember about him is that yes, he was a flawed human like many of us. But more importantly he was a prayer warrior and had a heart for God. I pray that God has forgiven him of all of his sins, and that he is finally able to rest from the hardships of life. I know he loved God and God loved him and I am sure he is enjoying the blissfulness of heaven.

25

At the time, I was working, but I was also an author as well. On Feb 14, 2008, I published my first book "Ny Street Religion." When the book came out, I was living in GA and went hard in the Atlanta area selling my books hand to hand. I remember driving around with a box full of books and going up to people and selling them or dropping them off to people who wanted them. I had received so much love and support in the streets, and it gave me so much confidence, on top of the fact that my book was getting awesome feedback and the readers loved it. I had met with a girl from Clark Atlanta who was a part of a book club there, and she and her group members read it, and we had a book meeting downtown. These women were studying to be doctors and lawyers and were very intelligent, so it was an honor for them to be featuring me in their book club, and personally inviting me to the venue to talk about the book. They asked questions and gave me their feedback. The experience was great, and I had a good time.

Soon after, I was a part of a social media club that I cannot remember the name of. But they were so supportive. The owner of the site had promoted my books, and I received so much love. He even threw me a book signing party at a Venue in Norcross, GA, and it was set up so nice. There was a whole table with my books on it for me to sign. I sat there and signed them and took pictures as people purchased them. The vibe was awesome, and the experience was unmatched. There was a DJ there and the turnout was great. I could not believe that all those people had come out to support me. I really felt like a celebrity, and I am thankful for the experience. I had taken lots of pictures that night for memories but unfortunately when my daughter Najah was little, she was playing with my camera and she accidentally deleted all the pictures which was devastating to me.

All the memories from that night were gone. On top of the fact that. I was with a self-publishing company, and they told me the agreement was I got 90% royalty and they would get 10%. I was selling books on Amazon, Barnes and Noble. As well as schools and libraries were ordering them, so I just knew for sure that my royalties would be awesome. I figured that I would for sure be getting a nice royalty check. When the company sent my check, I was sick to my stomach. It was $100. I almost flipped my lid. I called them extremely upset and they made up some bogus excuse as to where all my money was. Come to find out, the royalties with them in that quarter was close to $9000 and they kept it all yet sent me $100. I was so discouraged and heartbroken, so much so that I did not want to sell another book under that company, so I pulled my book and went a different route. I self-published under CreateSpace at the time, got a new ISBN # and solely sold my books on Amazon. I had been burned by the other company and I did not want to lose any more money as I was putting in hard work.

My mom was my manager at the time, and she booked me a "Book" tour back home in NJ. I had a whole itinerary. I did a book signing at the soldier's home in Atlantic City. I did a book signing at the Borders at the Hamilton Mall in Mays Landing. I had a book signing at Urban books in Pleasantville NJ. I had a book signing at a club in Philly and a lounge in Camden. I received a lot of love. Once I got back to GA, I kept getting feedback and people were constantly asking me questions about the book, and they wanted more. At that point, I knew I had to write a part two to the book that would answer all the readers' questions. In 2009 I had published "Queen Religion" which was part 2 of "Ny Street Religion. Both "Ny" Street Religion and "Queen" Street Religion can be purchased on Amazon.

I was in the process of beginning to promote part 2, so I had reached out to Atlanta's station V103 to try to get on the show to promote my books. Talking to the show's producer was very discouraging. I told her I wanted to see how I could go about getting on the show, and she told me that to get on my book had to be "Relevant." Her words were very hurtful, and she made me feel so low like me, and my books were nothing. I know they were used to dealing with celebrities, and I was not one at the time, but she should have used a better choice of words. Words are powerful, and when there is a young entrepreneur or anyone with a dream, one of the easiest ways to kill their dream and their spirit is to tell them that they are not relevant. That is exactly what her words did to me. They killed my spirit. I was so hurt that I reached out to the show's hosts at the time Frank and Wanda, and they were very apologetic. Wanda had very kind and encouraging words for me, as well as so did Frank and he even gave me an address to send my book to him which I appreciated.

It was so funny because a week later me and a couple of friends went to Suite lounge for a "Mars VS Venus battle. Hosted by Frank Ski and the show's producer who hurt my feelings. I was one of the contestants chosen and the DJ called my name and I walked on stage. Frank Ski and the producer looked like they seen a ghost when they see me. I waved to them when I walked past them and said "Yes it's me" because I knew they were thinking "is this the same girl who has been reaching out to us over the past week". I went on stage and did the battle and had a great time and I was over all the drama with the producer, and I enjoyed my night and put it all behind me.

26

Meanwhile, at home Damian and I were still at each other's throats, and things were getting worse. We were still arguing all the time, and tensions were high. Before him moving down to GA, we would have disagreements, but we never just flat out disrespected each other as we did once we moved together. One day we were arguing, and he called me a "Bitch" for the first time ever. I was in such shock that anger came all over me. I began throwing all types of things at him. We had a glass wall unit, and we had a cute picture in there that we took in the mall when we first got together. The picture was in a gold and black glass frame that had "Forever" on it. I loved that picture of us. I was so angry I had grabbed it and threw it at him. He was by the door and he moved, and the glass had shattered everywhere. "Look what you did," he said in shock. You throwing sh*t now, you buggin," he said to me in disappointment, and he began cleaning it up. It was silent at the point as the glass was literally all over the living room. Thankfully Najah was not there; she was at my grand mom's house spending time with her.

After Damian cleaned up the mess, he had left to get a breather because the air was so thick. That was the first time I had gotten so angry with him that I began breaking things, but it was not the last. After that, when we would get into arguments, I would get so enraged that I would throw, knock over or break anything that was in my sight. It was a very toxic thing for me to do, but I would be so upset that breaking things felt like a release for me. He and I were both toxic. It was a sad and horrible way to be.

The energy in the apartment was so bad and dark. I always felt like someone was watching us, especially in the hallway in the back where Najah's room was. Her room was set up so cute with her bed and all her Dora the explorer decor. She would play in the room in the daytime and watch tv and everything, but at night I did not like her to sleep in there by herself. Her room and my room were pretty far apart, and I didn't want to leave her back there by herself, so she slept in our room with us. A lot of times, Damian was not home, so it was just her and me there. I hated being in the living room by myself because of the energy coming from the hallway, so when he was not home, I spent a lot of time in my room.

One night I was in my room in my bed, and I had my door open, and it was dark in the living room and kitchen. I had heard a noise that sounded like two pots had clicked in the cabinet, which would have been impossible for them to do unless someone picked them up and did it. That threw me off and scared me, so I didn't want to get up and close the door. Where my bed was in the room, there was a wall where the bathroom was, and it blocked you from seeing the room door, so I could not look out into the living room, but I could hear. Najah was in the room with me, so I turned the tv up and tried to ignore what I had just heard; then, a few minutes later, it sounded like someone had thrown something in the trash can. Because I heard the lid move. At that point, I had chills and couldn't take it anymore, so I got up and hurried up and ran to close the door and got back in the bed. After that point, I always kept my door closed when I was in my room at night. I would leave the light on over the stove, but I still hated when I forgot something and had to open my door to go back out there. If Damian was home, I would tell him to get it, or when he wasn't there, I would hurry up and run out there and run back to my room.

One night I got off of work I was so tired. All I wanted to do was come in the house and take a shower and go to bed. It was about 9 pm. I had Najah with me, and she was sleeping, so I was carrying her in my arms. When I got to the door, I went to open it, and it would not open. I had tried and tried, but nothing was happening. I was in shock, so I had called maintenance to come and open it, but it was after hours, so I had to leave a message and wait for them to get back to me. In the meantime, it was cold, I was tired, and my arms were hurting from holding Najah. She had woken up and was sitting on the steps as I tried to get in.

It was mind-boggling to me because the only way that the door would not open was as if someone had locked the bolt lock. The only way our bolt lock locked was from the inside, meaning someone had to lock in from the inside, and no one was home. Damian was out of town, and no one was in the apartment. By then, it was 10 pm, and maintenance had not called, and I was getting restless. I had seen a couple of young guys in the neighborhood and asked them if they could climb on my balcony and open the door for me. I didn't tell them, but even when we locked our balcony, if we pushed it real hard, it would pop the lock.

Normally we had a broom there for extra security but thank God that night I did not have the broom keeping the sliding door closed. I lived on the second floor, and the boy's friend gave him a boost, and he got in my house and opened the door for me, and sure enough, he told me the top bolt lock was locked, and an eerie feeling came all over my body. I didn't even want me or Najah to go in the house, and I began to pray. "Lord, if there are any spirits in here, I rebuke them, and they have to leave now," I said as I came into the house, trying to take authority even though I was scared. Najah and I came in, and I turned on all the lights and went to her room to get her clothes for her bath and hurried up and went to my room and closed the door.

I had a bathroom in my room, so I gave her a bath and took a shower, and we both went to bed. I had called Damian while he was in NJ and told him what had happened, and he was tripped out too. All I kept thinking was, "there has to be a ghost in this house who locked the door" there was no other logical explanation for that to happen. Every night I came home that week, I was scared that the same thing would happen, so I made sure I did not put the broom on the door to keep it closed at night just in case I needed to get back in. But then I worried all day because the boys knew how to climb on my balcony and get in my house. Damian was barely ever home, so I could not depend on him to keep us safe.

Even though we were in a relationship a lot of times, I felt like a single mom. He was always out of town in Jersey, and when he was home in GA, he still never wanted to watch Najah while I worked or ran errands. No matter what I had to do, whether it was handling business or just needing leisure time to myself, his signature phrase was "take Najah with you," and even if he was sitting right there in the house, I had to get Najah dressed and lug her with me everywhere I went, rain sleet or snow, it did not matter to him, and the fact that he did that made me angry. He was a parent as well, but he always put all the responsibility of having a child on me, and that was frustrating to me and made me feel a lot of resentment towards him. Thank God for my family and my cousins Will and Quanie. Najah spent a lot of time at their house with her older cousin, their daughter. My grandmom also kept Najah a lot and took her to church with her on Saturdays, which gave me a break, and I appreciated it. A lot of times, when Najah stayed with my grandmom, Damian and I would hang out and go to dinner or the club. We used that time as US time, even though he always had a break, and I didn't.

Even though we fought a lot, we still had happy and fun moments. We would get dressed and go out all the time. We would get sections and go clubbing downtown, or we would kick it at a lounge close to us where we lived. Where we lived was full of spots, and we used to have a lot of fun. He would take me to nice places to eat with great ambiances. When we were not at odds, Damian could be so sweet and super romantic. He always knew how to charm me, and even though I would be mad at him, I would get a glimpse of the old him, and it made me fall in love with him all over again. He knew how to make me feel comfortable and safe with him. He knew how to make me laugh and smile. He always got me flowers and did sweet things for me. That was the Damian that I knew and loved. On the flip side, he could be a monster. Mean and ruthless with his words and the same lips that built me up and put me on a pedestal were the same lips that would curse me and tear me down to the point my self-esteem was torn.

When Damian would be mean towards me, I would get sad and feel anxious. I would shut down a lot and walk around with my head down, and he could tell that his actions were bothering me. So, when he had enough of mentally torturing me, and he saw that I was breaking, that is when he would flip it and start trying to be nice. He would buy me things and be flirtatious, and the biggest thing that he did was always come to me and ask me to talk. He would sit me down, and most times he would make us drinks. He made very good cocktails, and he would set the mood, whether it was dimming the lights and lighting a candle or putting on some R&B that we grew up on while he prepared for his speeches. He would make sure I was comfortable, and he would sit next to me and talk for hours. I would just drink my drink and listen to him.

A lot of times, his talks were about how he loves me so much, but I need to change and get myself together, and if I wasn't the way I was, then our relationship would be better and things like that. His talks would always make me feel on edge. The whole time I felt judged and beat up. Most of the time, by the end of his talks, I was crying real tears and apologizing to him and pleading to him how much I was going to change. He would tell me that it was "ok" and that he would give me another chance to get it right, and when he would say that I felt so relieved on the inside and would try to do my best to make him happy. I listened to all his talks and took all his advice and did everything he asked me to. But no matter what, he was never satisfied, and nothing I did was ever good enough. He would always tell me what I was doing wrong, and I always felt like a kid who was in trouble. Damian had a lot of mind control over me. The only thing I wanted to do was get his approval and make him happy, but it never went that way. I was used to the dysfunction of our relationship, and I just looked forward to the good days and prayed that they would last. I wanted my relationship to work, and I was doing everything in my power to be a good girlfriend.

There were a lot of toxic memories in the apartment, so we began looking for somewhere else to live. I remember one day coming home being out somewhere with Najah during the day, and when she and I came through the door, she started saying "hi" and looking around waving to people. "Who is she talking to?" I was thinking in my head, but I did not want to ask her, afraid of her response. Whoever she was waving at, it seemed like a lot of people, and they seemed to be friendly. She kept waving, and I eventually told her to stop, and she did, and she went to her room to play. I had prayed and used the anointing oil that my grandmom gave me.

I opened the sliding door and told whoever, and whatever was in my apartment that they had to go. The energy was beginning to be too much, and it didn't help that at night the guy that lived upstairs from me would walk in circles stomping for hours chanting, and then he would scream. I could not ever get any sleep on top of whatever he was doing sounded scary. He may have been doing voodoo or witchcraft, and I did not want any of those spirits coming down to my apartment where my child and I were. Of course, a lot of times Damian was not home to knock on his door, so I had to endure it for about a week straight. Thankfully either he got evicted or moved out. I had seen him in the breezeway carrying his mattress down the steps. That was my first time seeing him, and he looked hideous. I was almost sure he was up there practicing witchcraft, and I was glad to see him go.

In the meantime, Damian had come back from Jersey. I was happy he was back, but that was short-lived as usual. We got into a huge fight one night, and he had left and was gone for hours. I was texting his phone, cursing him out, and eventually he began ignoring me. I was calling him and he was sending me straight to voicemail, and that was making me angrier and angrier. I wanted to lash out and tear the house up again, but I had remembered the last time when I had to clean everything up, and I did not feel like doing all that. I paced back and forth to see what I could do, and a light bulb went off. I went to the closet and took all of his clothes out and threw them over the balcony outside on the ground. We had lived in an apartment with plenty of people around us, and someone could take his stuff at any time, and I didn't care. I kept throwing everything; his clothes, his shoes, and whatever else belonged to him.

After I was done, it sat out there for about an hour; then I calmed down. Once I came to my senses, I realized I didn't want his things taken, so I sat on the balcony and watched everything so no one would take it. While I was out there, I took a picture with my phone of his stuff outside and sent it to him. He came home almost immediately. "What the f*ck," he said as he pulled up and got out of the car and started picking his clothes up. "You buggin," he kept saying, and I saw in his face that he was furious. "Yo, I should f*ck you up," he said when he came through the door, and he mushed me. "All your stuff is already outside, get out!" I yelled at him. "Get out?" he asked me, confused. "Shamirah, I came to GA for YOU, I have no family and nowhere to go, but you telling me to get out?" he asked, shocked, and I could tell he was hurt too. "Yup, get the f*ck out. I'm tired of your BS and tired of you talking to me crazy, and then you take my car and leave and don't answer the phone," I yelled at him. "Are you serious?" he asked me as his tone changed.

I knew Damian like the back of my hand. I knew when he was angry, and I knew when he was hurt. At that moment, he was talking aggressively, but he was hurt. Before that moment, we had not ever had that type of interaction before. "I can't believe you threw my stuff outside, and I can't believe you are telling me to get out with nowhere to go, I'm baffled," he said as he went back outside to pick up the rest of his stuff. While he was out there, I did feel really bad. I had let my emotions get the best of me. I had seen him coming back up, so I had sat on the couch, and when he came into the house, there was silence. He was putting his stuff in suitcases and calling people to get a ride. The whole time I was just looking at him, and I felt sick to my stomach. Deep down inside, I did not want him to go, and I knew I had taken it overboard this time. "We need to talk," he said to me as he looked me in my eyes. He and I had this special connection where we looked into each other's eyes, and we could read each other's emotions. It is something I cannot explain, but it is something special we have between us. I would look in his eyes and read everything I needed to know and vice versa. Sometimes when I was really mad, I would look into his eyes, and he would look away because he knew I meant business, and I think looking into my eyes scared him sometimes. "

What do you want to talk about?" I asked him as he sat down. "US," he said, looking right at me. "We can't keep going on like this," he said to me, and I saw so much sincerity in his eyes. "I love you, and I love my daughter, and I want this family to work, but Shamirah, I cannot mentally keep going through this, you hear me?" he said as he looked directly into me with his eyes. "Yeah, you're right, and I am sorry for throwing your stuff out, and I really don't want you to leave. I just don't know what else to do," I said to him as I began to cry. "We are going to be good. We just can't keep doing this," he said as he consoled me. "I love you, and I want to be here with you," he reassured me, and I felt better. We had made up and cleared the air, and I took all his stuff out of the suitcase and hung everything back up and put his things back where they belonged. We both knew we needed a change from the vibes in the apartment, so I went to the rental office the next day to fill out the application for the townhouses they had available.

About a month later, I got approved for the townhome. It was in the same neighborhood we already lived in, and I was so excited. My apartment was set up really cute, and it was nice and cozy. It was a two-bedroom 2 bathroom with a kitchen, dining room, and computer nook area, and the living room and bedrooms were spacious with walk-in closets. It was nice, but the townhomes were even nicer. It was bigger with a nicer kitchen and an upstairs and downstairs, plus I lived right by the pool and the other amenities. I showed Najah where we would be moving, and she saw her new room, which was huge, and she was so happy. Damian and I were happy to be moving in as well. He and I had a talk, and we agreed that the new place would be a new start and that we would leave the drama behind.

"Ok, wow, that was a lot," the therapist said as she sat up and chimed in. "Yeah, it was," I said as I exhaled. "I am sorry that you were dealing with so many emotional issues. It seems like you all had good intentions but went on a downhill spiral, and it is hard to hear, so I could just imagine how little Najah felt growing up in such a toxic environment," the therapist said with compassion. "Yes, it was really hard at the time to keep my emotions in check. They were all over the place. I was frustrated, angry, overwhelmed, and in love and wanted my relationship to work all at the same time. A lot of time, we did not consider that Najah was right there taking in all the mean words we were saying to one another.

She was so innocent and adorable, and she didn't deserve to be subjected to our toxic-ness. For a long time; I felt guilty and beat myself up about it. That is why I think I overcompensated her and spoiled her the way I did. I just wanted her to feel loved, and I wanted her to feel comfortable. There was no doubt that her dad and I both loved her, and she definitely was daddy's baby, and for the most part, Najah had an awesome life. I just wish we would have kept the arguing and fighting away from her. "I understand," the therapist said as she shook her head in agreement and compassion. "I know you mentioned you all moved to a new home to get a new start. How did that go?" she asked me as she sat back and listened with her pen and paper.

27

When we first moved into the townhome, it was a new start, and the energy was great. I had set up the house really nice and comfortable, and Najah's room was super cute. The house had a lot of windows, so it was always nice and bright. I was so happy to be there. After moving in, my job had wrongfully fired me, so I was able to receive unemployment, and I was able to afford my rent and bills without Damian's help. Although after we moved into the townhouse, he did agree to step it up and began paying half the rent and bills, plus fund all of our fun activities. Which was a huge help because since he first moved in with me in the apartment, I was the one who paid the rent and all the bills. He didn't pay anything.

Being able to receive unemployment was very important to me because it meant I could survive, because I did not know if I could depend on Damian to pay bills because that is not a responsibility, he took on living with me. I had been at my job for over 5 years, and I had a 401k. After being fired, I had withdrawn my 401k. After paying the penalty I walked away with close to 9k, so I put it in the bank as emergency money, so between that and my unemployment, I was cool.

I was happy and in a good place. I had a gym membership with golds gym for about two years, but a lot of times it was hard to go because I had to work. Since I wasn't working, I was able to go to the gym more frequently. At that time, I did the cabbage soup diet a lot, and I was at one of the best weights in my life. I loved how I looked and felt, and I was in an all-around good place. Najah was in school and the bus came right in front of the house, which was perfect. Damian and I were in a positive space, and everything was all-around great.

In the neighborhood we lived in, my cousins were there, my aunt lived there, and eventually, my mom and sisters moved there too, so I had a lot of support and family around me. In the summer we would all go to the pool and have so much fun. My mom would get in and swim with Najah and my nephew JoJo, and we all just had a good time. I would pack a small lunch in the cooler with some frozen juices for me, and Najah and I would sit at the pool for hours, letting her play. By the time we left, it was time for her to take a bath and eat, and she would be ready to go to sleep. I loved our little neighborhood. It was homey and perfect, and the fact that my family was there was even better.

In the winter, I would walk across the parking lot to my mom's house, and we would make cookies and play games and just enjoy each other. Since we always had a babysitter, Damian and I would be out with our friends all the time on the town. I loved getting dressed up, and I always looked nice in my clothes. At that time, we were having a blast and going to all the clubs, and we didn't go out unless we had a section. Damian and his friends all had money. We got sections and popped bottles. Sometimes we got limos to ride to the clubs, and it would be a gang of us. Just out and about with good energy having a ball.

One night it was his friend's girlfriend's 30th birthday and her man went all out. He got the stretch hummer that was loaded, and we drank Patron and cruised the city on the way to the strip club. That night was lit. There were strippers everywhere, and the vibe was dope. The people we were with had good energy, and the night was just all-around epic. It was definitely a night to remember. Damian took me out all the time. We were boyfriend and girlfriend, but we were friends as well. We had a good relationship where we laughed and liked being around each other.

We were homies. Every birthday he made special for me. He always went all out with my cake and flowers. He always took me to nice places to eat and to party. One Birthday he had taken me to Pappadeaux and then to the hotel room next to it, and we went to an African hookah lounge. We had so much fun. We were out like every weekend on top of our house was a hot spot. We were always having parties and Christmas and Thanksgiving dinners. The house was not super big, but it was always full of people and making good memories.

Christmas of 2012, we had a house full of people. My whole family was there, and a bunch of Damian's close friends was there as well. That Christmas, Damian had cooked, and the food was bomb. Everyone was amazed at how good he did, and everyone was praising him. He always was a great cook. Throughout the years he is the one who taught me how to cook. Our very first Thanksgiving together was comical. I had never cooked a whole Thanksgiving meal before, but since I now had my own little family, I decided to give it a try.

I got some advice from my mom, and she kept asking me was I sure that we would not be coming to her house instead because my mom cooked really well. I told her that I was sure and that I wanted to cook for my own family. Since it was only me, Damian, and Najah. I had made a Cornish hen, macaroni and cheese, stuffing, greens, and yams. My cooking nothing like my moms, and when it was time to sit down and eat, and I presented them the food. I must admit it looked disgusting. I made my macaroni all wrong and the noodles ended up burning in the oven. My yams were out the can and nasty. My stuffing was all wrong. The only thing that came out decent was the Cornish hen.

I remember one of my cousins came over and knocked on the door.

When I answered, he said happy Thanksgiving and told me he was hit-ting up everybody's house for a plate. I told him to go in the kitchen and help himself to whatever he wanted. Damian and I watched him as he lifted the lids off the pots seeing what he wanted. I remember him looking at the food and saying, "Oh ard cuz, I think I'm good; I don't want a plate." Me and Damian burst out laughing and I told my cousin I understood, and he left. "Is it that bad?" I asked Damian. "Yeah babe," he said as he was trying not to hurt my feelings. "Aww, and you were still going to eat it?" I said to him, happy that he was being supportive. "Yeah, my babe cooked it, you did your best" he said to me as he smiled at me from across the table. "Aww, thank you," I said to him as I smiled back. "Do you want to just go to my mom's house?" I said to him as I looked at the food. "Yeah, let's go over there," he said, and we all put on our coats to leave. That is a memory that me and Damian always joked about. My cooking had come a long long way since that day and I owe it to Damian for showing me and helping me get my cooking skills up.

But on that day of our Christmas party the vibe was awesome. We were surrounded by family and people we love. We were drinking, taking pictures and playing games. It could not get more perfect, until we looked out the window and it was snowing. I had opened the door, and we all watched the snow coming down and we went outside to take pictures. It was absolutely beautiful. Prior to that day, I had never experienced a snowy Christmas in Georgia. All of us at my house were from Jersey, so we definitely appreciated the snowy winter vibes that we were used to.

28

A few weeks later it was Valentine's Day and Damian had gone all out like he always did. He ordered some roses that came to the door, and I was so surprised. They were beautiful. He was not home when they came so when he came through the door, I thanked him and gave him a big hug as he was smiling from ear to ear. Najah and I were sitting in the living room, and when he came through the door, he had bags. He had a teddy bear and chocolate for Najah, and she was so excited. Then he looked over to me and handed me my gift.

He handed me a heart-shaped box of my favorite chocolates. I thanked him and he pulled out another bag that said Pandora. I opened it and there was a pandora box with two charms in it. On Christmas two months before, he had bought me a Pandora Bracelet with the gift box and a heart charm. The next month in January for my birthday he had got me the Pandora 30th Birthday charm, and the cake charm. They were so cute. I was a Pandora addict at the time, and I loved the way he paid attention to what I liked. When I opened the box there were more charms, and I loved them. "Thank you!" I said to him as I hugged him and gave him a kiss. I gave him his gift which was Polo boxers and pajama pants and slippers. I always bought him stuff like that because Damian had everything. He was very hard to shop for because he was picky. Everything he wanted was always expensive so he would buy it for himself.

234

Later that day we went out to dinner as a family. We went to Carrabba's Italian restaurant and everything was so good. On the way back home, we had dropped Najah off at my grand mom's house so we could enjoy the rest of our night. Normally we would get a room or go somewhere special, but Damian said we were going home because he had a surprise. "Come in and sit down," he said when we got to our house and came through the door. "Ok" I said as I smiled and sat on the couch as he went upstairs. "Ok, come up," he said as he grabbed my hand and walked me to our bathroom in our room. He had run the bathwater and put the roses in it and had candles lit. "Aww this is so nice" I said to him as I smiled from ear to ear.

At that point I had been with him for about 12 or 13 years, but he still gave me butterflies and I still looked at him with love in my eyes. He was so romantic and never ceased to amaze me. "Get in," he said as he helped me take off my clothes and I got in and he poured me a glass of Moet, and I sat in the tub and relaxed. "I will be back, don't come downstairs until I come and get you," he said, smiling as he left the bathroom and went back downstairs.

I sat there and enjoyed my bath and played some music on my phone. When I got out, I had put on the lingerie I had bought. I put in a satin red one-piece teddy with the red thigh highs and the garter belt. I put on my Victoria secret pure seduction lotion and spray, that was his favorite fragrance that he liked on me. I sprayed on some Victoria's Secret body shimmer. I had a long sew-in, so I curled my hair in big flowing curls and put on some lip gloss and waited for him to come and get me. "You ready?" he said as he came into the room smiling. "Yes" I said smiling and he grabbed my hand and walked me downstairs. All down the steps were Roses leading into the living room. When I came down, he had changed the living room light bulb to a red-light bulb making the ambiance super sexy. Damian made a message area in the living room and had it all set up with oils and candles. There were roses all over the floor and couch and he had our favorite album Beyoncé's

"Dangerously in Love" playing. He had chocolate-covered strawberries on the coffee table with two glasses of Moet already poured, and he put strawberries in my glass. Everything was perfect. "This is soo nice!" I said to him as I kissed him. Damian didn't normally say much, he always just had a huge smile on his face and his smile said it all.

He was happy and wanted to make sure I had a good night. He was dressed like a male masseuse. He had taken a shower and had oiled up his body and was wearing nothing but a towel wrapped around his waist. "Lay down" he said as he helped me on the table, and I laid there and he took my lingerie off and began massaging my whole body. His strong hands felt so good and then he began massaging my feet which he knew foot messages were my favorite. "Are you enjoying yourself?" He said as the music played in the background. "Yup" I said as I was enjoying every moment. "Ok good. I love you," he said as he gave me a kiss. He had walked away to the kitchen and brought a chair into the living room, and he helped me off the table and sat me on the chair. "I am so greasy; I don't want to sit on this chair" I said to him as I laughed and was confused at what he was doing.

Damian had gone upstairs and got me a towel and put it over the chair and then he sat me down. I was sitting there Naked as he changed the music from Beyoncé to "Pretty Ricky" a group we used to like from back in the day and I burst out laughing as "Grind on me" began to play on the speakers. He walked over to me and started giving me a private dance. He was trying to be romantic but all we both could do was laugh. He had changed the music back and put on Jodeci. As he was dancing, he took off his towel and he was naked. He pulled me up and he sat down and pulled me on top of him to dance from him so I did, and we were laughing and caressing each other and enjoying the moment.

He was getting super aroused and began kissing all over me and sucking on my breast. We both were so greasy from the message oil that we didn't want to lay on the couch or the bed, so he sat me on top of him in the chair and began to slide his penis inside of me. It hurt a little because of the position we were in, so he was so gentle and romantic and once it was in; we just began making love to the music. Eventually he stood me up and I bent over the coffee table and he stood up behind me so we didn't get the furniture messy and we had great sex and eventually we both nutted and it was nice. We had gone upstairs and got into the shower together and we had sex again.

When we got out it was about 2 o lock in the morning. We went back downstairs to the living room and sat there in our robes and chilled and drank the rest of the Moet. "I got us something," Damian said, smiling. "What?" I asked curious and he went into the kitchen and came back with a small blunt. "What is that? Weed?" I asked curious as I burst out laughing. "Damian, we don't even smoke" I said to him in shock. Neither me nor him smoked weed at all, so I was surprised that he would even get it for us to smoke. "Well, I figured it's a special occasion" he said smiling. "You want to try it?" he said, pointing the blunt at me with the lighter in his hand. "Yeah, I'll try it" I said, nervous like a kid.

He lit it and we sat on the couch and smoked. As a little time had passed, I started feeling paranoid. "You see that?" I asked him as I pointed to the steps. "Nah, I don't see nothing" he said, staring at the steps. "Omg Damian I think something is coming down the steps" I said to him as I clutched his arm. "Ok, I'm about to go and see" he said as he got up. He stood at the steps cracking up laughing. I was too scared to get up because I was paranoid. But seeing him laugh made me laugh, and me and him literally laughed the whole night, literally everything was hilarious. We didn't go to bed until about 6am and we woke up about 1pm in the afternoon and recapped the night. "Did you have fun?" He asked me as he smiled. "Yeah, I did. Thank you so much for everything" I said to him. "You was paranoid as hell off that bud" he said to me as he laughed. "I know right, that's why I don't smoke. I can never enjoy the high, it always feels like something is touching me or trying to get me" I said to him as I laughed. "Damian you wasn't any better, you just laughed the whole time" I said to him as we both laughed. "Word" he said to me as he agreed.

"We going to take a ride and chill for the day," he said to me, as he pulled out our box of jewelry. He had a pinky ring with diamonds in it that he wore when we went out or got dressed up for the day. We also had a his and hers matching watch set that he bought for us. It was beautiful, it was white gold flooded with diamonds. He had handed me my watch and I had got dressed. I put on a Chanel off the shoulder sweater with my favorite high waisted stretch jeans that hit every curb and a pair of my favorite heels. Damian was dressed really nice too. We both had matching Versace sunglasses that he bought for us, and we put on our watches and we had left. We had drove to Dawsonville Ga to the outlets. We went to SAKS and shopped then to Michael Kors and Kate Spade where he got me purses and afterwards, we had gone to dinner, came back home that night. Everything was so much fun and that was the usual. Me and him were like best friends. We always had so much fun with one another. He always bought me things and spoiled me. If it was not the two of us being together, then we were together doing this with Najah as a family.

Damian would always do romantic things for me. I was the love of his life, and he always made sure to show it. I always wanted to ride the horse and carriage downtown in Centennial Park. One day Damian told me to get dressed, and we went downtown and parked in a parking garage, and he said we were going to take a walk and enjoy the Atlanta breeze. It was cool with me, as we walked and held hands. When we turned the corner, I saw the big Ferris wheel and people riding pass us on the horses. "Aww I wish were were doing that" I said to Damian as I looked at the people. Just as I finished saying it, we turned another corner, and there was a man dressed in a suit with white gloves on. He was looking at me smiling, and he had his hands stretched out. "Is this the lady?" the man said to Damian still smiling. "Yup, this is her"

Damian said as he smiled back at him. "Suprise" Damian said to me excited. "Aww Damian, what is going on?" I asked him as I was surprised. "I know you always wanted to get on the horse and carriage so I surprised you today" he said to me smiling. "Aww Damian, thank you" I said as I hugged him, and the man helped us up onto the backseat of the horse. We got on and Damian was making jokes and enjoying himself. It was night time and the Atlanta air was cool, so he handed me a blanket. We did not use the blanket because we didnt know who else had been using it, so Damian just wrapped his arms around me, and we cuddled the whole time, as we cruised the city.

The ride was so romantic. People were beeping at us, and admiring us and showing so much love. I felt like a princess with my prince, on the horse and carriage. Me and Damian, talked and laughed and took video's and had an awesome time. He definatley surprised me, because I had no idea that he planned it. After the ride was over, we walked down Centennial Park and enjoyed the vendors, and the lights. We did not get on the Ferris wheel, because I was too scared. The whole night was absolutely amazing and one of the best dates that Damian had ever taken me on, and I was so appreciative to him for it.

Outside of our romantic dates, we drove to Florida many times together just me and him. We had bought Niyah with us on our first family trip to Panama City Beach. We drove there in my car and played music and laughed the whole way there. We stayed at the Palmetto hotel, and it was beautiful. The first thing we did when we came through the door was go on the balcony and look at our view of the ocean. We were on the 7th floor and the view was amazing. The water was turquoise blue and the ocean stretched for miles and miles. It was breathtaking to be there, and we could not wait to hit the beach and get into the pretty water. When we looked down, we could see the Cabanas, the tiki torches, the pool, and the Palm trees. There was a nice hot tub and a Pavilion with grills to cook out on. Everything was so nice, and we could not wait to enjoy it.

Our room was set up like a house with a kitchen it had a stove and everything fully loaded. Before we left, I had went shopping and bought a cooler and all types of Hawaiian style accessories and we had liquor with us. We had our bathing suits and Damien took Najah downstairs to the shop and bought water tubes and goggles and all sorts of fun stuff for the beach. Once we got settled in the room since there was a refrigerator and cooking utensils, we decided to go food shopping. We had gone to Piggly Wiggle's not too far from the room and bought hotdogs hamburgers, chips, juices, popsicles, chicken, Belgium waffles eggs, thick cut turkey bacon. We had gone all out and had a cart full, so while we were there, we did not have to worry about buying food.

When we got back, we put everything away and put on our bathing suits and got all our water stuff and hit the beach. The water felt so good. It was so warm and clear. Najah and Damian were swimming far, and I was a little scared, so I did not go past my waist in the water. Damian wanted me to go farther so he put me on his back and swam me to the sand dunes where I was able to stand. To my surprise, we were out really far but the water was not as deep as I thought it would be, so I got comfortable enough to get in and my feet actually touched the ground. While I was in there, I noticed a school of fish swimming pass me. They were beautiful but I had a phobia of fish, so I wanted to go back to the shore and relax in the shallow parts of the water.

I watched Damian and Najah play, and scuba dive and they were having so much fun. Eventually Damian came to me with the tube that was made for two and told me to get on and Najah stayed on the sand playing with her beach toys while we watched her as we cruised in the water on the tube. It was so pretty and relaxing. It felt like we were in Paradise. That was our first time being at a beach that beautiful with the water, the Palm trees, and the scenery. We were used to Atlantic City beach water, which was wavy, salty, and dirty. I hate going to the beach back home, it was full of seaweed and constantly stepping on seashells. But this beach was beautiful and perfect.

We got there about 11am, which in the Panama City time zone was 10 am. All day I was wondering why it kept feeling early until I realized they had a 1-hour time difference, so it gave us more time to enjoy the day. It was about 4pm and it had begun to get a little cool, so we decided to go back to the hotel to take showers and get ready to eat dinner. Once we all had got clean and changed our clothes, we got the cooler and put the hamburgers and hot dogs and all our food in it and went downstairs and set everything up at the pavilion, and we sat down there and grilled out on the deck. The sun was starting to set so they lit the Tiki torches, and it was so beautiful. The vibe was so tropical and nice. The weather was perfect. We grilled as the sun began to go down, and we looked out at the water as people were walking on the beach and the hotel guests were in the pool and the hot tub, and everything was lit up. It was truly an awesome feeling, and to be spending it with the man I loved, and my daughter made it even better.

We sat there and ate and enjoyed each other's company then we went back up to the room and sat on the balcony and enjoyed the night sky and watched everybody swim. Najah and Damian wanted to go on an adventure hunt with their hats with the lights on them to find fish that come out at night, so they went on the beach, and I stayed and watched them from the balcony. I watched everyone swim and enjoy themselves as music played and people sat out the deck enjoying the ambiance. I went downstairs to put my feet in the pool because the hot tub was full, and everyone was so nice and welcoming.

When Najah and Damian came back we all went back to the room, and we all were tired from the day, so Najah got on her bed and went to sleep and me and Damian got out our liquor that we bought with us and sat on the balcony and enjoyed the breeze and drank and had good time. "This is dope," he said as he drank his liquor. "Yeah it is' 'I said as I smiled and we drank then eventually we went in and went to sleep. We stayed there for about 4 days and every day we spent the whole day at the beach and in the pool. We had a blast. We had cruised Panama's strip and went to the pier and an Oyster restaurant and Najah even got a chance to open a clam and get a pearl from one of the vendors on the strip. On the third day we drove to the Marina because Damian wanted to rent a boat. He took the class and the guy took us to the boat dock and I was scared out of my mind.

I had never been on a pontoon boat before, let alone one that Damian was driving. I knew he could drive a car, but I didn't know that he could drive a boat. "Don't be scared. I got you" he said as the guy handed him the boat key and told us to have a good time. We got on and I immediately put on me and Najah's life jackets. "You good. My uncle taught me to drive a boat. It's not hard" he reassured me. As we cruised from the dock my stomach was turning as we were no longer near land but surrounded by nothing but water. Every time the boat rocked from the waves; I would get nervous. "Relax" he told me, as Najah was not scared at all. She was enjoying herself eating a strawberry shortcake ice cream looking into the water and she even saw Dolphins. "Come here, you want to try it?" Damian asked me coaxing me to get in the driver's seat and he stood behind me and showed me how to steer. Although I would never drive a boat by myself it was fun, and it helped me relax.

We had drove for a long time and I sat back and enjoyed it. We had come to these sand dunes that was like an Island and boats were docked there, so Damian had pulled over and docked our boat on a sand dune as well and we had got off and walked the small Island. I got in the water and swam a little as Najah played and wrote her name in the sand.

We had stayed there for a while, and it was so peaceful. We were literally on a small piece of sand surrounded by the Gulf of Mexico.

It was magical just to know I was chilling in the middle of the ocean. Eventually we had got back on the boat, and it was so funny because when we got off where Damien docked, it was surrounded by water so we jumped off not realizing we had to swim to get back on. I don't know what was wrong with me but for some reason I had a hard time getting back onto the boat, and Damian thought it was funny to yell "Shark" I was so mad at him, and I hopped on like my life depended on it. On the way back the drive was peaceful. We hit a couple of waves, but I got through it and me and Najah watched the Dolphins. We got back safely to land, then drove from the Marina back to the hotel. We were so tired. It was our last night there, so we went downstairs and relaxed in the pool and then took showers and packed to check out the next morning. We took pictures and everything before we left, and we got on the road back home and that was the end to an awesome trip.

"Wow, that sounds like it was really nice," My Therapist said to me, smiling as she sat up in her chair. "It sounds like you all had fun. It sounds like you all had finally got on track in your relationship," she said, still smiling. "Yes, the trip was awesome. We had a great time and built great memories, but nothing ever stays consistent," I said to her. "What do you mean? She asked me. "You would think with a trip like that, that we would have come back on cloud nine. Which we did for a few days then shortly after, there was drama again," I said to her. "Oh no, well tell me what happened," she said, concerned and picked up her pen again as I began talking.

When we had got back, everything was cool between Damian and I, but I wasn't feeling too good. I figured I was just tired from the trip, so I had rested a lot. I was always falling asleep and that was not like me. I was on the birth control pill, but I did remember missing a few so I had gone and bought a first response pregnancy test. I was so nervous to take it, but I knew I had too because I was not feeling right. I went in the bathroom and secretly took the test and sure enough it was positive. "Oh no" I thought to myself, and I immediately began googling abortion clinics because I did not want to have a baby at that time. I called the clinic and made the appointment which was about a week away and as the days went by, I got sicker and sicker. Eventually, Damian started to question my sickness, so I told him. "I already made the appointment to get an abortion," I told him because I did not want to hear what he had to say, because I already knew he didn't want to have a baby. "You made that decision on your own?" he asked me. "Yes, why?" he asked, I'm just making sure it's your decision, so you don't try and blame me, he said. I didn't pay him too much mind. I was sick and didn't want to be bothered.

It just so happened that the day of the abortion was on Damian's birthday in April. He had a section at Compound Nightclub for his birthday and I was looking forward to it. "You know you can't come tonight because you are not going to be feeling good after you do this" he said to me. "I'm still coming, I will be fine" I told him as we were getting dressed to go to the clinic. We were in there for what felt like forever. Finally, I was in the back going over all my aftercare rules. The lady told me to go home and rest. Do not lift anything. Do not drink alcohol, and do not have sex. Afterward I got my gown and I sat in the room and waited to go to the back to get my abortion. When I came to the room, I remember laying on the table, and they put a white light over me and all I can remember last was the mask coming with the anesthesia in it and I was asleep. When I woke up, I was in the recovery room. They had given me pain medication and I knew I needed to heal but all I could do was look at the clock because time was winding down to get ready for Damian's birthday party, and I still needed to pick up his cake and run errands.

When I got out, Damian pulled up in the car to get me from the back where they released me, and we drove home. When we got there, it was about 5pm. I had left home to run to Walmart to get his cake and then I came home and took a shower and laid down before I and started getting dressed. "What you doing?" Damian asked, concerned. "I'm getting my stuff out so I can get dressed and start doing my hair" I told him. "Didn't they tell you to relax," he said to me. "I'm not worried about what they are talking about, I feel ok" I told him as I laid my clothes out on the bed. "You sure, because I'm not trying to be taking you to the hospital. "Damian, I'm ok," I told him as I got dressed and we left. He had a section, and there were a lot of people there. He introduced me to who would later become one of his best friends named Terrance and his wife Michelle, as well as one of Terrance's artists at the time named Shanice. His other close friend Theo and his wife Nichole were there as well.

We all had a ball and celebrated. At the club, I was drinking and dancing even though the doctors had told me not to. I had only had the abortion about four hours before then, but I felt fine. At the end of the night, I was so drunk, and we all left the club. When Damian and I got home, we had sex, again against the doctor's orders. It did feel weird, but overall, I was ok. Over the next few days, I was in small pain, but I healed and got over the abortion physically and mentally very quickly. At that time, I did not want to have a baby, so I was fine with the abortion, and I went about my life.

29

At the time Damian and Terrance were getting really close and since Terrance was into music him and Damian would be in the studio a lot. Damian was like an A&R finding talent all the time, so him and Terrance would be really busy. I would mention to Damian about spending more time with me, but he was really not trying to hear it. He had even become really distant and cocky. I did not know what his problem was. I felt like since Terrance had money and Damian became his sidekick, that Damian started feeling himself. He would fly to NY with Terrance and have meetings with major labels, and he would go to all these fancy places, and he definitely gained a cocky complex, especially when it came to me. He would sit on the porch a lot in her townhouse, and he would talk on the phone outside.

One day he was outside on the phone pacing back and forth smoking his black and mild. I heard him talking about somebody, but I was not sure who it was. He was saying very mean things and expressing things like how the person gets on his nerves and so on and so forth. The more I listened, the more I realized he was talking about Me! I sat and listened and eventually, I could not take any more of him bashing me, so I opened the door and confronted him. "Why are you outside kicking my back in?" I asked him as I was angry, and he looked like he saw a ghost. "Here she go right now bro" he said to the person on the phone. "Bro, she's crazy. I call you back," he said to the person on the phone, and he hung up. "That's messed up that you really out here talking about me like that, and lying," I scolded him. "I ain't lie about nothing, and you should not have been listening and all in my business," he said rudely. "Don't sit and talk about me anymore. I can't image two guys sitting on the phone kicking my back in; that's female traits," I said to him. B*tch f*ck you" he said as now we were in the house, and he was getting his clothes out ready to leave. "Don't call me a b*tch" I yelled at him. "Don't yell at me, b*tch" he said, getting in my face. "Damian get out my face," I said to him as I saw him getting aggressive like he wanted to hit me.

When he got mad at me, he would have this evil demeanor about him. It was like he turned into a whole different person. His eyes even looked different. I saw him getting revved up and it was making me get revved up. We began to have words back and forth and things began to get heated. "You are a b*tch a*s n*gga" I told him as I was walking away. In the argument, he had called me about fifty b*tches but the one time I said it to him, he went berserk. "Oh, I'm a b*tch a*s n*gga?" he said as he went into the closet and pulled out a stack of money and began waving it in my face. Just like I thought, every time he had money, he would be very cocky and rude. "Damian, I don't care about your money. I am not impressed. You still a bum broke b*tch a*s nigga" I said to him as I was a few feet away from him. "Oh yeah," he said to me, as he did the thing with his lip and he had the evil look in his eyes. "B*tch, I will show you broke," he said and before I knew it, he had taken the stack of money and smacked me in my face with it.

He had hit me so hard that the rubber band on the money had popped, and the money burst everywhere like a strip club scene in a movie. I was in shock. I couldn't hit him. I couldn't cry. I could barely move. "Call me a broke nigga again, and I will f*ck you up," he said to me, getting in my face with his fist balled up. "F*ck you!" Get out of my face!" I screamed at him. "You need to watch your mouth," he said to me, as he was picking up the money off of the floor. I felt numb at the moment and didn't know what to say. He had picked up all his money and was getting dressed to go out. "You hit me; God is going to get you for that. Since you hit me in my face, tonight somebody is going to hit you in yours," I said to him so calmly and with a sense of peace in my spirit. "Nobody is going to do sh*t to me," he said cocky, and he got dressed and left shortly afterward in my car.

He would pop so much trash to me, yet still, leave in MY car. There are so many times I would try to stop him, but he was so disrespectful that he would take it anyway as if it were his. He left about 10 pm and I got a called about 12 am in morning. I wasn't sleep; I was up watching tv. "Hello?" I said as I didn't recognize the number. "Mirah, this is Terrance," the voice said on the other end of the phone. "Ok," I said, wondering why he was calling me. "Are you good?" he asked me. "Yeah, I'm fine" I told him. "I'm on my way to park up by your house, something happened and I want to make sure you and Najah are safe," he told me. "Ok" I said. "What's going on?" I asked him. "Damian is on his way to the hospital. He got hit in the head with a brick," Terrance told me. When he said it, I didn't even flinch nor feel bad for Damian. I told him that since he hit me that someone was going to hit him.

He smacked me with a brick of money, and someone smacked him with a real brick. That's how karma works. I was a firm believer in God and how calm I was when he hit me, let me know that God was not going to let him get away with it. "Oh ok, where's my car?" I asked Terrance, not even asking if Damian was ok. In my heart I knew he was ok, but I also felt like that is what he got for putting his hands on me. "Dag Mirah, you not even going to ask if he's ok?" Terrance asked a little surprised. "What hospital is he going to?" I asked, and Terrance told me. I asked him again where my car was and he had let me know that Damian drove the car to the hospital, and that was where it was parked.

We had hung up, and shortly after our convo him and a few other guys were outside my house. Terrance knocked on the door to let me know he was there, and I told him ok and I closed the door and finished watching tv and I was peaceful. Normally in a situation like that I would have been worried and felt bad for Damian, but in that situation I didn't. Before he left, he was being a tyrant to me and hitting me with the money was the ultimate disrespect, so as long as he was ok, I didn't mind him sitting in the hospital. Hopefully he would always think about that the next time he decided to put his hands on me or hit me with anything.

A few hours later Terrance and the guys had left, and Damian had come home with his head wrapped. When he came through the door I was still up, and I didn't really say anything to him. "So, you didn't even care that I got hit huh?" he asked me. "What?" I answered him, barely looking at him. "Terrance told me how you was acting and he said he was shocked," Damian said to me. "Oh well, did you tell him before you left that you hit me with a brick of money? I told you that since you hit me, that somebody was going to hit you" I said to him firmly. "So, you think you did some type of Voodoo?" he said, as he seemed upset with me that he got hit. "No, I don't do voodoo, but I do know that you can't mess with God's children and get away with it" I told him. Damian wanted to go back and forth but I was not having it. It was about 4 am and I was ready to go to bed, so I did.

The next day I still didn't have much to say to him at all, but it seemed like he just kept picking with me. I had gone outside to get something out of my car, and I noticed there was so much blood on my driver's side window, and at that moment, I knew that he was hit hard, and I was thankful that he was ok. I went back in the house and didn't mention it to Damian. I had just got some Windex and went outside to clean it. I was not driving around with blood on my window. I came in and he was still trying to agitate me, so I just ignored him. Thank God he had eventually left, and I had the house to myself.

It was the weekend, so Najah was with my grand mom. I was having some me time and was playing music and cleaning up the house. After I finished cleaning, I got into the shower and washed my hair, blow-dried it, and flat ironed it. It was a long process, but my hair looked so nice, and I was ready to go out to meet up with my friend for some girl time. As I was getting dressed, Damian had come home and like usual when he came in; it was like a dark cloud came with him. He had horrible energy, and all I wanted to do was finish getting dressed so I could get away from him. He said something to me. I was not sure exactly what it was, but it sparked us to have some words.

Next thing you know, despite him being hit with a brick the night before, he was still threatening me and trying to fight with me. "Damian, leave me alone!" I was yelling at him as he just looked like a hateful monster. I could just see the evil spirit on him, and it was disgusting. I tried to go out the front door and he kept closing it so I couldn't get out. I was not sure why we had gotten into it, but at that point it was really heated. He seemed like he wanted to really hurt me. I went upstairs to my room to close the door, but he kept blocking it to where I couldn't shut it. He came in and we both were screaming at each other.

I had just got dressed, and I used to use baby powder, and it was lying on my bed as we were yelling at each other. Damian picked up the powder and poured it all over my hair and it got all in my face and my eyes. I was horrified. I could not see; on top of I had just washed and done all of that to my hair. I was pissed beyond measure. "Oh, you f*cked up today!" I kept yelling as I was trying to get out of my room door, but he kept blocking me from getting out. "Move!" I kept yelling as I began to push him out my way, but he was too strong. "Ok, I got something for your a*s" I said to him as I opened the window and yelled "Help me!!" to the whole neighborhood. Damian had run to the window so fast and pulled me away from it by my hair, and he slammed it shut. "B*tch, is you crazy?!" he was yelling at me as he kept pulling my hair.

At that point, I was terrified and I felt trapped. Damian did not even look like himself. He was a whole demon, and I was not sure what he was going to do to me at that point. He cursed me out for opening the window and eventually he left. I had got in the shower and washed out all the powder that was matted in my hair like clay. I did not get to meet up with my friend, and I was emotionally drained. After I got out the shower I had gone to sleep. Damian had left.

Later on, I had got up to get something to eat. As I was in the kitchen, he had come home, and we didn't say anything to one another. I tried to not even look at him. I was in the kitchen making my food and he came in there and just stood there. I felt his energy and could tell he was in a different spirit. That evil spirit was resting, and it was the real him standing there. He had too much pride to say he was sorry, so he just sat in the chair and chuckled like a crazy person. I still ignored him. I was over him at that point.

Earlier he had acted like a maniac, and I wanted nothing else to do with him. "Come here" he said as he sat there coaxing me to sit on his lap, but I didn't come. I was standing in the kitchen by the microwave, which was in the corner. I had my back to him as I was still making my food. He had got up and walked over to me and went in the drawer and got a big steak knife and stood close to me as I was cornered by the microwave. "Why you have that knife? Are you going to stab me?" I asked him as I had no idea what he was doing. "No babe, I wouldn't do that to you," he said, still standing in front of me blocking me in the corner. "Do you know how much pain I feel?" he said to me staring into my eyes and when I looked back into his, I saw numbness. "No, I don't know what you are talking about" I said to him. "I lost my brother, and it still hurts. Look in my eyes" he said as he tried to drop a tear, but it wouldn't come down.

"Damian you are not even crying" I said to him as it was hard to have compassion for him at that moment because he was acting scary. "I am crying, look," he said as he bent down to let me get a closer look at his eyes. They were becoming watery, but still no tears. "Ok Damian, I miss Drew too," referring to his little brother who had passed. "You missing him does not give you a reason to act out towards me. "I know, I know, and I'm sorry" he said to me as he finally put the knife down and sat back down and was in his own thoughts. I let him be, and gave him his time because I knew anything that I said would be a trigger, and I did not want any more drama from him.

"Let me interrupt you there," my therapist said as she sat up in the chair with her legs crossed. "That was a lot" she added. "I know, it was" I agreed with her as I was almost embarrassed by exposing so much of our toxic-ness in the relationship. "At that point, you all were very harsh to one another, and Shamirah, I do want to add, he did some very mean things to you. What made you stay in the relationship?" she asked me sincerely. "I had taken a minute to pause and think about it. "Umm, I really don't know. I think I was so submerged in the toxic-ness that I didn't realize how toxic it was. I was always just hoping that things would get better. Sometimes it did, but only for a short while.

I wanted the fairy tale life. I wanted to be with him and always hoped that he would change his attitude towards me and not be so mean" I told her sincerely. "Right, I understand," she said as she was nodding her head in agreement. "Ok, well I did interrupt. After all of that I wanted to be able to recap with you. Please continue" she said as he picked up her pen and I begin talking and she began writing.

30

A few weeks later, Damian had flown his baby brother Khris down to Atlanta to stay with us for a little bit. Damian loved Chris and Khris loved him. It was nice having him down. He spent time with Najah and walked her to the store and they built memories together. Khris could sing so while he was here Damian and Terrance had taken him to the studio and Damian was enjoying his baby brother and so was I. Damian and Khris talked about him moving down to Atlanta with his kids and his girlfriend. Khris was a great dad; he loved his kids with all his heart. He had told Damian that he wanted to come back when he got things straight for him and the kids that he would be back. Damian didn't want his brother to go back to Jersey, but Khris had missed his kids and Damian understood that he had to go. Damian had taken him to the airport and I knew they both were going to miss each other. They had a very special bond. While Khris stayed with us for those few days me and Damian did not argue or have any issues.

The day Damian dropped Khris off he had left with Terrance and was gone the entire day until nighttime. I was calling his phone but he was not answering so I was worried about him. Finally, after many hours had passed, he had walked through the door with a pair of Carrera shades on and an Armani exchange bag. Before he had walked in, I had heated up some shrimp fettuccine that I had. I was about to eat it because he wasn't home. Damian was allergic to seafood so I tried not to bring it in the house. In the past I had been eating crabs at my mom's house and when I got home Damian was drinking a sprite and I asked him for a sip forgetting that I just ate seafood hours earlier and he drank after me and wound up in the hospital from an allergic reaction. After that I was very cautious. After I ate seafood, I made sure I brushed my teeth, changed my clothes, washed my hands and even bleached the surfaces just to be on the safe side.

"Where you been?" I have been calling you all day," I said to him. "Yeah you was blowing my phone up" he said. "So, you know I was calling you and you still ignored me" I said to him as he was ignoring me in that moment as well. "Damian you hear me talking to you" I said to him as he took his clothes out the bag and laid them on the couch. "I'm about to get dressed, I'm not worried about nothing you saying" he said to me rudely still with his shades on in the house.

I could not believe the way he was acting. I had gone into the kitchen to get my fettuccine and I didn't care that he was there. I was going to eat my shrimp anyway. "So, you know seafood almost killed me last time, and you still eating it around me?" he said finally taking his glasses off. "I will do what I want. Just like you doing what you want" I said to him as I sat down on the couch to eat. "Ok cool, I'm out anyway" he said to me. "So, you been gone all day and you're going to leave again?" I asked him. "Yup" he said cocky. I was so upset and annoyed at his arrogance that I had got up and I wanted to hit him. "I dare you to hit me, I will knock you out" he warned me. "Shut up" I said to him and instead of hitting him I took my bowl of shrimp fettuccine and threw it all over his brand-new clothes. "Ayo wtf you doing!?" he said in shock.

"Now you not going nowhere since you want to threaten me and pop trash" I lashed out at him. "Yo, you really are crazy" he said to me as he tried to salvage his clothes that was drenched in sauce. "And you threw seafood on it at that! I swear you are the worst" he said to me as he began throwing his clothes in the washing machine in the kitchen. "So, what, you stay out all day ignore my calls and then talk to me crazy, you were asking for it" I told him.

"I can't believe you did that" he said as he was upset and he called Terrance on the phone and told him what I did and that he wasn't sure if he was going to be coming out or not. "This ain't even going to fit the same. I had to wash a brand-new outfit" he said as he took it out the washer not wanting to put it in the dryer. When we did laundry, especially our nice items we either took them to the cleaners or sat them on the drying rack. We never put them in the dryer. Damian was pressed for time, so he had no choice to put his stuff in the dryer and he was pissed.

He had wound up wearing something else and he still got dressed to leave and Terrance had come to pick him up. "It's a damn shame a brand-new outfit was ruined" he said as he put his watch on to go out the door as Terrance was outside waiting for him. "Whatever" I said as I was annoyed that he was leaving. "You tried to kill me tonight with Shrimp" he said to me as he laughed. "No, I didn't" I said as he made me laugh too. "Even though you crazy and ruined my clothes and tried to kill me, I still love you" he said to me as he gave me a hug but I did not want to hug him back. "Me and Terrance have a meeting downtown and afterwards I'm coming straight back, so you don't have nothing to worry about" he said to me and he hugged me and left.

I sat there on the couch listening to "Its 4am and my lover won't answer" and vibed out. I did feel a little bad for throwing food on his clothes but only because it had shrimp in it other than that I didn't care. He was texting me for most of the night being lovely dovey. He had come home a few hours later and we cuddled and played and had sex and we acted like nothing toxic had happened earlier. That was our cycle. We would fight, then make up. Damian would be a tyrant to me and it seemed like it turned him on because after every fight no matter how heated it was, he wanted to have sex afterwards and I would always give in. We were like each other's triggers and toxic drugs.

The very next day we got into an altercation, and I was screaming at the top of my lungs. It had gotten so heated that I was sweating, and I became light-headed. I sat on the floor trying to catch my breath, but my heart was beating so fast that I was feeling like I was suffocating. "Breathe" is what I kept telling myself and I realized that I had a panic attack and I could not control it. I had gotten so scared that I had called my pastor at the time and I asked him to pray for me because in that moment, I had felt like I was being attacked by so many demons and I felt helpless. He prayed for me and gave me advice and we hung up, and in that very moment I knew that I had to get away from Damian because I could no longer live in chaos with him.

It was starting to affect my health and I was turning into someone that I wasn't. I was a nice, humble, kind-hearted person and arguing with Damian all the time was turning me into a toxic monster. Damian must have felt out of control as well because he asked to set up a meeting with my Pastor and his wife, and they agreed. They came over to our house and counseled us. They were very helpful. Damian had even told me that he had meetings with the Pastor without me to get counsel. He had also reached out to Terrance and his wife Michelle to counsel us as well.

Us four sat down in my living room and I was very transparent whereas all Damian was trying to do was attack my character and tell lies. I guess he felt that since Terrance was his friend that he would automatically take his side. But it did not work out that way, all Damian did was expose himself and all the truth was coming out about a lot of his own toxic actions and I think they got to see him in a different light. In the meeting with the Pastor and his wife, he held it together, but the meeting with Michelle and Terrance, he kept getting angry and defensive and he was telling on himself with his own actions. They tried to help him see things from my point of view but he wasn't hearing it. "So, Damian, I do want to say this to you" Michelle said. "Shamirah is sitting here taking responsibility for all her actions, but I didn't hear you take responsibility yet" she said to him sincerely and I was so glad that she picked up on that, because that's how he was.

He was a blamer and he never took responsibility. He would just constantly deflect. After she said it, me, Terrance and Michelle were looking at him for a response and the best he could do was look at me and say verbatim "your good." "What do you mean by that?" Michelle asked him. "She's good, she's a good liar, she even got y'all believing her lies" he said to them, and we all looked puzzled. I had told no lies; he was just mad that he was the liar but the truth about him was exposed and he was pissed. At that point I was tired of talking because clearly, we were not getting anywhere. I think Terrance and Michelle felt the same way and we wrapped up the meeting. I hugged them and thanked them for coming as they were going out the door. Damian sat there still looking salty. His goal was to sabotage me to his friends but it didn't work because the truth will always prevail. I felt good after the meeting and I felt like Damian played himself. After they left, I went upstairs to my room and closed my door. He was a mess and I was sick of his crap at that point.

In the midst of the drama that we had already had going on, Damian had got a phone call from his son's mom stating the state was trying to take him due to an incident that had happened so she needed Damian to come and get him. He flew up there the next day to get his son Branden and bought him to live with us. It was all sudden for me and was a big adjustment. We lived in a two-bedroom town house and Najah had her own room and her own space, but Damian had to get bunk beds and make space in Najah's room for his son. Branden and Najah fussed all the time over the room, toys and everything else. The whole situation took some getting used to for us all.

Even though Damian had his son there he was still ripping and running the streets and doing what he wanted to do. I explained to him that Branden was now there and he needed to step up more with parenting him. I was working full time and going to school as a medical assistant which I did get my certification as a patient care technician, a phlebotomist and an EKG tech. I was also very involved in Najah's schooling and dropping her off and picking her up from her after school activities. Throughout elementary school she was in dance, choir and all types of other programs that kept me and her busy, so for Damian to bring his son to live with us and expect me to take a whole another child on full time was not fair to me, and I expressed that to him. He would get upset when I told him how I felt and that just created more tension between us. The arguments were getting worse and even more frequent.

There started to be resentment being built up on both sides. He resented me for not stepping up and taking on the responsibility of his son, and I resented him for putting that responsibility on me. I had no problem with helping him with his son, but I was not ready to fully be his mom and take on that role 100%. I still was not even healed from finding out that he had a child period and now to ask me to be that child's mother was just too much for me mentally at the time.

Me and Damian had grown farther and farther apart, and he talked about getting his own place and I agreed. One day while the kids were at school me and Damian had got into a heated argument and just so happened my mom had popped up at my house in the midst of it. We were going back and forth and my mom jumped in, in my defense and after she did that world war 3 had broken out. and Her and Damian had got into it and they both were slandering each other and trying to break the other down with their words. It was horrible, it was like watching a train wreck before my eyes and I could not make them stop.

In the midst of the argument my mom had told Damien to pack his sh*t and get out.

We talked about him leaving but I was not ready for him to go at that moment, but once she said it, he started gathering his stuff. "I'm out, f*ck you and your mom" he said as he looked me in my face as he was packing. I felt helpless and the situation was beyond out of control at that point. Eventually everything calmed down and my mom had left and me and Damian did not speak. While he was packing you could hear a pin drop. He had got his stuff and put it in his rental car and he drove off. I sat there in my empty living room and played back all the chaos that just happened. All I could do was sit there and cry. I felt so broken and defeated and empty.

I was mad at my mom, but I was also relieved because she had said everything to him that I had been wanting to say to him, that I did not have the courage to. I sat there for a while then I began cleaning up the mess that he had made from moving when Najah and his son had walked through the door from school. They were talking and looked happy like kids did and before the door could close Damian was outside beeping his horn and he told his son to get in the car and they drove off. "Where is my dad going?" Najah said sadly. "He will be back" I said, comforting her not wanting her to know that he had moved out.

Damian was Najah's best friend and she was crazy about her dad. A few minutes later he called my phone and asked to speak to her. "Daddy will be back to pick you up soon ok; I have some stuff to handle and then I will be back to get you ok" he said comforting her. "Ok daddy" she said as she began to smile and I could tell she felt better. She had hung up and handed me the phone and she ran upstairs happily to play with her toys. I felt bad because I did not know what was going to happen next. I didn't know what the future held for all of us. Days had passed and I had not heard from Damian. He would not talk to me, but every day after school he would be outside waiting for Najah to get off the bus and she would sit in the car with him and spend time with him. Sometimes they would drive off and get ice cream and eventually she would come in the house and he would leave. Time had passed and I was working and in school and I had the house to myself. It was just me and Najah there and there was no arguing and no drama. The air in the house was clean and there was good energy all throughout the place and it felt good.

About a month had passed since Damian was gone and I had not talked to him the whole time. One day I was cleaning out my closet and I had come across my box filled with photo albums and I had come across a lot of our old pictures and it brought back a lot of memories and I had begun to break down and cry. Even though I didn't know if he was still mad or not, I had picked up the phone and called him. "Hello?" he said sounding surprised to hear my voice. I was on the other end crying and I could not get my words out. "What's wrong? Why are you crying? He asked me. "I was just looking at some pictures and they brought back memories and it made me sad because we don't even talk anymore, I told him. "Word, I definitely understand" he said agreeing with me and I could tell he was glad that I called, because his pride would have never allowed him to pick up the phone and call first.

While I was on the phone, he started to talk to me and the conversation was going well. He had his own place and Najah would go there with him and his son on the weekends. "Why don't you come and chill when Najah comes this weekend" he said to me to my surprise. "Are you inviting me to your house?" I asked as I chuckled. "Yeah" he said as I could tell he was smiling on the other end. Days had passed and Saturday had come and he finally gave me his address and I drove Najah to his house and saw his apartment for the first time. It was nice, a typically guys house. He showed me around and the kids went to the room to play. We sat and talked and he ordered food and we watched a movie and vibed out. He was being very nice to my surprise, and it seemed like any bad feelings that he had, had went away. I had spent the night and we had sex and it was nice. He was really romantic and caring.

The next day we got up and I made everyone breakfast and eventually it was time to go back home so I could get ready for my work week and Najah could get ready for school. I worked Monday-Friday from 9am-3pm and was off on Saturday and Sundays and from that weekend on I had spent every weekend with Damian at his house. When Najah got out of school on Fridays we would go there and stay until Sunday and we always had a good time. Throughout the week Damian would come over to my house almost every day. He would come to see Najah and he would also come to spend the night to have sex with me. He called me all the time and flirted with me, and he even took me out on cute dates. Our relationship had begun to get a lot better and things were looking up. It was nice living in separate houses, we only had to deal with each other when we wanted to and the time, we spent with each other and we actually enjoyed it.

31

One day Damian had got a call that one of his good friends got killed so he flew up to Jersey for the funeral. While he was there, he spent time with his little brother Khris. Damian was telling him he needed to leave the city because there was too much violence and that he could bring the kids and come and live with him in his apartment. Khris had agreed but needed to tie up some loose ends before he left. While in Jersey Damian had got a call that his other little brother Rich had got shot in the stomach. Rich was in the hospital so Damian, Khris and my cousin Nayshawn had jumped on the road asap to Greensboro NC to be by Rich's side. They had stayed there for a few days while Rich recovered and then they went back to Jersey.

While they were there Damien kept trying to persuade Khris to leave with him when he went back to GA in a few days. Khris had business in reference to his kids a few days later so he told Damian that after everything was handled, he would come and Damian was satisfied with the answer. "I'm going back to GA now bro, so you should be flying down in a few days, right? Damian asked him for reassurance. "Yeah big bro, I will be there" Khris said as he smiled. "Ok then" Damian said to him as he gave him a hug and came back to GA.

When Damian got home, I went to his house and he had told me all about it and he told me he was excited to have Khris down in GA with him. All I remember Damian saying was "My lil nigga got killed, he was the same age as Khris, if something happens to my little brother, I'm going to lose it" and I knew he was sincere because I knew the way he felt about Khris. He loved him with his whole heart. There was a shooting in A.C later on that night and Damian had called Khris to make sure he was in the house and out the way. "I'm good big bro, I'm in the crib" Khris reassured him. "Ok then, I love you lil bro" Damian said to him and they hung up. They talked every day until it was closer to the time for him to come.

Over the weekend Damian came to my house early to pick up Najah to take her and Brandon to the movies. I had the whole day to myself, and I was loving it. I was in a good mood and the energy of the day felt amazing so I turned on some gospel music and took a shower and relaxed. Hours had passed and they still did not come back. I had sent Damian a text and he told me they had not gone to the movies yet; he had taken them a few other places first. I told him Ok, and I continued about my day. Eventually it was nighttime and my best friend had called me and we talked and laughed for hours. I had looked up and before I knew it, it was after 9 pm and Damian still had not come back with Najah. I had sent him a text and he didn't respond back but I didn't even notice because I was on the phone with my bestie. I had got a call on the other line from a number that I did not recognize so I didn't answer it. The number kept calling me back to back so I finally told my bestie to hold on and I clicked over.

"Hello?" I said wondering who it was. "Mirah, it's Terrance," the voice said. "Hey Terrance, what's up?" I said to him curious why he was calling me. "Is Damian there? I been trying to hit his phone but it keeps going to voicemail" he told me. "No, he's not here, he's been out with the kids all day" I told him, and then I remembered that Damian never texted me back either. "Let me try to call him," I told Terrance and we hung up. I called him and it was going straight to voicemail and I began to get an anxious feeling. I kept trying to call but was not able to reach him. As I was calling him Terrance had called me back. "Sorry to keep

calling you Mirah, but it's about Khris" he told me. "What about Khris?"
I asked curious. "Somebody called me and said somebody got shot and
they think it's Khris" he told me. "Oh my God what?!" I said shocked. "I
don't think it's Khris, I'm about to call his phone" I told Terrance and I
hung up and called and there was no answer. I hung up and called their
sister and she didn't answer either. I began to panic on the inside and I
called my bestie to tell her what Terrance told me. She said somebody
was just shot but it was an older guy with dreads and I felt better.

I was waiting for Khris to call me back so when I heard my other
line beep, I thought it was him, but it was Terrance again. "Hello" I
answered, and this time Terrance was hesitant and I heard worry and
stress in his voice. "Mirah" he said. "What happened?" I asked him scared
of his response. "It's definitely Khris for sure" he said, like it pained
him to have to even say it. "No!!!" I yelled and my heart dropped into
my stomach and I felt nauseous. I began to cry hysterically as Terrance
tried to calm me down over the phone. "Me and Vernon(also know as
Chef Vernon) are on our way there right now" Terrance told me referring to him and one of Damian's other close friends were on the way
and I hung up. I had the eeriest feeling come over me.

By now it was about 10 pm. Damian was still not answering and I
was worried. I ran upstairs to throw on some sweatpants and a shirt
and still with my scarf on I ran out the house to find him. I had
no clue where he was. I had drove up the street to the movie theater
hoping that he was there because if he wasn't, I didn't know where
else to go. Thankfully when I pulled into the parking lot his car was
there. I had called Terrance and told him I found Damian and him and
Chef Vernon pulled into the parking lot soon after. "Mirah, I'm sorry"
Terrance said as he walked up to me and hugged me. Him and Vernon
stood there looking sad and in shock. None of us wanted to be the ones
to tell Damian and I was still crying hysterically. I could not even think
about looking him in his face and telling him that Khris was dead, it
broke my heart just thinking about it. Finally, we all saw Damian come

out the theater with the kids holding popcorn and a slushy, as soon as I saw his face I started crying even more. My heart was broken into pieces that night.

Terrance and Vernon had walked over to him to tell him and I was scared to look at Damian's face and see his reaction because it was too painful. To my surprise he was calm and actually seemed numb. He told the kids to get in the car with me. I tried to hug him, and he had no expression in his eyes. He looked blank. He didn't say anything. He was silent and he got in the car with Terrance and Vernon and they drove away and went to Jersey asap. His son Branden was with me the week he was gone and I had barely talked to Damian. Finally, he called me the day before the funeral as he was on the avenue shopping for clothes for Khris's burial. It was so sad and I was still in disbelief. I was not able to go to the funeral. I didn't do death well and I did not want to see Khris lying in a casket. My heart was broken even knowing he was gone. He was sweet and he was the baby of the family.

At the time he got killed he was working at the boys and girls club with the youth. He was not into the streets. He was a stand-up young guy who was all about his kids and was making plans to come to GA for a better life and he didn't deserve to die the way he did. He was walking home that night. He made a store run for his girlfriend and while on his way home some guys tried to rob him and he told them that he only had $10 on him, as he was talking to the guy in front of him a guy in the back of him had pulled out a gun and shot him in the back of his head, point blank for no reason at all. Khris had dreads and he laid there in the streets with his dreads covering his face and no one knew who he was. It was the saddest day ever for me. The family was heartbroken, they had already lost their brother Drew a few years before that.

Their mom was sick at the time and got even sicker after Khris passed. It was a nightmare for the family and for me as well. I always remember Khris' smile and his spirit. I missed hearing him call me sis and I missed watching him with his sons that he loved dearly. To this day I pray that whoever did that to him pays for their sin a million-fold and even if they get away with it in this life, I pray that they pay for it in the afterlife as well. Khris didn't deserve to die like that. Whoever did it broke a lot of hearts by killing him in cold blood for no apparent reason at all.

After Damian came back from Jersey from the funeral, I took his son back to his house and I visited him. He was in a low mood and I could tell he was still trying to process everything. He had shown me pictures in his phone of when he went to see Khris' body and he looked so peaceful. He looked like he was sleeping and that bought me comfort. Even though it was still painful knowing that he was gone. I tried to comfort Damian the best way I could but there were literally no words to ease the pain. I stayed there with him for a few days to make sure he was Ok. Terrance had come over too, and spent a lot of time with Damian as well as for comfort.

Damian's dad was heartbroken as well and a few weeks later his dad had moved in with him. Him and his dad were close, so I think his dad moving in was a good idea as they were a comfort to one another. Having his dad around seemed to put him in better spirits. His dad lived there for almost a year and throughout the time me and Damian were still close. We still dated and took the kids out on family functions and visited each other and spent Holidays and attended Najah's school events together. Things were very good between Damian and I for the most part.

One night I was at home getting ready for bed for work in the morning and I had got a call from Damian. "Hello?" I answered figuring he wanted to come over. "I been shot" he said so calm that I thought he was playing. "What?" I asked confused. "I just been shot in my back and I'm on my way to the hospital" he said calmly. "Oh my God!" I said as I started panic. "Calm down, I'm good. I love you and tell Najah I love her" he said, still calm. "What hospital you going to?" I asked as I was putting on my clothes. "The one not too far from us" he said as he hung up and I rushed to my mom's house who was thankfully in the same neighborhood and dropped Najah off. I was in such a panic that I could not drive so my sister drove me down there. We rushed to the emergency room and I got there and got up and ran through the doors and I saw Terrance, Damian's dad and his son Brandon waiting in the lobby. Terrance had hugged me, and I hugged Damian's son and I asked for updates. The doctor had come out and told us that he was shot in the lower back next to his spine and the bullet grazed his spine and a few more inches he would not have been able to walk so it was a miracle. I was relieved that he was ok, but my anxiety would not subside until I actually seen and spoke to him in person.

I had flashbacks of when he was stabbed back in 2003 and I was in the hospital with him. It brought back so many sad memories of him being stabbed and Drew and Khris being shot. I felt so bad as his dad sat there and I could tell that he was worried. He held it together well, but I knew he was tired of being in hospitals concerning his boy's lives. "You ok Mr. B?" I asked his dad and he half smiled. "Yeah, I'm ok" he said. "I'm just glad he's alive," his dad added. "I know what you mean, it's a blessing" I said to him as I smiled. Even though I was smiling I had broken out into tears because the whole situation was just overwhelming. Brandon had got up and got me a tissue and I thanked him. He sat calmly, he was about 9 or 10 at the time and I was not sure if he was fully aware of what was going on, but he was sitting there being strong.

After a while they had let us back to see Damian and he was in the hospital bed with tubes. When his son walked in that was the first time, I saw concern on his face. "What's up boy" Damian said to him, acting normal to let him know he was ok, and his son smiled and I could tell he felt better. Terrance had left to drop Damian's dad and his son off and my sister waited for me in the waiting room as I talked to him alone. "What happened?" I asked him, trying not to cry. "Somebody shot me" he said. "Why?" I asked him and before he could answer two detectives had walked in and announced themselves and asked Damian what happened and he told them he was shot and they asked did he see the person who shot him and he said no, they asked a few more questions but he could not remember anything, and they eventually left.

He had got out of the hospital the next day and I came to his house to help take care of him. "You Ok?" I asked him as we sat on his bed and he had his back where he was shot all bandaged up. "I'm Ok, it just hurts, " he said as he took a pain pill. "You want to see it? He asked me. "No not really" I answered. I hated blood and I did not want to see his bullet wound. Despite me saying I did not want to see it he had begun to peel the covering off and show me anyway. He had almost a quarter sized hole in his lower back, and it was still open where he was shot. "Ok, put the bandage back on!" I yelled to him as I could not take seeing it any longer. He had stood up in front of me and he had his shirt up and I saw the scars from when he was stabbed that went from his stomach to his back and now, he had a bullet wound too. "You got all your battle scars huh?" I said as I joked with him. "Yeah" he said as he joked back as we both tried to make light of the situation. Eventually I had to go home and get back to work so his dad had looked after him while I was not there. I had called and checked on him all day and for the most part he was ok.

Shortly after Damian being shot, he got into a bind and he wound up having to move out of his place. He didn't have anywhere to go so I offered him to come back and stay with me until he got back on his feet. His dad had moved to NC, and Brandon went with his mom, so he back to Jersey with his mom went back to Jersey for a little while to spend time with her. Damian now had his own car too, because before Khris died, he was given a car by his girlfriend's mom, and his girlfriend gave the car to Damian to have. He was grateful and it was a reminder of Khris.

One night while Damian was still living in his apartment, we were sitting in the car in the parking lot talking and the car was off, and it suddenly just started up by itself. "You see that?" Damian asked me as it spooked both of us. "Khris if this is you, turn the car off" Damian said out loud and the car turned off. "Turn it back on " Damian said and the car came back on. I sat there in disbelief at what was happening, but I did believe in energy and I knew it was most likely Khris visiting us, so after a while it didn't spook us, it gave us a sense of comfort. "I love you little bro" Damian said out loud and after that the car did not turn on and off ever again. Damian being back home with me was nice, and it felt like we were a family again. Us living in separate houses is what we needed, and it actually made us grow closer and appreciated each other more. When he came back home there was not really too much drama at the time.

One night I had cooked a nice steak dinner and me and Najah had baked cupcakes with blue icing and I planned on having dinner as a family. "You ready to eat?" I asked Damian as he came through the door. "Nah, I have to run out really quick" he said to me as he was in a hurry. "Where you going? we are about to eat" I said to him as I showed him his plate. "I know, and I appreciate it" he said smiling. "You and Najah go ahead and eat and I will be right back" he told me. I wasn't hungry anymore and I felt uneasy as he walked out the door. I made Najah her plate and let her eat one of the cupcakes and I waited for Damian. He left out at about 6pm and time had passed. I had called him around 10pm and he didn't answer. I figured he would call me right back like he normally did, but he didn't. I called him back around 11pm, then 12am and still no answer. I told myself maybe he was at a lounge or something and couldn't hear his phone. I was getting worried so I tried to go to sleep to stop stressing and figured he would be there by the time I got up. I went to sleep around 1am and woke back up around 3am. I figured if he was at a lounge then it was over at 3am and he would pick up. I called him and still no answer. I called back at 3:30pm and still no answer. At that point I began to get nervous and panic. I kept looking out the window expecting his car to pull up but it didn't. It was not like Damian at all to not answer my calls, let alone stay out that long especially without calling me. In my head I began thinking the worst and kept trying to keep myself from panicking. I laid there in bed and tears came down my eyes and I began praying.

About an hour and a half passed and it was now about 5:00 am. I had got a call from a government number and I started to not answer it, but something said pick it up so I did. "Hello" I said with the cry voice. "Hello" I heard the voice say and it was Damian. My heart felt so relieved to hear his voice. "Where are you?" I asked worried. "I'm in jail at Rice Street," he told me. Rice street is a jail in Atlanta, and I had no clue why he was there. "I was driving to see my peoples and I got pulled over, and they took me to jail" he said to me. "Oh my God, for what?" I asked him and he told me. "Do you have a bail?" I asked him. "No, not yet. I have to see the judge first" he told me. I was so sad that he was in jail, but relieved that he was ok. "I will see the judge in the morning and when I do, I will call you and let you know how much it is, and you can come and bail me out" he told me and I agreed. "I love you, and when Najah get up tell her I love her too" he said to me and I told him I loved him and we hung up.

In the morning I had called the jail to see if he had a bail and I waited for him to call. When he finally did, he sounded bummed out. "Did you see the judge? How much is your bail?" I asked him optimistically. "The judge didn't give me a bail" he said to me. "Damian stop playing, how much is it?" I asked still optimistic. "I'm serious, when I went before the judge the state picked up the case and I was indicted on higher charges. The judge I went before was a municipal judge so I have to wait to see the criminal judge. I don't know when that will be" he told me. "What?" I said as my heart dropped. "So, you don't have a bail and you don't know at all when you will have one?!" I said to him as I began to cry. "Calm down, everything will be Ok. I got the money to bail out when I get a bail, all I need you to do is be strong and hold you and Najah down while I'm gone" he said to me and I tried to dry my tears. He had not been in jail since we were in NJ and that was years and years ago. Since we had been in GA and Najah was born he was never in jail and Najah was used to seeing her dad every day even when he had his own place.

She was in school at the time, and I didn't want to tell her that her dad was in jail. "I love you; I will call you later when Najah gets home from school" he said to me and I told him I loved him and we hung up. I had put money on the phone so he would be able to call whenever he wanted and later that day, he called Najah and told her he loved her and that he would see her soon. I went and detained him a lawyer to fight the case for him and made sure he had money on his books to eat and get what he needed while he was in there. Also, when he got locked up his car was towed. I had called the police lot where his car was and an officer or whoever I was talking to let me know what his charges were and that he was not able to get his car out, and that for now it was their property. I was disappointed when I got off of the call, but I also had an overwhelming sense of peace and God had told me that everything would work out.

In the meantime, I was working and got off at 3pm so I was always home before Najah. When she got home from school, I made sure to keep her spirits up and she kept my spirits up as well. I was so sad, and I missed Damian but I knew I had to be a strong mother for our daughter. If I worried, she would worry and I didn't want her to sense that anything was wrong, especially with her dad because they were close and that was her best friend. Damians' cousin Lonnie would call me every day to check on me and I kept him updated and he would always encourage me and tell me to tell Damian that he loved him. He was also waiting to see what the bail amount was just in case he needed to help out and I appreciated that. Damian would call me all the time, even when I was at work.

Some days he sounded ok, and some days he sounded down and I would try to encourage him. I could tell that being in jail away from his family was bothering him because none of us were used to being apart that long. I wanted to see him and I didn't know how jail worked in GA. I thought it was like the county jail back in Atlantic County NJ where you could see each other through the glass, but it was not like that. When I pulled up to Rice street I got searched and everything and the area to do the visit was a video call. I didn't like it but I was willing to sit there and video chat with Damian versus seeing him through a glass, but I guess his video chat was not set up so I could not see him and I was so disappointed, not to mention I drove all the way from Gwinnett to Rice Street for nothing. One of the guards let me know that I could get the video chat set up on my phone and I did not have to come all the way down their next time, and I wish I had known that info ahead of time. Najah was still in school so I hurried home and Damian called me and I told him what happened. "Don't even worry about it. Thank you for coming, I didn't know how it was set up either." he said as we talked for a while.

He was in jail a little over a month when one day he called me and told me he had a bail. We both were so excited. I immediately got up and called a bails bondsman. A lot of bail bondsmen told me they could not get him out and I was getting so discouraged. Finally, I had found one downtown and I drove straight to Atlanta to post his bail. As I was sitting at the bail bondsman office, the lady was pulling up his paperwork and she showed his mugshot on the screen of the night he got locked up. All over his face was sadness and I could read his mind and, in the moment, I knew he was thinking about me and Najah and was thinking to himself "I messed up." His mugshot made me feel bad and I was glad he was coming home. She did all the paperwork on the computer and she got to the end and basically told me what all the other bail bondsman told me which was he was "un bailable" and I was getting frustrated because I did not know what that meant. The lady told me that she would keep working on it and that she would call me when she got it all squared away and I left the office.

When I left something told me to call the jail and figure out what was going on. The clerk had let me know that he could not go through a bail bondsman because he had to bail out straight from the jail. I was relieved that I finally got an answer but I wish the bail bondsman had just told me that themselves and it would have saved me a lot of time. It was almost night time so I needed to get home in all the traffic. Damian called and I told him what happened and that I would get up early and go to the jail in the morning. He was calm and understood that I was getting the run around and he said ok just try again tomorrow. I got up early the next morning and got dressed and left for Rice Street after I had put Najah on the bus.

When I got there, I had parked and went into the jail and when I walked in, I saw Porcha Williams from the Real housewives of Atlanta, her sister Lauren and Porcha's attorney's. I think there maybe even were two attorneys. When I first saw Porscha I was shocked and happy to see her so I instinctively said "Hi Porscha" and I smiled at her. She was standing by the guards about to be handcuffed and she turned around to me and smiled and said "Hi" in a very nice tone. Her attorney said a few words to her and shortly after she went through the door to the back in handcuffs. I was waiting in line to bail Damian out and all that was going through my mind was first was wow Porcha was way shorter in person that she looked on tv and that her waist was super tiny. She was going to jail but she looked so pretty. She had on pink lipstick, her hair had a side part with flowing curls and she had on black pants and a black top.

At the time the media was talking about her going to jail but I believe she came in early to beat the press. It was real lowkey and there was no press there. Secondly in that moment I had admired Porscha because she was literally seconds from being cuffed and had a lot going on with going to jail and I could imagine how scary that could have been for her, but she was still smiling and had a humble spirit about herself. I could tell that she had a lot of faith that things were going to be ok and the fact that she still spoke to me even when she didn't have to spoke volumes about her character. I was going through my own trial at the moment and in that moment, I had drawn my strength from her and she didn't even know it, so I thank Porscha for that. That small act of kindness really made a big impact in my heart.

When I got up to the window I had gave them Damian's info and they pulled his file and his picture was literally on top of Porcha's picture and I chuckled to myself because most people would have tried to take a picture and post it on social media, but I was not like that, I don't believe in invading people's personal privacy all I wanted to do was get Damian home. They took the money and posted the bail and I was so excited. It was $5000 that we had to give them and I was ready for him to come home! The clerk let me know that it would be a while so I went home. Damian had called me and I let him know that the bail was posted and I could hear the happiness in his voice.

I had posted the bail on April 14th and what made it more exciting was that the next day was his birthday so he him coming home was his gift. We waited and waited the whole night and he still was not out. The next day on his birthday he called and we were optimistic that he was getting out at any moment and I was going to be driving there to get him. The day had turned into night, and he still wasn't home. He had called me that night and we both were confused as to why it was taking him so long to get out, and he wound up spending his birthday in Rice Street. His cousin Lonnie and everybody was calling me to see if he was home yet and I had to keep telling them he wasn't and it was becoming discouraging.

The next day April 16th, he had called me from somewhere downtown and let me know he was out but he didn't have his phone because all his stuff was at another location. Once he told me where he was. It was later in the afternoon and me and Najah got in the car and drove to get him and when I saw him that was one of the happiest moments ever. I pulled up and he immediately told me to get in the driver's seat and he drove my car. "Daddy!" Najah said excitedly in the backseat. We were all in the car laughing and smiling as Damian was cracking jokes and happy to be free. I had called his cousin Lonnie and they laughed and were chopping it up. "Mirah, I know you happy as hell that Damian is home" Lonnie said as he was smiling over the phone. "Yeah I am" I said as I smiled. "You want something to eat?" I asked him and we pulled into Boston Market to sit and eat. I didn't like Boston Market, but I didn't care where we were as long as we were together. We ate and Damian smiled the whole time.

He was just so happy to be back reunited with us and we were happy to have him back. We had got home and he looked around the house like he had never been there before then he got in the shower and spent time with Najah and later he got in the bed with me and laid on his side and said "Bismillah" which means "Thank You God" in Islam and I turned to him and smiled and laid on his chest and we hugged each other tight and went to sleep. We did not have sex that night, we literally just hugged one another and was just so grateful to be back with one another and we just enjoyed the moment. Damian being back home was nice and everything was positive for the most part.

"Wow that was a lot" my therapist said to me as she intervened. "What were his charges? If you don't mind me asking" and I told her. "Ok" she said. "I am happy that everything worked out. I could imagine that him being gone for a period of time was overwhelming, especially for your daughter but you handled it very well" she told me. "It seems like when he came home things were positive and that was great. So how did the case end? If you don't mind me asking" she said to me as she sat back in the chair and listened.

"As I stated earlier, I had detained a lawyer for Damian. A little while passed and his court date came up and it was a trial by a judge meaning there was no jury, the judge would make the decision if he was guilty or not. On the day of the trial I did not go because there would have been no one home to watch Najah when she got out of school, so me and Damian agreed that I should stay home. I had prayed for him before he left. I was praying and worshipping the whole time he was gone. He was in court so I was not able to talk to him so I had no clue how everything was going. I had played "Shifting the Atmosphere" by Jason Nelson and I was worshipping and I felt a feeling of supernatural peace coming over me. I continued to stand on my faith that everything would work out in that courtroom and refused to be worried or anxious. A few hours later when Damian got out of court, he called me. "What happened?" I asked curious. "It's dismissed, I will tell you about it when I get home" he said to me and we hung up and I immediately began praising God. When he got home, he told me that the cop who pulled him over was there and testified to what happened that night and what was found.

Damian's lawyer argued that his car was illegally searched because Damian did not give consent. The cop lied and said he pulled him over because his tail light was out and that he searched the car because he smelled weed, which was a lie because Damian did not smoke weed and also while he was in jail his lawyer ordered a weed test for him to take as evidence and it came back negative so that proved that the officer was lying. Also, his lawyer had got the copy of the dashcam from that night and Damian's tail light was not in fact out at all. So, the cop had no probable cause to stop him nor search his car. After the judge saw all the evidence, she threw out the case and Damian was free to go accept, he did have some community service to do for a few weeks. Damian told me that even his lawyer was shocked that his case was just thrown out because that rarely happens and I told him that it was because of prayer and the favor of God and he agreed.

After it was all over, we were able to go down to Rice street and get the bail money back, even though the jail took a percentage. The rest of the $4500 we got back and every Tuesday for about a month Damian went down to Peachtree street to go to his community service probation which didn't take long at all. We used to make a day out of it. We would drive downtown, go to probation and then leave and walk around down there and sight see and go get something to eat and spend time. Most of all since his case was thrown out, he was able to get his car back from the police lot. They had to release it back to him which they were not expecting to do.

The lot was in Alpharetta and I drove him there to pick up his car and he was like a kid in the candy store. He was so excited to have his car back and I was very happy for him as well. God was showing up and showing out in his life and we were able to be a happy family again, and the jail and court cases were behind us." I explained to the therapist. "That is awesome" she said as she was happy to hear the good news. "I am so glad that everything worked out. I truly am" she said as he smiled. So how was everything moving forward?" Did things stay positive?" she asked me as he picked up her pen and pad. Yes, I would say things were positive for the most part. After the whole ordeal we put all of that behind us.

Damian and all his cousins planned a lake house cabin trip at an Airbnb for his dad's 60th Birthday. There were a lot of us who attended. There was me, Najah, Damian, his son, his dad. His two older brothers. His cousin and his girlfriend and their two kids. His other cousin and his girlfriend and their three kids. We were deep. The lake house was huge and beautiful. It had 6 bedrooms, huge living spaces, a hot tub downstairs and access to the lake and a boat. It was nice. Me and Damian had the best room. Our room had a fireplace and a jetted stone tub. All the kids loved being together and playing in the huge house, and us adults cooked and drank liquor and had a ball. Everyone was in a good mood before we came and we all were having a great time. Suddenly his cousin and his cousin's girlfriend got into it and things got heated. After we all diffused that situation his other cousin and his girl got into it, so we had to break up that argument as well. Right before our eyes everyone was fighting and Me Damian and his dad were the only ones who were civil and we had to continue to be mediators.

The next day we all got up and took the kids to Lanier world at lake Lanier and they had a blast. Outside of the house everyone was having a great time and there was no arguing. We had all got back and cooked out on the grill and suddenly the arguing started again between everyone. Me and Damian thought it was funny and we were just happy that it wasn't us with all the drama. Overall, the lake house was so much fun and I enjoyed being with everyone. The next day we drove to Port Royale Marina to get on some Jet skis. Everyone had Jet skied before and they were so excited. I had never been on one before and I was terrified of the water especially since we were at Lake Lanier where there were so many deaths. We did the Jets ski class on the computer then they gave us our life jackets and took us out to the port where the jet skis were.

On the same Marina were all types of different boats porting and it was giving me anxiety. The instructor was telling us what to do and everyone started to get on their jet skis and the kids got on with their parents or older adults. Damian had got on his jet ski and Najah got on the back with him. "Who Am I getting on with?" I asked Damian confused. "You got your own jet ski" he said as he smiled and pointed to the empty jet ski. "No, I can't ride it by myself," I said to him. "Yes, you can, it's fun, just try it" he told me trying to get me to have fun. "Damian, I can't" I said to him as I was scared. They were all getting ready to ride out and leave me so I had no choice but to get on. I got on and the instructor showed me how to start it up and what gears to use. I was scared out my mind as they jet ski started moving and I followed the crew out as they were ready to have a ball in the water. I was riding so slow in the water as we left the dock and I could feel every wave and all the water under me and it terrified me.

I got pass the dock where it led to the open lake. People were driving their jet skis fast and on speed boats and everything and the water was going haywire and my jet ski was rocking back and forth and I panicked. "Take me back, take me back!" I yelled as I did not want to be in the water anymore because I did not know how to control the jet ski and I felt like I was going to fall. I was only out there for about five minutes and Damian helped me get back to the dock and I had to park my Jets ski and I got off and took off my life jacket and was finally on safe land and I felt so relieved. "You sure you want to sit here on the dock by yourself? Damian asked. "Yup" I'm great right here" I said to him as I sat under the shade and he sped off into the water with Najah on the back and they were having a ball.

The Jets ski rental was two hours and I did not care that I was sitting on the dock, I was just happy to not be in the water. On the dock was a tiki restaurant so I had gone and got some food and enjoyed watching everyone have a good time. I saw people partying on their boats and dancing to the music at the bar. I was watching shows on my phone and enjoying myself. The two hours had gone by fast. There was about 20 minutes left until the time was up and I saw Damian riding to the dock as he looked like he was having a blast. "Come just try it, we only have a few minutes left, you will be ok, it's fun" he said as he persuaded me. "Ok" I said against my better judgement and I hopped on the back.

As we got out of the dock area to the open water all the cousins and everyone was out there to greet me and they were ready to ride out. "Hold on tight" Damian said to me as he was about to speed off. "Yo cuz, she don't have her life jacket on!" one of his cousins had reminded us. I had totally forgot that I had took my life jacket off at the dock and I did not put it back on when I hopped on the jet ski. "Stay right here cuz I will go back and get it for you" his cousin said to me as he sped off to get my life jacket. As we were in the water Damian was telling me how much fun the jet skis were and all the tricks he was doing. As he is telling me this the water is rocking back and forth. "Ok, just relax until I get my life jacket. " I told him as I was scared but I was trying not to panic. "You good" he said as I was holding on to the back of him for dear life and he decided to stand up and fix his pants. "Sit down!" I pleaded with him as the jet ski was rocking from side to side. "This will not tip over" he said as he is still standing up and the jet ski is still rocking side to side. "Damian sit down!" I pleaded again and he went to speak. He said "The boat wont......." and before he could get Tip out his mouth before I knew it the jet ski had tipped over and I fell in to rapid Moving water with no life jacket on and I was beyond petrified.

I was in so much shock that I tried to scream but nothing would come out. I was struggling to stay above water because of all of the waves and I could not swim that good. I felt myself sinking and all I kept seeing was me being another death on the news at Lake Lanier. "God please do not let me die in this lake" is what I kept pleading and praying. I asked my angels to save me as I was getting weaker and weaker. The jet ski was flipped over and floating and I saw Damian in the water too, and even though I didn't know if I was going to make it or not I was more worried about him than my own life, and I asked God to not let him die. He was swimming towards me and he grabbed me and was holding me up. "Damian, I'm dying" I kept saying to him as I was panicking. "You not dying just hold onto me" he kept saying. Damian had a life jacket on and he was not going to drown but I did not realize that in the moment and I was holding onto him for dear life as if I could save him and at the time, I was not worried about myself. The jet ski was floating away and getting farther and farther. "I have to get the jet ski so I can save you. I have to let go of you for a minute so I can get it" he said. "No!" I tried to scream to him but nothing would come out. Next thing I knew he let go off me and I saw him swim away as I began to sink. I had seen a boat floating by that was kind of far away and I mustered up enough energy to scream "help!" I think they looked over and I remember hearing one of his cousins yell to them that I was ok. I didn't have enough breath to tell them that I wasn't and they kept on riding. I felt like I was going to die at that moment. I was so tired and literally out of breath and I felt myself sinking and mentally fading away. Damian had finally tipped over the jet ski and got it close to me. "Grab my hand" he said as he came to the back of the jet ski reaching out his hand for me to grab it. I was so weak that I could not lift my arm. "Come on Shamirah, you can do it" he said to me trying to encourage me.

He reached down into the water and helped me latch onto the back of the boat steps. I grabbed on but did not have any energy to pull myself up. I got far enough where Damian was able to pull me up the rest of the way and I fell onto the back of the jet ski and tried to catch my breath and I thanked God for being out of the water. "You ok?" he asked me as I still could barely talk and my body was still in shock. "No" I said as I tried to muster up the energy to speak. "Please take me back to the dock. I begged him as my hands and legs were shaking. His cousin had ridden up to our jet ski and handed me my life jacket finally, and I hurried up and put it on. "Ok, take me to the dock now" I told Damian. "Ok hold on tight to me" he said as he started up the jet ski. "You good? You ready?" he asked me, making sure I was all secured. "Yes, I'm ready" I said to him and instead of going in the direction of the dock he darted off into the water at full speed hitting every wave. "Damian, what are you doing? Take me back!" I was screaming. "You are good, you're safe, you have a life jacket on" he said as he was smiling and laughing as his cousins were on a trail behind us and everyone was having fun. I was terrified and I wanted to throw up. Damian was going fast and doing all types of tricks and all I could do was close my eyes and pray for it all to be over. Thank God the time was up and we had to head back to the dock.

On the way back I was pissed that I had fallen into the water because of him and instead of him taking me to the dock he drove the jet ski even farther out. When we got to the dock there were a lot of people there waiting for their boats and jet skis and I don't know what happened when Damian tried to jump the jet ski on the parking area but for some reason he missed and the jet ski tipped over again. Thank God that time I had on my life jacket but I still panicked on top of the fact I was so embarrassed. At that point I was over being there and I was ready to go. Damian and everyone else thought it was funny but they did not realize how traumatized I was. Falling off of the jet ski that day was an experience that I would never forget and it haunted me and traumatized me for a very long time and large bodies of water had become a huge fear for me. I loved the beach but I would not go in it past my knees. I think my original fear of water came from growing up in Atlantic City. I lived in the inlet right up the street from the beach and when it would flood, I could look out the window down the street and see the water coming. The city would flood all the time and it was so scary to me. Ever since I was little, I knew how powerful the ocean was and how one minute it could look calm and the next minute you could be under water.

"That must have been a very traumatic experience for you" my therapist said as she chimed in. "I am so glad that you are ok, because yes Lake Lanier does have a lot of deaths" she said to me with compassion. "So, is that still a fear of your?" she asked me, and I answered her. "Well a couple of years had passed and his cousins would constantly come down to GA and they would rent jet skis and I would always go and sit on the dock until they were finished or not go at all. One summer day about three years later, I had just woken up and said to Damian "Let's ride some jet skis today." "Are you sure?" he asked me. I told him that I was sure. I told him I was tired of reliving that day and I wanted to conquer the jet ski, so he called Port Royale and booked the jet ski and we made a date out of it and rode there. I put on my life jacket and took all the precautions and although I was terrified, I got on the back and Damian drove. At first, he went at a slow pace and worked his way up to a high speed and doing donuts and all types of water tricks. I was scared but I loosened up and tried to have fun because that is what I was there for, to face my fear. We had ridden for miles and miles at top speed.

We had stopped at a few Islands a couple of times so I could regroup and we sat and talked and kicked it and Damian was being really sweet and compassionate and making sure I was comfortable. We would get back on the Jet Ski and ride some more. We had stopped in the middle of the water where nobody was and he just waded in the water and chilled. "You ready?" he asked me out of nowhere. "Ready for what?" I asked him. "Ready to jump" he said to me. "Jump into the water? Hell no, I'm not jumping in" I said to him resistant. "If you want to fully face your fear then you have to jump in. You have your life jacket on, I want to show you that you cannot drown with your life jacket on" he said as he got up and got prepared to jump. Next thing I knew he was in the water and he popped back up. "Now you go" he said to me as I did not want to go, but I took a chance and I jumped anyway and I landed right next to him and I popped right up. "See you are good right" he said to me as he seemed proud of me. "I'm good but I want to get out, I told him." "We going to do it a few more times' ' he said to me and we jumped several times and we swam to the island and we actually had a great time.

After we were done, we got back on the jet ski and went back to the dock and we left. "Today was a good day, right?" he said as we drove home. "Yeah it was fun, I am glad I did it. I still don't think I will be riding jet skis like that but I am glad that I got it out of my system" I said to him. "Word, I'm glad too he said and we went to get something to eat and went home" I told my therapist. "Oh wow, I am proud of you for facing your fear" she said to me smiling. "I am glad you did that; I know it was very scary for you to do, but you did it anyway and you should be proud of yourself" she told me smiling. "Thank you," I said to her. "Ok so you and your husband, then boyfriend at the time were on good terms and everything was going great at that point" she said to me. "Well I did not get to tell you the ending to the lake house" I said to her as I smirked. "Oh ok, please do" she said as she sat back in her chair and picked up her pen and began to listen.

On the way back to the lake house Damian and his older brother Evan had got into it and they were arguing and it was so comical. I had never seen them have a disagreement and it was so petty and hilarious, everyone was laughing because we could not take them seriously. Damian saw his brother getting more and more upset so he finally calmed down and shook his brother's hand to show there was no hard feelings. When we all got back to the lake house, we all took showers and got the kids ready to eat and put some food on the grill. Afterwards the plan was to go take a boat ride on the lake. While everyone was eating and enjoying themselves, me and Damian sat on the boat by ourselves and took pictures and spent time. "This boat ride later is going to be nice" he said as he sat in the driver's seat of the boat. "Yeah it is" I agreed with him as I looked out into the water. His brother Greg had got on the boat with us, and we all talked and laughed and enjoyed each other's company.

The day with me and Damian had been perfect and even though everyone had got into an altercation at that point, me and him had no drama and nothing but good vibes. Evening had come and we were all getting ready to go, as me and him were in our room. I had said something and I don't remember exactly what is what, but whatever I said made him respond in a way that had caused us to go back and forth. Next thing you knew we were now arguing and it spilled out of the room to the main areas where everyone else was and it got so heated that the ladies were trying to hold me back, and the men were trying to hold him back. Before we knew it, we were outside screaming at the top of our lungs. I was so upset that I could not breathe and felt like I was having an anxiety attack. The lake house was in the middle of the woods down a steep hill with nothing else around it and Damian decided to take my luggage out the house and roll it up the hill and tell me to leave and find my way home. Mind you, we drove. there in MY car. "I am not going anywhere" I yelled to him as I rolled my luggage back down the hill and put it on the porch. "You not coming on the boat with us, " he said as everyone headed to the small dock. "I don't want to go anyway" I said to him as I walked the other way. "Come on cuz, you don't have to stay here" the ladies were saying as they were trying to get me to get on the boat. "No, F him, I'm not going nowhere with him" I told them as I walked away, and everybody got on the boat and sailed off.

I was all alone in the woods by myself. The sun was starting to set and I refused to go back in that scary demonic haunted house by myself so I went and sat in my car and called my mom. I had told her what happened and we talked for a while. It had become dark and it was pitch black outside. The only lights were the lights from my car. At that point I knew I was not getting out of the car until they got back and it seemed like it took them forever. Thankfully my mom stayed on the phone with me the whole time, so I didn't focus on being scared because we talked and laughed the whole time. I saw a group walking to the front door so finally they were back and I got off the phone with my mom and went into the house. I still wasn't talking to Damian but I asked the girls how it was and they said it was fun. I had chilled with them and we made mimosas and all spent time together and laughed and had a good time without the guys.

The next day it was time to pack up and leave. I still wasn't speaking to Damian and all the other couples had their tension as well. On the ride home me and Damian finally talked and we still could not figure out why we started arguing in the first place. "That house had a lot of bad energy, right?" he asked me as he was driving. "Yeah it did" I said as I thought about it. "Everybody was cool until we all got into that house?" I told him. "Word, it's like that house had mad Jinns" he said to me and I agreed. Damian was Muslim, and jinn was the term Muslims used for demons.

I agreed with him the house had strong negative energy, not to mention it was in the middle of nowhere and by a lake. Spiritually lakes are known for having spirits lingering around them as well as spirits that come from out of the water. A lot of earth's mysteries are buried in the oceans and seas and we were aware of that. The lake house was right off of lake Lanier which was notorious for deaths so I would not be surprised at all if the house was haunted. Me and him talked about it the whole hour ride home. We were both into the spirit realm and we both believe in extraterrestrial life. We fussed a lot but me and Damian had so much in common. We could sit and talk about the origins of the world, aliens and other things that people would find weird. We didn't find a lot of things weird. We were knowledge seekers and we found a lot of things especially related to science very fascinating. When we pulled up to our house, we had way better energy and were in a more positive space with one another.

Everyone else had pulled up beside us and began to get out of their cars. Before I could step foot out of the car, I had heard Damian's brother snapping on his cousin. "What's the problem? Damian asked them as he got out of the car and his brother turned his attention on him and became aggressive. Before I knew it Damian and his brother were arguing and his brother started taking his shirt off to fight. "Nigga I will beat the sh*t out of you" Damian said as he was trying to contain himself. At that point his cousin had got in between them to diffuse the situation. Finally, the situation had calmed down and Damian got a phone call and he had to run to Atlanta. His dad and his older brother were outside on the porch and the kids went upstairs to play. Me, his two cousins who were brothers, and their girlfriends chilled downstairs. Damian's one cousin had got into it with his brother's girlfriend and they were having a war of words.

They were in my house yelling and his brother's girlfriend was picking up things and trying to throw it at her boyfriend's brother. Their fight had lingered from the lake house, and tensions had never died down. They exchanged words and someone spit on someone. I could not remember if his cousin spit on the brother's girlfriend or if she spit on him. Either way spit was exchanged and it was on from there. His cousin's girlfriend went bonkers and her boyfriend intervened and told her and his brother to chill out. The girlfriend was mad at her boyfriend for not taking up for her and letting his brother talk to her any kind of way, so she began to yell at him. He was calm at first and really didn't want any problems but she kept calling him names and saying he was scared of his brother and that's why he didn't take up for her. He got heated after a while and I remember him leaning on the stove with his back against it and her being in his face pointing her fingers and cursing him out.

I kept telling them to chill the whole time because they were doing all this in my house and it was becoming disrespectful to me and my belongings. She was in his face yelling and he was silent, next thing I knew he had pushed her. He had pushed her so hard that it was like she flew from the stove all the way to the washing area and she fell into the doors and there was a dent in my washer and dryer door area. They were the type of closet doors that you open sideways, I am not sure of the material, but they were a type of metal and they were ruined with a dent in them. After that she was still snapping and she began to cry out of shock.

I could not take any more drama so I had called Damian and told him what was going on and he told me to tell everyone to get out the house and that he was on his way. I told everyone to get out and when Damian got home, he was pissed. No one really said anything while he was there, it was silent. I was just happy that all the commotion was over and eventually everyone left and headed back to Jersey. I cleaned up the house and prayed over it to remove any bad energy. "That was a lot. These whole last couple of days were a lot over all" I told Damian. "Word, it was" he said, relieved to be at home peacefully.

3 2

"We need a new start" I told him. "What do you mean? He asked. "We need to move, " I said to him. My mom was about to move from the area. All my family that was in the neighborhood had already moved away, it was going to be just me and my aunt Tina left living around there and I was ready to move. The neighborhood went downhill from what it used to be, plus the townhome was becoming too small and I wanted something bigger with a garage because I was so tired of arguing with the neighbors about parking in my parking space. Damian had agreed on the move and we began to search for houses. We had lived in Gwinnett and my mom had moved to Stone Mountain. We looked for houses all over Gwinnett but they were out of our budget.

One day I was searching on Zillow and a house popped up in Stone Mountain and it was perfect. It looked huge in the pictures. It was a two level three-bedroom cottage style home with hardwood floor, a fireplace, a kitchen and separate dining room, two car garage, garden tub and a yard. The house had so much character and the best thing about it was the high cathedral ceilings it made the house feel grand. I had been looking all over and this house had felt right. When we went to see it, it was even better in person. The rooms were spacious and the bathrooms were huge. The washer and dryer area had a space of its own and all together the house was awesome. To make things even better my mom only lived eight minutes away. The only downfall was that the house was not attractive on the outside but it was awesome on the inside and the price to rent it was perfect too. I told the realtor that I wanted it and I put in the application and was approved a little while later. We began packing up our townhouse to move. Me and Damian were excited, it was like our fresh start, we had wanted to put all of our toxicness behind us and elevate in life and our relationship. We had lived in an apartment and we upgraded to a townhouse, now we were going from a townhouse, to a single-family home and we were proud of that.

We had moved all of our stuff in and I had decorated the house and it was so nice and comfortable. I cooked our first meal there to really make it feel like home and me, Damian and Najah sat down in the dining room and ate at the table like a family. Once everything was all settled, I had wanted to drive around and get to know my area. Around the time we began moving in I was always not feeling well. I figured I was moving and had a lot going on so I didn't really pay much attention to how I was feeling. It had been draining to get up and get dressed so I rested a lot in the living room on the couch. Hanging from the cathedral ceiling was a nice fan and I would get a big blanket and turn the fan on and fall asleep watching tv. One day I had decided to get dressed and look nice. I did my hair and everything and cruised the area but I did not stay out as long as I wanted to because I wasn't feeling good.

A few days later Damian's dad and his sister had come to town to visit us and me and his sister decided to cook a big dinner, while Damian and his dad were in the backyard talking about yard work that needed to be done. As we were cooking and laughing, I started to feel bad again. "Girl I need to go and lay down I don't feel that good" I told his sister. Me and her went upstairs to my room and I sat on my bed as I felt a little dizzy. "Girl you pregnant" she said out of nowhere. "Huh?" I asked confused. "You are sick because you are pregnant" she said again nonchalantly and confidently. "Girl what, I am not pregnant" I said to her as I laughed because the thought of being pregnant had never even crossed my mind. "I bet you, you are. Here" she said, going into her purse and handing me a pregnancy test. "Why are you walking around with pregnancy tests in your purse?" I asked her as I laughed. "Girl because you just never know, " she said as we both laughed and I went into the bathroom to take the test.

I came out and sat on the bed and waited for the time to check the results. "I am not going to look at it" I told his sister as I laughed but was nervous at the same time. I had no intention of taking a pregnancy test because I had never considered that I wasn't feeling well due to pregnancy. "Ok, I'll look at it" she said as she smiled and went into the bathroom and I saw her pick it up and look at it and she had a mysterious smile on her face so I couldn't read her. She walked out the bathroom still smiling and she handed me the test and I looked at it and surly it was positive. "Oh my God!" I said in complete shock, I definitely was not expected to find out I was pregnant. "Congratulations!" she said being funny, but she was genuinely happy for me at the same time. "Oh my God, I cannot believe it" I kept saying.

It took a few minutes to sink in that I was actually having a baby and when it did, I had got excited. In the upstairs part of the house was my room and Najah' room and there was also a loft area that we had turned into a living room sitting area with the couch and end tables. Me and his sister had walked around and I was telling her the ideas I was having about turning the loft area into the baby's room since it was right next to my room. I would have considered the downstairs guest room as an option but it was too huge, and I didn't like the fact of putting the baby downstairs. I had so many ideas running through my head. I had a daughter already, but I had also wanted a son, and I felt like I could have been pregnant with my boy finally and I began getting even more excited. I had fell in love with being pregnant and I had felt so blessed. It definitely was unexpected but for me it was a pleasant surprise. In my eyes it was perfect timing. We had just moved into this huge home and there was more than enough room for a new baby. I was working a good job full time. Damian had money coming in and was getting into flipping houses. We were happy and in a good space and everything felt right, and I was looking forward to my pregnancy journey. "When are you going to tell my brother?" she asked me. "I want to tell him now, but I am so nervous, " I said to her as I was smiling. I was not sure what his reaction was going to be. I figured that he would be just as shocked as I am, so I was nervous to tell him.

I had put the test in my pocket and me and his sister headed back downstairs to check on the food. We talked the whole time about baby names and all of that fun stuff and I was more and more happy by the minute. I had looked around the house and, in my mind, I saw a little baby running around and it made my soul happy. Also, I knew that Najah would be ecstatic to have a baby brother or sister. She always asked me to have a baby for her to play with so I could not wait to let her know the news. When the food was done, we had made everybody's plate and I had walked out to the yard to let Damian and his dad know to come and eat. As his dad walked away, I told Damian I had to tell him something as I was smiling from ear to ear. "What?" he asked me, looking curious. I didn't speak, I had just pulled the test out of my pocket and smiled. "Get that sh*t out of here" he said as he shewed me away. "Damian, I'm serious, I'm pregnant" I said to him still smiling. "I'm serious too. Get that sh*t out of my face. You all smiling and sh*t. I'm not trying to have no baby" he said to me in a rude tone and I could tell that he was serious.

My smile had turned upside down in the blink of an eye and it felt like my stomach had dropped into my shoe and I had felt nauseous. Not from pregnancy but from his reaction. "Damian are you really acting like this?" I had asked him in disbelief. "Hell yeah, you buggin, thinking it's funny" he said as he started walking away. I didn't want to argue in front of his dad so I had let it go when we got in the house, but my body language let everyone know that I was upset. I didn't even want to eat. All I wanted to do was go in my room and cry. I went upstairs and his sister came with me and asked me what happened and I told her. "Wow, I didn't think that he would react like that" she said to me as she seemed like she felt bad. "You were just so excited. At the end of the day you can still be excited, don't let his reaction change how you feel" she said to me. I heard what she was saying, but she did not know her brother like I did. She didn't know that he was a bully and tried to control my every decision, so by the way he acted it let me know that I was about to have a huge problem on my hands.

When his dad and sister had left, Damian let me know how out of pocket I was for taking the pregnancy test in the first place. He said that I put his sister in our business when I didn't. She offered the test. Also, he was mad that I told him while his dad was there, again also saying that I was telling his business, when I didn't even tell him in front of his father. He said his father "just knew" what it was. I told him that I didn't understand why he was upset. We were both two grown adults living on our own, so I didn't know why it was such a big deal to him that his sister and father knew about it. "Well, I don't want any more kids so you know what you have to do" he said to me. "No, I don't know," I said to him confused. "You getting an abortion asap" he told me as he was angry. "No, I am not. I am keeping my baby" I said to him as I began to get upset because I could not believe he had the audacity to tell me to get rid of my baby.

"Look at me" he said to me as I was sitting down at the edge of the bed, and he got in my face like he normally did when he was trying to intimidate me. "Look at me. I'm telling you now, if you have the baby and I am telling you not to, I promise I am going to make your life a living hell. You will raise the baby by yourself and I'll never speak to you again" he threatened me as he was looking into my eyes. At that time in life I hated when Damian got upset with me. As much as I wanted to keep my baby. His words kept playing in my head and day after day I tossed and turned about the decision to keep the baby or have the abortion.

Damian had left for a few days. He had taken a small trip to Jersey. He had called me every day while he was there and he was really nice, so I thought maybe he was loosening up about the abortion idea. When he came back it was a few days before his birthday so I figured he was focused on his birthday and not the abortion. "Did you make the appointment yet? He asked me as we were in the kitchen sitting at the breakfast bar. "No" I said to him as I began feeling anxious. "Well you need to make it soon. I got the bread right here" he said to me as he pulled the money out his pocket and put it on the table. Because of his abortion suggestion, we argued back to back and he really was making my life hell and being so evil towards me. I could not take it anymore so I finally called the abortion clinic and made an appointment and the appointment happened to be on his birthday.

We got up early and drove there. I was crying the whole time. I did not want to abort my baby at all and it ate me up inside. We had got there and the abortion protesters were out there with their signs and were yelling "murderers' ' as we drove in. I was ashamed and did not want to be there in the first place so I put my head down as they continued to chant. I had looked up and one of the protesters had made eye contact with me and he went to hand me a pamphlet through the window and Damian had sped up to get him away from the car and he began chasing us. "Ma'am, ma'am please ask God to forgive you!" he was yelling and at that point I broke down crying. I was crying so hard that it felt like I could not breathe. Damian had calmed me down and said a few encouraging words. I was not trying to hear anything he had to say, he was the reason I was there in the first place.

There was no reason for me to be at the abortion clinic other than he was selfish. His reasoning for wanting me to get an abortion was selfish as well. But I was in love with him at the time and I didn't want him to be angry at me, so even though it was tearing me apart mentally and emotionally I still wanted to please him so I got the abortion anyway. When we went in, I gave them my ID and filled out all the paperwork and we sat and waited. Damian waited with me the whole time and he would crack jokes to make me laugh as he tried to get my mind off of the reality that I was actually waiting to kill my unborn baby. I would laugh at his jokes and forget for a split second where I was, then I was kindly reminded when a wave of nausea would come over me, and it didn't help that I didn't eat because I couldn't eat anything after midnight due to me having to get anesthesia.

We got there about 8am and I didn't begin the process of being called to the back until around noon. They called us back to take the payment and Damian payed for the abortion and after that I was called in the sonogram room to hear the baby's heartbeat and they let me know I was eight weeks. I sat there and looked at the baby on the screen and saw the heart beating and I tried my best not to break down. Everything in my soul did not want to get an abortion. After she was done, she wiped the gel off of my stomach and printed out the sonogram picture and I reached my hand out to ask her if I could have it and she said "no". "Why?" I asked her disappointed. "It is policy that we don't give the pictures out" she said as she dropped the picture in the trash can with what looked like hundreds of other sonogram pictures.

After I left out the room, I felt empty. I walked back into the waiting room where Damian was and I began to cry. "What's wrong?" he asked me as my whole demeanor was somber. "I saw the baby on the screen" I said to him as I wiped my tears. "It's going to be ok, this is just not the right time" he said trying to reassure me that I was doing the right thing. I sat there for the rest of the time silent and on the inside, I was angry at him. Angry at him for even having me there. Angry that he did not want our baby that we made together. As I sat there, I was getting angry and angrier and I wanted to leave, but his voice kept playing in my head of how he was going to leave me and make my life miserable and I did not want that. In a lot of ways, I feared him. I didn't fear that he would do anything bad to me like kill me. But I feared making him angry and at the time I feared being without him so I tried my best not to be on his bad side.

I had a lot of thoughts running through my head but my anger quickly turned to nervousness once I was called back to the room where I was going to get changed to get ready to go into the actual abortion room. "I'm scared" I told him as I was getting up to go back. He could not go at that point, he had to wait in the waiting room until it was time to pick me up from the back door after the abortion was done. "You going to be good Allah got you. I love you" he said as he hugged me and I walked with the nurse to the room. She had stuck me to prepare my arm for my IV and had took my vitals and gave me a pain pill and some antibiotics and she gave me my hospital gown, my hospital cap and shoes and a blanket. She gave me a bag to put my clothes in and took me to the waiting room with the rest of the ladies waiting.

One by one girls were leaving to get their abortions. Finally, I was the only one left and I sat there scared. I said as prayer to God that he forgives me for what I was doing and that he kept me safe and that I woke up afterwards. I kept fearing that I was going to die on the table. I had felt so bad for getting my abortion that I felt like my punishment was going to be death and I felt so scared that I felt like I was going to throw up. But thankfully God is so merciful and he gave me a sense of comfort and told me not to fear dying because I was not going to die and I felt a little bit better. The nurse had come out and it was my turn to go in the back. I laid on the table and put my legs up and it was so uncomfortable. As I laid there I stared at the light in the ceiling and said another prayer. Soon after the anesthesiologist came in and began putting the anesthesia in my IV and before I knew it, I was out.

When I woke up, I was in the recovery room and they were handing me some animal crackers and juice. "Are you feeling ok Ms. Smith?" one of the nurses asked me. "Yes, I'm doing Ok, I am still a little woozy from the anesthesia, I wish I was waking up from a BBL instead of an abortion" I said out loud and every one had started laughing. They had given me my Rhogam shot since I am Rh-negative and I went to the bathroom to change and they put me in the wheelchair and wheeled me out and Damian was out there waiting. Him and the nurse helped me in the car and it was all over. "You good babe? That took a long time. I was starting to get worried" he said to me. "I am in pain" I told him as I felt crampy.

I was super hungry so we had gone to Taco Bell to get something to eat and then we drove home. When I got to my house, I went straight upstairs to my room and cried. I couldn't not believe that I woke up in the morning pregnant and now in the evening I was not pregnant and miserable. I felt like there was an empty hole inside of me. Damian kept coming into the room and checking on me to make sure I was ok. I could not stop crying so I cried for the rest of the night. He laid in bed with me and must have heard the sniffles of me trying to hold my tears back and I remember him turning over to me with my back towards him and he reached over my face and felt my eyes and they were soaking wet. At that moment he sighed and turned back over. Damian knew me, and at that moment he knew that he had messed up. He knew that this was a situation that a few jokes and gifts would not just wash away.

When I got up the next day my heart was still heavy but I told myself that today would be a better day and that I would move forward and try to be happy instead of wallowing in my sadness. I had got up and cleaned the house and it seemed like every commercial was about babies. It seemed like babies were everywhere. To make matters worse I had logged onto FB and all I saw down my timeline was Congratulations and baby bumps and baby showers. It had seemed like all the pregnant people had come out the woodworks. It was so depressing to see, all I wanted to do was get my baby back and be pregnant again. I had told Damian about all the pregnancies and he tried to encourage me the best way he could. Then soon after, close people in our lives were becoming pregnant. I could not understand for the life of me how we were in a nice home, a good relationship, we both had money and were in a happy place and I still had to get an abortion, that bothered me and I nagged him about it every chance I got.

My mom would come and visit me since she lived so close. One day she came over and gave me some black curtains to hang up in my room. That was not out of the ordinary because my mom always helped me decorate my house. She had helped me hang them up and we had talked for a while and then she left. I was the type of person who always had the house bright. I always had the curtains and blinds open to let the sunlight in. For some reason when we hung up those black curtains, I didn't keep them open. I had closed them. When I closed them, the room had become pitched black in the middle of the day. I had laid in my bed and I began thinking all types of thoughts about Damian and how he made me get an abortion.

Me and Damian got into an argument one day and in so many words, he revealed that he wanted me to get an abortion as a retaliation for his son Branden not living with us at the time. At the time his son was living with his mother. I thought about his words he said about making my life miserable. I thought about killing my baby, that I wanted with my whole heart. I thought about it all and it drove me crazy. I laid in that bed and cried and cried and I felt trapped in my own head, and I could not get out. The pain was consuming me. After I closed those curtains, I left them closed and I sat in my room in the dark day after day getting more and more depressed until I fell into a dark place.

Months had passed and I got deeper and deeper into depression. It would be bright sunny days and I still did not want to get out of bed. Damian would come into the room and check on me to make sure I was ok. Sometimes he would literally make me get up and get dressed and come outside in the garage which was his man cave to get some fresh air. He spent a lot of time in the garage smoking his mild's and that was the hang out spot when his friends came over. I would come outside with him from time to time and we would laugh and have good talks. Damian's best friend Terrance was over our house almost every day. He was Muslim just like Damian was and he would always talk to me about Islam and how Allah SWT is merciful and that I should stop beating myself up about the abortion because Allah already forgave me. As a Christian at the time I had already knew the word. It still didn't change the fact that it hurt and I thought about my baby every day.

We always had lot of company at the house. They were mostly Damian's male friends who were all Muslim, and they all had the same encouraging words for me, and they always had talks about Islam and the Quran, and when prayer time came in, they would offer salat together in our front room. It was beautiful to see. During Ramadan they would all fast and me and Damian would cook so they could eat Sahur at our house. Our house was full of love and life. Our house was the hotspot and I loved it. I appreciated Terrance at the time because even though he was Damian's best friend, he was my friend as well. I talked to him about a lot, especially regarding religion, because he had a love for Islam and he talked about Allah all the time, so I was able to ask him many questions and he was always willing to answer them for me.

Terrance always gave me his undivided attention and he always listened to me and made me feel like he cared about what I had to say. He knew about the abortion and how hurt I was, and he always showed compassion. He had two twin boys and I loved it when he brought them to the house to see me. They made me feel good. They were cute and happy babies. I always wondered if my baby was a boy, and being around his boys made my spirit happy. They were about two at the time and they would run around the house and play and I loved every minute of it. I had always prayed to God that he allowed me to get pregnant again. As time passed, I would go to work and all my coworkers were so supportive of what I was going through. Alot about me had changed. It was like my spirit had died. I was still present enough to be a good mom to Najah and be there for all her school events and birthday parties and everything. I didn't let Najah know my pain. She was my baby and I made sure that she knew it.

Months had passed after the abortion and one day while at work I was having sharp pains in my stomach and they lasted for about a week. I began to get worried, so I made a doctor's appointment at one of the clinics not too far from my house. I had taken off from work and went. The last time I had been to the doctor before the abortion I was a healthy 27-year-old, with no weight issues, no reproductive issues and all my organs were fine. The doctor's office had run tests and did an ultrasound and drew blood to see why I was having this pain. I sat in the room waiting for all my test results knowing they would be normal like they always are.

The lady came into the room stern and direct with a piece of paper in her hand. "Ms. Smith?" she said as she introduced herself and got straight to the point. "I got your test results back and you have PCOS, " she said to me very direct. "PCOS? What is that? I never even heard of that before" I told her. "PCOS is a reproductive disorder you get when you have cysts on your ovaries and that's why you have been in pain" the lady told me. "What?" I said as I sat there in disbelief trying to process what she was telling me. "Ok so how do I get rid of it?" I asked her. "There is no cure" she told me. "I will write you a prescription for Metformin," she said to me. "What is Metformin" I asked as I kept getting more and more shocking information. "Metformin is a medication to regulate your blood and your weight, you are overweight" she said to me directly.

Before having the abortion, I was about 155 and I liked my size and weight. After I found out I was pregnant I gained about ten pounds. After I had the abortion, I wanted to be pregnant again so bad that every month I tricked my body into thinking I was pregnant so I didn't work out or eat healthy like I used to. I ate like a pregnant woman because I convinced myself that there was still a baby inside me. I went from about 155 to 176 is what the scale said at the doctor's office. I knew I had gained weight and I felt different and that was one of the things that depressed me as well. I didn't like my new body. I did not feel like myself. I was 5 foot even, and even though 155 looked good on me I still was trying to get down to about 140, so to be 176 really made me disgusted with myself.

I sat there taking in all this heartbreaking information that I was not expecting to hear and I wanted to cry so bad, but the lady was so cold that I did not want to show any emotion. I just wanted to get out of there. "Here is a picture of your ovaries and all the cists on it" she told me as she handed me a paper with black and white images on it and all I saw were different size balls. These are my ovaries? I asked shocked. "Yes" she said. "Oh my God " I said and at that moment I did not believe it. My stomach was hurting but it wasn't hurting that bad, and to see all this going on inside of me felt unreal so again I was speechless. "Well I want to have a baby, so will these cists affect anything?' I asked her. Immediately she responded with no remorse "Oh no Ms. Smith, you will never have a baby again with your ovaries looking like that" she said and when I heard those words, it felt like life had stopped.

Ever since I had the abortion, I feared that I would not be able to have a baby again and, in that moment, my worst fears came true and I felt sick with grief. "So, I can't have kids anymore?" I asked her somberly and afraid to hear her repeat herself. "No, you won't. You have PCOS and cysts on your ovaries so you are not ovulating. I want you to take the metformin to regulate your blood sugar and hopefully it will make you ovulate too" she told me as I was so confused and mentally drained from all the information. She handed me the script for the metformin and gave me a summary of my visit and I left the office feeling defeated.

I went to the pharmacy to pick up my script and I went back to work. My job was really lenient, and my manager was like family so she let me take the time I needed to see the doctor. When I got to work, I told my manager and close co-workers the news and they were encouraging. "I know how much you want a baby. We serve God, you continue to trust God and not what the doctor says" my manager said to me as I was crying and disappointed. They all huddled around me with encouragement and I got my emotions together so I can get back to work.

When I got off, I had told Damian what the doctor said. "Wow, that's crazy. Don't let that get you down, Allah has the last say and if it is Allah's will then you will get pregnant again" he said to me as we sat in the garage and looked outside at the stars. I appreciated his words but always in the back of my head I felt like it was all his fault that I was in this situation in the first place. After getting the news from the doctor my depression had worsened and I kept hearing her voice play in my head. I had taken the metformin for about four days and it gave me a horrible pain in my back. Something inside me told me that it was not for me and that I need to stop taking it so I did. After getting off of the metformin the pain in my back had gone away but, not the pain in my heart.

It had been about a year since the abortion and I was still obsessed with getting pregnant. I did not take birth control and every single month I would take a pregnancy test to see if I was pregnant and it was always negative. I tracked my ovulation. I watched baby stories and videos of women with PCOS on YouTube to get more information. I was totally obsessed at that point. The more PCOS videos I watched. The more I did not identify with it. I had felt in my heart that everything the doctor said at the clinic was not true and it was eating away at me. Finally, after pondering and being tired of being depressed and obsessed. I decided to make an appointment with my regular Primary care physician. He is usually booked up, which is why I did not book with him in the first place.

I went to his office and explained to him about the abortion and all that I was told at the clinic about having PCOS etc. He looked right at me in my face and said "Ms. Smith, you do not have PCOS, and as far as your ovaries are concerned, I will send you to an image lab to get an ultrasound and I will look at it myself" he said to me. They did my blood work right there in the office and all my labs came back normal. He did mention to me about my weight though which I knew I needed to work on. I was not used to being fat and since I had gained weight, I hated how I looked. I still looked and dressed nice, but my weight gained was noticed by myself and others. They just thought I was gaining weight just because, but they did not know that I was fighting a silent battle of depression and my weight was a result of it. No one knew my pain except Damian because I always expressed to him my regret and he saw how my life spiraled since making the unwanted decision.

In a lot of ways, I knew he felt bad because he would do everything in his power to try to make me happy and keep me peaceful. Even though he was the cause of my pain, I still found comfort in him and appreciated his love and his kind words. I appreciated the times we laid in bed and laughed and played. I appreciated the long rides we would go on just laughing and enjoying each other's company. I appreciated him taking me out on dates and us vibing and making memories with our friends. I was going through a hard time but he made it easier. He made sure he was gentle with my feelings and he put me first. Me, him and Najah were a little happy family and I was grateful for them. Shortly after, we had went on a trip to Disney with his cousin and his wife who is one of my very close friends and we all had a blast.

Me, Damian and Najah were always going on trips and spending time and I enjoyed it. When we were home, we would cook out and just chill and do family things. I would watch him show Najah how to cut the grass, then me and him would sit outside and watch her play with her friends in the neighborhood. Though I was battling depression

I found joy in the moments and was very greatful for the family that we created.

Damian could also be a sweetheart at times. When he loved you, he made sure to show it. Mother's Day had come and Damian threw a big brunch at our house for me, my mom, my grand mom, my aunts and my sister. It was beautiful. We had a long buffet table that sat about 12 people, and he decorated it really nice. When I woke up that morning, he gave me my bouquet of flowers and a charm for my pandora bracelet, and Najah got me earrings and a necklace. He then showed me the gifts he got for everyone else, and I knew that everyone would be happy. I had got dressed up really nice and did my hair and put on a flower vail and I felt really pretty. As I was getting dressed Damian and Najah were in the kitchen cooking, and everything smelled so good. I had come downstairs to help but they told me to relax and handed me a mimosa. As all the guests started coming Najah greeted everyone at the door with their bouquet of flowers. Once everyone was there, we all sat down at the table and admired how beautiful everything was.

It was a bright sunny day, and the house was lit up with sunlight and it was so clean and smelled good. The table and everything were decorated so pretty. There was sliced fruit sat out on the table for us to nibble on while we waited for our brunch. Najah was our server and she started us off with orange juice, and some of us had mimosa's. Damian had made Belgian waffles, eggs, turkey bacon and grits and Najah served us our food and made sure we had syrup, butter and everything else we needed. My grand mom and everyone was thanking her and telling her how cute she was. We sat and ate and laughed and enjoyed each other on Mother's Day and when we were done Najah cleared the table and her and Damian cleaned the kitchen while me, my grand mom, my mom, my sister and my aunts sat in the living room and talked and laughed.

After Damian was done cleaning the kitchen, he had made an

announcement and gave everyone their gifts which was a gift bag with pandora boxes in it. He had bought each person a pandora bracelet and a charm and everyone was so grateful and thanked him and hugged him. Damian had made our Mother's Day very special and I appreciated him for it. We all had took pictures then eventually everyone went home and I spent the rest of the day with him and Najah having quality time and it got my mind off of being depressed.

A few days later I was scheduled to go back into the doctor's office for all my lab results. I was so nervous because I did not know what news to expect to hear. When I got there and sat in the room, I had butterflies. The doctor walked in and greeted me and smiled like he always did. "Hello Ms. Smith" he said to me as he sat down. "Hello Dr" I said to him as I anticipated my results. "So, I got your results back and just like I told you, you don't have PCOS" he told me. "Yay!" I said as I was so relieved, and he smiled at me. "Also, the ultrasound from your ovaries showed no cysts at all and you are perfectly fine" he told me. "That's great, so why did the other place I went to say I had PCOS and cysts on my ovaries?" I asked him. "I don't know why they told you that, but all the lab work came back 100% fine. You are healthy and have nothing to worry about" he said as he smiled. I was hesitant but I had to ask him the question. "So, Dr," I said to him, nervous. "Since I have no cists and everything is fine, does that mean I can get pregnant if I wanted to? I asked him. "Yes, you absolutely can get pregnant, you are a healthy woman and your reproductive system is working just fine" he reassured me as he smiled. I sat there feeling joy in my soul.

I was ecstatic to get the news that my lab work was normal. I thanked the Dr, and I went to my car and called Damian and told him the good news and he was happy for me. The Dr.s office was literally 5 minutes from my house. On the way home I couldn't help but to think that they gave me the wrong results at the other clinic. Everything about the visit that day felt off and I really felt like they gave me someone else's results. The clinic was always overcrowded and understaffed and seemed to be unprofessional so I would not put it past them. I could not prove it to sue or anything, I was just happy to hear I was healthy, and I could have a baby and I was on cloud nine from that point on.

"Wow, ok let's stop there" my therapist interrupted. There were a lot of traumatic events that happened. I am sorry that the clinic was so harsh with you and potentially gave you the wrong results. I am glad you went to your PCP and got a second opinion. I do want to address you spiraling into depression. You went through some traumatic events with the abortion and dealing with your grief and depression so I understand how it could have changed your mood. I empathize with what you went through, and I did want to address when you said "Even though he was the cause of my pain, I still found comfort in him" my therapist said as she read my words verbatim from her notes. "From what I heard you say, it is almost just like the situation when you fell of the jet ski and he saved you.

You fell off the jet ski due to his actions, he made it tip over. Since it tipped over and you were in the water, he had to save you and in saving you in his perspective he was the hero, but had his actions not put you in the water in the first place there would have been nothing to save you from" she said to me and I agreed. "Just as in the abortion, you leaned on him for support because of the trauma the abortion caused, but it was his idea to get the abortion in the first place. The lack of wanting to get the abortion and doing it anyway is what caused the depression and so on and so forth and it was a snowball effect from the predicament that he put you in, yet you needed to be saved by him and he felt the need to save you. That seems like a constant pattern in your relationship and not to cast judgement but that is very unhealthy.

It seems from the things you have told me even leading up to this point that you and your husband had formed a trauma bond early on. It seems as there were things, he needed from you as well as there were things you needed from him, and you both fed off of each other emotionally. It also seems as you wanted to be saved as well as he felt the need to save you. You also were very influenced by him, his words and opinions mattered to you very much. So much so that you put your feelings aside even if it hurt you. But on the contrary from what you are telling me, it does not seem as though he valued your feelings as much as you did his. Does that make sense?" she asked me. "It makes a lot of sense" I responded to her. "So how did him not validating your feelings but feel the need to comfort you in your time of trauma which he played a part in, make you feel?" she asked me.

I had sat there and thought about it briefly as I never looked at it that way before. "It made me feel horrible and dumb. It made me feel useless because no matter what I said it was his way or no way. Sometimes he would even verbally say "It's my way or no way" and that was his way of thinking because he knew he could control me and he felt dominant over me. I also never really put up a fight. I just let him have his way to keep peace "I told her slightly ashamed. "I understand" my therapist said as she looked at me with her legs crossed and shook her head in an understanding motion. "We have to work on you loving you, and you validating you, because there is a disconnect there, because when you love self, you do not allow others to treat you any kind of way. Shamirah has to learn to love Shamirah and understand that your feelings matter" she said to me sincerely and I nodded my head in agreeance. "So, you left off at the point where you received your results and they were good, I am so happy to hear that" she said as she smiled. "Please tell me how that went?" she said as she sat back and listened.

"After I got my results back, I told Damian and I was excited. I wanted to try to start making a baby asap. After all that I had been through I thought he wanted to make another baby as well, but he didn't. We would have talks about it and he still said it wasn't a good time. I was still obsessed with being pregnant so every time we had sex, I thought that was the moment I would be pregnant and have my baby, especially since I was tracking my ovulation so heavy. But even after getting the good news my periods were still not regular. The only thing that regulated my periods was birth control and I absolutely did not want to be on any birth control. Trying to get pregnant was exhausting and mentally draining. Every time I missed my period, I thought I was pregnant, and I was spending a lot of money on pregnancy tests just for them to be negative. I now knew I was capable of having a baby so I couldn't understand why I wasn't pregnant. We were having sex all the time and it was becoming stressful.

One night I had watched a video on YouTube of girls having positive pregnancy tests and I got excited and took one and of course it was negative. As I looked down at it and felt defeated. I had said a prayer to God "God, I come to you humbly asking that you forgive me for all my sins. Lord, I ask you to please allow me to have my baby. Please allow me to be a mother again. I am sorry for what I did in the past and I promise I won't do it again" I said with tears in my eyes and I went to sleep. After that point I was living life and was a little bit more optimistic and not so indulged in depression. I was going to work and having fun and being a normal person.

I had started not to feel good again, so I made another appointment with my doctor. When I went in, I thought I may be pregnant so he did blood work and everything right there in his office. Everything came back about forty minutes later and he told me I was not pregnant and I felt defeated again. On the way home I literally fantasized that the doctor's office called me and told me they made a mistake and that I really was pregnant. I waited for that phone call for the rest of the day but it never came. Pregnancy was always on my mind all day every day, especially as people were having their babies left and right and me and Damian would be around babies all the time. About two years had passed since I got the abortion and I was still obsessed.

One day I had went to my PCPs office for a regular checkup and while I was there, they did lab work as they always. I waited in the room for my results as usual. My doctor came in and told me all my lab and blood work were fine, but he was talking about my weight any my diet and exercise. He told me that my weight was too high. At that time, I was about 190. The biggest I had ever been in my life. I didn't really look it because I always kept myself up, but I felt it and I hated being that weight.

We had gone over a diet plan and he gave me my paperwork and I was ready to go. As he walked out the office the door was cracked and I heard him talking to his assistant but I could not make out what they were saying, but it sounded serious. Before I knew it, him and his assistant walked back into the room and the doctor had a smile on his face. "Ms. Smith, we made a mistake on your bloodwork. According to your bloodwork, you are pregnant!" his assistant said excited as she knew my pregnancy journey. "What?" I said shocked as I sat there in disbelief and she handed me the paperwork. "According to the numbers you are really, really early though" she told me as she smiled. I did not care that I was early, I was just ecstatic to hear I was pregnant, and I wanted to shout. "So, Ms. Smith disregard everything we talked about, about the weight loss. You are pregnant so just eat healthy but do not go on a diet ok" the doctor told me and I nodded and I got my paperwork and left.

As soon as I got out, I had called Damian and told him the news and he was very nonchalant but shocked just like I was. This time around, he was not rude about it. He was very supportive to the idea we were having a baby. I was on cloud nine and I told everyone, and everyone was so happy for me. It was early and I didn't really have any symptoms like I normally do when I was pregnant, but I just figured with time it would come. Plus, the fact that my bloodwork was positive for pregnancy. I knew I had nothing to worry about.

A few weeks had passed and one day I was at work and I began to bleed and it was dark and almost looked black. I tried not to panic because I read in early pregnancy dark blood was common, but as the day went on it did not stop, it was actually getting worse. I had told my coworkers about it and my manager had let me leave to go to the hospital which was right around the corner from the job. I really did not want to go there because I had not heard good things about that hospital, but I did not have a choice. I had called Damian and told him what was going on and he asked me if I wanted him to come to the hospital with me and I told him no. When I got there, I was triaged. There were not many people there so I was hoping that I would be in and out. My bleeding had gotten worse, and I was panicking on the inside.

When they took me to the back I changed into my gown and I sat there and waited for the doctor to come in. The curtains were closed but I could see a figure walking back and forth and he was rapping rap songs and when I looked down, I could see his sneakers behind the curtain. He had on a pair of Jordans. "Wtf, this better not be my doctor" I was thinking to myself. Sure enough a few minutes later he came walking through the curtain. When I saw him, he looked like he was in his late 20's early 30's, he was brown skinned with a low cut. He had on a black polo shirt with a red polo logo on it. Black jeans and a pair of white black and red Jordans and he had on a doctor's coat. He was really cute until he opened his mouth. Firstly, he didn't introduce himself to me, he just wrote his name on the board.

"So, what brings you here?" he asked me without even giving me eye contact. I had told him that I was pregnant and I was bleeding and I thought I was having a miscarriage. "You are not pregnant" he said to me, looking at me like I was crazy. "Yes, I am" I said to him. "No, you're not, who told you, you were pregnant?" he asked me. "My doctor told me. I did blood work and it came up positive for pregnancy, so if I am bleeding then I think I am having a miscarriage I told him again. "Ms. Smith, you are not pregnant, but I need to do a vaginal exam on you to make sure everything is ok " he told me as he began getting prepared to do the exam. "No, I don't want an exam. I want to get bloodwork, because my doctor told me I was pregnant and you are saying I am not. I need bloodwork to see what is going on" I told him as I wanted to cry.

"Look Ms. Smith " he said as he propped one foot up on the chair and leaned toward me like he was just chilling kicking with somebody in the hood. I had looked him up and down because I could not believe how ghetto this man was acting. "Either you going to let me check you or not " he said talking to me like he was my man or something. At that point he was pissing me off. "No, I don't want you to check me. All I want to do is get bloodwork" I told him. I don't know what you want to get bloodwork for, it's going to say the same thing I already told you " he said to me as if he was getting frustrated. "All I have to do is examine you and we will be good," he said to me. "No" I said to him as everything inside of me wanted to snap on him as I was holding my tears back. I was already trying to process the fact that he said I wasn't pregnant which was devastating. Then I had to deal with him being an uncompassionate butt hole on top of it. "Ok If you insist. I will get you the bloodwork. You lucky I don't have much to do today, so I will give you that" he said cocky as he walked out the room. I could not believe how rude and ghetto this doctor was. All I wanted was my bloodwork to get the hell out of there.

The phlebotomist had come in to take my blood and she saw that I was sad and without even saying anything she gave me a hug and I burst out crying. "It's going to be ok baby" she said as she comforted me. "I heard how he was talking to you, don't worry about him. Just stay strong" she said to me as she took my blood, and I waited a few hours until the results came back. It felt like it took forever and finally the doctor came back in and I did not want to see his face. "You good now Ms. Smith?" he asked me in a slick tone. "I'm alright" I answered back in a slick tone. He had propped his leg up on the chair again and it irked me. "So, you want to hear the results?" he asked me this time having a calmer tone. "What is it?" I asked. "You are not pregnant. I don't know why your doctor told you that you were, but the proof is right here" he said to me as he handed me the paperwork.

Everything in me wanted to cry, but I was not going to drop a tear in front of him because I knew that he low key wanted to say "I told you so". "So why I am bleeding black blood?" I asked him. "I am not sure Ms. Smith; I keep telling you that I need to examine you. Now will you let me examine you so I can see what is going on?" he asked me sounding like a narcissist. He was so mean and cocky earlier now he wanted to pretend like he wanted to talk sweet and have compassion. "Go ahead" I said to him, and he left the room so I could take my bottoms off and he came in and did the exam. I was so annoyed for him to have his fingers in my vagina and I couldn't wait for it to be over. "Well Ms. Smith, your insides feel fine, so I would say you are just having a heavy period" he said to me. "A heavy period that is Black?" I said to him. "It's not black, it is just really dark because there is a lot of old blood coming down. It's nothing to worry about" he told me, and he left the room.

I began to get dressed and I was in disbelief, here I was not pregnant again and I had to go back to the drawing board. I had cried all the way home because I needed to get it out. When I got home, I told Damian about the whole experience and how the doctor acted, and he couldn't believe I had gone through all of that. "Well you know what, everything happens for a reason. Thank God you are healthy and nothing is wrong with you. Everything will be ok" he reassured me as I sat on his lap and we talked in the garage. "Ok" I said to him as I found comfort in his words. "Damian, I just don't understand why all this time I have been having a hard time getting pregnant" I expressed to him. "Well, if it makes you feel any better, the reason why you ain't getting pregnant is because I don't nut in you. I pull out every time" he told me. "I know you pull out, but even in the past with you pulling out I still ended up pregnant" I said to him. "Nah this time I pull out as soon as I get the urge. So, it's not that you are doing anything wrong. I just don't be nutting in you" he said to me, and it all made sense. Receiving news like that probably should have upset me, but it didn't. It actually made me feel better and it answered why I was not getting pregnant. "So, my promise to you is when the time is right, I will start nutting in you and you will get pregnant and we are going to be good" he said as I sat on his lap and he comforted me. "So, you are saying you want a baby?" I asked him as I smiled. "I'm not opposed to it" he said as he took a puff of his black and mild and he smiled a little bit. That was all I needed to hear and I felt so much better.

After that whole two-year pregnancy ordeal and my crazy experience at the hospital. I had decided to chill on trying to have a baby and just focus on me, Damian and Najah and start being happy again. I decided to start focusing on my weight and I began to go to my doctor's office to get the b12 weight loss shots and I was watching what I ate, and I began feeling so much better. I had finally somewhat put the abortion behind me and began living life again.

33

It was Damian's cousin's girlfriend's 30th birthday. She was having a big event so we flew up to Jersey. We went to the party and had a great time. While we were there my dad had heard I was up there, and he called me. I was not close with my dad at all, and I was not going to let him know I was in town. He called me and sounded so happy over the phone. "I heard you was up here, " he said to me on the other end of the phone. "Yeah, I came for a party. We are not going to be up here that long" I told him. "Ok, I just wanted to be able to holler at you while you were here. " he said to me. I could tell that he was very happy to be talking to me, because before then I had not talked to him in a while. Me and my dad did not have a good relationship, so I always kept him at a distance. Especially since I had a daughter of my own and I didn't want him in and out of her life like he was in mine, so to keep him from disappointing her I kept him at bay. "I wanted to take you out to dinner somewhere nice, to spend time with you, " he said to me. "Really?" I said as I smiled, because I had never heard him talk like that before, and I thought that was really nice of him. I told him ok, and that I would call him to set up a day and time. He told me he was looking forward to it and we hung up.

I stayed in Jersey for another two days then me and Damian got on a flight and we left. I never called my dad and set up dinner with him. I did not feel bad about it, because he had stood me up so many times in life. I low key wanted to give him a dose of his own medicine. I tried to remain cordial, but inwardly I had a lot of resentment towards my dad. One of my main resentments was that he was never consistent. He always made promises to me and got my hopes up and then he would disappear. He would go on these spurts when he would call me and want to talk to me, and as soon as I got comfortable, he would go ghost. I would call him, and he would not pick up and he would ignore my texts. He would treat me so cold so when he wanted to reach out to me, I gave him the same energy. There were times I would really need to talk to him, and he was never available on purpose and that hurt me, so every chance I got, I made a point to hurt him too. I know it was petty but that was just how our relationship operated. We were petty and hurtful to one another.

When me and Damian got back to GA, everything was cool and life was very happy and optimistic. His friends that were Muslim, were always around and at the house and I spent a lot of time with them. One night it was Damian, Terrance and his cousin Kain at the house and they had offered salat and were talking in the living room, so I had stayed upstairs because I didn't like sitting up under a bunch of men. When Damian's friends were there, I gave them their space. It was about 11 pm and Damian had called me downstairs where they all were. "What's up?" I asked him curiously. "We were all talking about Islam, and I know you had some questions so I wanted to know if there was anything you wanted to ask Kain and Terrance while we all here?" he said to me. I was thrown off because I wasn't expecting him to put me on the spot like that.

I had thought about it, and I thought it would be good to take advantage of the opportunity. I was Christian so I knew little about Islam. Damian was Muslim and was always talking about it, but he never forced it on me. Even though he was Muslim he never pressured me. He always excepted me for being Christian. At the time I had not been in church in about three years so even though I had my faith, and I was a praying woman, I was not actively getting the word outside of watching bishop TD Jakes on YouTube on Sundays. I was around Islam on a daily basis, and I was naturally a curious person who asked a lot of questions, so the more I asked the more I learned and the more I learned the more I was intrigued.

"Damian let me talk to you for a minute" I said to him as we went on the porch and talked in private. "What do you want me to ask them?" I asked him for support. "Whatever you want to know about Islam. I know you have a lot of questions that I may not be able to answer, but Kain and Terrance are super knowledgeable in Islam" he told me. "Ok, but I don't want to be disrespectful and asking a bunch of questions that they may think are dumb" I told him. "They are not going to think that. They know you, and they know you are not trying to be disrespectful" he reassured me and we came in and he sat on the couch right next to me, and stayed close to me the whole time. Kain started us off with a prayer and then they opened up the floor to me, and I asked things I wanted to know and they explained things to me. The thing that got to my heart was the fact that I saw these men almost every day. I saw them in their element and heard how they talked and knew their demeanors. They were regular men with egos and macho tendencies, but when they talked to me about God. Allah SWT, they had a meek humbleness about them and it was so genuine. The love they had for Allah was so real and I could tell that they took pleasure in talking about him. The energy in the house was so pure.

We started talking at about 11pm and we did not finish until about 4am. It felt like the time flew by. Before the sun came up, they offered salat for Fajr and they left. Me and Damian went to our room and got in the bed and recapped the conversation. "So how you feel?" he asked me. "I feel good. I feel like I got a lot of questions answered. I was surprised at how open they were" I told him. "Word, well I'm glad it went good for you. That's what the brothers are here for, to give you knowledge" he told me. "I really appreciate it because my dad is Muslim, and I was not even able to have those deep conversations about it with him" I said to him in disappointment. "It's all good, Allah knows best" Damian said to me as I laid on his chest. We had had sex and went to sleep.

The next day I got up and kept thinking about our conversation. Later that night I had laid in bed and asked God did he want me to be Muslim. He did not give me an answer right away, so it was something I had thought about every day. Me and Damian's cousin's girlfriend were very close and they came down from Jersey all the time. Damian's cousin was Christian then converted to Islam, and his girlfriend was Christian. When they visited they would stay in our guestroom. While they were there, I had got up to go downstairs to tell his girlfriend what I was feeling about becoming Muslim, but before I could get it out she had changed the subject, then his cousin came in the room and I left. We all had got dressed to go out for the day and I never got to have the convo with her.

The next time I saw her a few weeks later when they came back down, to my surprise she was Muslim, and all I could do was smile. Clearly, she was feeling the same way I was, but we never got a chance to talk about it. I was so happy for her, and it just made me think about Islam even more. One of my good friends had also became Muslim at the time as well. She was engaged to a Muslim man, so before I knew it everyone around me was Muslim. I was still waiting to hear from God on what he wanted me to do, and that was Damian's advice to me as well. He always told me to follow my heart and seek God first. I talked to Terrance more and more about it and he would get so excited. He told me whenever I was ready that he would give me my Shahada.

One night I had went to sleep and dreamt about my dad and it was as clear as day. I was in NJ and I saw him at a gas station. He was sitting in the car, and I went to hug him through the window but I couldn't so I told him to get out, and he told me that he couldn't because he didn't have any pants on. In the dream I had went to his house and he wanted to give me my Shahada. In the dream I told him I was not doing it unless Damian was there. In the dream I said to him verbatim "I will only take my Shahada if you gave it to me, and Damian is here" and in the dream he said Ok. In my dream Damian was not there so I did not take my Shahada and I woke up. My dream felt so real. When I woke up, I laughed to myself. I said out loud to myself, "that dream had to be a joke, I don't even live in Jersey and I don't even talk to my dad" I said as I could not believe I had a dream like that. I had told Damian about it and he was like "Wow Ok" he didn't think much of the dream because it was just a dream. We were in GA and had no plans at that time on going to Jersey, so we felt like it would be something far down the line to happen or it was just a dream, and it would not happen at all and we went about our lives.

About two weeks had passed since the dream and we got a last-minute phone call that Damian's cousin Lonnie's daughter was having a sweet 16 and they wanted us to come. Damian was debating if we were going to go since it was such short notice, but he ended up booking a flight the same day of the party and we flew up there. The party was an All-white, so we bought our outfits from the mall and went straight to the airport. When we landed, we went to our room and changed asap and hurried to the party so we didn't miss it. When we got there everything was beautiful and Lonnie was in the middle of the floor dancing with his daughter. When they were done Lonnie started dancing and I ran to the dance floor to surprise him. When he saw my face, he gave me the biggest hug and then Damian came up from behind me and Lonnie was so happy to see him. We mingled and talked to the family and saw a lot of people and had a great time.

When it ended, Me and Damian drove to Atlantic City to chill out and go to the Casino and enjoy the summer night. We had parked by the boardwalk by club Deja vu and reminisced about how we used to party there. The line was packed. We were going to go in but the crowd didn't look like the type of crowd we wanted to vibe with, so we went into the Casino, and got some drinks like old times and played some games. Damian loved the Casino, he played for hours. We got to the city at about 1 am and stayed in the Casino until about 5am. He had won about $1000. I told him I was ready to go because I had wanted to walk on the boardwalk and catch the sunset. He played a little bit more and then we left and walked the boardwalk and took billboard pictures and rode on the carts and everything. We were having a great time just being silly and happy. Damian had guided me towards the beach, and I took my shoes off to feel the sand.

We both were still in our all white and we walked the beach holding hands. The sun started coming up and it was absolutely beautiful. We stood there and a couple had walked by, and we got them to take a picture of us and it came out really nice with the sunset in the background. As the sun came up, I had put my feet in the water and enjoyed the ambiance. Being there with Damian made it even better. I was focused on the waves and the breeze, and I was not paying Damian too much mind. He was behind me. "Turn around" he said to me as he smiled. When I turned around, he had written "Will you marry me" in the sand. "Damian are you joking?" I asked him in shock. "No, I'm serious. Will you marry me" he asked me with the cutest, most sincere smile on his face. "Yes!!" I said to him, as I was so excited.

His proposal was so romantic. I had pulled my phone out and recorded the moment and the writing in the sand. It was the spare of the moment so he told me that he would get me a ring later. I did not care about a ring though. Damian had proposed to me before, and he had bought me plenty of rings. I was so blown away that he asked me to Marry him, and I was on cloud nine. We had been through so much at that point, so I did not even know that marriage was on his mind. But the timing was perfect, we were in Jersey in the city where we met. We were under the sunset and everything was absolutely beautiful.

It was about a little after 6am. The sun was coming up and it was becoming morning. Our flight to go back home was at 12 so we decided to leave to get breakfast and see his cousins before we left. As we were driving down Madison Avenue in the city. We had stopped at a red light. I was looking down in my phone when Damian said to me "look on the side of you, there's your dad" he said to me. I didn't look up because I thought he was joking. "Nah for real, that's your dad" he said to me, and he rolled down the window and yelled "Assalamualaikum" to my dad and my dad rolled his window down and smiled and said "Wa Alaikum Assalam" the light had turned green so my dad yelled for us to meet him at the gas station by the McDonalds.

We had followed him and when we pulled in, we pulled beside him, and he told us he was getting gas. I told him to get out so I could hug him, and he laughed and said he only had his boxers on so he couldn't get out. "How long y'all going to be here? He asked Damian. "Our flight leaves at 12 pm so we have to be at the airport at 11am" he told my dad. "Ok, y'all should stop by my house and holla at me before y'all leave" he said to Damian and Damian said ok, and we pulled off to go off-shore to meet his cousins. "You want to go over there?" Damian asked me. "I don't know" I said to him as I was hesitant. "It's up to you, if you want to go, I will take you" he reassured me. We met with everybody we wanted to see. It was about 10am and our flight was leaving out of Atlantic City so we headed back to the city to the airport. Before we go to the airport, I can take you to see your pops" he said to me, and I thought about it and I said "Ok".

We had pulled up to my dad's house, and he had come on the porch and we talked for a while and I told him about the proposal that Damian did and he said "Masha Allah" and he was so happy. My dad loved Damian like a son. They had a lot of history and my dad would not want to see me with anyone other than him. Damian asked him for his approval to marry me and my dad said yes with no hesitation. I had gone into the house to see my little brother and my dad's girlfriend, but they were not there. My dad came in the house and talked to me. I told him about the dream I had two weeks earlier and he smiled and said

"Alhamdulillah" which means praise God in Islam. "If you ever wanted to take your Shahada, I would be more than honored to give it to you" My dad told me. "Well, just like in my dream, if I were to take my Shahada it would be with my you and Damian present" I said to him. "Word, word, exactly, it shouldn't be any other way" he said to me. I stood there with him and said again "I would take my Shahada as long as you and Damian were present" and I looked at him and he caught on. "Oh, you saying you want to take it now?" he asked, shocked. "Yes, I want to do it now. Right now just feels right" I said to him, and I could not believe what I was saying, but in that moment, it was perfect and it felt right. I felt like God had given me the answer I was praying for. I had the dream with no intentions of seeing or talking to my dad or coming to Jersey, yet we were NJ and standing in front of him. I believed everything happened for a reason. Everything happened in real life almost identical to how they happened in my dream, and I felt like that was my confirmation. Damian was on the porch on the phone and I went outside to tell him. "Word? Are you serious?" he asked as he smiled from ear to ear.

I stood at the top of the steps on the porch with my dad. Damian stood at the bottom of the step and watched as my dad took my hand and said repeat after me and we said the Shahada in Arabic and then in English. As I was standing there with my hands in my dad's hands reciting that I bear witness there is no one worthy of worship but God, I felt so much peace and love. That moment was pivotal and it felt surreal. When I looked down at the bottom of the step, I saw Damian standing there proud and his spirit was so humbled. He looked like he wanted to cry. It all was so beautiful and perfect. As we finished, my dad looked at me and gave me a hug and I fell into his arms and started crying. I cried like a baby, and I could not stop. "Get it out" I heard him say as he was hugging me tight. Damian had walked up to the step to console me as well. I had both of the Muslim men in my life supporting me, and the moment was epic and something that I will never forget.

In that moment all the hurt from my dad in the past had gone away and I forgave him, and it felt like a new beginning. Now with me being Muslim like he was I was excited to embark on a new journey with him, and I was very happy and optimistic. We talked for a little bit, then we had to leave for our flight. We said our goodbyes to my dad and headed to the airport and got on the plane. "This trip was crazy" I said to Damian as I laid on his arm as we were up in the sky looking at the clouds. "Word" he said as he agreed. "We got engaged and I took my Shahada, I was not expecting either" I said as I smiled and felt so warm inside. "Yup, the best things are unexpected, you know" he said to me in a sweet way. The flight attendant came and me and Damian ordered a patron and cranberry and we toasted to the moment and we both fell asleep until the flight landed. We both had not slept since the day before and we were tired.

When we got back to GA we drove home, and Terrance and all the other brothers had come over and congratulated me on my Shahada. I got to tell them about the engagement and all the other excitement. They were all happy for me and I was happy as well. I had told my good friend that I was Muslim, and she bought some garbs and pins to my house to show me how to wrap my hair up. We talked and laughed and we both could not believe we were Muslim. The next day Damian and Terrance had taken me to the Islamic Market in Stone Mountain. Damian was taking me shopping for Garbs and Overgarments so I could pray and go to the Masjid.

I had tried on several things and every time I came out to show him and Terrance they were oohing and awing like I was a princess. Both of them looked so proud. Damian bought what I picked out and he got me a prayer rug and some oils. When we got home, he showed me how to make Wudu and we all offered Salat. Damian and Terrance were in the front and me and Najah were in the back. Terrance did the recitation, afterwards we prayed and it all was so beautiful. Once I became Muslim, I had spent a lot of time learning the Deen. I wanted to know everything, it was all so exciting to me, and it made it even better that I was around all Muslims so I was constantly getting more and more knowledge.

A few months had passed and as me and Damian were growing closer in the religion. We both started having guilt because we were committing xena. Also known as fornication. Every time we had sex it would feel dirty and after having a conversation about it, we discovered that we both were feeling conviction. "I think it's time that we got married" Damian said to me as we were in the garage, and he was sweeping. "What!?" I said as I sat in the chair thrown off. "Are you serious?" I said to him as I smiled. "Yeah I'm serious" he said as he smiled and I felt his energy and we were having a moment. "Ok" I said to him as I agreed. The thought of getting married was exciting. When he was done sweeping, we sat down at the table with a pen and paper and made out a guest list. We talked about the decor and how we wanted something special there for his mom, Drew. Khris and my Grand pop since they all had passed away.

We were so excited about our wedding. We had talked about my wedding dress and our wedding colors and the more we talked the more expensive it got. "This is adding up" I said to him as I laughed. "Right. What we should do is get married at the Masjid and then have the wedding later" he told me. "Ok, that does sound like a good idea. We can get married at the Masjid now, then have a nice reception with all our family later" I said to him as I agreed. "Maybe sometime next year it will give us time to do everything right" I added. "Word" he said as he agreed. Terrance had come over and him and Damian were talking about the marriage at the Masjid, and he asked Terrance to be his best man and of course he said yes, and they talked about getting everything set up.

Me and Damian thought it would be an easy process, but it wound up getting really overwhelming. For whatever reason it was hard to get in contact with the Imam at the Masjid. It took about two weeks for Damian to finally be able to talk to him. When he finally did, he expressed that he wanted the Imam to marry us and the Imam agreed and they set up a date which was about a week later. In the midst of the conversation, I guess Damian mentioned to the Imam that my father was Muslim. Once the Imam knew that my dad was Muslim, he let Damian know that my dad would have to be present for him to perform the marriage. Damian had let him know that he was not sure if my dad would make it because he was in New Jersey, and at that point my dad had got ghost again so we weren't even sure if we would be able to find him. Damian told me he expressed that to the Imam, and the Imam's response was "It doesn't matter if her father was at the bottom of the sea, you must find him. It is his right as a Muslim man to be at his daughters "Nika" which means marriage ceremony in Islam, and he let Damian know that without my dad present that we could not get married.

When Damian told me what the Imam said I was upset, because for one it was our marriage, and I didn't understand why we had to wait for my dad. Secondly, I was really upset because after I took my Shahada, I thought it would be me and my dad's new beginning. I was reaching out to him and he began ignoring me again, and we fell into the same toxic cycle as from before. I was upset with my dad and I had cut him off and I did not want him at my wedding, so to be forced to have him there really bothered me. "Can't we get married somewhere else then?" I asked Damian as I was annoyed. "We could, but I thought about it, your dad is Muslim and it would be good for him to be here" Damian told me. "What? Are you serious?" I blurted out to him. "I do not want him here" I insisted to him. "I know how you feel, but you may just feel like that now, if anything ever happened to your dad you would wish he was around for a time like your wedding. I know y'all be beefing, but I think you should let him be here" Damian told me. "No" I said to him as I was ending the conversation. "You sure?" he asked me. "Yes, I'm sure, let's find another Masjid then we can get married asap.

This is our marriage so it shouldn't be dictated by if my dad is here or not " I told him as I was upset. "You right" he agreed with me.

"Can you do me one favor though?" Damian asked me. "What?" I said to him giving him the look and he started nervously smirking, because he knew I was not playing when I gave him the look. "The favor is: if I find your dad and he agreed to come I will pay for him to get down here to be at the wedding, is that ok?" he asked me. "Damian you are getting on my nerves" I responded, and he started smiling. "I'm serious. I will find your dad and get him down here; you don't have to worry about anything Ok" he reassured me. I looked at him for a minute. I knew him, he was not going to give up and he was going to keep bothering me about it. The longer we prolonged this thing was the longer it was going to take to be married. "Ok Damian, if you can find him and get him here, then he can come" I said to him. "Ok cool, I will handle it" he told me and he walked out the room and went downstairs. I was annoyed but I had no other choice, so I just had to trust the fact that everything would work out. He had got in touch with my dad about a week later and my dad agreed to come. He told Damian that he had a couple of things to handle in Jersey first and then he would let him know how soon he could fly out.

A few weeks had passed and finally my dad told Damian that he was ready, and Damian booked the flight. We were supposed to get married at the Masjid on that Friday. The previous week me Michelle, Terrance and Damian went to the Masjid and prayed. Afterwards we were supposed to get something to eat, but I told them that I had to go and start shopping for the wedding. I had invited all my family to the Masjid. Even though they were not Muslim they all still agreed to garb up and come. I left Damian and them and headed to shop for some dresses. I had gone from store to store to find the perfect dress because getting married at the masjid I did not need a traditional western wedding dress, but I also did not want to wear an Islamic garb as my dress either. Finally, I found the perfect dress, I loved it. When I got home, I showed

Damian and he liked it. A few days later he had gone to the Islamic shop to get a Garb and Koofi to match it. I still needed a long shawl to go around me, so I went to the Islamic shop to buy one and my mom came with me, and she bought a garb to wear to my wedding as well. I thought that was really nice of her and it showed a lot of support. My mom did not like the fact that I was Muslim, but she did show support when she could. I had found the perfect long hijab and it covered my head and my body and it was appropriate for the Masjid. At that point we all had everything we needed and I began getting excited.

I had imagined getting married and looking Damian in his eyes and both of us reading our vowels to one another. I wrote out my vowels on my phone, and he said he was going to do the same. We both imagined our close family and friends there watching us in our union. We pictured bringing food and our wedding cake there and having a small celebration until we had our big reception. Me and Damian were both excited about our day. We vowed to each other and to God that we would not have sex until after we were married, and that gave us a little thrill and something to anticipate. After the wedding we planned on going to a hotel downtown and to have dinner and a small honeymoon with just the two of us. We had it all planned out and we were ready. We were just waiting on my dad.

He was supposed to fly in on that Thursday before the wedding and when the day came, he had called Damian and told him that he had missed the flight and I was pissed. The next flight was not coming until the next day which would have made him miss the wedding. "I knew it! I knew he was going to mess up the wedding" I said to Damian as I was crying and angry. "Calm down, we are going to figure something out" he said, as I could see on his face that he was concerned too. "Let me make some phone calls" Damian said to me as he went into the garage and got on the phone. I was so pissed I had called my mom. "Mom guess what? " I said to her angrily. "What?" she said, worried. "My dad missed his flight" I told her. "Oh my God, wow that's a damn shame. How did he miss it?" she asked me. "I don't know, he knew what time he had to be at the airport. Damian already paid for everything, all he had to do was show up and he couldn't even do that" I said to her disappointed. "Wow, I'm sorry, so are you still going to be able to get married tomorrow?" she asked me. "Mom, I have no idea what's going on. Damian said he is trying to figure it out, so I guess I'll have to wait and see" I told her as I was extremely upset. "Ok, well calm down, everything will work out" she told me, and we hung up.

Damian had come into the house and came into the living room where I was, and sat next to me to comfort me. "You good?" he asked me. "No, not really. This is exactly why I didn't want to base it on my dad coming because he is always a disappointment" I told him as I was frustrated. "Us getting married is for Us. He has nothing to do with it, and he is messing it up" I told Damian. "I understand how you feel, but that is still your dad and he should be there with us," he said in my dad's defense. "Ok, then he should make sure that he is here then. There was no reason for him to miss his flight" I said to him. "I understand and I talked to him. I sent him some bread so since he missed the flight him, his girlfriend and your little brother are on their way here now. They're just going to drive to make it here on time" Damian told me hoping that would cheer me up. Drive?" I asked confused. "Yeah, they leaving out now and should be here sometime in the middle of the night," he told me. "Yeah ok, well I will believe it when I see it" I told him as I had no faith in my dad at that point. I was annoyed for the rest of the day. I didn't even want to mentally prepare myself to get married, because I was not sure if there would even be a wedding. I would not feel confident until I saw my dad standing in my face.

The next day I had heard Damian opening up the door for them around 6am. I had heard my dad's voice while I was still half asleep and I felt relieved. I got up a few hours later around nine and I came downstairs to the front room to greet them. "Sorry for missing the flight babe. I know you were pissed thinking I wasn't coming" my dad said as he was smiling, happy to see me. "Yeah, I didn't think you would make it after Damian told me you missed your flight" I told him. "I would never miss your wedding, even if I had to walk here, " he said as he gave me a kiss on the side of my forehead. "Well, I'm just glad y'all made it, " I said to his girlfriend and my little brother, as I gave them both a hug. "Make y'all self at home. Its food and stuff in the refrigerator, and its snacks in the cabinet" I told them as I left the room and went upstairs. It was a Friday, and we were supposed to be at the Masjid around 1pm for prayer. So, I had started getting me and Najah dressed around 11am. Najah wore a long white dress with tulle and a white hijab with spar-kles on it, as she was supposed to represent my flower girl. She was so excited that me and her dad were getting married, and she was excited to wear her dress and shoes, and we had girl talk while we got ready.

Najah was about 8 at the time and she was a mommy and a daddy's girl. After I was finished with her, I took my shower and began to get ready. Once I got out, I had put on my best lotion, and my best perfume then I did my hair. Which was parted in the middle to just show a little bit under my hijab. I had put on my dress and it fit perfectly. Then I did my makeup really light and put on my hijab then put on my jewel piece over it. I had looked in the mirror and looked like an Arabic princess. I was so nervous for Damian to see me, but I was excited at the same time. When I opened my room door, I saw that everyone was in the living room. As I came down, they all clapped and looked at me in Aww. "You look so pretty" my little brother said to me, then my dad said I looked pretty as well. Damian had come in from the garage, and he was dressed in his outfit too and he looked really handsome. When he saw me, he was smiling from ear to ear, and I could tell he thought I looked nice. "You look beautiful" he said as he was still smiling. "You ready to get married?" I asked him as I smiled nervously. "Alhumdulilah, Insha Allah, I'm ready" he said smiling.

It was time to head to the Masjid, so we took some pictures and then left to be there on time. Prayer was over at about 2pm, so I had told all my family to meet me there at that time since they were not Muslim and were not coming to pray. When I got to the Masjid for prayer my friend was there, and she had just come from having her wedding in Jersey and I was so happy to see her. Also, Terrence's wife Michelle was there, and my dad's girlfriend E was with us too. Since we were getting married I thought that the other women in the Masjid would know as well, and I figured they would be a part of listening to the Nika(marriage prayer) but when I came into the prayer room every-one just looked at me like "why was I so dressed up" and it was really awkward. After we finished listening to the lecture from the Imam and we prayed. I thought they were going to announce the Nika, but they never did and all the sisters started leaving. At that point I was super confused and so was Michelle, my friend and my dad's girlfriend. We had all walked outside to the men's side to find Damian and Terrance to see what was going on. Finally, I saw Damian in the crowd and waved him down.

"Damian, I thought they were going to announce us being married, what happened?" I asked him confused. "I thought so too" he said. "I'm trying to find the Imam now, hold on stay right here" he told me as he went back into the men's door. My dad, Terrance, my cousin Nayshawn and a few of the other brothers as well as us women, were standing outside waiting. Damian had finally come out and said he found the Imam. "Ok so are we getting married?" My family is about to pull up at any minute" I reminded Damian. "Yeah, he said hold on because he forgot about the Nika" Damian told me. "What, he forgot?" we all said confused. We all stood outside and waited and by this time everyone had left, and the parking lot was empty. It was just me, Damian and our crew waiting, and then my grand mom, grandpop and my mom and aunt had pulled up and they all were garbed and ready to see us get married.

The Imam had finally come out and we all were prepared to go in, and I began to get butterflies. "It's finally happening" I said to myself as

I was excited. "No ladies" I heard the Imams voice say as I was walking side by side with Damian holding his arm because I was so nervous. "What he mean no ladies?" I asked confused, as all the men went in and Damian stood there with me, and then he eventually went in too. I stood by the men's door, and he came out a few minutes later and looked disappointed. "What's going on?" I asked him confused, and he looked hesitant to tell me. "Since this is the men's side y'all can't come in" he said as my mom, grand mom, and all us women out there heard him, and you could hear everyone say "what?" as we were all confused. "Damian, they came all the way here to see us get married" I said as I was beginning to panic. I was already nervous, and the day had already been hectic. First, I wasn't sure if my dad would be there. Then they didn't even announce the Nika so no one knew I was getting married, when normally the sisters would greet you and congratulate me and stay for the Nika. Then Damian tells me the Imam forgets the wedding was supposed to happen period, and now I had my family outside the Masjid and can't even see us get married. I was upset and embarrassed.

"Ok Damian since they can't come in, I guess only the guys will see us get married then?" I asked him, and he was hesitant again, as he had a nervous smile on his face like he was scared to tell me something. "What?" I asked him, as I read his face. "You can't come in either" he said to me, and I almost flipped my lid. "So, you mean to tell me that I can't be at my own wedding?" I blurted out as it felt like I was about to faint. I was in disbelief. "I know, I'm sorry, I didn't know it was going to be like this" Damian said, and I could tell he was very disappointed as well. "I gotta go. I will call you" he said to me as he kissed me and went back in. "I cannot believe this" I said to Michelle and my friend because they were both Muslim, and had been Muslim longer than me. I was I was trying to make sense of the whole thing. "It's ok Mirah, just stay calm" Michelle said to me as she saw I was panicking. My friend Shyneice and Erin comforted me as I stood outside in the parking lot on my wedding day. They were having a wedding prayer for my wedding, and I was not even a part of it.

On my wedding day I was not able to hold my husband's hand and look into his eyes and see his smile. I was not able to say our vows together and have butterflies. I did not get the opportunity to know what it felt like to be a bride, and to get those first pictures with my husband as we said "I do". I did not get any of that. Instead, I was in the parking lot with my mom and aunt fussing about how it was ridiculous to be outside. I was beyond embarrassed. I was just so thankful to Michelle for helping me keep a cool head, because I wanted to lose it. I wanted to snap on my family and tell them to shut up! And I wanted to break down and cry. I had waited for the moment to marry Damian for a long time, and he was in the building getting married without me, and I was so sad. They were in there for a very long time. I think about two hours. When all the men came out, they were smiling and looked happy. Damian was smiling and walked straight to me and took my hand and put a ring on my finger. It was beautiful but I still was clueless as to what happened while they were in there. I guess while I was in the parking lot I got married.

My dad came up to me and hugged me and congratulated me, then all the men hugged me too. They all seemed in good spirits. I just wish I was inside to experience my own marriage as well. Terrance and Theo were Damian's best men. My dad and grandpop were all in there. Damian's good friend J, and my cousin Nayshawn and my little brother all were able to experience it, and all of us women were outside clueless. We took lots of pictures in the parking lot and eventually left to go back to my house. Everyone came but we had no food or cake because we did not plan on being there, so we ended up ordering pizza and everyone kicked it in the house and the garage and they were so excited for us. We ended up not going to dinner, and to the room like we planned because the day had been so mentally draining, that I did not want to do anything. I really just wanted to be left alone to ask Damian a million questions about how it went, but we were surrounded by people. My mom and dad were there, and I hadn't been around them both at the same time in years. We all laughed and took pictures and it ended up being a fun night overall. I just wish I could have felt like it was my wedding day instead of a kickback. When me and Damian went to bed that night, I don't even remember if we had sex or not. It was all a blur, and there were so many emotions. Plus, we had a house full of people and I was not feeling sexy at all.

For the next few days Damian was on cloud nine and we eventually consummated our marriage. He was so happy to be married and I was too. It was a new feeling. We no longer felt convicted after having sex, and everything was now permissible in the eyes of God. It was so much fun learning about marriage in Islam and being married period. We shared so much newness with one another and it was an experience that bonded us closer together. My dad had stayed a few days and they left to go back to Jersey and life was back to normal.

34

Things after the marriage were going pretty well. One day Damian had come to me and was talking about his son coming to visit. I had agreed and a couple of days later he had flown him down. He had stayed with us for the summer and me and Damian began to bump heads. Me and Damian were close and were supposed to be a team but when it came to me being a parent figure to his son, he had an issue and it was causing tension between us. For example if Brandon needed to clean the room, and if I were the one to tell him to clean it, Damian would say things like "I don't like your tone with my son, or don't tell him nothing, I will tell him" and that went on in almost every situation, and that started arguments between us because I felt like he constantly under minded my authority. We were married and I was a parent figure to Brandon as well, and I should have been able to treat Brandon just as I treated Najah as far as a parent and authority figure. I was not the type of parent who gave beatings or hit my kids, so I had no intention of hurting him or Najah. But when I told them to do something, I expected it to be done.

I noticed a lot of times with Brandon, if I said something to him about anything, he would always go to his dad and make it seem as if I was doing something wrong. That really would frustate me and hurt my feelings. I felt like he only did it, because of the way Damian would respond. Damian never verbally said it in front of me, but his actions showed to me and Branden that I was not an authority figure to Branden, Damian was, and Branden did not have to listen to me, and that was not right on Damian's part, because he is the one who set the tone for Branden to feel that way. It is not easy trying to mother another woman's child, I tried my best, but Damian sure did not make it any easier. I started to get stressed, and felt like I was stuck between a rock and a hard place, so to keep me and Damian from getting into it, and to keep from getting my feelings hurt, I stopped trying to help raise Brandon and when his dad wasn't around, he did whatever he wanted and he knew there was nothing I could do about it or I would have to deal with Damian.

It was not that Brandon was a bad kid, because he wasnt. He just needed motherly guidance and discipline. He needed to know how to clean and to pick up after himself, small things that kids are taught, the same way I was teaching Najah, to pick up after herself as well. They were getting older and needed small choirs. Damian always took it as I was being mean, when that was never the case. We had an argument one time, and I asked him what was the problem with me giving Brandon rules? His response to me was "You don't like my son, so don't say anything to him" when he said that to me my feelings were so hurt. I never said I didn't like his son, nor did I feel that way so for him to say that was a smack in the face. I felt like Damian was making issues that were not there, and the fact that I was a humble person and loved everyone's kids and my own husband felt like he had to protect his son from me of all people, really hurt.

There were times when Brandon was failing in school and I am very great at academics so I tried to give him advice on how to get back on track as well as I told Damian how he needed to get in touch with the teachers for makeup work and be more proactive in Brandon's schooling and he shut me down and said that he would handle it. I wanted to communicate to Brandon's teachers because as a mom that is what I did. Najah had been an A'B student all her life, and I had close relationships with all her teachers to the point where they could call me on the phone, and they knew that I was on point with Najah's education, and we got things done and I wanted to do the same with Brandon, but Damian did not allow me to do all of that. He made it seem to the school as if he was a single dad raising his son by himself, and that was not the case. Even though the situation with Brandon was hard for me because in the beginning of our relationship finding out he had a son on the way hurt me very badly, and it was something I had a terribly hard time healing from because of the trauma in my own life from my own issues that had nothing to do with him. I still loved Brandon. I still was there as a mother figure to Brandon and a wife to Damian and I was hurt that my husband felt the way that he did.

Damian would talk so bad about me to other people, he made them think I didn't like his son and I was the reason that his son didn't live with us throughout the years and that was not the case. He lived with his mom sometimes, and he lived with us sometimes, they had joint custody. Damian's life was so busy and he was always ripping and running. The majority of time I had Najah while Damian was handling his business, so to make it seem like I was the sole reason was not fair. Damian barely had time for me and Najah because he would be handling his own affairs. Whenever I did have the opportunity to have one on ones with Brandon, I always showed him love and had small talks affirming to him that I loved him, and I gave him hugs.

Me and Brandon's relationship was not tainted. We were good. Damian's perspective on how he assumed I felt was where the tension came from. I expressed pain to Damian about finding out he had a son, and then his son's mom moving in with Damian and his mother, as well as me having to get an abortion because Damian felt like he didn't want another child in the house since his son was not there. In my opinion those were all valid reasons to feel hurt. But I never came out to Damian and told him out of my mouth that I did not like his son nor did my actions show it either. Things that happened were not his sons fault and he had nothing to do with it. I was just pained due to circumstances that surrounded him.

The whole summer Brandon was there was stress and tension between me and Damian, and as the summer ended and Brandon was going back home with his mom, I felt like there would be some relief. But right before he was supposed to go home, Damian came to me, and told me that he wanted him to stay. "What?" I asked him, as we sat in our room on our bed and talked about it. A few weeks before that, we were in Jersey and went to my dad's house and had a heart to heart about the whole situation. Damian poured his heart out to my dad about how he wanted Brandon to live with us and I expressed to my dad the stress that Damian puts on me when Brandon is there, and my dad understood both sides. "Mirah", my dad said, as he sat next to me with his arm on my leg, and he looked me in my eyes, "just give it a chance and maybe things will be different" my dad said to me. "I don't have a problem with Brandon being there. I have a problem with how Damian acts towards me when he's there" I said to Damian and my dad at the same time and my dad looked at Damian. "Son, you have to trust her" my dad said as he looked at Damian who was sitting across from us. "Damian just bring him and trust the process, my daughter has a good heart and y'all will be ok," my dad said to him.

After the talked we left and about a week later is when Brandon came for the summer. "I decided to keep Brandon here with me. Your dad said I should just give it a try so that's what I'm going to do" Damian said to me. "Yes, this summer was rough, if we are going to do a whole school year then you are going to have to stop thinking I don't like Brandon, and let me be comfortable with him the same way I am with Najah" I told him. "Ok" Damian agreed and we didn't really say much after that, and he left the room. He told Brandon he was staying and school had started and we went from there.

Things were on and off between me and Damian and we were arguing a lot. I had felt depression starting to set back in and tensions were
high between us for a lot of different reasons. Since depression began to
set in again. I started spending a lot of time in my room again. I would
come home from work and go straight to my bed because being at home
had become mentally draining. As I would be in my room so many
thoughts would come to my head. Damian's mean words would play in
my head and I would get angrier and angrier. Also, the abortion would
play in my head as well. I would think about how old my baby would
have been and Damian's words would play in my head about how I had
to get an abortion because his son did not live there at the time and I
would get upset about that as well. I was extremely upset with myself
for allowing Damian to bully me to get an abortion especially for a
dumb reason like that, because at any time his son could have moved
in just like he did. Sometimes seeing his son would trigger sadness and
depression in me as well, because I always felt like Damian made me kill
my baby because of him. It was not his son's fault at all. Alot of me and
Damian's issues stemmed around the abortion he forced me to get.

One day me and Damian had a conversation because he noticed
that I was showing signs of depression again and he asked me what the
reason was. I was completely honest with him and told him that I was
stressed that we were fighting all the time and that I was struggling with
the abortion again. "Why are you still struggling with the abortion? I
thought you got over it" he said to me as we sat on the bed and talked.
"That is something I will never get over, especially since I didn't want
to get it and you forced me to do it" I told him. "I didn't know you still
felt away about that, " he said to me. "Yeah I do and to be honest when
I see Brandon it triggers my depression, because you told me to get an
abortion because of him not living here at the time and the fact that I
wanted a boy so bad, so to see him makes me sad because it brings up
hurtful memories. Brandon didn't do anything wrong, and it's not his
fault at all, but seeing him does remind me of having to abort my baby"
I sincerely expressed to Damian. He had sat there on the bed silent for a

minute, as he was processing what I was saying, because he never heard me talk like that before. I held a lot in and didn't express my feelings about how he used his son to force to me get an abortion, but I needed to get it out because I was tired of carrying around the pain, and seeing his son every day was painful to me. I hate that I felt that way, but I had to acknowledge my truth, and the truth was having his son there was painful and brought back hurtful memories throughout the whole relationship even before the abortion.

"Ok, let's stop there for a second" my therapist said, as she sat up in her chair. "I heard you say that his son being there was painful because your husband used the fact that his son was not in the home at the time as a reason for you to get an abortion, correct?" she asked me. "That's correct" I said. "And what I heard you say was, your husband felt like he did not want to bring another child in the home because he felt guilty that his son was not there and to bring in another child would not be right in his eyes, correct? She asked me. "That's is correct" I said to her. "Also, what I heard you say is because your husband used the fact that his son was not there as a valid reason to say "if my son is not here another child will not be here either", correct?" she asked me. "Yes, that is correct" I said to her. "So, what I hear you saying is you did not have anything against his son, but the circumstances around his son triggered the trauma of you having to abort your baby, correct?" she asked me with compassion. "That is correct" I said to her as I thought about it and began getting a little emotional. "What are the emotions for?" she asked me with compassion. "I am getting emotionally because none of it was his sons' fault, but my husband used his son not being there as a means to hurt me. I aborted my baby, but his son wound up living with us anyway, and I felt like I was played for a fool.

I am not a mean person, and it hurt me to see his son; and instead of being able to fully enjoy him all I saw was pain. I hated to have to live that way day in and day out, it cringed my soul. I wanted things to be normal and I tried to get past it, but Damian did not make it any better by making it seem like my resentment was towards his son when it was actually towards him, and he knew it. The narcissist in him would not allow him to admit that he was wrong for forcing me to get an abortion, so he found every excuse to deflect the light off of him. Him falsely accusing me of not liking his son made me feel like we were not a family and everything felt so divided, and it didn't help that when we got into arguments that he would threaten to leave me. He would always say "I'm moving and getting a place with me and my son." I already had abandonment issues, and I loved him so much at the time so him threatening to leave me would tear me up inside, and made me fearful and insecure. "It all was so overwhelming" I said to my therapist. "I totally understand, that would be overwhelming for anyone" she said with compassion. "So just to be clear I heard you correctly, it was not the fact that you had an issue with his son, but you had a lot of trauma due to the abortion, and him using his son not living with you all at the time as an excuse for you to have an abortion brought about pain in you?" she asked me. "Yes, that is correct" I told her.

His friends would always ask me; why do I have an issue with his son being there so on and so forth. I never really gave my side of the story because I didn't want everyone to know certain things because they were hard for me to talk about, so instead of giving my side I just took the blame as the bad guy. Damian gave everyone the impression that I did not like his son, and that was not the case. "So, what was the case? What is your truth?" My therapist asked me sincerely. "My truth is; I was a young girl looking for love, when I got with Damian I was his everything. His world was all about me and mine was all about him. We had plans for the future together, and he treated me like a princess. I got with him under the impression that he had no kids and when I found out he had a son, it tore me to pieces, but I still stayed through the pain. I didn't have my dad and Damian was my boyfriend and though it may sound weird in a lot of ways he was a dad figure to me, and I did not want to share him with anyone.

A child is a big responsibility and I was not ready to be with a man with a child. I didn't want kids myself because I had my whole life ahead of me, but I stayed with him anyway. Through me staying I was hurt on top of embarrassed and humiliated especially when his son's mom moved into the house with them. Throughout the years, I felt hurt after hurt, and still stayed and to fast forward years later now having to abort my baby because of your son too, and him bringing him to live in the same household with us but basically stripping all my rights as a parent to his son, and making me feel like I had no authority as a parental figure, and that hurt because I felt like I was not respected. So from my point of view it was drama after drama, pain after pain regarding his son and Damian never made me feel safe because due to the drama, he always threatened to leave me, and it brought about a lot of hurt and resentment and that is my truth" I told my therapist. "Very well said, and I am proud of you for acknowledging it and getting it out" she said as she smiled. "I know that was a lot. " I said, as I laughed, "Yeah but that's ok, that's what you're here for" she said as she smiled. "Ok tell me what happened next" she said as she picked up her pen and paper and I began talking.

35

One day me and Damian were in the kitchen, and he was talking to me about how he feels like I have a brain disorder, and that I have emotional issues and I need help. I listened to him as he spoke these things about me and at the time, I valued his words so much that I believed everything he said about me. I had no real self-identity. My identity was whoever he said I was, and on that day, he identified me as a broken woman with mind issues. "I think you are a good person, you just don't got it all" he said to me, as he stood next to me while I washed dishes. "What you mean?" I asked him. "You be getting depressed and spazzing out. I be trying to help you, but I don't know what else to do" he said to me, as if he was concerned. "I think you should see a therapist," he said to me. "A therapist for what?" I asked confused. "So, they can help you get your mind right, you are a good person, but you have a lot of issues and I think you should seek help" he said to me. "Ok I will find a counselor" I said to him without hesitation. "That's good, I look forward to seeing your progress and seeing you become the woman that I know you can be. You are a writer and one day when you are healed from all the stuff you got in you, I see you writing a book about it and I see you becoming really successful" he told me out of nowhere. "Oh wow, that's crazy you see that" I said to him as I heard what he was saying but I did not see the same vision he had for me for myself, so it went in one ear and out the other.

The next day at work I was online and I found a therapist that I thought I might like. I emailed her and she responded later that evening, and I set the appointment and went to see her about a week later. I went to her office in Druid Hills and it was really cozy. That was my first time at a therapist office and it was pretty much what I expected. There was a couch and some candles and a safe vibe. She asked me some intake questions to dig deeper into my life and we went over my relationship with my mother and my siblings and everything was fine, but when she got to my dad I burst out in tears. She asked me some very deep questions, and that was my first time in life actually expressing how I felt about my dad and his absence. It was very emotional and she gave me a tissue and she dug a little deeper and got into the session. She gave me a lot of insight and I felt comfortable with her so I came back weekly for about a month and we talked a lot about family and my husband and what was going on at the house, and she gave me advice through it and I felt like things were going ok.

Damian would ask me about my sessions and I would tell him. It was the beginning stages so me and my therapist were getting to know each other. She focused on my life, my past, my family and issues that surrounded me as an individual to learn who I was as a person. Damian was not satisfied with that, he wanted her to address our issues and the things about me that he felt like were a problem, so he asked if he could come to a session. In my next session I let my therapist know that he wanted to come and she was very hesitant because she said we were not at the stage to bring in family yet, so she declined. When I got home, I told him that he could not come and he practically begged, and told me to call her and ask how much it would be for a private session and he would pay out of his own pocket. She was hesitant but with my approval she agreed to see him, and he paid her and we went to the session. My therapist was a very nice, classy, laid back woman and our sessions together flowed and we had good energy. I was transparent and always left her office with an understanding and that was our flow.

When Damian came and we sat down on her couch, she greeted us and began to ask questions and already I could feel that Damian's energy was on high. He was ready to explode and basically tell on me. She gave him the floor and he talked about a lot of different issues he had with me, and told her how he felt like I had mental disorders and she would stop him every time to confirm to him that I did not have any mental disorders and she was constantly reiterating to him to not slander me. Basically, he was in her office throwing me under the bus and she made a statement saying "wow this is opening Pandora's box" and when she said that Damian took the opportunity to pour his heart out. The more he talked, the more he exposed his own trauma and the therapist suggested that he saw someone one on one for himself just as I was doing, but he told her he didn't need to see a therapist. I was the one who needed therapy and that was the only reason he was there. The more she talked to him about his own issues, the more he deflected and took the light off of him and kept putting it back on me. He was trying to paint a picture to her that I was not the humble person that she knew in therapy and that I was actually a monster, especially at home and he wanted her to know it. We got on the issues regarding his son and Damian told so many lies and painted me out as if I were abusing his son and I wasn't. At that point she was tuned in and taking every word he said in. "Well Damian from what you tell me there are just things you have to work out regarding your son to get on the same page and have better communication" she told him and that wasn't good enough for him.

One day we were in the house and I was cleaning by the fireplace where the tv was. On the mantle was a three-piece vase set. When I went to move the vase, I noticed someone broke it and tried to put it back without telling me. My sister had bought me the set and I really liked it, so I was annoyed. I went to the garage to get the broom and Damian and his son were sitting out there. I came in to sweep up the rest of the pieces and throw it in the trash in the garage. When I came out to the garage, I told Damian about my vase and he said something smart because his son was the one who broke it and tried to hide it. I was so upset with Damian because he was popping trash to me instead of telling his son he should have told us the vase was broken or at least cleaned it up because it fell and glass was all over the place and someone could have gotten hurt. Instead, Damian was being rude to me. I was still in my rage stage of life where I would break everything. I used to break and tear up whatever was next to me. I did not control my emotions. I had so much bottled anger, and breaking things was the only way I knew how to release. With that being said Damian was pissing me off so I opened the door to the garage and threw one of the small vases at him and he blocked it and it hit the floor and broke. It did not hit his son; his son was sitting across from him. "Bitch you threw glass at me and my son" he yelled at me and I slammed the door and went in the house to my room. When I came back downstairs a few hours later, he had cleaned up the glass and by that time Terrance was at the house. Damian, Terrance and Brandon were in the garage listening to music and that was that.

The next day I apologized to Damian, and he said somebody could have got hurt and I needed to control my anger and I agreed, and that was the end of it. In the therapist's office he told her about me throwing the small vase and made it seem as if I threw it at his son, which was not true. I should not have thrown the vase period and my actions were undeniably wrong, and if I could take it back, I would. I would and have never intentionally tried to hurt his son or him. I was just a hot head who did not know how to control myself. When I first came to see my therapist on our first visit, she read the disclaimer to me and basically said I could tell her anything and it would be confidential except if I expressed that I wanted to hurt myself or if it involved hurting children then she would have to get DCFS involved and I agreed to the terms. With that being said once Damian told her about throwing the vase, her whole demeanor changed towards me. She stated that, it was a form of abuse and that if it happened again then DCFS would be notified. The look on Damian's face was that he finally got satisfaction, because he finally was able to tell her something that would make her look at me different. I was horrified and disgusted by him, because he told a lie and painted a false picture, at that point I was ready to go. I was totally uncomfortable and appalled.

I was a mother and I loved kids. I was the type of person to protect kids and for someone to threaten to report me to DCFS was insulting and hurtful, and it was all because of Damian and his hateful ways towards me. His mission was complete and his job of sabotaging me was done. On our way out the door, the therapist pulled me aside, but Damian could still hear her, and she said "Shamirah, your issues have little to do with him, and everything to do with You, you understand?" She said to me giving me genuine advice. In a nutshell, she was telling me to work on myself so I won't be easily triggered by others. She told me that once I heal, that others have no power, and that was a jewel to me from her. But of course, Damian took it as she was saying he had no issues, and I was the one who was the problem. He would always bring up what she said to throw it in my face. He used it as if she validated HIM when she didn't. He came to my session and sabotaged it. Though I was able to book more sessions with my therapist I didn't. The threat of DCFS was too much for me. I would not risk Damian telling more lies and making me out to be an abuser, and them trying to take his son and Najah because of his lies. After his lies, I was no longer comfortable with his son staying with us either since Damian put out false accusations. At that point I was ready for his son to go home with his mom. It was either that or Damian needed to stick to his word and move out with his son. After the accusations on top of everything else, it had really become too much. I began looking at Damian side eyed too. The fact that he would even say something like that about me knowing he was lying. But at the time, I was still in love with him so I forgave him like I always did for the mean things he would do to me.

It was the end of the school year in GA and his son was in danger of failing the 8th grade so to ensure that he made it to high school, I suggested to Damian to send him back to NJ where they were still in school in hopes that that will give him more time to catch up in school and get promoted. Damian took my advice and on the last day of school Najah had a 6th grade graduation at her school, and we attended and celebrated her and later that night Me Damian, Najah and Brandon got on the road and drove to NJ. When we got there, we had dropped him off with his mom and Damian gave her all the paperwork she needed and we said our goodbyes and we left. Brandon was in fact able to catch up on his work, and he did get promoted to high school and it all ended up working out for him.

Prior to me coming to NJ I had been so stressed that I hadn't got my period in a few months, yet every time I took a pregnancy test it was negative. While we were up there having fun, I had woken up one morning and my stomach was killing me, and it hurt for most of the day. In the afternoon we were driving and I had felt a warm gush out of nowhere as I was sitting in the passenger seat. When we got to where we were going, I went to the bathroom and I was soaked with dark blood. I was so annoyed because I did not want to be on my period while I was out of town. My period didn't come when I was home in GA, but it decided to come at the worst time. I was bleeding for the rest of the trip and when we got home my period stopped. For some reason I got the feeling I was "back to normal" my body had felt like it had been reset and I felt great. The tension in the home had lessened, and me and Damian did not argue as much and things between us were a lot better. We were actually having fun again.

I had planned a day trip for me and him at the Evergreen Spa on the Stone Mountain property and we got massages and ate at the buffet and talked. I expressed to him how frustrated I was with my dad. Especially since we were married and I was Muslim, and my dad was supposed to be the over seer of me and Damian, yet he never answered my calls or texts and I was upset about it. Damian gave me words of encouragement and told me it would get better and he would see what he could do. "You don't have to do anything, it's not your problem to fix, you keep coming to my dad's rescue when it concerns me, he is a grown man and needs to fix things with me himself" I expressed to Damian. "Yeah you are right, but as your husband when you tell me that something hurts you, it's in my nature as a man to want to fix it" he told me. "I know, and I appreciate it, but my dad has to want it. I don't want you to force him to love me because then it's not genuine" I expressed to him. "Yeah you right, well let's enjoy our time together here, and we will deal with that when it comes'" he told me and we finished our dinner. We went outside to the pool area to enjoy our time at the resort. We had left full and refreshed. The massages were nice and the buffet food was so good.

A few weeks had passed and I was in the car with Damian and he bought up my dad. He asked me how I would feel if my dad surprised me, and I went ballistic. "If my dad popped up in GA I would be pissed" I told him as we drove in the car. "Why?" he asked me with a sneaky smile. When Damian had that smile, I knew he was up to something. "You shouldn't be mad if your dad popped up on you. You said you want him to reach out so what's the problem if he came to see you? he asked. "First of all, the problem is I would not be mentally prepared if he popped up right now, and secondly that would not be a surprise to me, it would be devastating" I told him, and he just sat there driving with the same sneaky smirk on his face. "Damian, I know that look, don't play with me. I swear to God you better not be trying to bring my dad here to surprise me or I will have an issue with You" I told him sternly as I was dead serious. "Ok, I contacted your dad and paid for him a flight and he will be here tomorrow" Damian confessed to me. "You did what?!" I said to him as I became angry. "I cannot believe you did that without talking to me first" I said to him as I was about to cry. "Wow, don't cry I did not know you would be this mad, my bad" Damian said as he felt bad. "He is only going to be here for a few days, just take this time to get everything off your chest that you want to say to him. Just make it a positive situation. If I knew it would hurt you, I would not have bought him here" he said, still feeling bad. "Damian you don't understand, talking to my dad is pointless, he twists stuff and does not care about anything I have to say" I told him. "Well if it makes you feel any better when you talk to him, I will be there with you the whole time" he reassured me. "You promise?" I asked him. "Wilahi, I promise" he reassured me.

The next day my dad flew into town and we picked him up from the airport. It was raining and the vibe was super off. We saw my dad and Damian got out to greet him and helped him put his bags in the car. I didn't get out nor did I get out of the passenger seat to let him sit in the front. I was already upset he was there, so I did not give him any courtesy. He got in the backseat and we barely spoke and the energy was super awkward. Damian made small talk with him on the way home, and when we got there I did not stay downstairs to talk to my dad. I went straight upstairs to my room and stayed there. While I was in my room by myself, I was crying. I cried because being around my dad and his energy towards me always made me feel like that rejected little girl. He was always stand offish to me and I could never read his energy, and that always made me feel uncomfortable. As a grown woman in my own home I was feeling the same exact way as I did as a little girl. I did not want him to be there and I was mad at Damian as well so I just wanted to be by myself. Damian and Najah were downstairs entertaining my dad and I went to sleep for work the next morning.

I had to be to work by 8am so I got up and left. I usually get off of work at 3pm and I didn't stay a minute longer, and all my co-workers knew that about me. My manager had asked another co-worker of mine if she could stay until 9pm for overtime and before my co-worker could answer I said "I'll stay" and everyone looked at me like they saw a ghost. "What?" they all said in shock and I laughed. "I will stay and cover the shift" I told them. "Shamirah, are you Ok?" my manager asked me, thinking I was joking. "Yes, I'm ok, I want to stay and cover the shift" I told her and she gave it to me and everyone had packed up to go home, and I stayed with the nurses and I didn't mind. Normally I would have never stayed, but I did not want to go home and have to see my dad, so I was trying to avoid my dad at all cost. If I did not stay at work I was going to go walk around the mall or go and get a pedicure or something to kill time. Since I was already at work it was better to stay and make money versus going out and spending money. Normally the days at work would drag, especially on second shift, but that day nine o'clock came super-fast and it was time for me to go home. I had talked to Damian on the phone throughout the day and I told him how I was feeling and why I stayed at work late and he understood.

On my way home my stomach was in knots. I was just praying that when I got home that my dad was not in the garage because that is where I parked my car and I would not be able to avoid him. Our garage was huge. It was a two-car garage so even when I parked my car inside there was still room for people to sit and relax in it. Thank God when I pulled up my dad was not in there. He was in the room with the door closed. I hurried up and went upstairs in my room and closed the door and took a shower and went to bed for work the next day. By now my dad had been there three days and I pretty much avoided him the whole time. Damian and Najah entertained him amongst the company that would be over like Terrance and a few of Damian's other close friends. I had done overtime literally the whole time that my dad was there.

One particular night I came home and closed my door and Damian came in behind me. "So, you just not going to talk to your dad the whole time he is here?" he asked me concerned. "Damian I already told you I don't want to" I said to him as I was taking my clothes off getting ready to take a shower. "I know, but I think you need to," he said to me. "I don't need to do anything, you invited him here, not me" I said to him as I was getting annoyed. "I know, but he did say he wanted to talk to you. You come home and go straight to the room so he hasn't had a chance to spend time with you" Damian said. "That's because I don't want to spend time with him" I told him. "Your dad is going home soon, and he came here to see you so I think you should talk to him tonight" Damian told me trying to plead with me. "Tonight? No, I'm about to go to bed" I said to him. "Just do it please, the sooner you do it, the sooner he can leave " Damian reassured me. I stood there and thought about it for a minute and agreed only because he said my dad will leave. "I took my shower and changed my clothes.

Before I came downstairs, I sat in the room with Damian and told him all the concerns I had with talking to my dad and he reassured me that he would stay by my side the whole time. "I got you, you're going to be ok. Just hear him out and see what he has to say and you say what you feel too and hopefully y'all can work it out" he said humbly to me. I trusted him to protect me and support me, so even though I had butterflies I went downstairs and out to the garage where my dad was. Damian had set up the chairs in a circle for us to have a discussion. My dad was sitting closer to the wall, I sat not too far from him, and Damian sat in between us. It was us three in the garage and our dog Prada. Prada was in her cage because it was night time and she was normally lying down, but this time she was up and facing us. Prada was a Pitbull and she was laid back unless you were playing with her and then she was really rambunctious. Prada looked at me and she looked at Damian and she sat down. Although she never laid down because I could tell she was not comfortable. My dad sat there with a smile on his face. Damian had a nervous smirk and my face was numb and annoyed.

"I guess you can start" I said to my dad giving him the floor and he began to talk, about 30 seconds into him talking Damian's phone rang and he got up from being next to me, and he walked in the house leaving me out there with my dad, which he promised me he would not do. At that point I was alone and I was pissed.

My dad had switched from whatever spill he was about to say when Damian was out there, to basically trying to blame me for things the same way he did when I was seventeen years old when he told me he was not in my life because of "Me". I felt myself getting anxious and overwhelmed in my mind and anger was starting to take over my body. Prada felt my energy too because she came all the way to the end of her cage closer to where I was, and her body was at attention and she paced back and forth growling. "It's ok Prada" I said to her, coaxing her to calm down. If Prada were out of her cage at that moment, I do believe she would have attacked my dad, because she felt my energy and she was in protective mode. "I did not want to be in there with my dad, so I went into the house where Damian was. "What are you doing?" I asked him angrily, as I looked dead in his eyes. "I'm so sorry, I had to take this call" he said to me apologetically. "You left me out there with him and he did the same BS that I told you he was going to do" I told Damian as I wanted to cry. "I will call you back bro" he said as he got off the phone. "My bad for real. That was an important call, c'mon and let's go back out there and get all this handled right now" he said to me and he went out before me and I stood behind him.

We had both sat down and Damian began to talk. "I brought you here because Mirah carries a lot of pain from you, this is my wife and I watch how she is hurting. A lot of things affect our relationship because she has daddy issues, so I brought you here to clear the air in hopes that y'all can resolve some stuff face to face" Damian said to my dad trying to get the conversation back on track. "Absolutely" my dad agreed. "Mirah, I came here because I love you. I know I was not always there, but my issues had nothing to do with you. I'm here now and I want to do better and be here for you and my grandbaby" he said to me, and I immediately responded. "That's not true because every time I call you, you don't pick up, when I reach out to you as my Wali and to get advice about my marriage, you are never there. When I call you don't pick up, but when Damian calls you pick up every time. So you say you love me and everything but you don't show it, and you say all this now, but when Damian went in the house you was blaming me for everything like you always do" I said as I was hype and had to calm myself down. I had so much built up anger towards him that I wanted to explode.

My dad had chimed in and responded and said he was not blaming me and began to try to twist the truth so I began to get frustrated and wanted to end the conversation, because it was going nowhere. I sat there silent and I wanted to cry but I did not let a tear drop from my face. I was not going to let him see me vulnerable so I just sat there angry. "You good?" Damian asked me and I ignored him. My dad leaned over and put his hand on my knee and said "I love you" to me as I was looking down and I did not say it back, and he said it again and I still didn't say it back. He had a smile on his face and he acted as if my feelings were a game and I was just so done at that point. My dad got up and hugged me and I did not hug him back.

I got up and went upstairs and called my mom and cried and told her everything that happened. She encouraged me and told me not to worry about it. Damian had come into the room and hugged me and comforted me. He saw how hard all of that was for me and I think at that moment he really felt bad for bringing my dad there because it had opened up a lot of emotions. Damian was supportive of me and my dad's relationship and he saw the good in my dad and had a certain respect for him. Which I understood, but Damian also needed to understand that there were emotions in me, that I was not ready to deal with, and that though his intentions were pure, he could not force my dad on me, because it was too much for me. I appreciated his effort, but his timing was just wrong. My father had left and went to back to New Jersey a few days later, and we didn't speak much after that.

36

A few months had passed since my dad had left. I was on to bigger and more exciting things. My little sister was on her way to college at ASU: Albany State University and she was having dance tryouts so me and my family were going for support. As we were driving on the way there out of nowhere a car came on the side of us almost pushing us off of the road. It was about 10 pm and after that happened, I had the most eerie feeling. I felt uneasy the whole ride there, but I just said a prayer for protection and tried to brush it off.

When we got there, it was late so we checked into our hotel room to get some sleep because we had to get up early to make it to my sister Jamilah's competition at about 9 am. We had got up early and me, my mom. My grand mom Ernestine, and my sister Jaleesah got up to get breakfast before we got dressed. It was about 6:30 am and we were walking down the hotel hallway when I got a text from my bestie, and she sent me a screenshot from FB that said R.I.P Terrance. "Ain't this Damian's best friend?" is what the text read. When I saw it, my stomach dropped and I felt nauseous. I didn't not believe it. Terrance was so humble, everybody loved him. I could not imagine who would have wanted to hurt him. Before I got emotional, I decided to call Damian. When he picked up the phone before I could even ask him, I knew it was true.

When he answered I could hear in his voice that he was crying. "So, it's true?" I said to him, "Yeah" he said and I began to cry. "You Ok?" I asked him. "Not really" he said to me and that broke my heart even more. I was so sad because I could not be there with him and Najah. I was supposed to stay in Albany until Monday and it was only Saturday. I wanted to go home so badly to mourn with them, but it was my sister's competition and I knew that my mom was not going to take me back home. I was so hurt that I did not want breakfast anymore. I cried most of the morning, just thinking about Terrance and the conversations we used to have. Terrance wasn't just Damian's friend; he was my friend as well, and when I heard how he died it really broke my heart. The news article said he was shot in a gas station. I could not believe it. I text his wife Michelle and gave her my condolences and Damian's number so he can help her with the Janazah since we were all Muslim. It was soon time to go to the competition and my head was not there at all, but I tried to be present and supportive while I was there.

We had a lot of fun and we enjoyed watching the dancers. Afterwards we went to the mall and to get something to eat. I did not want to go anywhere but I tried to stay present and be in the moment, but every time I talked to Damian I would break down and cry and I just wanted to be alone. I did not want to talk to anyone. I just kept thinking about my friend, who was Damian's best friend and Najah's God dad. She loved Terrance and her little heart was hurting, and I was not there to console her and that ate me up. I talked and laughed with everyone as I was mourning. I tried to be normal but I had my moments. Everyone I was with had known Terrance, and knew that he had passed and they had compassion, but for some reason my mom was getting upset with me. I did have my moments when I was sad and I did not want to talk. I was surrounded by them the whole time whether in the car or in the hotel room, so I was just taking mental moments to myself and when I did, I guess she took it as I was being stand offish.

The way she was acting towards me was really hurting my feelings because she literally had no regards for me being in mourning. She was pissing me off and I did not like her energy and how she was treating me so that really made me want to go home. Finally, the trip was over and I got back home to see Damian and Najah and the energy in the house was so sad and somber. I knew that Terrance had passed but being home and seeing their faces made reality set in for me. I was going to miss him being at the house and looking out the window and seeing his car and having the talks we used to have about life and Islam. My heart was truly hurting. The day after I came home Damian had left to go to Jersey to Terrance's Janazah and I stayed home with Najah.

After Damian came back a few weeks later. Terrance's sons had come to spend the night at our house. They were about three or four at the time. Damian had a nerf gun fight with them and Najah and they had a ball. When it was time for bed, they stayed with me in my room and watched "Rugrats" and ate popcorn. They had always made me happy ever since they were little babies, and they were so smart. We were talking and one of the twins asked me, why was there talking babies on the show and his brother said it's just a cartoon it's not real and I laughed. The older twin asked me if I had a baby and I told him that Najah was my baby and he said "Najah is too big" and I laughed. "Why you ask me if I have a baby? You think should have a baby?" I asked him jokingly. "Yes!" both of the twins said at the same time. "Ok when should I have a baby?" I asked them, and the youngest twin answered and said "You will have a baby when Allah is ready." We were joking and having fun, but when he said that it hit my heart in a special way and I said humbly "Yes you are right, I will have one when Allah is ready" and I gave him a hug and we finished watching the show and before I knew it we all were knocked out.

The next day Damian took the boys home. About two days later Damian had left to go to Jersey to handle some business. I was home in GA taking care of Najah and living my everyday life. I had woken up one morning and I had felt crampy, so I went to the bathroom to see if there was blood and there wasn't. I had looked on the calendar in my phone and realized I was about two days late for my period. Since I had been back from my last trip to Jersey my period had come every month like clockwork for three months straight. With it now being late. I did not think much of it because my period was always off and on so I figured it had gotten off again. I had brushed it off and figured that it would come when it came. At that point I had went about my normal day and when I woke up the next morning there was still no period and I was still campy. At that point I was no longer addicted to taking pregnancy tests so I did not want to go to the store and waste money like I did in the past. I was feeling some type of way all that day and I could not sleep that night thinking about if I could possibly be pregnant.

I had woken up early that morning and went to Walmart and got three 88 cent pregnancy tests because I refused to spend money on any more expensive brands. I took the first test and sat in on the sink and left it there while I took a shower. I was so anxious to see the results, but I tried to not think much about it. When I got out, I look at the test sitting there and I almost fainted, there was two lines!!! I could not believe it! Oh my God I said to myself in disbelief. I wanted to be sure so I took another 88 cent one and watched it and sure enough I watched as the second line popped up and I got excited again! "Yes!!" I said to myself as I was overwhelmed with joy. The third test I took I recorded it and sent it to Damian because he was still in Jersey. "Did you get my video?" I asked him as I called him with excitement. "Yeah" I got it" he said in an upbeat voice. "I'm pregnant!" I said to him as I was overjoyed.

This time around I did not care what Damian said, I was not getting an abortion. I did not care if he was mad about me being pregnant, all I knew is that it took me three years to get pregnant since the last abortion and I was ecstatic and I was keeping my baby. "Ok, that's what's up" he said to my surprise. "Are you happy?" I asked him. "Yeah, it's cool" he responded. "Oh my God I can't believe it finally happened!"

I said to him as I was happy. "Yup, I'm glad, that's what's up" he said to me. "I'm beyond happy" I told him. "I knew you was pregnant" he told me. "What you mean?" I asked him. "I made sure I nutted in you, so you could get pregnant" he said to me. "So, you did it on purpose?" I asked him. "Yeah, you could say that. I knew how much you wanted a baby and I was tired of seeing my wife sad" he told me compassionately. "So, I figured I wouldn't pull out like I normally do, so you can get pregnant" he said to me. I didn't know how to feel about the information that he was purposely making sure I didn't get pregnant. I was just trying to be in the moment and in that moment, I was on cloud nine and nothing could bring me down. I got off the phone with Damian and called my mom and sisters and told them and they were so excited!

When Najah got home from school I set up a game to reveal the news to her and she was so happy. I went to Walmart and bought the clear blue test that reads yes or no, just to see the YES pop up! I had watched so many pregnancy test reveals on YouTube and I would watch the lines pop up or the test would say yes and I wanted that feeling so bad and I finally was able to see the YES pop up on mine and it was the best feeling ever. A few days later Damian came home, and I was able to take the test in front of him. I was so excited and in baby mode. He was on board so that made it even better. When I first found out it was all smiles and happiness and I felt great, but as the weeks passed by, I began to get sicker and sicker. I am the type of person that when I get pregnant my sickness is so horrible that I have to be put on medication for the nausea, and even the medication did not work so I was just miserable. I went for my first check up and Damian came with me and we saw the baby on the screen and heard the heartbeat. I was about 9 weeks at the time and even though I was sick as a dog. Seeing the baby made it all worth it.

As the weeks went on my sickness didn't get any better and I mostly stayed in bed. I was a secretary at the time, and mainly worked from home, but my hours were drastically cut, because I was always so sick.

Damian was doing construction flipping houses, plus he had a cleaning business so at that time he took care of the rent and the bills. I pretty much stayed in bed all day miserable. Every single day before he left out for the day, he would go to Dunkin Donuts and get me a turkey egg and cheese sandwich on a croissant and an orange juice. He would bring it upstairs and sit it by me on the nightstand to make sure I had something to eat, and at dinner time he always made sure he cooked or brought something home so me him and Najah would have something to eat. He was really sweet when I was pregnant. I would be so sick but I couldn't throw up, so he would stick his finger down my throat to make me vomit so I could feel better. I would get the worst constipation and he would run my warm bath water for me to soak so it could help my muscles relax and a lot of times that would help me go to the bathroom. He was very helpful with making sure that I did not have to worry about too much of anything.

"I want to move, I am tired of living here, " I said to him as we sat in the garage talking. "Where do you want to move to? He asked me. "I don't know, I wish we could move back to Gwinnett" I told him as I laughed. "I don't want to go back to Gwinnett, but I do want to move," he told me. "With the new baby and how the balcony is set up I would always be worried about the baby falling, and that fact that the whole downstairs is hardwood floor is not good for when the baby starts crawling" I told him. "Plus, I don't want Najah going to Junior High in this school system" I added. "Word" he said to me as he agreed with me. "Well the lease will be up soon, so we can look online for some places, " he told me and we got on the tablet and started looking. The next day Damian had went to the worksite and was talking to his colleagues about moving and they all suggested with his credit score being a little over 800 that we should consider buying a house instead of renting.

A few months prior to that I had fixed my credit as well and was at a 730. So, we both agreed that buying a home would be a good option.

I was pregnant so I was blessed to have my receptionist job making pretty good money as well as Damian was doing good with contracts, so we both felt ready to purchase a home. Since Damian was getting into the buying and flipping business, he suggested that he used his credit for the business, and I used my credit to buy a house and I agreed. I had spoken with the lender and they gave me my approval letter with the amount I was approved for and we began working with a realtor to find homes. At this point I was about six months pregnant and it was beginning to be summer so it was hot. Big and all I got up every day to look for houses with Damian and the realtor. I wanted a move-in ready home and Damian wanted a fixer upper. I was pregnant and I did not want to live in a home that was being renovated, nor did we have the option to stay in our current home because we were already on a month to month lease and time was winding down for the baby to come. All I wanted to do was get a house, move in and get it set up before the baby came. The home buying process was more stressful than I thought.

We would find homes that we liked and put offers in and they were not getting accepted so we would have to start all over, and I was getting overwhelmed. When I would be at home, I would notice I was getting sicker and sicker and it became harder for me to do things. When I was upstairs it was not as bad, but as soon as I came downstairs, especially in the kitchen, I would get beyond nauseous to the point I had to stop coming down there. I stayed in my room most of the time, and I was not able to come downstairs and cook and clean like I normally did, so out of character for me the house was getting a little messy, because I had left the upkeep of the house up to Damian and Najah and they were way more laxed on cleaning then I was. I had noticed when I was not in the house, I did not feel sick, but as soon as I got back, I would feel that nauseating faint feeling again. "You good? Damian asked me as I could barely breathe as we walked through the front door and I headed straight upstairs. "I'm not sure why you are only sick when we are home, but there are a lot of water issues with this house, I am going to get a mold inspector to come out because something is not right" he said to me. "Ok" I said to him as I laid down because I was getting a headache.

Damian called an inspector and they came out and tested the things they needed to test and we had to wait a few days for the results to come back and when it came back, sure enough the kitchen tested positive for black mold. Just hearing the results made my skin crawl and instantly made me sick and to know me and my family was breathing the air made me want to just pack up and leave. I notified the rental office and they would not get us a hotel room or anything. They suggested we get a humidifier and some air vents to protect the air from the particles coming in and they supposedly sent someone out to get rid of the mold. The person came out and basically sprayed a substance and left and it pissed me off because they needed to replace wood and sheetrock and they did nothing. At that point I was ready to go and I needed a house as soon as possible. After a long and disappointing search there was finally light at the end of the tunnel. Damian was out of town when my realtor called me and said that there was a brand-new development being built in Rockdale county and he wanted me to come and see it. Since Damian was not home, my mom and my sister Jamilah came with me. When we got to the neighborhood there were construction workers everywhere and there were a few houses up and many being built.

I pulled up to the house and the realtor was already inside and he opened the door for us and when we came in, we all instantly were in awe. The smell of the new wood and paint smelled so good. When we walked in the home it had an open concept and it was very classy and modern. It was not originally what I wanted but it was so cute and I could see myself living there. The house we were looking at was actually the Demo house. Our home was a few doors down and it was not finished being built. We had walked down to the lot where my house would be and the frame was up and that was it. I was excited to have a brand-new construction so I had put the offer in and a few days later my realtor had told me it was accepted. We had begun the home buying process which was super stressful at that time. All I remember is submitting document after document to the lender as well as packing up the old house to move.

It was a very hectic time. I was in the process of closing on a home, packing and being seven months pregnant all at the same time. I had no peace or no rest because there was so much to get done before the baby was born. Through all the stress I will never forget the day when the Lender called us and told us that we had closed on the house and to meet at the lawyer's office to sign the final documents and get keys and in that moment all the stress was worth it. A few days later we met in Atlanta at the Lawyers office. It was me, Damian, our realtor and our Lender sitting at the round table. We all signed what needed to be signed and we were given the keys and that was such a proud moment for me and Damian.

We were finally home owners! In the lawyer's office Damian did not sign off on the deed, only I did so even though we got the house together the house was only in my name. I asked him to sign as well but he did not want to, which I felt was odd. We were married and we accomplished this together so I thought it was only right for both of our names to be on the house but I did not want to make a big deal about it so I just signed my name and went from there. We had all taken a picture together in the attorney's office as everyone congratulated us and afterwards, we went across the street to a restaurant to celebrate. "Are you happy?" I asked him as we ate. "Yeah" he said to me as he had a drink. "I am so happy and proud of us, now we can finally move and get ready for this baby" I told him as I smiled. Damian sat there and had really no emotion, he was always nonchalant so I really could not read him. Pulling his emotions out of him was always like pulling teeth, so I didn't even try to read much into it. We had gone home and began packing and the house was a mess.

Over the next few days, we had packed but we had so much stuff that it had all become overwhelming. My mom came and helped us get some stuff into boxes and the rest of the stuff Damian had just thrown into totes and said we would sort everything out at the new house. On moving day, the movers came and the house was in disarray there was so much stuff still not even packed. The movers just began taking stuff and throwing it in the truck and just dumped everything at the new house. When the move was finally over, I had come into the house and there was stuff everywhere.

The new house was so packed all I could do was look around and cry. I was almost eight months pregnant and I did not have the mental or physical strength to unpack and organize the whole house. Thankfully my mom, my grand mom and my sisters came over and unpacked everything and got the house in order and everything looked so beautiful and finally my new house felt like a home. It took them a few days and when they were done, I thanked them and hugged them and when they left, I lit a candle and relaxed. Najah had been gone for the summer and wouldn't be home for another three weeks when school started so it was just me and Damian. We spent a lot of time together sitting out in the yard talking and it seemed like we were going to Walmart every five minutes to get things for the house. I would cook for us and we really enjoyed each other's company. We were all we had. We had moved far from our family and friends and since our neighborhood was a new development it felt deserted.

There were a few houses up and just us, and our neighbors Haily and Brett that lived to the right of us. Other than that, the neighborhood was empty. At night we would sit on the porch and talk to Brett and Haily. Across from our house it was just a dirt lot before they built houses on it and it would be dark except for our porch lights, that's how empty the neighborhood was. One night we were sitting outside and out of nowhere in the dark sky was a large orange light that shot from the sky and we all looked and it faded away. We were in awe and assumed it was a shooting star. We were way out in the country and were not used to seeing stuff like that.

Everything was cool, me and Damian were getting used to our new surroundings. I went out and got new bedroom furniture for ours and Najah's room and I set her room up really cute for when she came back. When she came home, school started. The neighborhood was so new that she was the only child who lived in it, so her school had to create a new bus route for her which was perfect because the bus came right up to our door and picked her up and dropped her off. With me being pregnant, I was so grateful that I did not have to drive her to a far bus stop. Najah liked her new school and she adjusted very well. Damian's contracts and business started to slow up so to make up for money, he had got a job not too far from the house.

While they were at work and school, I was home trying to get every-thing ready for the new baby. I had begun to get excited and it began to sink in that soon there will be a little baby running around the house. My mom bought the baby's bedding and her curtains and most of her room decor and the changing table. My sister Jaleesah had bought her crib and the mattress. I was so grateful to them for helping me because a lot of me and Damian's money had gone into buying the house. I was pregnant so most of the financial responsibility was on Damian, so all the help from my family was more than appreciated.

One evening after Damian got off of work, he had come home and was putting up the crib in the baby's room. As Najah helped him put the crib together, we all laughed and talked about how excited we were about the baby coming. We also talked about what was the labor plan, in case I went into labor while he was at work. After they were finished, they put the crib in place where it was supposed to be, and me and Damian went into our room and took a shower and chilled out. I had such a nice time and the vibe was so perfect. But it was short lived because the next day he was upset about something. "What's wrong?" I asked him concerned. "Nothing," he said at first. "Damian, I heard you talking on the phone, and now you are in a bad mood, what happened?" I asked again. "It's something going on with my son" he told me. "Is he ok?" I asked. "He good, he just got in some trouble at home with his mom" Damian said and then he was silent. "Oh Ok, do you want to talk about it?" I asked him. "No not really" he said to me and I could tell he was annoyed. "Am I annoying you?" I asked him.

"Nah, it's just that my son needs to be here with me" he blurted out. "I know Damian, we had tried to find four-bedroom houses but none were available and the ones that were, we put the offers in but did not get them" I said to him. "I know but I still feel like he should be here," he said. "We tried our best to get the four bedrooms, but with the time crunch of the baby coming, you agreed that a three bedroom was fine and that your son would stay with his mom, since he has a room and everything with her" I told him, and he sat there and smoked his black and mild and was silent for a minute. "I don't see why a new baby has to have their own room, what baby do you know that needs a whole room? That could have been Brandon's room" he said suddenly. "Well first of all the baby has a lot of stuff so she needs her own space. It would be too crowded to put the baby's stuff in our room and Najah is a pre-teen, she does not need to be cooped up in a room with a crying baby and her space would be crowded too.

"We have a three bedroom, It makes sense for it to be the baby's room. On top of it, you knew that I was doing a nursery for the baby" I told him. "It just doesn't make sense to me when my son could have got the room," he said. "If your son got the room, where was I supposed to put the baby? On top of the fact that you agreed to buy a three bedroom instead of a four bedroom, and you specifically said that it was ok. You said that your son would live with his mom since we couldn't get the four bedrooms. I completely under stand how you are feeling right now. I truly do, and I have compassion for what you are feeling as a father. It just makes everything complicated now, because there is completely no room. This new house is half the size of the old house, and we already had to downsize everything" I explained to him. "Niyah's room is small as it is, and definitely cant fit a crib and the baby's stuff. Plus I would not want to cram Niyah's space like that, it is not fair to her. I'm confused, because you made it clear that your son was not coming, now you spring all of this on me" I said to him. "Well now I changed my mind. He's having issues at his mom's house, and I want to bring him with me" Damian said to me. "I'll figure it out, I'm probably going to get a place for me and my son" he said to me. "You are going to move out?" I asked him surprised. "I don't know yet, I am thinking about it" he told me. "Why would you have me get this house just for you to move out? On top of we are about to have a new baby" I said to him disappointed. "I have to get my son here so I have to figure something out. " he told me and I was so hurt by him saying that he was leaving that I didn't ask any more questions and I left the conversation alone.

After that point there was tension about the baby's room. Every time my mom or sister would drop something off, and I would put it up in the room there was an issue. I would have to sneak and decorate the room when Damian was at work, because when he was there and I was in the room it was uncomfortable. I would hear him on the phone with his friends or family and they would be talking about how it was dumb for me to give a baby their own room and they would be talking about me.

"Ok, let's stop right there, my therapist said to me, as she sat up in her chair. "You mentioned that you would hear your husband on the phone talking badly about you to his friends. How did that make you feel?" she asked curiously. "It would hurt my feelings, but it still didn't stop me from preparing the nursery. I had prayed to God to bless me with a baby for three years straight and he finally did, and Damian was taking all of the joy out of it. God had blessed us with a new home, and a new baby and it was a very stressful but exciting time for all of us but Damian was making a blessing began to feel like a nightmare.

Najah was super excited to be having a baby sister and I thought that Damian was excited too. When I was pregnant with Najah, Damian gave me hell. One minute he would be nice to me and the next minute he would be rude and super mean to me, I thought things would be different with the new baby, especially since we were older, but clearly it wasnt. Damian was still up to his toxic ways when it came to me being pregnant, and bearing his kids. He would say how he didn't want the baby and how he wasn't going to do anything for her. He was always wishy washy.

One minute he would be good with the idea of the baby coming and the next minute he would be rude and I would tell him to keep that same energy when she was born. I didn't know how Damian was going to react when the new baby came. I didn't know if he was going to love her or bond with her, or even want to be bothered with her at all, because he would tell me that he wasnt. And how nasty he began acting towards the end of my pregnancy made me believe him, so I had put it in my mind that I was going to be my baby's rock and love her with all my heart. because I was not sure if her dad was going to receive her or not. Damian became funny acting and I did not put anything past him.

Even with all the hardship that he gave me during my pregnancy especially towards the end. I still was hopeful for the fairy tale ending and having the family, and all the memories that I always wanted. When I was pregnant with Najah, I was in GA and he was in NC. I didn't see him from three months pregnant, all the way up until I was eight months pregnant, and then I did not see him again until I was in labor with her. He stayed in the hospital with me for one day, and he left to go back to NC because he was still grieving his brother who had passed. So I say all of that to say being pregnant this time we were actually married and lived together and were already a family, so I felt like this was my chance to do it over, and to do it the right way, and have all of those special moments that I wish I had when I was pregnant with Najah.

When I had Najah, I lived at my mom's house. She slept in the room with me, and slept in my bed, and when I moved with my grandmother it was the same thing. I did not get a chance to have a nursery with her and do all the fun things before she was born, so being pregnant with the new baby and having my own home, and her having her own room. I was excited to do a nursery and everything else I did not get to do with Najah, and Damian could not seem to understand that" I said to my therapist. "I do understand how you felt, and it is not unusual for a baby to have a nursery, " she said to me. "I know it's not, and the fact that Damian was trying to take all my joy away by saying his son should have the room when he already had a room at his mom's house made me feel some type of way.

I felt like he wanted to make the rest of the house cramped and uncomfortable for his son to have a room, when he had already agreed that since we had a three bedroom instead of a four that his son would not be living with us, because he was comfortable at his mom's house. Damian made it seem like everything was ok, and the nursery was fine, and then he threw a monkey wrench in the game and flipped it on me and really blindsided me, by telling me he was going to move out to be with his son. It was all overwhelming having to deal with while I was pregnant, and I felt that it was not fair" I told her. "What part did you think was unfair? " she asked me compassionately. "I felt like it was unfair that he said his son was not coming to live permanently, and he agreed to buy the three bedroom and made me believe everything was fine. Then at the last minute tell me that the nursery is his sons room and to cram the babies stuff either in our room or Najah's room when we did not have to do that because the baby had her own space. I also thought it was unfair that his son had a room where he lived with his mother, and he was comfortable but Damian would make me and my kids uncomfortable to bring his son and give him the bedroom. It was all too much, " I said to her. "I see, I understand, " my therapist said to me. "So ultimately what wind up happening?" she asked me as she sat back in her chair and listened. "I wound up finishing the nursery. My mom and sisters came and decorated and put up the curtains and the decor and everything came out beautiful.

Damian was upset but he got over it, and we continued to prepare for the baby to come. I had told everyone that I did not want a baby shower, but my mom and my old coworkers had surprised me with one anyway. It was so beautiful and everything was decorated so nicely. My old friends were there, and we played baby shower games and ate and I got a lot of gifts. It was an all-around great time, and I was so thankful to each and every one of them for giving me a shower, especially my mom, because she put the whole thing together. They had packed the car for me and I bought all my gifts home and was officially ready to welcome my new baby to the world.

37

A few weeks had pasts and I was huge, my back and my whole body hurt and I was miserable and over being pregnant. The baby showed no signs of being ready to be born so my doctor set a date for me to get induced. Every day Damian went to work and Najah was in school. Damian would call me all day to make sure I was ok and that I did not go into labor. On the day of my induction we got up in the morning like it was Christmas. My appointment at the hospital was at 5pm and we waited for Najah to get out of school and we left and drove to Decatur and went to eat at Moe's for my last pregnancy meal. I was so nervous but Damian and Najah were there with me the whole way. We had checked in at the hospital and I was taken to the delivery room and got prepared for labor. The nurses came in and I was given the IV for Pitocin to get the delivery rolling. My mom had come to the hospital for a while and she decided to leave so Damian could be there for me during the labor since he was my husband. When I had Najah my mom had helped me the whole way, so this time now that me and him were married she wanted him to be there for the labor and delivery.

Throughout the night me Damian and Najah laughed and talked until the morning. By the time morning came I had felt my water break and I began feeling the contractions and I was given the epidural and I was dilated to 10 centimeters so my labor had begun. Damian stood by me and held my hand and all I wanted to do was get the baby out. I was pushing with all my strength but she still would not come out. In the middle of my labor my epidural wore off and I felt all of my labor pains and I was losing my mind; the pain was unbearable. In the middle of labor, I had to get the epidural again but the pain did not go away. The nurse told me that the baby was on my nerve and that was where the pain was coming from and the only way to make the pain go away was to push the baby out. The nurses counted down for me to push and I was pushing with all my heart but still nothing.

The nurses began to talk amongst each other and Damian overheard them. "Shamirah Push" he said to me very sternly and authoritatively in his voice and I knew he meant business and I knew he knew something that I didn't know and it was urgent for me to push. After he said that I had pushed with all my soul and finally the baby began to come out. "She got a lot of hair" I heard Damian say as he was smiling. The nurse pulled her out and laid her on my chest and I looked at her and she was so white. She was so cute and we named her Aaniyah. I looked at her and it was so weird seeing her outside of my stomach. Najah had cut Aaniyah's umbilical cord and they cleaned her up and swaddled her and put her hat on and Damian held her. I was so excited to finally have her in the world and I was so happy to not be pregnant anymore. Eventually they took me to my recovery room and my mom came to see us. Damian stayed for a while and then he had to leave to go back to work. Najah stayed in the hospital with me overnight and I was not able to get any rest because she slept in my hospital bed and I sat up most of the night. The baby was given a baby bed but she didn't want to sleep in it and she was very uncomfortable so I held her for most of the night. The nurses were not helpful at all.

I had to do everything for the baby myself and it was overwhelming. The next day we got up and I got Aaniyah dressed and Damian came to see us. I had felt uncomfortable the whole night, it felt like bugs were crawling all over me. I had looked over on the table and there was a line of ants on it and when I looked around there were ants everywhere and I was pissed off. I had let the nurse know and they were going to move me to a new floor but I was so annoyed being there that I had just wanted to go home. I told them I wanted to leave and they said they had to run tests first to see if I was ok to go and if so then I could be discharged.

In the meantime I had went to take a shower and as I was getting in, the picture lady had come to the door and I let her know I was taking a shower and she said she would come back in a half an hour and I agreed. I took my shower and got out and got dressed and got Aaniyah ready for her hospital pictures. Najah was sitting in the hospital bed and she was holding Aaniyah as I was getting something out of the bathroom. The picture lady came in and gave me some paperwork and as I was signing it, she gave me a consent form and told me to put the parents name on it so I signed my name. She let me know that she could not take the pictures without a parent's consent and I said Ok. When it was time for Aaniyah to take the pictures, I told Najah to get up so I could lay the baby on the bed and the lady asked ``how old is the mom?" I told her I was 33. She looked at me and said "oh YOU are the mom?" I said "yes, who did you think was the mother?" I asked confused. "Oh, I came into the room and saw her sitting on the bed and I thought She was the mom" the lady said pointing to Najah. "Oh no, that's my daughter she is only 12" I said to the lady as I laughed. "I was confused as to why you gave me these consent forms now it makes sense. You thought my 12-year-old was the mother of the baby. Oh no these both are my daughters' ' I said as me and the lady laughed. "I am so sorry, I have seen it all, you just never know these days. I didn't want to be rude and ask, but I was thinking wow she sure is young" the lady said to me.

After we got that all settled Aaniyah got her pictures done and I waited for my results to go home. The doctor said everything was fine and that I could be discharged. Damian came up to the hospital to sign the birth certificate and we left. I was rolled out in a wheelchair, and when we drove out the hospital garage it was bright and sunny and I felt free. It was surreal having Aaniyah in her car seat in the backseat, and

I was excited to get home and start our lives with the new baby. When we got to the house, we put her in her crib and took pictures. Little by little, family came to see her and we were overjoyed. I was happy to be home but I had not rested at the hospital, and when I got home I was constantly up and down the steps. I was cleaning and handling the baby so I had begun to swell really bad. About 3 days had passed and the swelling had gotten worse. It was so bad that my feet had swelled up to the point where my skin was ripping. "You need to go to the hospital" Damian had told me as he looked at my feet. I did go and I was admitted and they ran test and gave me an IV and told me I had severe edema so they flushed out all the fluid and I was able to see my ankles again. Finally, when I got out of the hospital, they gave me a script for water bills and all my bloat was gone. I came home and tried on my old jeans and I was ecstatic that they fit. Damian had to go to work the next day. Thankfully Najah was on fall break so she stayed home with me all week, and helped me with the baby. But the next week she had to go back to school, and it was just me and the baby home. Although I was happy to have her, it was a lot having her alone all day.

My life had gone from getting up and doing what I wanted to do when I wanted to now having a newborn. My days were filled with making bottles, feeding her, bathing her, changing her diapers, listening to her cry and she was always constipated so I was constantly on the phone with the doctor's office to see how I could get rid of her constipation. When she would go to sleep is when I would clean the house and cook to have food ready for when Damian and Najah got home. Damian's days were exhausting. he would come home and get the baby for a while and then he would eat and relax for a little bit before it was time for him to get ready for work. He had to get up at 5:30am and a lot of nights he would be up with me taking care of her especially when she was constipated. When Aaniyah was a newborn she wouldn't let anyone hold her but me, so it was frustrating because even when Damian tried to take her, she would cry and he would give her back to me. That went on for a while and finally she was used to him and he bonded with her and she no longer cried giving me a break from time to time. The whole house was consumed with the new baby. Damian's outlet was work and Najah's outlet was school, but I did not have an outlet and overtime I think postpartum began to set in. I was happy to have my baby but I was not happy with my finances or my social life or my weight. I was overall getting depressed. I had a lot to be grateful for but I would have low moods a lot of the time.

After Aaniyah was born, me and Damian's relationship had begun to change. I think we were both stressed about money and having a new baby, and not being able to do the things we used to do. When Najah was little we had tons of support and tons of baby sitters. But when Aaniyah was born everyone had grew up and was living their own lives, so no one had time to babysit for us. On top of the fact that we lived so far. So most of the time I would just be at home with the baby. Damian would go out from time to time to get a breather. But I never went out, and never got to get a break. Even when I told him how I felt, he never offered to watch her so I could have some me time. He always told me to take her with me everywhere I went, and that was stressful having to lug a baby everywhere, especially when he was home and he could have watched her. He always made excuses, and that made me resent him because he used to do the same thing when Najah was little. That situation alone had caused a lot of tension between us. Despite the drama and even though I was not in an emotionally happy place with Damian. I still close tried to operate as a family with him.

A few months after Aaniyah was born it was my birthday. Damian got me balloons and a cake and took me out to a restaurant in Buck-head, and I had the most amazing time. The restaurant was so nice and I was able to get dressed for the night and I felt a little like myself again. I had dropped Aaniyah off to my mom earlier that day and I had gone to get a pedicure and I went to the hair salon and got a sew in and I felt amazing. My birthday dinner was so nice, the restaurant was lit dimly and there was a fireplace next to our table and the food was so good.

Me and Damian sat and talked and enjoyed each other's company and even saw a few of his friends he knew while we were there. The vibe was awesome, and I had missed having nights like that with him. He made my birthday very special and I appreciated him for that. When we got home, we chilled out and had birthday sex and Aaniyah came home the next day so I was back to my usual mom routine.

At that time, I had totally lost myself. I lived in an area far away from my family so I had not been seeing anyone much. I had no friends and no social life. I was not working. I was at home all the time with the baby. We had got a letter in the mail that the mortgage had went up because our property taxes in escrow had gone up so Damian got very frustrated since he was the only one working at the time. Even though he agreed that he would be the provider until I got on my feet. He began becoming resentful towards me and making remarks in reference to finding a job. Aaniyah was not even one yet at the time, but to take some of the stress off of him, I asked him that if I found a job could he drop Aaniyah off at daycare up the street before he went to work. He got upset and told me No. "Damian I am trying to find a job but we live far, so I have to leave early. I am trying to find something during the day so I can be home in the evening with Najah and the baby.

Najah had flag football practice and other activities she was in, so I needed to be home to pick her up, I explained to him. "That don't have nothing to do with me" he said brushing me off. "How don't it have anything to do with you, when you are telling me I need to work, and I am trying to but I can't be to work on time and drop Aaniyah off. The daycare opens before you go to work and you can just drop her off on your way to work" I pleaded to him. "No, I can't" he said rudely. "Damian you always do the same thing, you tell me something and when I do it, then you give me a hard time about it" I told him as I began getting upset. "How am I supposed to work if I can't drop Aaniyah off at daycare?" I asked him. "Figure it out" he said to me. "I am figuring it out, you are her dad, and I am asking you to drop her off" I said to him. "No, I'm not getting up an extra 45 minutes out my sleep to drop her off" he said to me. "Well if you don't want to help then don't complain that I am not working.

If I can't get her to daycare then I can't work, and I have to work during daycare hours because if I work a late shift then you will have to watch her and make sure you pick up Najah from her after school activities and make sure you cook and make sure Najah's homework is done and she gets ready for school" I said to him as I was angry at that point. "Well you have your mom and your grand mom" he said to me. "Why do you always bring them up?" I asked him as I was frustrated. "My mom lives 40 minutes away in Stone Mountain and my grand mom lives forty minutes in the other direction in Gwinnett. I am not going to drive all the way there and back to drop the baby off to them to get to work when you are right here, and you can just be a team player like real parents do. But no, you always have to make things hard for me and she is not just my baby. She is yours too" I told him. "Well I already told you I am not doing nothing; I have to be to work by 7am and I get up around 6am and I am not getting up earlier than that" he said to me as a matter of fact and he ended the conversation.

I was super annoyed with him about the fact that he would not even try to help with dropping her off especially since the fact that I was not even asking him to pay for it, so the least he could do was get her there. When I was not working, I had applied for Tanf since I had no income on top of the fact that I knew that being on Tanf would get me childcare asap. I did the application and had my interview and the caseworker let me know off top that if I received Tanf in the state of GA that it was mandatory that I put my child's father on child support. Me not wanting him getting jammed up on child support, I told the case worker that I did not want the benefits and to close the case so she did, and that meant no child care for me. Which left me having to pay out of pocket, all because I was looking out for him and yet he was not looking out for me nor the baby.

In the past Damian was a humble, giving guy but he had become very selfish. Ever since I had become pregnant and we bought the house he had changed. He was always angry and condescending to me. One of the things we used to do the most was going for car rides. We would drive wherever, and we would talk and listen to music, and get food and just enjoy each other's company. But when we moved to the house, he stopped asking me to go on car rides with him and he would only ask Najah and leave me in the house. After a while I had asked him why he didn't want me to ride with him anymore? He said it was because we had to bring the baby with us and Aaniyah always cried when we got in the car so it just made it easier for him to leave me and the baby home. Which was a bummer for me because that was really the only time I could get out of the house, plus the fact that I missed our time together. We had been taking rides ever since we got together and that was our thing.

As time went on, he got ruder and ruder and more and more distant. At night the baby would be up and he would be tired, so he started sleeping downstairs on the couch on the days he had to work but, on the days, he was off, he would sleep upstairs at night. I understood that having the baby broke his sleep so I didn't mind him being downstairs. A few weeks had passed and I noticed that he was still down there even when he was off. I would confront him and he would always say that he was coming up to bed but he never did. I would be upstairs trying to sleep which was hard because I was so used to sleeping next to him. He would send me texts asking me to come downstairs to spend time with him while the baby was asleep. I would come down there and he would want to be touchy feely and have sex. I would always ask him to come upstairs in our bedroom to have sex where we could have privacy and close the door, and he always refused. He preferred to have sex on the couch or the floor. The first couple of times I gave in but after a while it began to get frustrating because it was not romantic bonding sex. It always felt like a quickie and I began to feel like a jump off instead of a wife. He would text me to come down, when I got down there was never real foreplay to turn me on, he would pull his penis out and tell me to bend over either on the couch or the floor and we would do it, he would nut and get a rag to clean me off, then I would go upstairs to our room and he would stay down stairs and go to sleep and that became the pattern and I was over it.

One night Damian wanted to have sex and I told him that I was not doing anything with him unless he came upstairs and got in the bed. At first, he resisted and then he finally agreed. "I'm up here, what's up?" he said to me, as I laid on the bed and he stood over me. "Lay down" I said as I wanted him to get in the bed and cuddle and be how we used to be. It had been a couple of months at that point, and I missed bonding in the bed with him. "Nah, I'm good" he said, smiling. "Damian I'm serious, lay down" I said to him again. "Nah, I didn't come up here for all of that" he said to me as he pulled his penis out of his boxers. "Come on" he said to me. "Come on what? You just want to do it; you don't want to cuddle or anything?" I asked him disappointed. "I will cuddle next time, just come on" he said holding his penis as it was hard. "Ok" I said as I laid down on the bed, thinking we would have foreplay or something at least. "Nah just bend over" he said to me. "Bend over?" I said as I became angry. "You going to tell me to bend over? I am not wet or anything, do you think I'm just some kind of robot that you can just pounce on? Where is the foreplay? Where is the love? You don't do anything to make me feel wanted. You just come up here talking about bend over!" I said to him as I lashed out.

I was so angry and hurt by him. He made me feel like I was nothing. He made me feel like I was a piece of trash. He didn't care about my heart or my feelings. I wasn't upset about him wanting to have sex, I didn't mind being a whore for my husband in a good way, but in that moment, he just made me feel low. He didn't sleep in the same bed as me, he didn't show me affection, he did nothing to show me love from a husband to a wife, and he had the nerve to tell me to just bend over, and at that point I had had enough. "Why are you snapping?" he said as he was taken back. "Because Damian I am tired of you. You don't show me any love then have the nerve to say bend over with no remorse to the fact that I asked you to cuddle and you said no, and I am not wet or anything so I am just supposed to bend over and be in pain? You don't care about anybody but yourself? I yelled at him. "I thought you liked it when we be nasty and do stuff like this in the bathroom and wherever else," he said. "You are not being sexually nasty right now in a good way, we don't even have that connection anymore. At this point you are being degrading" I said to him, as I began to cry and his penis was no longer hard. "Ard, I'm just going to go out the room, because I don't know what just triggered you" he said as he was acting confused and I agreed that he should go out the room, and he left and he began texting me how he was sorry and I ignored his texts and went to sleep.

A few weeks later I was on the tablet that was connected to his email and I heard a ping and it was unusual because the tablet was rarely used. I went on it to see what the notification was and it was a message from the dating site POF. "What is this?" I thought to myself so I clicked on it and there was a message for Damian. I had opened up the profile and he had a different name and it said he was a male looking to date Muslim women. "Wow" I said to myself and I immediately went downstairs and woke him out of his sleep to confront him. "So, this is what you do? You lay down here and create profiles on dating sites?" I said to him as he was wiping his eyes. "What are you talking about?" he said, acting clueless. "This is your profile right here on POF" I said to him as I showed him in his face. "That is not my page" he said, as he sat up and was looking mad that I woke him up. "How is it not your page when it's your information and your email?" I said as I confronted him. "I made that for Tyriek, referencing his brother. He was going through something with his wife and he asked me to make him a page to find a new wife" he said to me. "Tyriek? That is BS, Tyriek know how to work the internet better than you. Why would he need YOU to make him a page when he can make his own page" I said to him as his story did not make any sense. "Wilahi, I did it for Tyriek" he insisted. "Whatever, you are a piece of sh*t" I said to him as I went upstairs.

I laid in my bed and my feelings were hurt. Out of all the years we've been together, I had never worried about him cheating or entertaining other women. He was very loyal to me, so him having a dating site was very out of the ordinary for him, especially since he did not do social media period. I did not know if he was lying or not, but what I did know was that he had changed and so did our relationship. It was becoming stressful. All we did was argue and fight. He would call me fat and call me bitches. He would call me broke and bum bitches. He would talk about my family and how my dad didn't love me. I would say things back to him as well but his words hurt. He would say things to intentionally cut deep.

I had, had a baby and was dealing with postpartum on top of all his putting me down and breaking my spirits. When Damian would say mean things to me, I would believe him. At that point I had no self-worth. All I saw myself as was a mom. All I did was cook clean and take care of Najah and the baby and the cycle repeated itself. I wasn't happy with my weight nor my life, I already thought negatively about myself, so when he would say things like I'm a waste of sperm and my parents should have aborted me I agreed with him. I was so unhappy that I did not want to live. I had nothing to live for. My only motivation for getting up every day was my kids. If I did not have them then my will to live would have been non-existent.

One day we were riding in the car and we were driving to Stone mountain going through Lithonia riding over the train tracks. I remember clear as day Damian playing a lecture video on blue tooth in the car like he normally did. He was always listening to lectures as he drove. He would listen to Islamic lectures, things on outer space and manifestations, all types of things. This particular day he was listening to a lecture on mental health, and the person was talking about Borderline

Personality Disorder. "Listen to this" Damian said, as he intentionally turned the radio up so I could hear. The man speaking was describing what BPD was and the characteristics of the people who had it. He was describing horrible toxic things, and I listened to it like I listened to most of the lectures he played. "What did you think of what he said?" Damian asked me when it went off as he turned the radio down. "I didn't think anything of it," I said to him. "Listen again" he said with a straight face as he played it again and turned the radio back up. As the man was talking, every time he described a behavior Damian would say to me "This is you, or this is what you do." As the man was talking, I began putting myself as the person he was talking about, and I began to feel worse and worse about myself to the point I began to cry. "Do you see yourself?" Damian asked me as he turned the radio down. "Yes' ' I said as I was still crying. "This is you; this is how you are, " he said in a low, calm convincing, manipulating voice. I just sat there not knowing what to say.

I was feeling bad and since Damian said I was like what the man described in the behaviors, I received it and did not try to defend myself. "I am sorry to have to be the one to tell you this, but Shamirah, I think you have borderline personality disorder" he said to me as if it was hard for him to say, and he felt bad for giving me the epiphany. "Wow" I said to him as I received the epiphany and I began to cry harder. "I always knew something was wrong with you. I just didn't know what it was, now I know" he said to me in his cunning, compassionate way. "Damian, I don't know what to do. I am sorry I was doing all of that. I don't know how to change" I said to him with remorse. "Well, you didn't know, but now that you do, I think you need to get help" he told me, as he put his hand on my leg. "Help from who?" I asked him, looking for the answer. "Maybe try to find you a psychologist" he said to me. "You want me to go back to therapy?" I said hesitant. "Yeah, it would be good for you. If you see the psychiatrist, they can diagnose you and you will have medications plus you can collect disability and you won't even have to work" he said as he dressed it up and tried to make it sound pretty. "I don't know Damian. I will think about it" I said as I was trying to process everything all at once.

When we got to where we were going, I had felt low, my self-worth was in the gutter, all that kept playing in my head was what the man was saying, and that Damian said I acted that way and I felt horrible. I was embarrassed and I just wanted to go under a rock. What Damian said about me and how he viewed me meant a lot to me, and since he said I had borderline personality disorder I believed him. When we got home we talked about it again and he told me how he felt bad for me, and how since now that he knows I have a problem that makes him able to have more compassion for me, and that when I got my medication that things would get a whole lot better, so I began to get optimistic about being on meds and I felt like I finally found the source to my problem that Damian told me that I had.

The next day I was upstairs in my room scrolling through google to find a therapist. At the time I did not know the difference between a psychiatrist and a phycologist so I just scrolled and picked who stood out to me and wrote their numbers down. One lady in particular had stood out to me and I read her bio and I felt like she would be a good fit for me. It's like her energy had popped off the screen and something inside of me said she is the one! Everything was perfect. I saw that she even took my insurance. I had went to email her and when I looked at my insurance card I had realized that the insurance that she actually took was my previous insurance, so I got a little discouraged but something on the inside said "just send the email anyway and see what happens" so I did and she responded the next day and informed me that she did not take my insurance BUT she would submit a pre-authorization form and see what happens, and if it was approved then she would set the appointment, so I just had to wait until I heard back from her.

I had told Damian about it and he was happy for me. "I'm glad you found somebody to talk to, now you can get the help that you need" he said to me. "Yup" I said, as I smiled and agreed. "I'm proud of you for seeking out help, once you get your meds you going to be good" he said to me and I smiled and agreed. A little over a week had passed and my therapist had told me that the insurance company approved the paperwork, and that she could take me on as a client and I was excited. "Damian, I have my therapy appointment tomorrow at 4pm" I told him as I was excited. "Ok that what's up" he said to me. "I have to be there about 3:30 to fill out some paperwork, so I'm going to leave the house at about 3:15pm" I told him. "Ok cool. You're taking Aaniyah with you right?" he said to me to my surprise. "Why would I take her to my therapy session?" I asked him. "Because I have stuff to do, and I can't watch her," he said to me very adamantly. "Damian, I don't think I can bring kids there, she is just a baby.

Aaniyah was only 8 months old when I began therapy. "It's crazy to me that you would tell me to seek help, and when I do and try to get myself together you are telling me to bring the baby with me. A therapist office is not somewhere that a baby should be and it's really not fair" I pleaded with him. "Well it is, what it is, if you want to go then you have to take the baby with you. I am not watching her and that's that" he said dismissing me. "When my appointment time came it was summer and it was super-hot. I lugged Aaniyah in her car seat and took her to my appointment and here I am!" I said to my Therapist and we both laughed. "That was an interesting story and I am so glad that you found me, and I am so glad that you are here, and I do not mind the baby coming. I understand how it is as a mother" she said, smiling at Aaniyah. "Firstly Shamirah, I want to tell you that you are a very bright young lady, and you have been through a lot. I am proud of you for coming and I look forward to your journey with me. Just speaking with you and doing the evaluation with you. I see absolutely no signs of Borderline Personality Disorder or any other disorder" she said as she smiled. "What I do see is a young woman who is hurting and what I would like to do is explore more of that hurt so we can begin the healing process" she said to me as she smiled.

The session was over and I scheduled another one with her for the following week. I had begun to see her on a weekly basis. Every session that I came to I would have Aaniyah with me. On the days I had therapy Damian would make a point to not be home so he did not have to watch her. It was frustrating because it was hard to focus, with Aaniyah being fussy and antsy. But my therapist was very kind and the more she got to know me the more she understood my relationship with Damian and his toxic behaviors. Going to see her had become an outlet for me, and it became a blessing. The more I came I began to feel lighter and lighter. I would come home and tell Damian about my sessions, but after he found out from my first session that I was not diagnosed with BPD and I was not going to be put on medication he was not so enthused after that.

Therapy was something that he in fact suggested for me so I thought that he would be happy for me, but it actually was the complete opposite. He made sure that I took Aaniyah with me even though I told him that it made it difficult with her there, but he didn't care. If it were not that then he would start arguments with me before my sessions and try to make me late. When I told him about my progress he would not act interested. It got to the point where he would get upset and say things like "You are not telling the therapist the truth; you need to let me come and talk to her". "I want to come to one of your sessions," he told me one day. "For what?" I asked him curiously. "Because I want to see what you're telling her, because I know something is wrong with you, and she is not seeing it, so she needs to hear my side, because I don't think you are telling her everything" he said to me and I got a little offended. "I am telling her everything she asks me, and you said you want to tell her your side? What's your side?" I asked him curious. "She needs to know how you really are, and that you're toxic" he said to me. "Wow, she's my therapist. I think it's her job to pick up on things like that, and if she hasn't picked up on anything yet then it's clear nothing is wrong" I told him. "Yeah well, just see if I can come to one of the appointments because I want to talk to her" he insisted. "I will ask her and see what she says, but I hope you do not think you are going to sabotage this appointment like you did with my other therapist" I warned him. "I am not going to sabotage anything; I am just going to tell the truth" he said to me. In my next appointment I asked my therapist about Damian coming to a session. She was apprehensive, but finally agreed with conditions. "He can come two weeks from now as long as the session stays respectful, if I feel like it is going left then I will end the session for the safety of your mental health" she reassured me.

A few weeks later Damian came in, and he had a lot of pinned up negative energy. She asked him a few questions to get into the session, and he immediately burst out with issue after issue that he had with me. My therapist was very patient with him and let him get his side off of his chest, and of course he bought up his son, and how I was toxic and used to throw things. Basically he bought up everything he told the previous therapist that made me not want to go see her anymore, so I am guessing he was trying to do the same thing with therapist as well. His thing was, she liked me but he wanted her to know the ugly parts of me as well. But little did he know she knew all the ugly parts because l was very transparent in my sessions with her. As Damian was saying all these nasty things to her about me. My therapist looked over to me, and put her hand on my knee and said "Shamirah, no matter what is expressed, I promise I will not look at you any different" she reassured me as she let him continue to speak.

He saw that none of his antics of sabotaging me were working, and I saw in his face that he was getting frustrated. I don't know if my therapist picked up on it, but I knew Damian and, in that moment, I knew that he did not come there to work anything out or express any feelings that would be beneficial for himself nor the relationship. He solely came there to throw dirt on my name and put a bad taste in my therapist's mouth, but it did not work. It came to the end of the session and Damian became annoyed. "How is the session over that fast? I didn't even get everything out" he said as he was upset. "I am sorry, but our time is up, " my therapist said to him very politely. "It don't make sense to come to y'all therapist because every time people begin to open up, the sessions end and they have to keep coming back to get things out little by little, that's y'all gimmick" he said to her. "I am sorry that you feel that way. I am Shamirah's therapist and I really think you could benefit from therapy too. You have a lot to get off of your chest, and I would love to recommend you to someone in our office" she offered him sincerely and he got upset and declined. "I don't need to see anybody, this is for her, I'm good" he blurted out to her. "Ok, I understand. I do want to see you win and be happy" she said to him as she gave him her undivided attention. "I want to see you both happy, and for you both to win, " she said to him as she smiled, and Damian just nodded his head and I could tell he was ready to go. His mission was not accomplished, it was actually backfiring on him because now he himself was recommended to see the therapist and with his ego, he did not like that. We had left the session and he did not say much on the way home.

38

In my future sessions me and her talked about my issues with Damian as well as my dad and my upbringing with my mom. My therapist had given me a lot of insights that I had not considered beforehand. I had issues with my mom growing up but, even more so I had a lot of issues with my father. When I began therapy me and my dad were not speaking because he would never answer my calls, so I just gave up on our relationship. My therapist would ask me to talk about how I felt about my dad and every time she mentioned him, I would break down and cry. I had never realized how much pain I was carrying from him. I expressed to her how I felt abandoned by him from a child all the way up to adulthood, and the different little mean things he did to me along the way.

Every session my therapist would see how emotional I got when we talked about him so she knew that my pain from him was unresolved and a lot of it had spilled into my relationship. "Shamirah. I see that talking about your father is very emotional for you" my therapist said, as she handed me a tissue. "Yes, it is, I didn't even know all these emotions were in here" I said to her as I cried. "Yeah, I understand and I want you to get it out," she said with compassion. "I am just angry," I admitted with tears in my eyes. "What are you angry about?" she asked me compassionately. "I am angry at the fact that my dad was never there for me, and he treated me like I was invisible, and when I do open up to him and think we are going to have a relationship he switches up on me. Dealing with him is emotionally exhausting" I said to her as I broke down. "It's ok, get it out" she said as she gave me my moment to get it all out. "So, tell me a little about your father," she asked me.

"From what I know, my dad has been in and out of jail starting from a juvenile. I am not sure of his upbringing and what caused him to be troubled. I remember my Nana, his mother telling me that he was always different and she did not know why he was standoffish, so when he was little, she put him in therapy, but I am guessing it did not work. He ran the streets and he spent a lot of time in jail. Even though he was locked up my mom still took me up there to see him and I have pictures from the time I was one until about four years old of jail pictures with him. My mom made sure he knew who I was and from looking at the pictures he seemed happy to have me. Him and my mom were never together but they had an ok relationship, good enough to where she was going to see him every week and they took a lot of pictures as if they were a couple. When my dad came home, he continued to run the streets and was not a part of my life. I would see him here and there" I explained to my therapist.

"See Shamirah here is the thing" she said seriously, "I know that your dad hurt you and you have all this pain and anger towards him, but it is best for you to let it go, and when I say let it go, I mean let it go for you. It has nothing to do with him. Forgiving and letting go allows you to be free" she said to me sincerely. "Even if he never apologizes or acknowledges your pain, you still have to be willing to say: you know what, it happened, I can't change it, I can't change him, all I can do is deal with me and my emotions. You have the power to decide what you let in or not, and you do not have to let in hurt, pain, anger and un-forgiveness. You have the power to say, "I am letting it go" she told me boldly. "You don't need anyone's validation to be happy or to forgive. You are in control of your own life" she told me boldly again. "You are right" I said, as I took in everything, she said to me. "When you look in that mirror YOU have to love who is looking back at you. You are in control. The past is the past. We all have to heal from it and grow, it's all a part of the process" she said to me as she smiled. I took in what she said and I agreed. "And also, Shamirah, let me tell you" she added.

Your father is human, he had a life and feelings before you were even born. From what you tell me it seems as though he has been through a lot. It seems as if he had his own unresolved issues. When a person becomes a parent, it does not make them magically these perfect people. They are just flawed and unhealed people who have children now" she said, as she smiled compassionately. "So, try to not look at your dad as "my dad who hurt me". Try to see him as a "hurt Human being " take the parent aspect out of it, and just try to understand him as a person she said to me. I listened to every word she said and when she said it, a light bulb went off and it made it easier for me to forgive him and my mother. I had put them on pedestals as parents and felt like they should have done things correctly because that's what parents do. I had never looked at them from the perspective of just being regular people who had unresolved issues just like everyone else.

I was angry at my mom for a lot of things she has done as a parent but looking at it from the point of view that my therapist gave me, it allowed me to see my mom as a woman just like me. A woman who had childhood issues. A woman who had lost her husband and was looking for love. A woman who had faced depression and lack of self-love and the list go on. So, it was not that my mom was not a good mom and did things intentionally. It was the fact that my mom was a mom carrying her own pains, and she did the best she knew how, and for that I began to be more appreciative of her. Especially with me being a mother and understanding that even on my worst days as I was fighting depression and anxiety, I still had to show up and be a Mother. Moms don't get mental health days off. We are still expected to be there and that can be a lot of pressure, and takes a lot of strength. I watched my mom struggle many days, but she never gave up so I began to look at her in a new more compassionate way. I also did with my father as well.

When my therapist gave me a new way of looking at things, I instantly felt compassion for his lack of self-love. I understood that he could not give what was not in him. I didn't know his childhood but clearly, he had issues that he never resolved. So he just went from an unhealed boy to an unhealed man, and did a lot of things he regretted and constantly beat himself up for it, and may have turned to drugs to not have to not feel. So not only was he an unhealed person but he had also been incarcerated and had unresolved trauma as well, so it was all a domino effect unfortunately.

Everyone would tell me how smart my dad was. He could have been anything he wanted to be in life, but unfortunately his life turned out the way it did. I knew in my heart that he did a lot of things that he regretted, and he beat himself up for it, and those things affected his life and self-worth, and I knew my dad struggled with depression because of it. I was good at reading energy and I could literally feel people's spirit. And in my spirit, I felt that my dad felt like he was not worthy of living because of the things he did, and he did not allow himself to forgive himself so he treated himself poorly. The part that made me feel the worst is when I felt that he felt he was not worthy of love and that made me break down. He was a fifty something year old man, but on the inside he was a hurt little boy with no self-love, and felt unworthy of receiving love so with that I had viewed him in a different light, and even though he had never apologized. I had forgiven him truly in my heart and when I forgave him sincerely, it felt like a ton of bricks had lifted off of me, and at that point I began to start to heal as I let things go.

When I came to my next therapy session, I had explained to my therapist the epiphany I had, and she was very proud of me. "I am so glad to hear that you forgave your mom and your dad, " she said as she smiled. "Now that you are in a better place with them mentally, I would like to do an exercise with you" she said to me as she smiled.

"What is it?" I asked her because I never knew what her exercises were going to be. "I know you have a good relationship with your mom, and you talk to her every day and that's great. Now I would like for you to begin to bridge the gap with your father as well" she said as she looked at me curious as to what response she was going to get. "Ok, but I told you he doesn't answer my calls' ' I told her. "I know and hopefully that will change, but for now I would like you to write him a letter" she told me. "A letter? How am I going to get it to him? I don't know where he is", I explained to her. "I understand, but this letter I want you to write is for you, not for him at the moment. I want you to write what you would like to say to him and express it in the letter and when you are ready and the time is right, I would like for you to read it to him" she told me, as she smiled and held my hand because she did not know how I was going to respond to what she wanted me to do. "Ok" I said to her as I agreed. "I don't want you to do it now, I want you to go home and think about it and in our next session I want you to bring it and read it. This is your safe place. I want you to read it out loud and give it to him when you are ready" she told me.

In our next session I had read her the letter that I typed up on my phone, and she was proud of me because she knew how far I had come. In the letter I talked about how I forgave him, and how I wanted him to forgive himself because he deserved to love himself and be loved. The letter was long and full of love, and I intended to read it to him. I had healed enough to take a chance and give him a call to read him the letter, and let him know what was on my heart, but yet again he did not answer. About two weeks went by and he sent me a text telling me that he had been on a journey and that was in a rehab facility of some sort and, that he was doing good and that he was getting his life together. I had read the text and I meant to respond but I had got sidetracked and I didn't.

My birthday had come and it was horrible. Everyone I had made plans with had bailed out on me. Damian did not take me anywhere like he normally did. He normally tried to save the day but this time he didn't. He didn't get me a cake or anything. I had reservations at the Ponce City Markets Winery, and my sister was supposed to come but she got her hair done and was running late so I just cancelled the reservations. It was my birthday and I was not about to be sitting at the table by myself waiting for her. My feelings were so hurt how everyone just stood me up especially Damian, that was definitely not like him. I had the kids with me and I took them to Chili's and we had dinner, and they were my dates. I was sad but I was thankful that I had my babies. We had gone home and Damian was not there. There was no cake or anything and I was so sad that all I wanted to do was go to bed. It was almost midnight when I looked at the time on my phone and I realized that my dad had not texted me all day and said Happy Birthday and it really hurt my feelings and made everything even worse.

The next day I got up and still there was no text from him. He texted me about a week later talking about how he was doing good etc. and I will admit that I was in my feelings again and I did not text him back on purpose. He kept texting me after that point, and I was intentionally ignoring him so he could see how it felt. Najah had an audition at a performing arts school which was on her birthday and he texted me to tell her happy birthday, and to send her a cash app. He texted and asked if he could talk to her. I did not want to be petty so I let her call him and they talked and she was happy, and he told her he loved her and that he was proud of her, and he wished her luck on her audition and they hung up. Najah's birthday was January 11th and my dad text me from time to time up until February. At that point I was texting him back having small talk but nothing much. He would always say he wanted to talk to me on the phone when the time was right. I always told him the time is right now and to call me, but he never did. I wanted to hear what he had to say as well as finally read him the letter.

On February 7th I was in my room taking a nap and while I was asleep, I had a phone call from my aunt. She had called me on Facebook.

I had got my number changed and forgot to give it to her. When I saw her call, I was so tired that I could not wake up, and I saw that she texted me as well. By the time I got up it was about 7 pm and I was woken up to Damian walking in the room with Najah and he flicked the light on. "Shamirah get up" he said to me and I saw the expression on his face and I knew something was wrong. "What?" I said to him as I knew something wasn't right. "I just got a call that your dad was killed" he said to me straight forward. "What?" I said, as it still had not processed to me what he was saying. "A few seconds later I got another call from my aunt and this time I answered. "Hello" I said to her. "Mirah" she said in a soft voice. "Hey" I said to her, waiting to hear what she had to say. "I have bad news," she said. "What's going on?" I asked her. "Your father was shot and he didn't make it" she said humbly and I could tell that she did not want to tell me that.

I sat on the phone silent for a few seconds trying to process everything. "You ok?" she asked me. "Yeah I'm ok" I said numb. "Are you ok?" I asked her. "I'm ok, I am just in disbelief" she said to me trying not to cry. "Ok, I'll call you back, thanks for letting me know" I told her as the news began sinking in and I began to panic on the inside, and I wanted to get off of the phone and we hung up. "You ok?" Damian asked me as he hugged me, and then Najah came over and gave me a hug as she looked so sad. "I'm Ok" I told him, as I sat there numb with a blank face. Damian did not know how to read me because he had never seen me that way before, so he sat next to me on the bed for a while to make sure I was in an ok headspace. "I just want to be by myself" I told him. "You sure?" he asked me. "Yes, I'm sure "I told him, and he left the room and closed the door. I laid there and thought about it and I began to cry.

All the memories kept rushing back. I had remembered the bad stuff and the good stuff. I kept seeing my dad's face and he was smiling and he was so happy. I could feel his presence and it was peaceful. It's like I could feel him saying it's Ok, I'm Ok and it felt like he was right there reassuring me. I felt like all the weight that he was carrying from this life had been lifted, and I felt like he was telling me to lift my weight as well. He was free now and I knew it in my soul, and with his peaceful presence I had found comfort. I got myself together enough to call my mom and let her know and she was so sad. "Wow he is gone" she said as I heard her crying a little bit. "Wow, I never thought that he would never not be here, I'm sad" she said. "Are you ok?" she asked me. "I'm ok" I told her and we told each other we loved each other, and she told me to call her if I needed her and we hung up. I had called my brother and sisters and let them know too and everyone gave me their condolences.

I called my dad's girlfriend to check on her and my brother and it took her a while to text me back which was understandable. When she finally called me, she had told me what happened and where she found him and clearly it was a homicide. She was crying but she was being strong. My dad was Muslim so he had to be buried within three days, so I had to get up to Jersey ASAP, but I did not have the money. My aunt told me that they would help me get up there and she would call me but I had not heard from her or anyone else in my family, so I figured I was just going to miss his Janazah. Damian did not have the money to help me get up there, my mom and no one else had it either. Things were so financially rough at that time and it was so sad, and the tickets were sky high because it was the last minute to fly up there. Thank God The day before the Janazah that his girlfriend called me and offered to buy me a ticket so I won't miss my dad's burial. I had booked the tickets and flew up there asap.

Normally when I fly to Jersey it is with Damian and we have a rental car and everything runs smooth. Since I was flying by myself and I didn't have a rental I had decided to catch the train from Philly to Atlantic City like I did back in the day, and it took me straight to A.C with no hassle. When I got off the plane things had changed. I had to take a train to another train station then from there take a train to Jersey, and it felt like it was taking forever. I was trying to hurry up and get to Jersey because my dad was having a viewing and I wanted to see him before his Janazah which was not like a traditional funeral where I would be able to view him. At the Janazah they kept the casket closed and the service was very short, so if I did not see him at his viewing it was a good chance that I would not get to see him at all until he was going into the ground.

On the train ride there it was dark and I was looking out the window. Every time I looked at the reflection in the window, I kept feeling like I was going to see my dad. That is how strong I felt his presence. It literally felt like he was sitting right next to me, and I kept hearing his voice say "stay strong, stay strong." That's how my dad was when he was alive, he would not want people to see me hurting and broken. He would want me to put on a strong face so that is what I did. When I got to the train station my cousin picked me up, and we went to my aunt's house and all my family was there and they greeted me and hugged me and asked how I was doing. I stayed in my aunt room most of the time helping her do my dad's obituary and then we went out and got vegan food. We talked and laughed and I enjoyed her company.

The next day was the Janazah and we got up real early so she could leave to get the obituaries printed and to be at the Soldiers Home on time where my dad's service was being held. We had all met up at my aunt's old house, and I saw all my cousins there that I had not seen in forever and it was so good to see everybody. Since it was a Janaza, I was in my Islamic Garbs to show respect to my dad. Most of my cousins and family on my dad's side were Muslim so we are all garbed up and headed out to go to the Janazah. When we got there, there was a crowd of people outside. My uncle pulled me to the side and told me to come in with him to see my dad before the service started. I was so nervous that I began to feel sick.

We went in and my dad's casket was behind a curtain and there were about four men back there in suits. They were all tall and me and my uncle were short so they kind of hovered over us. When I saw my dad's casket it was open, but I was on the side where I could not see him. "Come on and say bye to your dad" my uncle said, as he took my hand for me to walk with him. "As we turned the corner, I could see the top of my dad's head and I pulled away. "I can't do it" I said to my uncle as I began to panic. "You're Ok, you can do it" my uncle said, as he consoled me and tried to calm me down. At this point I could hear that the people were starting to come in, and at a Janazah you were not allowed to cry loudly or make a scene so I was trying to stay calm so people didn't hear me through the curtain that was separating us. "You can do it, don't cry, talk to your dad, he can hear you" my uncle said, as he hugged me then grabbed my hand and proceeded to take me to see my dad again. I took a deep breath and told myself to be strong and I walked around the casket where I could see him lying there and I lost it. I tried to hold it in but I couldn't.

The only way for me to muffle my cry was to bend over and put my face in my knees. I had cried so hard and when I got up, I looked around and the men that were around us were crying too. I guess it hurt them to see how much pain I was in. I stood over my dad's casket and put my hand on his sheet where his hands were and he felt so skinny. I just looked at him and said "I forgive you" in my head to him. I didn't say anything out loud because my uncle and the guys were standing right there, and I did not want to express my deepest emotions to my dad in front of them. My dad knew what it was and I left it at that. I touched him and I walked away and came from behind the curtain and went and got myself together to prepare for the Janazah prayer.

I sat in the front next to my Nana who was hilarious. My Nana was cracking jokes the whole time. I was just happy to see her smiling, especially since we were burying my dad who was her youngest son. The Janazah began and the Imam spoke and he was very emotional and passionate and had very kind words to say about my dad. Afterwards we did the prayer and it was time to take my dad's body to the grave-yard. Even though I was Muslim that was my first time at a Janazah, and it was unfortunate that my first time was burying my dad, but again I kept hearing his voice saying to be strong. We parked and I got out and walked towards where his hole was and I had changed my shoes because I knew I would be in dirt as it was custom in Islam for the family to help bury the body so I was prepared to do so.

There was a crowd standing around and the hearse pulled up and they slid the casket out of the back of it, but instead of the casket going down into the hole, they had lifted my dad's body out of it and put the casket back in the hearse. Now my uncles, the Imam and a few other men were holding my dad's body and all I kept hearing my uncle say was "do not let the sheet come off of his face, do not show his face" my uncle kept stressing, and they did their best and the sheet never exposed his face. In Islam they do not get buried in caskets. You go into the ground wrapped in a shroud with a tie around your torso and ankles just like they did back in the day of the prophets, peace and blessings be upon them all. That was my first time ever witnessing everything that I was seeing. I was standing next to my dad's girlfriend the whole time and we were consoling each other as our hands were on each other's backs.

My three cousins were in the grave ready to receive my dad's body and they lowered him down and I stood there and watched my dad's lifeless body in the grave and it felt surreal. All I kept hearing was my dad's voice saying "Don't panic, it's ok, I am ok, this is all a part of the process, it's ok, it's not scary or anything. When you die it is not scary" I heard his voice saying and the panic inside of me had calmed down. They had put the board over him to help with his decomposing process and it was time for us to start putting the dirt on him. Since I was the oldest, I went first and threw the dirt on him and then my little brother and all the family after that. After a while the graveyard people took over with their machine and filled up the whole and we all stood there as people said their last words. When it was over, I felt numb. I didn't know how to feel. All I wanted to do was go back home to GA to my house so I could process everything in private. But instead my flight didn't come until the next day so I went with my family to the repass as everyone ate and talked. I was super uncomfortable as the vibes were off. I wasn't really talking to anyone because at the end of the day I did not know who killed my dad so I wasn't trying to be friendly with anybody.

I remember sitting at the table with one of my cousins and I felt so alone. For the first time on the trip, I felt sad. I had looked around and saw all my uncles with their kids' taking pictures and reuniting, and even though me and my dad did not have the best relationship, I know if he was there we would have been taking pictures too, and he would have been showing me off to everybody saying "Look at my daughter, ain't she pretty" smiling like he always did. But at that moment we were all there because he was dead. I sat there and I refused to cry. I was holding it in and all I wanted to do was go home. As I sat there feeling lonely, suddenly it felt like my dad was sitting next to me saying "I'm here, you're not by yourself, you're good and you better not let them see you crying." I laughed to myself and I received what he said and I didn't cry. I stayed strong until it was time to go.

Once we left later that day, I spent time with my friends, then I spent the night at my dad's girlfriend's house so she could take me to Philly to the airport the next day. While I was there, we talked and she told me how happy she was that I was there and having me there felt like my dad was there, and that made me feel good that I was able to give her and my little brother comfort. The trip was a lot but I got through it. She dropped me off at the airport the next day and I hugged her and my brother and flew back to GA.

39

Damian picked me up from the Airport and I told him all about it. I came home and went to my room, and released the cry that I was holding the whole time while I was in Jersey. Damian was supportive the first few days I was home and then he was back to his BS. He was getting into arguments with me about the stupidest things. When we would fight, he would say things like "Who is going to do something to me? You don't have no one here to protect you" referencing my dad being dead, and he was so hurtful. He was supposed to be my husband and my protector, yet he treated me like a sworn enemy. He was filled with hate towards me, and it just kept getting worse.

While I was in Jersey, I got a phone call from a job and I told them I just had a death in the family so I would reach back out to them when I came back to GA. I had been home for about two weeks so I called the job back which was a teacher's assistant position at a preschool/daycare which worked out because I was able to bring Aaniyah to the daycare for a discounted fee. I met the director and I was hired on the spot. I had got a job and started thinking about saving money so that I could get away from Damian. He had become so disrespectful and unbearable that I no longer wanted to live with him and I wanted my own place.

One day while we were not arguing, Damian came to me and we talked about doing our taxes. He had claimed Aaniyah the year before, and I had claimed Najah. He came to me to get Aaniyah's social security card so he could claim her again. I let him know that I wanted to claim both Aaniyah and Najah and with the money I would pay up the mortgage which was behind a substancial amount at the time. Damian disagreed and insisted on claiming Aaniyah and his son. I told him the only way that I would let him claim Aaniyah was if he would agree to take the money he got from her, and I took the money I got from Najah and we went half and paid the back mortgage payments and he agreed, so I gave him the info he needed and he claimed her on his taxes. When we got the money back, he had never even told me that he got his. I had to keep asking him about it and he would say things like "it's none of my business" and "don't worry about his money."

Damian had a business account that he put me on, and the card is what I used when I needed to buy and pay things. One day he got mad and took the debit card from me because he was petty. Unbeknownst to both of us, the card expiration was up so they sent out new cards and I had the card to his account about a week later. I did not use it nor did I let him know I had it, but I did check it periodically. Since he did not tell me he got his taxes, I had called the card myself and sure enough his taxes were on there. I did not tell him I knew, but I did ask him when we were going to pay the mortgage. "Damian, another month of the mortgage is about to be due. When are you going to give me your half?" I asked him boldly. "What?" he said to me as if I were not allowed to ask him anything. "I said when are you going to give your half of the mortgage. I let you claim Aaniyah because that was the agreement" I reminded him. "You didn't let me claim nobody, that is my daughter and I live here and I have a right to claim her" he told me rudely. "You don't have a right to claim her. The only reason I let you claim her is because you agreed to pay half the mortgage. I could have claimed both of my kids and had all the money to pay the mortgage that's in my name that you stop paying " I said to him as I was getting upset. "I don't have it" he said as he lied.

He was getting dressed so he was moving around and intentionally trying to dismiss me. "What do you mean you don't have it? Yes, you do" I said to him as he was making me furious. "Well it don't matter if I have it or not, I ain't giving to sh*t" he said confidently. "What do you mean you're not giving me nothing. It's not your money and had I known that you were going to do this I would have claimed both my kids because that was the mortgage money" I told him as I was angry. "Oh well" he said as he was putting on deodorant and he shrugged his shoulders. I was so beyond furious that I just walked away. Everything inside of me was burning but I did not hit him nor react or anything. I was so disappointed that it made me numb. I went to my room and I prayed to God about it that's how upset I was that I needed God to step in. Time had passed and he still did not give me the money.

In the meantime, I was working at the daycare for a few weeks and I was in the toddler room. The job itself was ok, but the fact that Aaniyah was there too was making it hell for me because she wanted to be up under me but she couldn't. She was not in my class and I tried my best for her not to see me all day, which was hard because even when she didn't physically see me, her class was right next to mine so she would hear my voice and start to cry because she wanted me. Aaniyah literally cried all day at daycare. She wouldn't play with the kids or anything and, it made it even harder because she loved her pacifier and, in her class, they would not give it to her and that was her way of self-soothing. She cried so much that it made my job so much harder. One because I was trying to work as an employee and two, I was a mother and I wanted to comfort my baby while she was crying and the job would not let me. I knew why she was crying and the fact that they were telling me what and what not to do with my child was pissing me off.

I remember one day it was hell at work. I was left with the class and it was nap time, and for some reason all the kids decided they wanted to be bad. They were running around; some had peed on themselves. There was a particular little boy who was throwing stuff and it was mayhem on top of my child was in the next room screaming at the top of her lungs. The director and the teachers were in the room where Aaniyah was and no one was trying to comfort her, they were just letting her scream which was pissing me off, so it made it even harder for me to focus on the chaos in my room because I was focused on my child. The director was in the room watching me in my room from the camera, and he saw how off the hook the kids were and how frustrated I was. I went to him and asked him for help and he told me to figure it out which was even more frustrating.

At that point I had enough. Aaniyah had been crying for about a good hour. And at that point and I remember her saying she was thirsty so one of the teachers came to me to ask me where was her cup and I told her and next thing you know I hear the director say "oh no, she's not getting any water, it's not lunch time" meanwhile his kids were walking around with McDonald's cups, and it was not lunch time. Him and his wife ran the daycare and his kids attended as well. I knew my child was thirsty and, she was denied water and at that point I had had enough. The kids were off the hook and I did not care what they did from that point on. The director finally came in yelling at them and I am sure he was low key yelling at me too, because he said "What is going on! This is ridiculous" referring to how I could not control them.

I was new and they had no fear of me because I was nice and didn't yell at them. I asked him for help and he told me to figure it out so I did. I guess he had enough of Aaniyah crying too so he took the little boy who was the worst and told me to take Aaniyah and when I got my baby, she was hot and sweaty from crying and her nose was running and everything. I went in my bag and gave my baby some water from my water bottle, and I know he saw me on camera and I did not care. When the other teacher came back from her lunch I picked up Aaniyah and went on my lunch and went to her classroom and got her stuff to take her to my mother's house, because at that point I did not like how they were handling my baby and that was going to be her last day there.

I went on lunch and dropped her off at my mom's house and came back and I could tell they were talking about me because I felt the tension and I did not care. My baby came first. I didn't really talk to anyone; I just wanted to do my job and go home.

All that week all of the kids at daycare were sick and a lot of them went to the hospital but no one knew what was wrong. COVID had broken out in China and it was not a big deal because we were in America, but rapidly COVID spread and had reached the states. Aaniyah had become really sick so I had called out of work over the next two days. One night it was so scary. She was sick but she seemed to be doing ok. She had woken up in the middle of the night playing so I didn't think anything of it. When I felt her, she was burning up hot, but I was half asleep and since she was playing, I thought she was fine.

About an hour or so later I was woken up to her jerking and I tried to wake her and her eyes were rolled to the back of her head. I panicked and grabbed her in my arms and ran her downstairs to Damian who was asleep on the couch. He instantly got up and was calling her name as she was jerking "Aaniyah, Aaniyah" he was saying as I heard the fear in his voice and I called the ambulance. I could barely talk as I explained to them what was happening. "All I kept saying was God, please don't let my baby die" as I tried not to lose my mind because I did not know what was wrong with her. Eventually she stopped jerking and I panicked even more. "No!" I was saying to Damian as I looked to him for comfort. At that moment he had her in his arms and he was trying to stay calm as we waited for the ambulance to come. It felt like they took forever and they finally came and checked her and everything and they told me my baby had a seizure because her fever got too high. When they said that, I felt like crap. I had felt that she was hot but I did not get up and I beat myself up with guilt because of it.

They took her in the ambulance in her car seat and I came with her. They drove her to the children's hospital and they gave her Tylenol to get her fever back down. As I sat next to her in the ambulance, she was finally coming too. I was sitting next to her holding her little hand and she was trying to open her eyes and they seemed so heavy. She finally got them open and she looked over at me. She looked confused like she knew me but she couldn't figure out who I was. "Mommy here Baby " I said to her, and I kissed her on the cheek and she was staring at me but she seemed at peace. When we got to the hospital, they gave us a room and I sat there with her in the bed and hugged her tight. Damian and Najah had not gotten there yet. I sat in the room with Aaniyah as the lights were dim and I felt so guilty and I began to cry and tell her that I was sorry. The doctor came in and she saw that I was crying and she turned the light on. She looked at Aaniyah to make sure she was ok and she turned to me "I know it was scary mom" she said to me compassionately and I began to cry even more.

The doctor was so nice and she had so much empathy. "Everything is fine Ms. Smith, it is just that when the body reaches a certain temperature that it goes into a seizure to cool it down, we see that a lot in children and it is not to be concerned about. Aaniyah is very healthy and it's one of those things that just happens sometimes" she reassured me. "Thank you, I was just so scared, and I feel so bad because I felt that she was hot and I should have got up and given her some medicine" I said as I cried harder. "Ms. Smith you are doing an awesome job as a mom, please do not beat yourself up, it is ok, this is just one of those things that happen, it is not your fault" she told me trying to comfort me. "Thank you" I said to her as I was wiping the tears from my face. "We will run a few tests to make sure everything is good with her, and we will have you out of here soon, no need to worry Ok" she said to me as she smiled. "Ok" I said to her and she walked out of the room.

I sat there with Aaniyah and was kissing her when Damian and Najah walked through the door and Damian picked up Aaniyah and she laid on him. "Is da da baby ok?" he asked her as he kissed her. "Dada baby is ok " she said with her pacifier in her mouth, as she played with her ear. "Najah" Aaniyah said in her little voice. "Hey Aaniyah" Najah said to her as she kissed her. Aaniyah loved her some Najah. After a while she began to talk and act like herself again. Damian asked her to spell her name and count and say her ABC's and she did them all perfectly. She was playing and laughing so I began to feel a little better. The doctors ran tests and everything was fine and we were discharged. The whole day I was checking on her and I would not let her out of my sight. I kept her hydrated and gave her the Tylenol every few hours like the doctor told me to.

Over the next few days her fever was on and off and slowly she began to be healed. In the meantime, I had let my boss at the pre-school know what was going on and he instructed neither me nor Aaniyah come back until she was cleared by the doctor. Since Aaniyah was sick I began to not feel that well either, so my doctor gave me a note of when I could return back to work which was about three days later. Once Aaniyah was well, I was going to return to work but I was not going to bring her back, one because I didn't want her there and secondly her getting sick the way she did really made me not want her around any extra germs.

The night before I was to return to work the next day, my boss sent out a text for all of us employees to get on a conference call and he marked it urgent. The call was around 7:30 pm and he seemed really worried. "So, as you all know there has been an outbreak in China due to COVID 19, and now the virus has hit the U.S " he said and it felt like I was listening to a breaking news bulletin. "There has been a confirmed case here in GA in Fulton County so the commissioner has advised Dekalb, Fulton and all the surrounding counties to shut down immediately" he said and you could hear everyone on the call gasp. "So that means that we have to shut down the daycare so I do not want any of you to report to work until further notice" he said and everyone began asking how they were supposed to get paid and they all were in a frenzy. "Let me make it clear, " he interrupted as he advised everyone to put their microphones back on mute. "I want you all to come down in the morning and get the paperwork, I will approve everyone's unemployment so you all can still get paid until the daycare re-opens' ' he reassured everyone and they were asking how long it was going to take so on and so forth. He stated he did not know and that he hoped the virus would be over soon and that he would follow the instructions of the G.A governor Brian. Kemp but for now we all had to play it by ear. "I know everyone is worried and I know these are un chartered times, but we all have to keep our faith and trust God. You all still have a job, we just have to play everything by ear for now and I will be in contact with you all with any and all updates, and you all have a good night" he said and we ended the call.

When I got off the phone, I was relieved that I didn't not have to go to work and I had felt like they were going to get the virus under control and that things would be better before we knew it. But I had thought wrong. The next day I had woke up to a phone call from the Rockdale county school system letting us know that the schools were closing due to COVID, and county by county was announcing their school closing as well. It was all beginning to get serious as the students had went from in person to virtual and the whole process within itself was a culture shock and major adjustment. Things really began to get scary when the governor announced the closings of businesses and the stay at home order, at that point everyone began to panic and began going out and buying all the food and toilet paper as well as all the cleaning supplies and hand sanitizer. Initially I did not panic like everyone else, so I did not go to the store right away. I did call Damian and told him about the shutdown order and he went out and bought a bunch of food at least $500.00 worth to make sure we had what we needed. He did not shop the way I did so there were still certain things that we needed so I had to go out and get them because I was not sure if they were going to shut down the grocery stores too.

When I came out to shop the stores were literally empty and it was something I had never seen before. It was like doomsday and so surreal. The shelves and freezers were so scarce and I began to get discouraged, but by God's grace as I shopped each and everything that I needed to buy was there, to the point that there was only one left. For example when I went to get rice, there was only one bag left, when I went to get orange juice there was one left, when I went to get packs of chicken there was only a few left, when I went to get tuna fish there was enough cans for me to buy. The more I shopped the more I thanked God because I felt his favor on me and he supplied each and every one of our needs. I went to Walmart, Kroger, and BJ's and I walked out of each store with a cart full of food. I was able to get toilet paper, bleach and all my cleaning supplies. I came home and Damian got everything out the car and we put everything away and I was filled with gratefulness from God, because we had lacked nothing at all.

The governor had announced more and more shutdowns and we did have a stay at home order. I didn't really go out at that time but when I did the streets were empty. Atlanta traffic is normally bumper to bumper and at that time the traffic was so little that you could just flow on the highway which was so unusual in Atl. We had spent a lot of time at home, and I made sure that I kept the kids busy. We played in the yard and walked in the neighborhood and spent a lot of time at the park. Before COVID hit, life was hectic and busy and it was always something to do and somewhere we needed to be. But during COVID life had slowed down and it enabled us as a family to slow down and spend time with one another and appreciate the little things. I was always an appreciative person but COVID gave me a new appreciation for my family and my home and my circumstances. We were stuck in the house but we were blessed. Blessed to have one another, blessed to be healthy, blessed to be stuck in a home that was clean and had food and love and everything we needed. We would watch a lot of movies and have family time. Our home was a safe place filled with love.

Since Aaniyah had gotten sick I did not take her to any stores and

I was very conscious of exposing her to any germs so outside of being outside playing she did not go anywhere else and neither did I for the most part. During COVID, Walmart and a lot of other stores started having curbside pick-up where you did not have to get out of your car to get your groceries or supplies. Even clothing stores had curbside pick-up as a lot of the stores were closed to the public. I would order from old navy or Macy's and drive there and they would bring it to my car, so life was very convenient and kept out exposure very limited. I would cook almost every day and we would eat as a family.

Although me and Aaniyah stayed home a lot, Damian and Najah were constantly out and about, and I would always get on him about it. "Damian, it's COVID, you need to stop being out in the streets" I told him one day as him and Najah came through the door. "It's ok Shamirah, we have on our mask and our gloves and we constantly use hand sanitizer. We are good" he said to me. "Damian it doesn't matter, y'all are still out in the germs. Najah you don't need to be out and about either" I said as I looked over to her, as both of them were at the sink washing their hands. "Mom, I am fine" she said in her arrogant teenage manner as if she knew everything. "Y'all go out into the community and come here with y'all outside germs and I don't like it" I told both of them. They did not pay me any mind because they continued to do it.

Summertime had come and I had not seen my family in forever other than on facetime. Even when I went to visit my grandparents I had to stay in the driveway, and they stayed on the porch so we could socially distance. We were a very close family so to not see one another like we normally did was very hard for us. It was the 4th of July so I had decided to throw a luau in my backyard. I went to the dollar tree and bought a bunch of luau things and decorated and everything looked so nice and Hawaiian. I bought out the slip and slide for the kids and got a palm tree that was a water sprinkler for them to play in. We had a tent and tables and lots of food and everyone who came got lays. My brother Waheed and his two friends came down from N.C and my whole family came and we all celebrated and talked and laughed and my siblings played cards as the kids played in the water toys and the kiddie pool. It was a perfect day. When nighttime came my brother and Damian had lit the firecrackers and we all watched and had an awesome time. That day July 4th 2020 was a day to remember. It was filled with family and so much fun in a time when being around family was forbidden, but we had still built memories and had a great time.

About a week after the luau, I had begun to not feel well at all. I had become extremely tired and I slept a lot to the point I had taken a pregnancy test to see if I was pregnant. I took the test and it was negative so I could not figure out what was going on. I had begun to get headaches and I was never the type of person to constantly get headaches. I had laid down a lot hoping it would pass and eventually they went away so I thought I was getting better. I remember being in the kitchen cooking one day and I had put seasoning on my vegetables and I went to taste it and I couldn't. I thought that maybe I didn't put enough so I put even more and I still could not taste it and I didn't think anything of it at first.

I remember taking a shower later that night and I had just bought new dove soap, the white bar which I loved the smell of. I picked up the soap and went to smell the fragrance and I could not smell it at all. I thought I had just bought a weak bar so I washed up and got out and put on my bath and body works lotion like I always did. I had used champagne toast which I loved the smell but when I put it on, I did not smell it at all. "Am I tripping?" I thought to myself. I went around my room and started spraying stuff to see if I could smell and I could not. I went downstairs to the kitchen and began smelling the onions and the garlic, things I knew that had a strong smell and to my disappointment I could not smell them at all and I began to panic. COVID was so new and different symptoms would come out every day. As far as what was known at the moment of COVID that if you had it you would be in the hospital because it affected the respiratory system. I didn't need to go to the hospital for my breathing so COVID had never crossed my mind. I had immediately gone to google on my phone and decided to look up the symptoms of COVID and the normal symptoms we knew of showed up.

One of the articles explained that even more symptoms had been discovered and some of the new symptoms were lack of appetite and loss of taste and smell. When I saw loss of smell my heart dropped. I told Damian what I was feeling and the next day I had made a tele-health appointment with my doctor as they only saw people virtually and not in person due to the COVID 19 outbreak. I told my doctor of my symptoms and he recommended that I get a COVID test. At that time the COVID centers were still limited so I had to go to South Dekalb Mall to get the test through the medical center they had set up in the parking lot. We were in line and it took us six hours to get to the front to get tested because of how crowded it was. Me, Damian and Najah got tested and since Aaniyah was so little and I had heard that the test hurt, I did not want to put her through that so I did not get her tested. When they came to swab us, it was not that bad and I had wished that I had gotten Aaniyah tested as well but it was too late.

It took about a week to get our results back. I had called the clinic and they let us know that Damian and Najah had tested negative, but they did not have my results in, and that I needed to call them back in about a half an hour, so I did. When I called them back the lady, I spoke to was so nice and she was so hesitant. "Ms. Smith " she said in a nice way, but like she was scared to tell me something. "Yes?"" I said to her as I wanted to know what she had to say. "Ms. Smith are you sitting down?" she asked me. "Yes' ' I answered her as she was making me nervous. I had her on speaker as me Damian and Najah were sitting by my phone to get my results. "Ms. Smith, I hate to tell you this but you did test positive for COVID 19" she informed me. Damian and Najah looked at me like they felt bad for me. I was silent for a minute before I responded by saying "Wow" I did not know what else to say. She told me that I needed to quarantine and I did. Also, at my doctor's appointment he advised me to get some bloodwork done which revealed that my vitamin D was extremely low, so he put me on vitamin D deficiency pills.

After I learned I had COVID I continued to take my vitamin D as well as I drank a lot of immunity teas, and I made home remedies. I would boil onions, garlic and lemon peels in water and drink it, as well as I would boil orange peels and stand over the vapor of the pot and inhale it into my system and I made sure to stay hydrated. I also took sea moss and black seed oil Thankfully I did not have bad symptoms of COVID. The headaches lasted for about three days and the loss of taste and smell lasted about 11 days. The whole time I wasn't tasting or smelling I would wake up and hope that I was better and even though I wasn't better and did not know when I would get better I still kept my faith in God and no matter how I felt I did not complain. God was with me and I would pray for complete healing over myself. I knew they told me that I had COVID, but spiritually I did not receive the sickness. I trusted God's word and saw myself healed and tasting and smelling again and being COVID free.

You never realize how important something is until you lose it. Not being able to taste or smell was horrible. I would eat and couldn't taste anything and that was very frustrating and the worst of it for me was that Aaniyah was still so little and still in diapers and I remember one day we were in bed and she had pooped and I had no idea because I could not smell it. The only thing that made me notice was when she got up and I saw that her diaper looked heavy and I went to change her and there was a glob of poop in it, but the part that made me really feel bad was that the poop seemed old. I could tell that it was not fresh and I felt so bad because I did not know how long she had the poop on her and had I known; I would have changed her asap. I was not the type of mother who left soiled diapers on my babies and at that point I was determined to get better because I had had enough. Eventually

I got better and I was retested and it was negative and I praised God! Life with COVID changed the trajectory of so many people's lives in so many ways. In my own life it made me way more humble and grateful for a lot of things that I had previously taken for granted.

40

In the midst of the pandemic as the world was supposed to be at a halt, there was still racial injustice against black people in America. Donald Trump was President at the time and racial tension was at an all-time high. In Minneapolis MN, George Floyd, a black man, was pinned down on the concrete as white officer Derek Chauvin knelt on Floyd's neck for 9 minutes and 29 seconds. Due to cell phone recordings, the world watched as George pleaded for his life, and at one point he even cried "I want my mama!" in pain as life was slipping out of him. On the video you could see and hear people telling the officer to get off him because he was dying, but the officer still knelt on his neck and did not budge. After the 9 minutes, 29 seconds you could see George's body become lifeless, and he was taken by the paramedics and was pronounced dead.

After the police killing of George Floyd the world went nuts! Not just black people were outraged but all other races were too. We all watched his murder with our own eyes. It was inhumane, and people were fed up with the police and their brutality so America had begun to riot. It started in Minneapolis, they set police precincts on fire and looted and tore up everything in sight. Soon there were riots and burnings in many more cities in the U.S. They marched on Capitol Hill in front of the white house which was protected by armed soldiers with shields and guns. America had looked like a third world country. Here in Atlanta they protested and rioted as well. They burned cars and flipped them over. It was mayhem downtown. It had gotten so bad that Trump had to call in the national guard, and Atlanta was given a curfew, and no one could be on the street after that time. Atlanta Mayor Keisha Lance-Bottoms also encouraged the rioters and looters to stop because they were destroying the city. I remember watching her on the news and her message to the rioters was "Go Home!" The rapper Lil' Baby even made a song and a music video called "The bigger picture" depicting real life events from that time. It seemed like something out of a movie or, images and videos from back in the day, but it was happening in our generation and in real time. 2020 was an epic year that none of us who lived through it will forget.

Throughout all the madness of the pandemic my sister Jamilah was a part of a church called "Rhema International Ministries." Prior to the pandemic she would send me text messages of the sermons that the church had posted on YouTube. The church has their own channel "Pastor Scott TV" on YouTube. She would send them to me, some I would watch and some I didn't. When she first began sending them to me, I was still in limbo of being in Islam and trying to figure out where I was supposed to be spiritually and religious wise. When she was sending them to me, I was not interested in church nor organized religion. I was in a spiritually lost place honestly speaking. I came from Christianity and I had converted to Islam, so I had felt that I did all that I could do religion wise, yet my soul was still searching for something real and solid. I knew that spiritually I was missing something, but I could not figure out what it was.

When the pandemic first came in March of 2020 Pastor Scott Sanders had called a phone conference meeting for his members, and Jamilah had invited me to join the call so I did. When COVID first came about, it was a very scary time, and I will admit that hearing everything that was going on in the news was very frightening. There was so much new information and conspiracy theories surrounding COVID. People were saying that 5g towers were being built to kill us off. They were talking about the new world order and getting chipped, and calling in the national guards to force us to stay in our homes and so on and so forth. As a believer I was thinking about all the end time events that the bible spoke of, and I was fearful. When I got on the conference call with Pastor Scott Sanders, he was giving his members words of encouragement and instructions. I believe the cell call was on a Tuesday and he preached a bible study the next day on a Wednesday. He was talking about the pandemic and giving us the word of God to get through it, and his words gave me so much encouragement and my spirit looked forward to keep hearing what he had to say.

Even though I was not a member at the time, I had followed his instructions and I began to watch him faithfully every Wednesday and Sunday and the word was so fruitful and it was always on time. At the time I was so skeptical about church and Pastors and their agendas. There was so much negativity in church and religion all together, and as a Muslim I wanted nothing to do with church or Christianity. But Pastor was not at all your average bible thumping, whooping and hollering Pastor just trying to preach to get your money. He was genuine. He really cared about people's souls, and he was a shepherd that really loved his sheep.

God would always show me things in the spirit and I had the ability to read people and their energy. On the very first service that I watched him as he was preaching, in the spirit God had shown me Moses. Not in a physical sense as I saw what Moses looked like, but God showed me that Pastor had the spirit of Moses. I had laughed to myself and asked God why he showed me Moses?" God had answered me and said this man is sent here to lead the people. He is genuine and his heart is pure. He is not like what you are used to. I want you to follow this man" Is what I felt like I heard God saying to me, and in my spirit and I felt confirmation and peace.

At that point I had never seen his wife, because he always preached online in his office by himself. But God showed me her in the spirit as well, and her heart was so beautiful. She was such a kind spirit. "Her heart is like your heart" God told me and I smiled, because I knew my own heart, and I knew it was pure. I had been praying and asking God to surround me with women who were like me, and had the same heart as me. As I was soul searching one of my desires was to be connected with pure hearted women, so when God revealed her to me it made my spirit smile. "Ok God" I had said to myself. I felt peaceful and that I had gotten the confirmation that I was exactly where God wanted me to be. The more I had watched him the more my faith had grown. I did eventually see his wife Co-Pastor Cynthia Sanders, and her spirit was just as beautiful as I saw it in the spirit, and I could not wait to meet her in person.

Before watching Pastor Sanders, I was in a low and broken place of confusion, the more I received the word the more I began coming out of my dark place, and I finally had begun seeing the light. Before I began watching I was so broke financially. My bank account was so low. I had owed on all of my credit cards to the point they were almost maxed out. I had worked at UPS as a seasonal position during the Christmas holiday a couple of months before COVID hit. And of course I worked at the daycare that closed due to COVID. Since my job had closed, I had got a job working from home as a customer service representative. It was ok. It was not my ideal job but it gave me income so I dealt with it. Working that job made me feel so unfulfilled and I always knew the vision God gave to me to be an Author and screenplay writer and producer. I had all these ideas for content that God gave me, and all I wanted to do was walk in my purpose.

I began getting frustrated with my life and my situation. The year before I had gone to a Beauty supply business school to open my own black owned beauty supply store, and the instructor was supposed to teach us how to do it. I paid $1500 to attend that school and I was so excited, but nothing happened afterwards to my disappointment. All the things that were promised had never happened, and I wound up not opening my store. Needless to say, while in school we were told to come up with a name for our business. I had to come up with a name and get it LLC'd and I did. I named my beauty supply store "Beauty in the Mirah." The name came to me out of nowhere. When I registered it, I made sure to not just register it as a beauty supply store, but I selected the other option where I could run multiple types of businesses under that name. But after not opening my store I was discouraged, and I left the name dormant.

In the meantime, God had laid on my heart for me to begin writing a book and title it "Beauty in the Mirah" so I did. As I was sitting down at my work desk one day the customers were annoying me so bad, and I was so overwhelmed. "God why am I at this call center when you gave me all these visions for my life? What do you want me to do?" I said as I cried to God with real tears. Instantly God spoke to me. At work, I always had a notebook and a pen next to me and God said "open it" and I began to write. God gave me instruction after instruction. The first was to register my business with the secretary of state since I already had it LLC'd. The second one was to pay for the domain name for my website, and it kept going from there. Lastly God spoke to me clearly saying "finish the book and I will put a special anointing on it" and he showed me exactly what he wanted the book to look like, and gave me what he wanted the book to be about and I wrote it down and made it plain, then started to do everything on the list and got all my ducts in order.

Meanwhile as I was working and I was listening to Pastor. He was talking about the power of sowing seeds. He always talked about the importance of being a giver. He is not one of the types of Pastors who hound you for money, and try to manipulate you into giving. He always made it clear that it was God's word that tells us to give, and that giving is for our own benefit as our obedience and giving with a cheerful heart allowed the blessings to flow in our lives, because God gives seed to the

Sower. So, as I was working and even though my checks were not much. I always made sure when I got paid to give my tithes and offerings. I was not a stranger to giving as I always gave whether it was monetary or giving my time or doing a deed, and the list goes on. Growing up my mom would always give. She gave food to the homeless, she always gave away clothes, money and helped people in need. She also would take take us to church and I learned early about tithes and offerings, and the importance of having a giving heart.

I had my first paid babysitting job at the age of 13 and I had been giving ever since. I was blessed when I was younger. I always had money flow and favor. There was nothing that I asked God for that he did not allow me to have. God was always merciful to me, and I knew I had a special place with him, and I do believe that my heart had a lot to do with it. Even as a youth I was always a very humble and compassionate person. I was an empath, and had the ability to feel people's energy. I always felt like I needed to help and save people and throughout my life that became my gift and my curse. So, when Pastor talked about giving, I had already known the power in it and I began to give even though I had not been a member at the time. As I gave, I began to increase. I began to receive money from everywhere, and was being blessed from all angles. One of the biggest blessings was when the mortgage was backed up, I had got a letter that my house was in foreclosure. Prior to that letter I had been trying to get a forbearance or modifications on my mortgage for months, and they kept being denied. The mortgage company let me know that since nothing was approved that there was nothing they could do and I guess from that point on they sent it over to an attorney to start the foreclosure process unbeknownst to me.

When I received the foreclosure letter I had immediately called the attorney's office and the secretary let me know that there was a mistake and that my house was in fact not in foreclosure. I was so confused, so I called my mortgage company back and let them know what I was told and they looked into my account and let me know that due to

COVID that they had given me a 6 months forbearance and that my home was not in foreclosure and that all was well, and that even after the six months they would give me a chance to catch up on my mortgage. When I got off the phone I was so relieved and felt like a ton of bricks had lifted off of me as I was no longer in danger of losing my home. After that point COVID had spread rapidly in California where my online job was based. A lot of departments had to shut down, and since I had no seniority, I was one of the first ones to be laid off. But by the grace of God I was able to collect unemployment which at the time they were adding the extra $600 thankfully I was still able to pay my bills, and take care of the girls.

Since I had begun listening to Pastor and making positive changes in my life, I also changed how I responded to Damian and his negativity. Since I was no longer being toxic with him, he could no longer push my buttons because I did not respond to him. That made him upset, and he began to get even meaner to me. I was not feeding into his negativity like I normally did, and I was resisting him more instead of arguing and that would get under his skin. He was not used to me taking a stand and not entertaining his toxicness. Even though he was mean to me and our relationship was changing, the money and the blessings just kept on coming into my life.

I remember the church went on the Daniel's fast for 30 days and even though I was not a member I still decided to fast with them. In the midst of the fast the word was awesome and was giving me a lot to think about. One day I had asked myself "If you are Muslim why are you watching Pastor and feel a connection? And why are you going on a fast with the church?" I asked myself, and I could not give myself an answer. "If you are Muslim, they why do you still have the ability to speak in tongues and are connected to the holy spirit?" I asked myself as well. I thought long and hard about it and still did not have an answer. So one of my prayers during the fast was for God to reveal to me if he wanted me to become a part of the church which would mean that I would no longer be in Islam which was big for me because Islam was my religion and my way of life so to become a part of the church would definitely have been a part of Gods will because I in my own will had no intentions of being a part of a church.

I had fasted and I believe it was a Friday night, two days before the fast was supposed to end on that Sunday. Pastor had did a worship service. He did not do any preaching, it was just all praise and worship unto God. As he was worshipping he had begun to cry. I was sitting there doing my daughters hair, and I had to stop because the worship was so powerful that it stopped me in my tracks. I got up and began to lift my hands and praise God and I began to cry, and all of a sudden, the Holy Spirit filled my house like a cloud and the feeling was so thick. It was so joyful and an overwhelming peace that filled my home and my heart. As I was praising and was in the spirit God had revealed to me plainly in that moment that he indeed wanted me to join the church and that Pastor Scott Sanders and Co-Pastor Cynthia Sanders were indeed sent in my life by God, and got indeed wanted me to be apart of their ministry. And in that moment I had my answer, and I was ready to join.

After the praise and worship service had gone off, I had called my sister Jamilah to tell her how beautiful it was, and what God had revealed to me. It was so crazy because she said her and her roommates experienced the same peace as well. I joined "Rhema International Ministries" about a week or two later. I lived about three and a half hours from the church so thank God during the Pandemic there was "Rhema Nation" for those of us who watched and wanted to join but did not live in the area. As a new member I had to attend new members orientation where I was able to meet Pastor and Co-Pastor and I was able to introduce myself to them as well as the other new members.

I was in the midst of watching Bible study when Pastor announced the Zoom for us new members to come on live. I still had my tv on in the living room, when I ran upstairs to get my laptop to log on. As I was upstairs, I fixed my hair and set up the laptop by the vanity in my bathroom and I logged on. The tv was still on downstairs and I guess at some point Damian came home. I waved and introduced myself and the new members zoom went very well and I was very excited. After logging off, Damian came into the bathroom where I was. "So, you joining churches now?" he said with a serious face. "What?" I said to him caught off guard. "I saw you on the tv downstairs" he said to me still looking serious. I could not lie or anything, I was caught. "Yeah I joined the church. My life changed since listening to my Pastor, and that is what God led me to do" I said to him in my defense. "Ok, well you know what that means" he scolded me. "What does it mean?" I asked curious. "I am a Muslim, and I don't want a Christian wife, so its either me or the church" he said to me firmly. "Damian this church is not religious, they are a church who preaches the word of God not Religion.

Gods word and Religion are two different things. I am not apart of a religion, I am apart of making my life better by the word of God. I do not want to be apart of any ones Religion. God delivered me from Religion and introduced me to what its like to have a real relationship with him." I told him. "Whatever, you heard what I said" Damian said to me. "Well Damian God led me to Rhema, so I cannot go against God" I told him. "Ok then" he said in a scolding way and he walked away. Damian was not pleased, and I was caught red handed and I did not care. Me being connected to Rhema saved my life and I was not turning back. I joined Rhema Nation and officially became a member! Rhema Nation has members from all over the country and I am sure in some other countries as well and we all stayed connected through zoom cell calls that we attend every Monday night to fellowship with one another.

A few months after joining I had taken a trip to Albany to attend the church in person. I did not want to drive so I decided to take the bus instead. I had gone by myself to stay with my sister and her roommates. I had caught the greyhound from the Atlanta Bus station. On the bus, I had sat by myself and there was an older black man sitting across from me. He was dressed ok. He had a hat and some white sneakers on and he looked clean. He kept looking at me and I waved to him and put my headphones in, because I did not want to talk. We drove for about an hour and we stopped at our first stop and everyone got off the bus to smoke or whatever else they needed to do. I had stayed on and so did the man across from me. I had taken my headphones out and I was getting up to adjust my blanket and. He saw that my headphones were out and he took the opportunity to tell me I was beautiful. He asked me how old I was and I thanked him and told him my age. He was nice but I did not want to hold a conversation.

I had fixed my blanket and put my headphones back on, and put my blanket over my head to get comfortable. As we began to drive again, I had lifted my blanket down and I happened to look over at the man as he was facing the other way looking out the window. I happened to look down at his hands, and when I did my spirit instantly said "he's a man of God, take care of him" and I instantly felt his spirit, and knew that he had a good heart. About another hour later we had stopped at another stop and this one was a gas station. I had brought some nuts and water with me in my bag so I was not hungry or thirsty, and there was a bathroom on the bus so there was no need for me to get off the bus, plus it was pouring down raining. But still, something told me to get off, and when I did the man had got off with me. "It's pouring" I said to him, as he walked beside me and tried to shield me with his coat. "Yeah it's raining hard" he said, as we were walking fast to get out of the rain.

"I am just going into the store; I don't have any money. I just didn't want you to walk by yourself" he said to me still shielding me from the rain. As he said it, instantly my spirit said "feed him." We walked into the store, and I saw that they had a buffet of food. They had chicken, mashed potatoes, green beans, cornbread and a couple of other things. "Get whatever you want," I told him. "Are you sure?" he said to me surprised and humble. "Yes, get whatever you want and I will pay for it" I told him. "Thank you" he said, as he went straight to the buffet. I had got me some funyuns and a grape juice and I waited for him to get his stuff. He had come to the register with his platter, "You want to get anything to drink?" I asked him, and he smiled and got a Pepsi and some chips. "Is that all you want?" I asked him. "Yes, sister this is enough, he said to me as he was so grateful." I had paid for everything and we walked back to the bus, and he told me how grateful he was. I told him that it was no problem and God bless him. We had got back on the bus and I was looking for something to watch on YouTube for the rest of the ride.

As I sat there, I looked over at the man and he kept thanking me, and I nodded my head to him saying "your welcome." We began to drive and I looked over at him again and he was crying and thanking God, and I instantly knew that what my spirit told me about him was true, that he was a man of God. "Can I come over and sit with you for a minute sister?" he asked as he leaned over to me. "Yes" I told him, as he sat next to me still crying. "Sister, I just want to Thank you," he said. "No problem" I had told him. "No, sister I THANK YOU" he stressed.

He had begun telling me about his life and different things he had been through and how he was a giver but life's circumstances had caused him to have hardship and he got addicted to drugs. He told me about his relationship with God and how even though he was on and off of drugs that he still loved God and was still a believer and still knew that God had favor upon him. "Sister I am on my way to rehab. They sent me a ticket to get there, all I have is my clothes and myself. I have no money to buy food or anything for myself. I told God that I trusted him and I knew that he would provide my needs. I didn't know how he was going to do it, but I knew he was going to do it, and he sent you to feed me" the man said as he began to cry from gratefulness. "It's no problem. "God is good" I said to him as I understood his tears and the praise that was coming from his heart.

When you got on the bus, I kept looking at you, it was just something special about you. I could just see the spirit on you" he said to me still crying. "Praise God" I said to him as I smiled. "You are special sister" he said to me, and I thanked him. "I don't want to take up too much of your time. I just wanted to Thank you. Do you mind if I pray with you?" he asked me, and I said yes. He held my hand and prayed over my life and my circumstances. As well as he prayed for himself, and his journey in life and he praised God and ended the prayer. "Amen" we both said at the same time. "Thank you, sister, God bless you" he said to me, as he hugged me and went back to his seat. I had put my blanket back on and when I looked over to him, he was still praying and thanking God. When I looked back over at him a while later, he was asleep. My spirit was at peace and I knew that God was with him, and that God would send people like me to help him on his journey. He had another 8-hour ride without me but I knew that he would be ok.

As he went to sleep another girl came to me for help because she thought I spoke Spanish and she needed to know how long it would take to get to her destination. Just so happened that I had my app on my phone that I used for my Spanish class and I was able to help her. It was not unusual that she came to me because no matter where I am, I am always ending up helping someone. After helping her I had fallen asleep for a short while and finally I was in Albany to my destination. "Hey sis!" Jamilah said as she pulled up and I put my suitcase in and got in the car. "Hey!" I am so happy to finally be here!" I said to her as I hugged her and we pulled off. We went back to her apartment on campus and it was my first time seeing it and it was so cute. She had introduced me to her roommates and they were all so sweet and powerful young women of God.

Me and Jamilah had talked for a while then we got ready to attend her friend's birthday dinner at a Hibachi place. When we got there, I met Jamilah's boyfriend for the first time as well as the Pastor's youngest son and his girlfriend and a lot of other young people from Rhema and it was so exciting. The birthday dinner was nice. The next day I got to go to the church for the first time in person, and it was so beautiful. Being there in person was so much better than watching it on tv. The building was so pretty on the inside. There was a long chandelier in the entrance and everything was so classy and clean. I had to use the bathroom, and even the bathrooms were nice. The sanctuary felt so peaceful and had an awesome presence of God in there.

As I saw everyone it was exciting because I watched them on YouTube so much that seeing them in person made me feel like they were celebrities. The service was great and I had an awesome time. It was COVID so Pastor was behind the shield. We had to social distance so at that time I did not get to personally get to meet Pastor and Co-Pastor, but it was a pleasure to be able to see them in person. Me and Jamilah had left and went to Cheddar's to eat and we met her roommates to go and see the new place they were moving to. I was going home later that evening so I spent time with the girls and asked them to pray for me as I went home. Those young women could pray! I had never heard young people pray with such power. They had prayed the roof of the place and when it was over, another one of her roommates had given me some anointing oil to take back home with me.

Later that night I got on the bus and went back home. It was a little after 11 pm when I got to Atlanta to the bus station. All the drug addicts were out and it was super scary downtown that time of night. I had called Damian to pick me up, but he refused and that was something that he had never done. He did not even want to pay for me an Uber either which again was not like him. I had wound up calling my own Uber. When I got home, he was sound asleep on the couch while I was in the hood in Atlanta. He did not even care if I got home safe or not, and that really hurt my feelings. It was chaos with him before I left for Albany. I did not want drama now that I was back so as he slept, I anointed him with the oil, and I went upstairs to go to bed.

When I got up the next day he was in an ok mood. We had a conversation about our living arrangements due to the situation with the mortgage. We both agreed that it would be best to just sell the house and go our separate ways because being together had become too toxic. Someone had told Damian that I was talking to someone on FB. It wasn't true but he still confronted me about it. "I know it's none of my business, but I don't think you should be talking to anybody right now while we are still living together" he said to me. "First of all, if you don't care, then why are you bringing it to me? Secondly I am not talking to anybody so I don't know why someone would tell you that" I said to him. "A couple of people told me, and I will always know what you are doing, because you don't know who I know" he said to me. "Well I don't talk to anybody so people should mind their business" I told him.

After Damian had approached me about supposedly talking to someone he had changed. He had begun showing a lot of interest in me. He was flirty and touchy feely and wanted to hang out with me all the time. We had got really really cool and it almost felt like old times. We even went to a cookout at our friends Theo and Nichole's house and had a good time and then went to a club afterwards and had fun with one another. It really felt like old times and was making me feel like maybe we could work after all.

41

One night my friend Neicy had called me to hang out with her and her cousins. At first, I was not going to go but she talked me into it and I met her at her house and we went out. We went to the Red Martini. Just so happened that same night Damian had told me he was going out as well to celebrate his friend's KB's birthday at a birthday dinner. Me and Neicy walked into the Martini and the first thing I heard the DJ say was "Happy Birthday KB!" from the DJ booth. "Oh my God my husband is in here" I said to her as I stopped her in her tracks. "Girl do we need to leave?" she asked me jokingly but serious at the same time. "No, we don't need to leave, we good" I told her. "Ok, well let's go to the bar and get you a drink so you can relax " she told me as she grabbed my hand and we went to the bar and she got me a patron and cranberry juice.

We were already in a club before that and we had a couple of drinks so when I drank the patron it made me really tipsy. I had called Damian to see if he was in there and sure enough when he answered the same music I was listening to was in the background. "Girl he IS here" I said to her as I hung up on him. He texted me "WYA" and I told him at the Red Martini and he texted me back "I know" because I am sure he heard the same music in my background too. "WYA in here I am about to come and get you" he asked me and I told him I was in the back by the bar and about five minutes later he was back there looking around like he was going to catch me with someone.

He had greeted Neicy and gave her a hug and looked at me to see what I was wearing. "I got a section with KB and Vernon and a few of my dudes, come on so I can introduce you to everybody" he said to me as he began to walk. I told Neicy that I would be right back and I knew that she was safe because her cousins were there so I left with Damian and went to the section. I hugged Vernon as I knew him forever and I said Happy Birthday to KB and Damian introduced me to everyone and I danced a little bit and took pictures and drank my drink. The more I drank the tipsier I got. I was feeling nice.

Patron was all I drunk and it always got me lit. "I am leaving" I told Damian as I whispered in his ear. "Where you going?" he asked. "I am going back with Neicy, I can't just leave her" I told him and I got up to leave and I stumbled a little. "You are drunk, " he said to me as he held my arm so I didn't fall. "No, I'm not" I told him. "What are you drinking?" he asked me. "Patron and Cranberry" I said to him. "Oh, you drunk" he confirmed because he knew how I got when I drank Patron. "You ain't going by yourself" he said to me, still holding my arm. "Yes, I am I been up here long enough, I am not just going to leave my friend and stay up here with you" I told him. "If you leave this section, then I am leaving too, and we are going home" he said to me authoritatively. "Damian, I came here with Neicy, I am not leaving with you" I told him and I waved to everyone and began walking out the section and he followed me. "Yo I promise we are leaving" he said to me in my ear firmly. When Damian said something, he expected me to do it and I did not want to leave with him so I was looking for my friend to hang out with her instead.

I had finally spotted her and before I could say anything to her Damian was whispering in her ear and she was agreeing with whatever he said. "I think you need to go home with your husband, " she said to me in her joking but serious way. "No Neicy, I came with you so I am leaving with you" I told her. "Shamirah, its Ok, leave with your husband, I am good, " she told me. Damian did not know she was there with her cousins so he offered her to go to the section with KB and them and he even offered to pay for her an Uber so she could get home safe. She thanked him and told him she was good. "Girl go ahead I am good" she reassured me and I knew her cousins were there so I finally gave in and decided to leave with Damian. Before we walked out the club, I had drunk the rest of my Patron and on the drive home I was getting drunker and drunker. Damian was talking my head off giving me lectures like he always did and I did not want to hear it or argue so I just blocked him out.

The kids were at my mom's house so when we got home it was just us. I was so drunk all I remember was making sure that Neicy got home safe and Damian poured me about 3 more shots of Patron from out the kitchen and I was wasted. I remember going upstairs and getting in the bed and I do remember that we had some bomb sex and we were doing all types of things after that I do not remember anything else. I had woken up and we both were naked and I was still feeling the liquor. My mom had called us to come and get the kids and I was still a little drunk so Damian drove.

When we got home, I laid down until my drunkenness wore off. The next few days after that were cool and we had no issues and I felt like maybe we didn't need to move and we could work things out. About two months before then me and Damian had got into a big altercation and he bought up the fact that it was tax season and that he was claiming Aaniyah. I told him that since he did not keep his word on paying the mortgage last tax season that he was not claiming her and that I was. He began to threaten me about how he was going to go to the person who did his taxes and hurry up and do them. And that he was going to call the IRS and tell them all these lies. He also tried to tell people that I didn't take care of my kids which was a complete lie.

I was always a great mother so those allegations were preposterous. I was their provider and they health insurance under me as well as I bought them clothes and everything else, they needed like mothers do. He tried to paint a picture to people like I was a bad mom which was far from the truth. Everyone knew I was an awesome mom and anyone who believed him was just as toxic as he was. I told him upfront that I was using my tax money to move with and since he threatened me. I was not about to let him beat me to the punch and leave me and my kids homeless, so I went and filed my taxes asap.

Everything had gone through and was approved for both kids and all I had to do was wait until I got it. I did not tell Damian. I figured he would find out when he went to his tax person being vindictive and they would have to tell him that the kids were already claimed. Whoever his tax person was, was supposedly telling him all these so-called tax laws to use against me which did not even make sense, especially when I am the legal mother and my kids were in my custody. Whoever was giving him advice was adding fuel to the fire and creating even worse of a monster. So, on a day when we were still cool, I had come to talk to him about something and he had bought up the taxes. "When are you filing taxes?" he asked me. "I already filed them. " I said to him as I was so scared of his reaction.

When I filed them we were not cool, and even if we were cool I would've still filed them because we had already agreed that we were moving separately and I explained to him that, that was my money to move and I was not going to change my decision because that money was for me and my kids livelihood. As a father Damian should have been able to understand that instead of being money hungry and not wanting me to have anything. "You did your taxes already? He asked shocked and I could see his body language get aggressive. "Yeah, I did" I told him as I wished I was not having that conversation because it was so uncomfortable. "Who did you claim?" he asked as he looked me dead in my face and I knew he was about to go bonkers. "I claimed Najah and Aaniyah like I said I was" I told him. "You did what?" he said as he began to flip his lid.

He had gone from a few minutes' prior being nice and talking regularly to the next moment he was cursing me out and calling me every name in the book. He was threatening my life and saying every mean thing under the sun. "Bitch you a Opp now, and I'm going to show you how I do Opps" he said as he got in my face like he wanted to punch me. "Damian get out of my face" I said to him as I pushed him. "Bitch don't touch me I will beat the sh*t out of you" he threatened me and then he threatened to call the IRS to have them stop it and he was saying all the things his tax person told him that he could do to stop me from getting the money. He was saying everything he could out of anger. "Damian, I had already told you since last year that I was claiming both of them so I don't understand why you mad" I yelled to him.

He was a grown man who only had to worry about himself when we split up, and I had to worry about two kids and he was mad about some income tax that I was using to take care of the kids. I was not asking him for anything nor any help so I could not understand why he was upset that I claimed the kids when they were my kids as well, on top of the fact that they were going to be moving with me and not him. He kept yelling about all the sneakers and toys he bought and telling me that he spent more money on them than me and that I "stole" from him. I did not steal anything from him. I claimed my kids to take care of them like a mom is supposed to. I am their mother and I had every right to claim them.

After that point Damian had slandered my name so bad and told so many lies on me that at that point I trusted no one that he dealt with because he would tell me how no one liked me, and that all his friends and family talked about how much a piece of sh*t I was for claiming the kids. I am sure he told his version and not the real story. He had women who were close to him such as his good friend and his sister and whatever other females he felt like he was cool with, and he would tell me how bad they would talk about me. He said they would tell him to leave me and that I am a bum and not a good woman when in fact they did not know the whole story. They only knew his side and never even reached out to me as his wife to even hear my side.

All these women called me sis but when things got rough between me and Damian, there was no sisterhood. There were no phone calls of encouragement towards me or to hear my part. They all took his side and believed him and talked about me like a dog without knowing the facts. I could not understand as mothers and as women how they could treat me that way when they knew how hard it is being a mom. Any of them would have done the same thing as me if they were in my shoes. What type of mother would let a man that she is not going to be with, and is moving on her own with two kids allow the man to take all the money leaving her and her kids to figure it out. No strong loving mother would do that.

Damian had claimed Aaniyah the first two years of her life, as my husband and her father he could have claimed her forever, I did not care. But once we agreed to part ways and that the girls were going with me, I had to go into survival mode because I could not just assume that Damian was going to help me. He had changed so much at that point that I did not know who he was. The old Damian I knew I could have faith that he would help me out and be there for me, but the new Damian was selfish and mean and a narcissist so I did not trust that he would be there if I needed him, because he showed me time after time that he did not care about me or my well being.

It was like he wanted me to suffer and he would even say out of his own mouth things like "Bitch when I leave you are going to suffer and fall on your face" so why would I allow him to claim my baby and hope he helps me when I could claim her myself and know that I am good. I trusted him the year before to pay the mortgage which was a huge responsibility and he didn't do it so I was not trusting him with anything else especially when it came to me and my kid's livelihood. So, to all those who judged me and back bit me for my decision instead of coming to me and asking me, especially the woman who called me "Sis." So many of you smiled in my face yet talked horrible about me behind my back. Y'all were his friends clearly and we were never sis's as y'all claimed. Every relationship I had was genuine and I am a loyal person, so to have been dismissed and talked about by women I trusted really did hurt. When we split up, I didn't get a phone call. No one asked if I was ok, no one checked on my kids, nothing. I have no hard feelings and thank you all for revealing who you really were to me and I forgive you with all my heart, but I can never ever forget. I wish everyone well, but the relationships definitely will never be the same."

After the altercation about the taxes me and Damian's relationship was torn beyond repair after that. One thing about him was that he was money hungry and he didn't like anyone messing with his money, especially me. He didn't want me to have anything and he wanted me to have to depend on him for everything. The fact that I claimed Aaniyah and not him had made him get to the point where he hated me and he made a point to show it. Damian always had more money than me and always knew how to get money so the way he was acting over taxes was blowing my mind. He kept telling me that it was not about the money it was about the fact that I stole from him. He treated me so nasty every chance he got, and it had got so unbearable that I was praying every day for peace. I would wake up to him torturing me by verbally abusing me and threatening me. No day did I have a piece of mind. As long as he was around me, he made a point to make my life hell.

I would sit in my therapy sessions with my therapist and cry, and we would talk about healthy options to move forward because the living situation had become unlivable. I was given an additional 6 months on the COVID mortgage forbearance plan which meant we were going to be living together even longer. After months of fighting in a stressful home I had prayed to God that Damian moved out. I could not move at the time because it was the end of Najah's 8th grade year and I didn't want to pull her out so late in the school year. Even though they were virtual. She still had upcoming eight grade events and ceremonies that I wanted her to attend with her friends. I felt that it made more sense for Damian to leave because he did not have to pack up the house and worry about Najah's schooling and where we were going to go whereas I did. So, I prayed to God and told him that I could not take it anymore and that if he could move Damian so I could have peace while I found somewhere to move to. I was also in school full time at GA state and I needed a clear head to complete my assignments.

A few weeks later Damian had told me that he was approved for a place and that he was moving. He had the place for about three weeks and he still did not move. He was still at my house being toxic. I could not understand if he had his own place, then why was he still at the house, especially being negative. "Damian, don't you have your own house?" I said to him one day as he was being toxic. "What does that mean?" he asked me. "It means if you have your own place then why are you not there?" I asked him. "Because I don't want to, this is my house and I will leave when I'm ready" he said to me rudely and he kept that attitude the whole time and he still stayed and wanted to argue. Finally I had had enough and told him he needed to go and he said he heard a conversation on the door camera that me and my sister were having about the fact that he was still here and after that he had started packing his stuff and moving it into his house. I was relieved but sad at the same time. I wish my relationship was not so toxic and that we could have worked things out but we couldn't. I did my part.

I went to Therapy and had been in it for almost two years at that point. I asked him if we could go to couples counseling and he refused. I asked him if we could sit and talk to the Imam and he refused that as well. Damian showed no effort to fixing his relationship and I guess he had gotten tired and gave up because, I felt it in every way. As he was taking his clothes, I was mentally preparing myself for him not being at the house anymore and I would have my moments. I was already used to not sleeping with him because he had been left the bed. I just had to get used to his presence not being at the house, and him not doing all the manly things like cutting the grass and washing the cars, and everything else he did in the household. I was going to miss those things. Once he took his stuff, I thought he was gone, but he still stayed even after that. He had taken most of his clothes but still had a lot of stuff in the room drawers and the garage. He stayed for a few more weeks, and I tried my best not to say anything to him, because he was always ready for a confrontation with me, and I mentally could not take any more drama. I had no more left in me.

It was the end of March and the beginning of April when I had gotten really sick. I had already had COVID but I was going to get tested again because I felt horrible and I was extremely tired. I was sick for about a week straight. Weeks prior to that I had switched from the Ortho Evra birth control patch to the pill. I had taken the pill faithfully but it was a really low dose because the pill always made me sick. I had been on the patch since Aaniyah was born and even in the past before then and I loved it. The patch was so convenient and I had never had any issues. I used to put the patch on my butt and rotate it every week. For some reason it had begun to itch and began to burn my skin. My doctor had taken me off of it immediately and switched me to the pill. After getting on the pill I did not get a period the first month which I thought was very odd. I had taken a pregnancy test and it was negative and I went to see my OBGYN and they took a pregnancy test at the office and it was negative as well. My doctor said maybe my dose was too low to produce a period, so she put me on a higher dose pill. I came home and began taking the pill and I took it faithfully for the whole month.

When it was time for my period to come there still was nothing which I thought was really odd. I had gone to the store to take a pregnancy test and it was negative so I could not figure out what was going on and that is why I was going to get the COVID test. I had made the

COVID test appointment but my heart was still unsettled and something told me to get up and go to Walmart and get another pregnancy test. I was so tired and nauseous but I mustered up the energy to go anyway. I had bought two tests, a first response and an 88-cent test. After I paid for it, I went into the bathroom and took the 88 cent one and to my shock the two lines came up asap. "What?" I said to myself as my mouth dropped. "This cannot be" I said in disbelief. Najah and Aaniyah were standing outside the bathroom waiting for me and I tried to stay calm so Najah didn't know. "Come let's go" I told her as I was ready to get out of Walmart. I already hated going into Walmart as it is. I forgot that Najah was in the car as I called my bestie and told what was going on. "How your old ass pregnant" she said as she laughed. We were always making fun of each other to make light of situations. "Girl I know right" this is crazy I said to her. "Mom your pregnant!" Najah asked me excitedly. "Oh my God Najah I forgot you were in here; you were not supposed to know" I said to her. "Wow, I am happy. Are you going to tell Daddy?" she asked me. "Yes, I will tell him, but don't get too happy Najah" I told her. "Why not?" she asked me and I did not answer her.

I had pulled up to the house and Damian was not home yet so I told Najah to get Aaniyah out of her car seat and for them to go in the house. When they got out, I was trying to get my thoughts together and trying to process the fact that I was pregnant. Damian was in the process of moving out and we were in a horrible space in our relationship and the timing of me being pregnant was horrible. My head was all over the place, on top of that I was scared to tell Damian because I knew his reaction was not going to be a good one. Even though I did not want to hear his rudeness, I had called him to tell him anyway. "Hello" he said as he answered his cell phone. "I have something to tell you" I said to him as I was so nervous on the inside. "What?" he asked in such a dry and monotone voice. "I have not been feeling that good, and I just came from Walmart getting a test, and guess what? I am pregnant" I told him. He was silent for a few seconds then he said "Well it ain't mine." "How is it not yours Damian? We were having sex a lot, but you know what I already knew you would say something stupid like that and that's why I am not keeping it anyway" I said to him as I hung up on him. "He is so stupid" I said to myself out loud.

I had already known he would say something rude because that's how he was. He was a butt hole and as much as I told myself I would never get an abortion again; I had felt like that was my only option. We were breaking up and I could not see myself being pregnant and sick with no help from him and then having to raise a baby by myself. I did not have the mental capacity to deal with anymore of his drama and I knew if I was pregnant that he was still going to treat me like trash and when I am pregnant I get extremely sick and would have definitely needed him with me for support and I knew he was not going to be there so I had to make a choice. Either keep on my journey to getting out of a toxic relationship and focusing on me and my two girls and my business to become successful or put a halt on all my future plans and be a single mom with my two girls and another baby and have to deal with Damian and his drama when I needed him the most. I didn't see the latter option as being good for the progress I have made already, nor did I see it being good for my mental health. I felt like if I bought a baby into the equation it would have made things ten times harder for me.

When Aaniyah was born Damian was there mentally physically and emotionally to help me with her and it was still hard, so with having a new baby and him not being there that is a task I did not want to take on and I did not feel that it was best especially with me being pregnant sick and alone. I would not have done well with that and with him being negative and disrespectful towards me during that time, it was all a recipe for disaster.

I had thought about all of it and while I was sitting in the car Damian had pulled up and sat in the driveway and he got out and was talking to someone on the phone. I looked at him and thought to myself that I would love for it all to have worked out where we were happy together and had a healthy relationship and we were excited to welcome a new baby in the family, but that was not my reality. My reality was that I was with a man who had narcissistic tendencies and he was selfish and unhealed at the moment, and he did everything in his power to make my life miserable. I came out of fantasy land of the "what if's" and faced the real facts of what was in front of me. Me being pregnant did explain a lot of why Damian was sleeping so much. He was not the type of person who slept during the day, but for the past few weeks he was always tired which I thought was odd. But it did begin to make sense because when I am pregnant, he gets my sick symptoms and my tiredness. But with all of that I still had to make a decision.

It was about 3 pm in the day so I had decided to call the abortion clinic before they closed to make an appt. I found out I was pregnant on a Tuesday and they scheduled my appointment for three days later on a Friday. Even though Damian was right outside I texted him and told him that my appointment was on Friday and the time for him to take me and he did not respond back to me. In the past he gave me hell about being pregnant and this time I was not going to give him the opportunity to harass me about getting an abortion like he always did so this time I decided to make the choice for myself.

When I got off the phone, I had a lot on my mind and I needed someone to talk to. I had not talked to Damian's sister in a while because I had so much going on in my life as well as I knew she had a lot going on in hers so I did not want to dump any of my issues on her, especially since it had a lot to do with her brother. I did not want to vent to her about her brother out of respect. I just let them have their relationship together as brother and sister and I stayed out of it to not cause any confusion between them. I did not want it to be a thing where I vented to her, and she gave her opinion and Damian found out and got upset with her. Nor did I want it to be a thing where she resented me for the ways I felt about her brother, so I decided to just leave the situation alone altogether. Him and his sister talked every day almost all day. I tried to reach out to her from time to time to check on her, but she would not answer my calls, so I figured whatever she was going through she did not want to talk to me about it, and I respected it. She had her brother to talk to and maybe did not want me in her business, even though I already knew some things because Damian would tell me. That is why I tried to reach out as a woman with compassion to let her know I was here also if she needed me.

In the past I had talked to her a lot, and she knew how Damian treated me when he found out I was pregnant, so out of all the people who I thought would understand, it would be her. I had called her and told her I found out I was pregnant, and she was shocked. I had told her that her brother's reaction was that "it wasn't his" and that I was getting an abortion. She told me that whatever decision I made just make it for myself, and that if I wanted to keep the baby then keep it, and if I wanted to get an abortion get it, if that is what I wanted, not because it was what Damian wanted like I had did in the past. Against my better judgement, I had vented to her about some things we were going through as far as him being upset with me for claiming both of our kids on my taxes. I explained to her that I claimed them because we were breaking up, and that I was using the money to move. I did not owe anyone an explanation, but I did want to talk to her about it because him and her talked a lot, and I knew that he gave her his own version which painted me out to be a money stealing monster, and that was not the case at all. Also, out of venting, I did tell her that I was in fact getting an abortion, and that it was indeed my choice and I did say to her that her brother "disgusted me" and that "I did not want to be with him anymore. I had vented many times in the past, and I did not think she would hold that against me. Especially as a woman who was hurting, we sometimes say things about our husbands that we don't mean. Sometimes things come out, out of pain and hurt. She said "I understand" and we got off the phone and that was that.

Later that day me and Damian had got into a small argument and he went on to call me a "user". "How am I a user?" I asked him confused. "You only call people when you need them, you're a user" he said to me again. "You think people feel bad for you, but they don't. People see right through your BS" he added. "And I disgust you right?" he said to me. I did not know what he was talking about at first, and then it dawned on me that I had talked to his sister earlier, and that clearly she had mentioned our conversation to him, and told him everything that I said. I should have not been surprised, that was the reason I had stopped venting to her in the first place. I was not upset with her for running back and telling her brother. I was upset with myself for letting my guard down. There was always drama in the past from me venting to her, and I learned my lesson. No matter how much I needed to talk to someone she was not the one I should have called, so that was definitely an L on my part. Me and Damian argued about what I said to her for a little bit and then I was over it. I was over the backbiting. I was over the drama and all I wanted was a peace of mind.

Friday had come and we got up early and Damian dropped me off at the abortion clinic. The protesters were out there with their signs, trying to block us from getting in. I sat there in the car numb. I did not want to be there at all and I could not even believe that I was about to go through this again. It felt so unreal. Due to COVID restrictions, Damian could not come in so this time I had to go through the whole process alone. I was there for about 8-9 hours and finally I went back to the surgery room and just like before I was given anesthesia and I was out. When I woke up, I was in a little pain and I was not pregnant anymore and I was glad that it was all over. When the nurses took me outside Damian was parked there waiting for me. The nurse helped me in the car and Damian did not even look at me. He did not ask me if I was ok, nothing. He just seemed like he was mad, but every time he was around me, he was mad so that was nothing new for me.

I was super hungry because I had not eaten since the night before so I asked him to take me to get something to eat and he didn't respond. He just kept driving. "Damian there's an Arby's right there, can we go there?" I asked him as we almost passed it and I knew there would be no more food places before we got home because we were about to get on the highway and I knew we would be stuck in traffic. Damian had spun his car around with an attitude and he went through the drive through. I was on the passenger side so I told him what I wanted so he could say it in the speaker. "You tell them" he said as he cut me off and I had to yell across him to the intercom and the lady kept telling me to repeat myself because she could not hear me. It hurt for me to talk loud or yell. I had literally just come from having my abortion and I was still in pain, but Damian was able to tell her what he wanted as he added to my order. So, he could have talked the whole time, he was just giving me a hard time like he always did. Finally, she got my order and we drove to the window and I paid with my card. Normally he would pay, but he made it a point not to this time, which was fine with me because I had my own money.

I was doing very well for myself at that time and I didn't ask nor need him for anything like I did in the past. I had paid for my own abortion that day as well, as he normally would pay for it, but this time he did not even offer. The lady had handed him the drink and the bag with the food in it. He looked in it to make sure his mozzarella sticks were in there and he sped off. "Damian you didn't even let me look to make sure all my food was in there" I said to him, as I looked in my bag. "You drove off so fast she didn't even give me mac n cheese" I said to him disappointed because the macaroni and cheese was the main thing I wanted. He just shrugged his shoulders like "Oh well" as he kept driving and was eating his mozzarella sticks. "You are so rude" I said to him in disappointed. I felt his negative energy but I was trying to bite my tongue because I did not want drama, but I could not hold it in anymore, and I had to say something to him. "I just came from getting an abortion and could have died, and this is how you treat me" I said to him. "Bitch shut up; I don't feel sorry for you" he said to me with so much anger in him. "I didn't ask you to feel sorry for me, I am telling you your attitude and rudeness is unnecessary" I said to him as he turned his music up so he couldn't hear me talk. "You're so miserable" I said to him as I shook my head and ate my food. I didn't say anything for the rest of the ride. When we got home, I came in and laid down and didn't say anything to him for the rest of the day.

A few days later, he wanted to take Najah and Aaniyah to Dave and Busters and Najah begged me to go with them so I agreed to make her happy. In the past before things got bad between us, I had talked to Damian about the music he played in front of the girls. He listened to a lot of vulgar rap with curse words and a lot of sexually explicit talk and I expressed to him that neither Najah nor Aaniyah need to be listening to that. First off Najah was a young teenager and she did not need to be listening to music where men are calling woman b*tches and hoes, and to suck their d*ck etc. It was totally inappropriate. I am very energy conscious and I am very careful what I expose myself as well as my girls to. After we talked about it, he agreed and said that he would not play vulgar music or let them watch anything that may not be good for their spirits and as their dad I trusted him.

We had all got in the car to go on our family outing and as we got on the highway Damian began playing vulgar music. I didn't say anything, but I did give him "the look". In the past when I gave him the "look" he knew what it meant and normally he would have changed the song. This time he gave me a "look" back as to say "I do want I want" and he kept the music playing. I tried to give him the benefit of the doubt that he would change it, but no, the next song came on and it was the same thing.

The words were making my soul cringe and to have my two daughters sitting back there being subjected to it was burning me up on the inside and I could not take it anymore. "Damian, I thought you agreed to not play music like this anymore with the kids in the car" I said to him. "This is my car; I play whatever I want" he scolded me. "I know it's your car, but do you think it's appropriate for your girls to be hearing men talk like this?" I asked him. "They alright" he said to me rudely. "Damian, can you please just change the songs to songs without all this vulgarity in it?" I asked him as I was frustrated but I was trying to be respectful. "No" he said to me bluntly. "Hmm" I said as I got an attitude. I had sat there listening to bad song after bad song and my heart began to hurt and I began to cry. Not for myself, but for my innocent babies, especially Aaniyah. She was so small and innocent and should not have to have been subjected to all that filth going into her spirit and what really hurt me the most was that as their father who was supposed to be their protector, yet was the one subjecting them to it and he did not even care, and the fact that if he did care because of his pride. He didn't turn it off to make a point to me. Me and his issues had absolutely nothing to do with the kids so the fact that they had to suffer for his pride and anger towards me was hard for me as a mom to watch.

We had drove from Rockdale to Gwinnett and the music still played. "I don't know why you sitting there with an attitude, you want me to take you home?" Damian asked and I ignored him. "Do you?" he asked again. "I don't care what you do, that's why I don't want to be with you now" I said to him. "What!" he said, going ballistic. "I'm taking you home" he said as he made a U-turn to go back on the highway and he drove me all the way back home in traffic and all. The whole time I did not say anything. I am sure he wanted me to plead with him to not take me home and he wanted to argue and be negative, but I was silent and I did not do any of that. The whole time I was just thinking in my head "I cannot wait to be done with him." I had enough of his toxicness. Damian used to be super sweet with a good heart, but he had become a mean, angry person. He was evil spirited and black hearted. His energy used to be so warm and loving and it had become cold and it was hard for me to be in his presence because of it. His energy was so nasty and it suffocated the life right out of me. It was horrible to be around and horrible to watch him go from such a good person to such an angry miserable soul. We got to the house and he let me out and I was glad to be out of his car. The energy was thick in there. I was happy I was out, but I was sad that my girls were still in there. I knew he would put up a fight if I told them to get out with me and that would be another issue, plus I did not want to ruin their day to have fun, so I just said a prayer to God for protection over them and sent their angels out to watch over them and I went into the house.

I texted Najah not too long after to make sure they were ok, and she told me they were good and that her dad had changed the music when I got out of the car. I was glad to hear that he did that but annoyed by his pride at the same time. I did not let Damian and his drama ruin my day, I was already dressed so I went out and went to the salon to get a pedicure and did some shopping and got me some seafood while I was out and I had a great time, plus it gave me a break from the kids. So, him dropping me off wound up being a true blessing and it gave me a much-needed peace of mind.

42

About two weeks had passed and Damian's woman friend Tracy who he called his sister, had come over to the house. She had been a friend of his for years and I was familiar with her as well as the kids were too. She was older and I did not think anything negative of their relationship. I knew they were strictly friends. In the past she would come over and me and her would hang out and talk or me, her and Damian would kick it and she loved to see Najah and Aaniyah. So, it was all love. Damian did mention to me a lot that none of the women in his life liked me and that they all thought I was trash. According to him, they had a lot to say after I claimed the kids on my taxes. So, me knowing exactly who the woman in his life that he was referring to, I chose to keep my distance. When she came over a lot of the times, I would be upstairs, and I did not make it a priority to come down and speak to her. When I did see her, I spoke but I did not sit there and laugh with her like I used to. "What's wrong with you chinadoll? Why you acting Boujee?" she would ask me as she always called me chinadoll. I did not tell her what was really on my mind because I did not want to start any drama between her and Damian so I just said less.

The reason I didn't sit and kick it with her was because I knew Damian always vented to her about me which I did not like. I felt like if I was his wife then he should have been talking to me about our problems and how we could fix them, not to another woman who was not a counselor or a professional and also the fact that he told me to my face that none of the woman in his life liked me and that I was trash, and she was def a woman who was in his life that he talked to. She made it clear that she was his friend and not mines. I knew where her loyalty lied so there was no telling what she said about me when I was not around, so I just decided to not do the fake dance and let him and her do them. He was telling her a bunch of lies and she never cared to hear my side which was fine because at that point I did not care who thought what about me.

Me and him were on the verge of being done and I was only focused on me and my girls. I knew that the truth always has a way of revealing itself. She had come over and I happened to be in the kitchen "Hey china doll!" she said as she gave me a hug. I had hugged her back nonchalantly. "Why you give me that fake hug?" she said in her country accent. Damian was in the kitchen with us and then he went outside to his car and the kids came with him leaving me and her in the house by ourselves. "What's going on with you girl? You look good" she said to me as she smiled and sat down. "I'm good" I said to her. "You always acting boujee" she said as she went to the cabinet to pour her a drink and she sat down to drink it and finish talking. "I'm not boujee" I said as I was wiping down the counters in the kitchen.

"I'm sure Damian already told you the business" I said to her as I could tell there was an elephant in the room and there was something she wanted to say. "What?" she asked shocked. "Don't even play, you know Damian told you I just got an abortion" I said to her. "No" she said she looked at me shocked. "Stop playing" I said to her. "Ok, ok Sis, he did tell me" she admitted. "I know he did" I said to her. "Ok well now that it's out there, why they hell did you do that?" she asked me disappointed. "Because we are not even together and he is moving, and I don't want to bring a baby into all of this mess" I told her. "I know sis, but y'all married" she said to me. "I know all of that, tell him that, I been trying for the longest. He is the one who gave up on us" I told her. "Well Sis, he did tell me that you took the income tax money, he was pissed about that" she told me. "First of all, I didn't take anything. Second of all he already knew this year he was not claiming Aaniyah. I had already told him last year after he didn't pay the mortgage like he was supposed to, that he was not claiming her so I don't know why he keeps telling people that I stole the income tax money. We are breaking up and moving and that is my money for me and my kids to move" I told her as I was tired of him portraying to people like I stole from him when I didn't.

He knew we were breaking up and moving and he knew what I was using the money for. Any real man would want to make sure their kids' mother has what she needs to take care of the kids and I was tired of him slandering my name and lying to anyone who would listen to his foolishness. "Oh, sis I didn't know all of that. I thought y'all was just breaking up because y'all have a lot of issues, and that the mortgage was backed up" she told me. "Yes, we have a lot of issues, but they could have been worked out. He has a lot of pride and I am tired of being the only one trying in this relationship.

He keeps making a huge issue about money and me claiming my kids and I am tired of it" I told her. "Sis, I just got a lawsuit and I have the money to catch up on the mortgage for y'all to stay together as a family and especially for the girls." she told me. "No that's Ok, he's moving now and I rather move too and get a fresh start. Thank you though" I told her. "I will be honest with you; I don't like him telling our business and then not telling the whole story. He only tells the parts that make me look bad and that's not right" I told her. "And also, I don't appreciate that he vents to you and whoever else and y'all form your own opinions without even talking to me, and that's hurtful to me" I told her. "Sis, I listen to Bro but I always tell him y'all husband and wife and I just try to stay out of it" she told me.

"Well he told me that all the women in his life have something negative to say about me and that y'all say I am trash based off of what he says and everything he says is not the truth" I told her. "What?" she said as she was taken back and her jaw dropped. "Sis I swear I never said you were trash and I never said nothing bad about you. I don't know why bro would tell you that. I'm about to go out there and say something to him" she said as he started getting up. "No, don't say anything right now because I don't want any drama. I just want you to know that when y'all talk about me especially without hearing my side it really hurts and it's not right how he is going from person to person trying to make me out to be a shady person when I am not" I told her. "Wow sis, I am shocked. No wonder you always act funny when I see you, now I know why" she said. "Yup, that's exactly why. I don't rock with people who sit around and talk about me" I told her. "Sis" she said to me as she grabbed my hand. "Sis, listen to me I promise you that I do not talk bad about you. I tell bro that's your wife and to work it out with you" she said to me as she looked me in my face, and I believed her and I knew she was not lying. Damian was the liar and the narcissist.

He was the one twisting the stories and trying to paint me out to be the bad guy, because he could not take responsibility for his part. It was so much easier to push all the blame on me like he did throughout the whole relationship, and I was tired of being his punching bag. She had eventually left, and I knew she said something to him because he mentioned it to me. He asked me why I told her what he said, and I told him because it was hurtful. He told me that he apologized to her for anything that he may have said that was not true. I was over him and his drama at that point. Even though I did not owe his friend an explanation it was nice to get some of my side out and clear up some of the lies and slander that he had told about me. Since I had claimed the kids, he began to move like he hated me. He had told me I was an Opp and I felt every bit of it. He made sure that I felt his wrath and he made it clear that he didn't like me and he was doing everything in his power to make sure that others did not like me as well.

43

It was April and it was close to Damians' birthday, and he kept getting packages at the door from Amazon. I did not think anything of it. As the packages continued to come, I noticed that they were from his sister. I did not mind him having a close relationship with his sister, but I did feel like he spent a lot of time talking to her and nurturing their relationship. He was always giving her advice in her relationships and even calling and reaching out to her spouse, yet he did not take his own advice in his own relationship and I will admit at times it was frustrating. I felt that he would rather sit and talk to his sister then sit and talk to me. On her end I did not understand why as a woman who had been going through her own relationship issues that she felt like it was ok to call him all the time, and dump all her problems on him when he had his own relationship problems.

As a woman I always wondered why it did not dawn on her that if she was on the phone with him all day then clearly, he was not spending time with his wife and being present in his own marriage. I concluded that she did not care about him nurturing his marriage as long as she had him to vent to, and I even mentioned it to him several times. After I mentioned it to him it became even more uncomfortable. Worst of all when he was on the phone with her and I was around. He would always make it seem like I was not around, or he would try to be rude to me to let her know that he didn't mess with me like that, when in all actuality Damian used to be all over me. Beefing and all, he was still attracted to me and was very sexual with me. It just confirmed to me that he talked about me badly to her. His whole demeanor would change with me when he was on the phone with her. Vibes and energy do not lie, and I could feel the tension from both of them, especially Damian.

It was a few days before his birthday and it was also a few days from Ramadan, which is the Islamic fasting month, so I wanted to get him gifts for his birthday that he could also use for Ramadan because I know that would have meant a lot to him. It was precisely three days before his birthday. Me and Najah were in the kitchen, and I told her the next day that we were going to go shopping for her dad. The next day was a Tuesday and I wanted to go that particular day because I had class all day on Wednesday and Damian's Birthday was on Thursday so Tuesday was the best day for me to go. "Najah, we are going to go to the Islamic shop tomorrow to get your dad some stuff for his birthday," I told her as she was washing the dishes. "Ok, what are we going to get him?" she asked me. "I want to get him a new prayer rug, some oils for prayer and a nice new Quran." I told her. "My aunt already got daddy a Quran " Najah told me as she was drying the dishes. "Ok, well we can get him the other stuff on the list then" I said to her. His sister had been sending Damian gifts about two weeks leading up to his birthday and they were in many different size boxes. So far, she had sent him twelve gifts in total. Since Niyah told me she already got him a Quran it made me think that she may have already gotten him more gifts that I had planned to get him already. "Do you know what else she got him?" I asked her. "No, I am not sure," she said to me. "Ok, I will call your aunt and see what she got so I don't buy him the same things she already got him" I told her.

Damian was sitting on the ottoman in the foyer and I didn't want to talk too loud because I did not want him to hear me talking about what I was going to get him so I went upstairs. It was about 11 pm, and I was ready to go to sleep but before I did, I texted his sister. I texted her "Hey sorry to text you so late. I was going shopping for Damian's birthday and I told her everything I was going to get him. I am reaching out so I do not double buy things you already got him." She had text me back and told me that she basically got him everything that I was going to get him except the prayer rug and the oils. Damian was very hard to shop for because he was very particular in what you bought him, and his sister knew that as well. "I stated to her verbatim with no malice, only pure intentions "Ok, you got him everything I was going to get him, he is hard to shop for, but I will figure it out, thanks." Me and her had known each other 19 years at that point. I had many talks with her and had asked her many questions in the past, so I did not think me asking her what she got him so that I did not double buy would be a big deal. But clearly it was. She had texted back "sorry" a little while after us texting and I had fallen asleep so I did not see it until I woke up the next morning.

I woke up to a text of her asking me if I intentionally made her feel bad about sending her brother gifts, then proceeded to go on a rant about how God led her to buy the gifts for her brother and how I need to take it up with God and not her and to please do not call her only about her brother or she would rather me not call at all. She was taking so many shots at me. I did not understand where all of this was coming from beings though me and her had never had an altercation in the 19 years that we knew each other, so I was very taken back. I text her back and told her; No I was not trying to hurt her feelings. I just genuinely did not want to get him things that she already got him, and I let her know that I did not appreciate her coming at me the way that she did, and it became a texting back and forth match.

She stated to me that I was writing a book for "Clout" and how she is his sister and it doesn't matter if I am his wife, that she will always be connected to him and come before me. I did remind her of the order of God which was: God, Husband/Wife, then family and she got very upset with me. She was asking me questions and I was answering her yet she was telling me that I was overwhelming her. In those moments dealing with her felt like I was dealing with Damian, and it was all too familiar and toxic so I proceeded to tell her that she needed to go and pray and get herself together.

She had said a lot of hurtful things to me. Things she was saying were beyond just taking up for her brother. What she was spilling out was personal, and she was exposing how she really felt about me. And it just confirmed what Damian was telling me and what I was already feeling that "she didn't like me". Damian would sit on the phone and talk about me to her for hours so clearly eventually she believed the things he told her, and began having ill feelings towards me. Even with knowing me for 19 years and having my phone number she still never called me to get my side, nor check on me, nothing, but proceeded in the conversation to tell me that I don't call her, and I let her know that the phone worked both ways. There were plenty of times that I called her to check on her, and she would not answer my call ,but a few minutes later she would be on the phone with her brother so clearly, she did not want to talk to me.

I remember one time she was going through something, and I called her to see how she was doing and she did not answer, but I heard Damian talking to her on the phone not too long after. I had told Damian that it seems like every time I call her she doesn't pick up, and that I had just called her right before he talked to her. and he let me know that she told him I called, but she did not feel like speaking to me. When he told me, I was offended and my feelings were a little hurt. I was trying to be there for her and she didn't want to talk to me, that was fine, but don't text me and act like I was just a bad friend when I wasn't. I reached out as much as I could and she ignored me. I felt the vibes, and I was not about to keep calling her and sweating her. I figured she would talk when she was ready.

I remember one time me and Damian had gotten into it and he said to me out his own mouth "that is MY sister, she doesn't have loyalty to you. She doesn't rock with you. She is MY sister not yours" and when he said it, I felt it in my soul. I had a thing where I thought people would love me how I loved them and when he said that it made me realize, no matter how cool me and her were, that at the end of the day she WAS in fact his SISTER, so for me to think I can confide in her, and have that sisterly bond with her was foolish of me. She was always going to have her brother's best interest over mine, which is understandable and I understood. So, after he said that, I began to play my position and not share certain things out of respect for their relationship. By her coming at me the way she did and saying the things she said. It really revealed her heart towards me and it broke a bond that will never be repaired.

As a woman who has had hardships in her own relationships and in life. I would have thought she would have had way more compassion for what I was going through with her brother woman to woman. But when I confided in her about my abortion she chose to run and tell him everything that I expressed to her, which was expressed out of pain. If anyone could understand what I was feeling I thought it would be her, but me talking to her actually made the situation worst. Her and Damian both played a part in hurting me very badly. But I forgive them both, and I have no bad feelings. It was a learning experience for me. I learned that sometimes in life your love and loyalty to others is not the same love that they have for you and that, that was ok. I just keep everything in my memory bank, forgive and move on.

After Damian's birthday came, he had opened all of his gifts that his sister bought him. She got him pots and pans, silverware, kitchen appliances, a robe slipper and everything else he needed to leave me and go to his own place. Once everything was opened, he packed his car and left for good this time. When he moved out the house was very peaceful. Finally, I felt free of all the drama and weight of all the arguing and pain we had caused each other over the years, especially in the last few years of living in the new house. We had a brand-new home, a brand-new baby and you would have thought that life would have been amazing, but it was not. After he left, I continued to go to therapy and continued to heal.

When he first left, I was a ball of emotions. Some days I would be happy and some days I would be angry and resentful. Some days I felt pain and hurt. Sometimes I missed him and sometimes I was glad he was gone. I did not miss his presence in bed because I was used to him not being next to me, which was wild because there was a point in life where I couldn't even sleep if he wasn't laid right next to me. Laying in the bed for couples is a form of intimacy and provides an unspoken closeness and bond, even without having sex. When he had decided to spitefully sleep on the couch to punish me, he did not understand the spiritual bonds between us that he was breaking. Damian was a Muslim and it was not permissible to deprive your spouse of intimacy and companionship. Just like it's not permissible in Christianity or any other religion.

There are so many Hadiths in Islam that explains how a husband should treat his wife. He should love her and honor her and respect her and be compassionate to her, yet he did not obey the rules of God in his own religion when it came to me, his wife, who was the other half of his Deen. Damian was mean to me and was a tyrant over me. He had no regard for my feelings as a wife or a woman. He was scornful and cold in his dealings with me. He treated me like an enemy that he hated vs the wife that God had given to him. When I was Muslim and even afterwards, I always reminded him of what God said as far as marriage, and how to treat each other, and he would always brush me off and not listen because he did not care. "Do you not fear your Lord?" I would ask him, and he would always have a smart remark or just ignore me all together.

The relationship became hopeless because he was not willing to change. He would just always push everything on me, and not take any responsibility for his actions, and his part in our relationship falling apart. I was already in Therapy and I asked him if we could go to couples therapy, he said "No". I asked him if he would be willing to go to his own individual therapy, he said "No". Since he was Muslim, I asked him if we could talk to the Imam he said "No" My father who was my Wali (my helper and advocate) in Islam was deceased so we could not go to him, so I was out of options. Damian did not care to fix the relationship so I had to come to terms that I could not be the only one fighting so I just stopped, and when I did that is when everything fell apart.

When he left, there was a lot of pain but relief as well. I enjoyed being in my home with my kids with no arguing or toxicness. The air felt clear and free, my spirit was much happier and so were my kids. Najah being 14, it was a struggle for her with us not being together like she was used to, but she was also glad to not have to hear arguing day in and day out. Me and the kids were upbeat. We talked and laughed and cooked and played games and spent time together in the house. Even though Damian did not live there anymore, he would still pop up and come in the house whenever he felt like it. A lot of times we would be having a good day and the kids would be excited to see him, but when it was time to go Aaniyah would start crying and Najah would get into her attitude moods and he was causing an uproar and creating chaos, that I had to deal with when he left. I had asked him to call me before he came and not just pop up out of respect, and he would get upset and tell me that his kids lived there, and he paid for the house so he could do what he wanted to do, and that would cause issues between us. I had begged to differ. On top of him popping up and getting the kids upset by him leaving, when he would come to the house, he would be mean and toxic and start arguments with me. It was like the same toxic cycle over and over again.

This went on for about a month and I could not take it anymore so I went out and bought a new top lock and changed it myself so he would not have access to just coming over whenever he felt like it. I did not mind him seeing the kids but I did not want him coming with his toxic energy and using the opportunity to start arguments with me. I wanted my home to be a safe place for myself and my girls. He was still with the same old same old angry man energy so I had to put a stop to it. He had come over one day and tried to get in. He still had the key to my storm door. I had only changed the bolt lock. He had finally realized the lock was changed and he got upset and began ringing the doorbell.

I had finally let him in because he threatened to kick the door in and when he came in, he was furious and began cursing at me. "So that's what we doing? We changing locks? Ok, watch this, he said as he began taking things. He took some more of his clothes and began taking things out the tv console and then he began unplugging the living room tv. "Bitch, I was being nice to you by letting you keep my tv, now I'm taking it" he said angrily. "Ok Damian and when you take it, I will buy another one" I said to him calmly. He was saying the rudest stuff to me to get a reaction out of me, but I stayed calm the whole time and let him take whatever he wanted and I did not put up a fight. He thought by taking the tv that it was going to hurt me, but it didn't. It was his TV, and he showed me his true colors.

When he got mad, he would always take things back or try to cut deep with his words, but this time I was not going to let him get to me. He was trying his best to do so but I stayed strong the whole time. Finally, he realized he was not fazing me and he took the tv outside and took the girls with him as he struggled to get the tv in the backseat because Aaniyah's car seat was back there. I just watched him from the door making a fool of himself and he finally got in and they left. I called Najah to make sure her and Aaniyah were ok and that they got to their dad's house safe. Once I knew they were good, I had relaxed and began writing some more on my book. I enjoyed my peace of mind and I was also proud of myself for finally staying strong while Damian was trying to break me.

The very next morning I got up and went to Walmart and bought me a brand new "55-inch tv which was way better than the one he took. I bought it home and put it up myself and I left the box by the door so he could see it. He had come a few hours later to drop the kids off and he came in and saw the box and the new TV on the tv stand. He did not say a word and neither did I. I hugged my kids and went about my business. Throughout the relationship Damian would get to me. He knew what to say to me to trigger me. He had a lot of mind control over me and I did not even realize it.

All I wanted to do was be pleasing to him and make him happy, so a lot of times I put my own feelings aside and silenced myself when it counted. Yes, I yelled and cursed at him and was toxic, but that was not the voice that counted. I needed to learn to set boundaries and communicate in an effective way and lashing out and having panic attacks was not the way to get heard. It was counterproductive. When I began to do the inner self, work is when I found myself. I found my true voice and I learned that I did not have to scream and shout to get my point across. I learned that sometimes silence is better and more effective. More importantly I learned that instead of venting to people I learned to take my issues to God and there is where I began to see real change and growth.

44

In life we teach people how to treat us, and throughout the relationship I allowed Damian to call me out of my name, and say hurtful things to me. I taught him that he could say whatever and treat me however he wanted and that there were no repercussions. I taught him these things because I was not aware of Self and I didn't think I was worthy of love and respect. I was just glad to have a man in my life, and I didn't want him to leave me, and even if I was right, I took on the role of being wrong to appease him. I taught him that no matter how much he hurt my feelings that it was ok. I taught him that I would always be his verbal punching bag and he obliged. He would say these hurtful things to me, and I taught him that as long as he was nice to me afterwards or bought me things that it was ok. I taught him that he did not have to respect me or have boundaries nor apologize to me.

The things I went through with Damian were hurtful especially during the end, but there is always a blessing in the storm. Him telling me that I was crazy and that I had borderline personality disorder and him telling me to see a therapist, though he said it for his own mean and selfish intentions, it wound up being a blessing because it changed the whole trajectory of my life. Going to therapy allowed me to clear my head enough to see the mess I was in, mentally physically and emotionally. Going to my sessions allowed me to sift through my baggage and clear the madness in my head, which allowed me to forgive, let go and heal from past trauma's. Once I began to come out of my depressed moods, I began to see the light of life again. I began to get my spark back and became enthusiastic about my future and my endeavors again. I began to slowly learn how to love Me.

I had begun therapy when I was about 34, and in 34 years I had finally got to know myself for myself, not for who people told me I was, especially Damian. I was getting to know Shamirah Shayonne Smith, and I liked who I was. Once I began to like me and respect me, I began to learn boundaries, and did not allow people to just treat me any kind of way anymore, especially Damian. With me turning from a caterpillar to a butterfly, he did not like it because he no longer had control. He was no longer the puppet master over my emotions, and that was too much for him to handle. Since he could no longer manipulate me and make me believe his lies, he had no choice but to turn and look at himself.

During our breakup he put me through things that crushed my heart. He made me feel pain and rejection that I had never felt from him before. Some days the hurt was so unbearable that I literally felt like I could not breathe. But even on my weakest days I knew I had to be strong for myself and my kids. I had to go inside of me and pull-on strength from within, and when I wanted to give up there was a still voice inside of me that always said "you can do it" and I listened to that voice, and I put my faith in God and I overcame all the obstacles that were stacked against me! When I wanted to give up, I fought! When I wanted to hate I loved! When I wanted to die, I praised God instead and decided to live with a purpose! I decided to walk in my truth instead of living a lie! Damian hurt me in so many ways, but I forgive him. But the biggest lesson of all that I learned, was that it had little to do with Damian and everything to do with me. Damian's actions and words only had power because I allowed them to.

Once I began to heal Self, I learned how much power I actually had. I had the power over my emotions. I had the power over what I let get to me, and what didn't. I had the power to know that a lot of things that others may do to me. have little to do with me and everything to do with them. I learned to not internalize everything and not to take everything so personal. I learned how to let go of fear, and embrace the positive possibilities. I also looked within and realized that in a relationship it takes two. I began to understand that I was hurtful and toxic to Damian in a lot of ways a well. Yes, he did a lot, but I took the same approach with him as I had to take with my father. Which was; even though he was my husband, he was a human first. And had his own traumas and unhealed parts of him.

Instead of me operating in hate with him, I had to operate in love and compassion, even if we were not together. I had to display love and respect from one human being to another. Damian is not a monster. He lost himself along the way, just like I did. At his best he is loving, compassionate, giving, kindhearted, funny, enthusiastic, nurturing, strong, romantic and loyal. He would literally give you the clothes off his back and shoes off his feet, and I have seen him do it. Damian gave me his whole heart, and I abused it in a lot of ways. I forgive him, just as well as he has forgiven me. I pray that he looks in his mirror and finds his happiness and self-worth as well, because he truly is a King and has an awesome calling on his life. He needs to heal from his own traumas and pain. His journey is his journey, and his healing is his own choice. All of us have a choice to heal.

We all may come from trauma and hurtful pasts full of pain, neglect, rejection, abuse, losing loved ones and the list goes on and on. We have a choice to look in the mirror and either hate what we see or to love what we see. No matter what people are saying around you, the choice is ultimately up to us to find our own beauty within and turn our war scars into beauty marks. Each and every one of us is special, and has a gift and something to offer the world. We just have to look within to find what that Is. The power lies in us, and we determine who we see looking back at us in the mirror.

I used to be a weak, insecure, unworthy girl, teenager and woman who needed validation from others, and did not see my worth in any way. But now when I look in the mirror, I see a strong woman who is loved by God, and values herself and is full of abundance and gifts to give to others. When I look at myself, I see strength and resilience. I see an over comer. Many tried to break me, but I stand strong as a diamond, and I am here to tell women and men that you have the same power within yourself. No matter what you've been through, do not give up. Give the battle to God, and trust that he will see you through, just as he did myself and many others. Our lives are testimonies to inspire others. God is not a respecter of persons. If he did it for someone else then he will do it for you too.

I had been through a lot in life and in my relationship. The day Damian moved out the house, his words to me were "Bitch you need me, and without me, you are going to fall on your face." Normally him saying something like that would have intimidated me, but I knew I was strong. I looked back at him and said, "I will never fall with the God I serve" and I meant every word because I knew that God would carry me and my girls and that we would be ok. My faith was stronger than my circumstance. Damian had walked out the door and I had a sense of peace in my spirit. After he left God began to bless me more and more. God blessed me financially and abundantly. I had my days of sadness but, for the most part I was great. God sent me new people and friends and family to pour into me and uplift me. I started having "girls' nights" out and began embracing other people in my life and valuing them.

I began to look at life from a brighter perspective. I had begun to work on my health and exercise more, and I began to lose weight and feel more confident. Eventually I got back to my goal weight and felt like the old me again, but an even better version. I had always had a gap, so I took the initiative to join the smile direct club and began to fix my teeth, which I loved and it took my confidence to an awesome level.

I began to love myself from the inside out. I had become more aware of self as I was healing and growing as a woman, and it felt amazing. When it was time to sell my house reality hit and it was sad, but even then, I had people around me pouring into me and guiding me along the way which I really appreciated.

Once the house was sold, I went to the closing and signed the paperwork to begin my new journey, and leave all the old memories behind. I loved my home but I had prayed and asked God that since I had to leave could he bless me with something even better and he did. My new home was beautiful. It was bigger and more spacious, and I had everything that I had asked God for. My bedroom was so big that it was bedroom and a small living room combined. My bathroom was top of the line, and I was just in awe of the place. One of my favorite things about the house was the front door. It was big and grand and when you walked in there was a huge arch way into the foyer and it made me feel rich. God had truly blessed me. The neighborhood was gorgeous and even had a pool and tennis court.

Everything truly was beautiful, and I lived in a very high-class upscale area to make it even more amazing. I never thought I could live where I lived, and I knew it was nothing but the favor of God. To even add more to my blessing, I had a 2001 Nissan Maxima that I had for over 12 years. I loved my car but it was old. It leaked oil and had a few other issues. About a week before it was time for me to move into my new place. God had laid it on my heart to go and get a new car. At first I was like "God are you sure?" and he reassured me that, that was what he wanted for me, and I begin to pray on what type of car he wanted me to have. He showed me online and I went to the dealership about two days later and as soon as I pulled up the car was sitting right there and I knew it was mine.

It was a 2021 Nissan. brand new with only 9 miles on it and I was the first owner. I test drove it and filled out the paperwork and everything went smooth and I drove away in my new car. God told me to trust him and not even worry about the payments because my car would be debt free and I received. So, I had a beautiful new place, a brand-new car, and so many blessings were surrounding me and it just kept getting better and better. Favor was coming from everywhere. Money was coming from everywhere. My girls were happy and healthy and we lacked nothing at all. Life had meant to leave me broken, with unbelief and no hope, but God is a restorer and what is meant to be bad, he will turn around for your good.

If you are reading this and you do not believe in God, then I would suggest you give him a try. He is a healer and a restorer. If you don't know what to say, just open up your mouth and say "God, I know I don't know you, but I want you to please come into my heart and show me who you are" and I promise he will, and he will blow your mind in an awesome way. I give all praise and glory to God, and I pray that each and every one of you who has touched his book is filled with love and peace. You are special, you are loved, and you are needed, wanted, and valued. Even if no one ever told you that. I am pouring into you today so have faith, smile, forgive, let go and have a heart full of gratefulness and embrace your inner beauty because it is in there. You are more powerful than you know. Let your energy vibrate at your highest level and give and receive all that life has to offer. The journey ALWAYS leads to a Destination.

Yours Truly, with LOVE,
Mirah.

"Thank You Page"

I would like to Thank all of those who were a part of me becoming the Woman that I am today.

Thank you so much to my mother Stephanie, who always believed in me and had my back throughout all my trials and tribulations.

Thank you to my siblings for supporting me, and loving me, even when I was at my lowest. Thank you Waheed, Jaleesah, little Stephanie, and Jamilah for always being there for me as a Family. I Love you All.

Thank you to my Therapist for kick starting my journey to becoming a better me. Thank you for believing in me, and holding my hand the whole way. Your words were jewels that allowed me to have a whole new outlook on life. You inspired me to want to help others, like you helped me. I thank you from the bottom of my heart for your caring and endless support.

Thank you to my Life Coaching instructor Brenda Underwood, the Owner of BtFL "Breakthrough for Life" Thank you for showing me how to be an extraordinary Life Coach, who leads with Gods Love. Thank you for challenging me, and pushing me to face and overcome my fears. I appreciate you and the wisdom you have brought to my life.

Thank You to my Spiritual leaders Pastor Scott Sanders and Co-

Pastor Cynthia Sanders. Pastor, thank you for being an awesome man of God and spiritual leader. Through your teachings I have been set free in so many ways. Thank you for creating Rhema Nation which allows me to be a part of something great. Co Pastor, thank you for allowing me to witness a classy, humble woman, who is strong yet loving at the same time. Thank you for allowing me to see what an example of a loving wife should look like. I admire you and love you. Thank you Both for being great examples, and continuously showing Gods Love to his people.

Lastly, I would like to thank those who hurt me and were a part of my pain. Thank you for tearing me down, because it allowed me to rebuild a new better, stronger me. Thank you for not believing in me, because it forced me to believe in myself. Thank you for misusing my trust, because it taught me to lean on God, and Trust him even more. Thank you for all the lessons that turned into blessings. Thank you for showing me You, without seeing the real You, I would have never been able to discover the real Me.

The Journey always leads to a Destination
Be Blessed
-Mirah

"Business Acknowlegement and Shout Out Page!"

Raymond Tyler (Radio Host)
The light with Raymond Tyler on FM 96.1 WTTH & FM 106.5
45's & 33's on FM 91.7 WLFR
www.mixcloud.com/raymond-tyler
raymondtyler@gmail.com

Mika English
(Hairstylist, Owner of Grew by Me Shampoo and Conditioner)
IG: grewbyme_
FB: Mika English

Sierra Muhammad/Taahirah Rivera (Lasor Lipo, Shape wear & More)
U Envy US Beauty Bar LLC.
117 New Jersey Avenue
Absecon NJ
uenvyus.com

Stephanie Coffey (Realtor)
609-665-8152

Haashim El-Amin (Author. Screenplay Writer, Director, Producer)
Owner of "INAACS Works"

Youtube: Hass El

Cymone Coker (Chef/Author)
Owner of "New Chick in the Kitchen" Dining and meal prep services
Author of "Grace's Mac and Cheese Please"
www.newchickinthekitchen.com

(Talk Show/Podcast Host)
Michelle Mosely/Producer of Sip and Discuss
with Co-host Khalidah J. Hunter
IG: sipanddiscuss
sipanddiscuss@gmail.com

Kashawn "Kash" McKinley
(Director of Constituent for the city of Atlantic City)
Services:
"Voice of the City" and "Dreams become Reality"
IG: chasinkash

Stephanie Hawkins (Nail Technician)
Owner of HoneyyBNails
IG: HoneyyBNails
HoneyyBNails@gmail.com

(Clothing & Fashion Designer)
Shyreka Ragland Owner/Designer of Booshie Raggz LLC
"Modesty" By Booshie Raggz
Nataty's Luxury CLoset
www.booshieraggz.com

Martina Martin (Selfie Museum)
Phantasm the Experience

phantasmtheexperience.com
609-481-5299

Malikah Thorpe (Apparel Designer)
The Queen & Kings Closet LLC.
Queenandkingcloset.com
IG: mekamami_

www.ingramcontent.com/pod-product-compliance
Lightning Source LLC
Chambersburg PA
CBHW020428130626
46549CB00001B/30